JEFF BECK
Crazy Fingers

Annette Carson

Backbeat
Books

San Francisco

Published by Backbeat Books
600 Harrison Street
San Francisco, CA 94107
www.backbeatbooks.com
Email: books@musicplayer.com
An imprint of Music Player Network
United Entertainment Media, Inc.
Publishers of *Guitar Player* magazine and MusicPlayer.com

Distributed to the book trade in the U.S and Canada by
Publishers Group West 1700 Fourth Street, Berkeley, CA 94710

Distributed to the music trade in the U.S. and Canada by
Hal Leonard Publishing P.O. Box 13819, Milwaukee, WI 53213

Cover Design by Richard Leeds
Front Cover Photo by Jim Marshall
Text Design and Composition by Nancy Tabor

Library of Congress Cataloging-in-Publication Data
Carson, Annette
  Jeff Beck: crazy fingers / Annette Carson
      p.   cm
  Includes bibliographical references (p.), discography (p.), and index.
  ISBN 0-87930-632-7 (alk. paper)
   1. Beck, Jeff. 2. Rock Musicians—Great Britian—Biography. I. Title

  ML421.B425 C37 2001
  787.87'166'092—dc21
  [B]

                                                    2001025142

Printed in the United States of America

01 02 03 04 05   5 4 3 2 1

Contents

Acknowledgements

THIS BOOK WOULD never have been possible without the dedication of two people: Dick Wyzanski and David Terralavoro. Their contribution was not merely unfailing help and encouragement—it was far more fundamental. Dick, editor of *The Jeff Beck Bulletin*, and David, who published *The Jeff Beck Fanzine*, were the original movers and shakers responsible for acquainting me with the uncharted side of Jeff Beck's career. Both of them steered my manuscript through the rocks and rapids of inaccuracy that lurked at every turn, and both generously permitted my wholesale plunder of their handiwork.

I am especially indebted to Dick Wyzanski for articles covering Beck's concerts, associates, recordings, and a wealth of biographical background. Thanks to Dick and his colleagues, fans can now catch up with all the latest news on the Internet at http://www.ainian.com. Dick was also a tireless facilitator in putting me in touch with many of the people credited below.

Before Dick's published work, there was *The Jeff Beck Fanzine*, for which David Terralavoro truly merits the title of The Man. Researcher and chronicler of Beck's career, David produced his magazine from 1990 to 1992, telling the entire Jeff Beck story with more detail and accuracy than ever previously known. David also compiled the most up-to-date, fully comprehensive Beck discography, which forms the basis of the one in this book, of which probably 90 percent is attributable to his years of work.

My gratitude also goes to many others who made my task easier and more enjoyable thanks to their valued input: Christopher Hjort and Toshiaki Igarashi take top honors for sharing their painstaking research with me, together with Bill Armstrong, Tony Bacon, Pete Bassett, Jennifer Batten, Bob Brunning, Chris Charlesworth, Alan Clayson, Michael Einhaus, Dan Erlewine (Stewart MacDonald's Guitar Shop Supply, Athens, Ohio), Ben Fisher, Gregg Geller, Charlie Gillett, Patrick Hilger, Doug Hinman, Alan Hope, Peter Jacob, Roger and Andy Jarvie, Richard Johnston, Sandra Kerwath, John B. Kinnemeyer (J. K. Lutherie, Harrison, Ohio), John and Paul Lucas, Richard Mackay, Wolf Marshall, Maggie Mundy, Rick Nielsen, Giacomo Piraino, Bob Potter, Chris Prior, Bill Rich, Marc Roberty, Steven Rosen, Kenny Sexton, Kathleen Shawcross (Sutton Central Library), David Sinclair, Mike Waddacor, Geoff Wall, and John Walsh.

Special thanks go to John Tobler and Stuart Grundy for permission to quote from the Jeff Beck profile in their excellent book, *The Guitar Greats*.

Such enthusiasm, support and generosity, from all five continents of the globe, are testament to the worldwide respect engendered by the subject of this book. To Jeff Beck, on behalf of all of us: thank you for the music.

Foreword

JEFF BECK IS a very private person. A dozen other writers before me received the standard reply when collaboration on a biography was suggested: "Thanks, but no thanks."

There are some celebrities who really don't givadamn what's said about them publicly, just as long as people are talking; who have a promotional machine that cooks up stunts and stories to keep them controversial. Jeff Beck is not one of them. And I wholeheartedly support his wish to guard his privacy. Having worked in the entertainment world for twenty years—for thirteen of those years directly representing the interests of performing artists—I maintain a staunch respect for their right to a private life.

In truth, show business personalities are among the most cynically exploited and manipulated people around, a fact to which Jeff Beck will readily attest. Because they are celebrities, the public enjoys hearing about them. So it's in the financial interests of those who sell newsprint, airtime and magazines to keep the public supplied with stories—the more titillating, the better.

Within these pages you'll find no tales of sexploits and druggery. Just the chronicle of a guitarist's life and career, which happens to have spanned the most interesting decades of rock history. Due in large part to Beck's own lapses of memory, what you *will* find are a myriad of details never before published— details about his activities and recordings, plus the most accurate, verified facts about the variety of instruments he has chosen to delight us with. Of Jeff Beck's personal life you'll find little that is not generally known already, most of it taken from his own accounts; more than this is not relevant to his role as a musician and performer.

A substantial book about Jeff Beck has long been overdue. I personally spent time looking for one, and discovered only that some smaller attempts and several false starts had been made, without doing full justice to their subject: it was time to rectify the position.

As to the contents of the book, I received plenty of input as well as plenty of support. I talked to many people who, as admirers of Beck, wanted to see him given due recognition; and who, being fascinated by his music, wanted to know more about its (and Beck's) background and sources.

Despite many long silences, Jeff Beck continues to tread the path of his musical calling—usually without looking back. I hope you will enjoy sharing the journey as we follow the trail left by his footprints.

Prologue

THE GUITARIST ONSTAGE is not alone in the spotlight. But he might as well be: all eyes are fixed on him.

His movements are economical, his gaze turned inward, seemingly unaware of the thousands packed into the hushed auditorium. He leans forward to coax a singing, shimmering phrase from the strings beneath his fingers, intense with concentration on tone and feeling. Still concentrated, he arches back, this time articulating a strand of tiny, exquisite sound-droplets. Infused with the subtle breath of music, they tremble and hang like iridescent bubbles in the receptive air. The effect is delicate, ethereal, mesmerizing. The song is "Where Were You." The guitarist is Jeff Beck.

As the echoes die away and the moment vanishes, Beck the man emerges momentarily from inside Beck the musician. Compact, narrow-hipped and light of step, his frame still has the lean, athletic look of youth. The body is sinewy, with the hands and forearms of an artisan; the angular face all but hidden by the tousled thatch of hair that's been his trademark for over thirty years. A brief acknowledgement of tumultuous applause, a puckish grin flashed toward the player at the keyboards, and with that fleeting grin a sudden burst of sunlight breaking through.

Then the features recompose themselves as a thunderous strutting bass sets out to rearrange the fillings in your teeth. The gentle troubadour is banished and a grimacing rock barbarian takes his place. He stalks and strides the stage, pumping up a blast furnace of scorching rough-house blues; now brandishing the guitar, totem-like, at arm's length before his face; now straddling his domain with legs spread wide, fluent hands hammering out torrents of outrageous licks . . .

To quantify the essence of Jeff Beck's guitar playing—the tone, the presence, the passion, the unsettling shifts of mood and coloration—is to describe an ever-changing spectrum of sound: from lunatic rock 'n' roll to delicate, filigreed elegance; from blistering ferocity to aching, savage beauty. How can you define a musician whose output, while topping a poll for Best Jazz Guitarist, finds a regular home in heavy metal catalogs? Yet despite an incredible disparity of styles, he's one of those rare players who have a quality that's instantly recognizable. It may be the unvarnished honesty of what he does. Or the sheer go-for-broke risk-taking that forever pushes the envelope further—not only musically, technically, sonically, but also in terms of what passes for his professional career.

Touring, sadly, is now becoming a rarity: Beck doesn't like touring, and his

Jeff Beck in classic pose, 1973, with famous Les Paul Goldtop.

constitution doesn't stand up well to it. Catching Beck on tour has lately exhibited a probability factor somewhat on a par with sighting Halley's Comet, only with less predictability.

In 1990, about to go on the road to promote the album *Guitar Shop,* he commented: "One of Eric Clapton's tours is more than the sum total of my live work since 1980. I just can't withstand endless nights playing. The pitch I play at is so intense that I just can't do it every night."

Of course, there are other forces that also conspire to keep him out of the public eye. One of them is his latter-day paucity of recorded output, and another is the burden of perfectionism which makes him by far his own harshest critic. That critical alter ego, always looking over his shoulder, has a voracious musical appetite, propelling him ever onward in a constant search for new frontiers to conquer.

For the true artist, there is no greater compulsion than the need to move his art forward. Jeff Beck has always been a pioneer, charting new frames of reference for himself and others. His pioneering explored, introduced, and popularized many of the effects and techniques that soon became part of everyday rock guitar language: feedback, distortion, orientalisms and modal scales, two-handed fretting, even his jokey voice box device. And his use of harmonics has become a personal signature. Who else would dream of developing harmonics and whammy bar as a medium for creating melody?

To be both pioneer and perfectionist can take a heavy toll, and one thing he's had to sacrifice is working within a regular group. If your music is in a constant state of flux, so is your choice of who you'll play it with. Marketability can be another problem: when you're not one to tie yourself to a single bankable style, you forgo the rewards of a large and loyal record-buying public. Fortunately, even in his farthest wanderings, Beck has never lost sight of his bedrock audience. And he's too steeped in rock 'n' roll to go way out on some esoteric limb.

Still, for him, the next challenge is all-important, even when it involves taking risks that anyone else in his shoes, with more of an eye on commercial success, would never countenance.

Conducting his career as a series of quantum leaps into the unknown has meant deliberately sidestepping the star image of conventional rock culture. Although often coupled with contemporaries Eric Clapton and Jimmy Page as "the Big Three of British rock guitar," his popularity, compared to their global fame, is (by choice) positively cultish. According to Ritchie Blackmore, a kindred spirit, "He's so fresh, so un-show business. That's what I love about Jeff."

Essentially he is a musician's musician, for whom the hype of star status gets severely in the way of down-to-earth credibility. He's also a fully self-contained individual with his feet planted firmly on the ground, and with too lively a sense of the ridiculous to embrace the excesses and posturings of the showbiz merry-go-round.

Offstage and outside the studio he has an engagingly wry, self-deprecating approach, frequently underscored by a quirky humor that tells you he doesn't take himself—or you—too seriously. He once described his risk-taking style as "bordering on total calamity."

But self-effacement isn't always wise in his particular line of trade. Many times he's paid the price for allowing circumstance to dictate the course of events.

The key to it all is he's governed by the emotions of the moment. He gets off on spontaneity. He needs the kick of the drum to set the pulses racing. Equally, he needs a frequent kick in the butt, often from others' musical creativity, to pry him away from his beloved hot rods, the great passion of his life that readily takes precedence over music.

Recognition from the industry has been late in arriving, but is welcomed with typical modesty. The year 1986 brought Beck his first Grammy Award, for the instrumental "Escape" from his album *Flash*—of which, characteristically, he remarked: "For what little amount of work I do, I don't deserve anything." He got his second Grammy in 1990 for *Guitar Shop,* this time for Best Rock Instrumental Album. And in 1993, for *Frankie's House,* he won a British Academy Award for Best Original TV Music.

But more important to Beck than music biz awards is the recognition of his peers. Nothing better typifies the esteem in which he is held than Eric Clapton's acceptance speech after winning a Best Guitarist award. "I think," he began simply, "this should have gone to Jeff."

And Eric Clapton is not by any means alone. A 1990 survey in *The Observer,* Britain's heavyweight Sunday newspaper, reveals Beck as conclusively the supreme choice for "best of the best" in the opinions of a cross section of widely differing lead guitarists including Phil Collen, David Gilmour, Tony Iommi, Brian May, and Gary Moore. As music journalist and broadcaster David Sinclair aptly summarizes in his book *Rock on CD,* "Jeff Beck is the greatest living rock guitarist, and that's official."

"Having given so sparingly of himself," Sinclair concludes, "he has, paradoxically, been able to preserve the take-no-prisoners approach that has long since deserted his contemporaries. . . . While the lack of a strategy has kept Beck out of the limelight, it is, ironically, his obstinate unwillingness to play the big numbers game that has enabled him to be, in the words of David Gilmour of Pink Floyd, 'the most consistently brilliant guitarist over the past 25 years.'"

1 Hail, Hail, Rock 'n' Roll

IN 1944, BRITAIN WAS a war-weary nation. After nearly five years of turmoil, people had grown tired of bombing raids, the interminable blackout, travel restrictions, ration books for food and clothing, and—in the cities especially—gaping, barren bomb sites where once ordinary suburban families had led ordinary suburban lives.

Midsummer Day, 24 June 1944, was not the most auspicious day for young Geoffrey Arnold Beck to make an entry to the world. Especially in Wallington in suburban Surrey—sandbagged, bombarded, fatigued, and threadbare.

Wallington, adjoining the busy center of Croydon, was one of London's environs that had long since lost its rural character, now engulfed in the urban sprawl to the south-west. The Beck family home at 206 Demesne Road was only a short distance from Croydon Airport, a key base within RAF Fighter Command. If anyone knew what World War II was all about, Jeff Beck's parents certainly did.

The British were adept at meeting adversity with a whistle and a song and dry, derisive humor. Thankfully there were plenty of professional bands, plus dance music combos from the armed forces, to keep the world of music alive and healthy during the war years; and BBC radio ensured that Broadway, Hollywood, and Tin Pan Alley were not forgotten either.

Dancing was the universal recreation, in town halls, dance halls, camps, cafés, or simply at home, and at one time the BBC was broadcasting twenty dance band programs a week. Amongst the young of every nationality—most of them in uniform—it was swing music and the new jitterbug dance they wanted. Glenn Miller, with his unique sound and great foot-tapping arrangements, was the wartime leader of swing until his sudden disappearance on Christmas Eve 1944: a sobering reminder that the peril of death was indiscriminate.

Nevertheless, by the time the new little boy was one year old, the incredible had happened. The Becks had joined their neighbors to celebrate the war's end with parades and dancing in the streets. Now it was time to pick up the pieces.

If Jeff remembered anything from his infant years it would be shortages and rationing. Commodities such as fresh oranges, bananas, and eggs were outright luxuries. Butter and tea were limited to a couple of ounces per week, and cream had been unheard-of for years. Worst of all, bread—unrestricted throughout the war—came on the ration books in 1946.

Though anxiety and austerity were the climate surrounding young Jeff Beck's early life, being a war baby gave him an advantage more precious than money could ever buy: that of living through the postwar discovery years when music started rocketing into a thousand different directions. It was the richest, most exciting formative period that any rock musician could experience.

The younger of two children, Jeff also had the advantage of parents who recognized the opportunities available in the new world of reconstructive Britain. With free secondary and technical school education being offered, Arnold and Ethel Beck were keen to give their offspring a good start in life that included the arts and music.

Annetta, four years older, was the apple of her dad's eye—perhaps leaving her brother a little overshadowed. "My sister's a brilliant pianist, she can ride horses and draw pictures of them—a genius, speaks five languages."

The thrill of discovering guitar music was first ignited when he heard that great innovator, Les Paul, whose hit "How High the Moon" was a radio signature tune. Jeff was transfixed by the myriad of clever effects he pioneered. "I remember hearing him on the radio and asking my parents what that strange noise was. They knew, of course, because he was quite big in the late '40s. I couldn't believe that slapback echo. I must've only been seven or eight, but I was really blown away by that sound. My parents told me it was all fake—just studio tricks. But I'm sure that was the first music that really caught my attention. Les is a funny boy. He's got humor all over it. He's responsible for a piece of my brain damage. . . . It was like a hurricane blowing through. I just thought of sparks flying and metal, which you'd never associate with a guitar."

This was heady stuff, and he was quick to try to emulate it—"stretching rubber bands over tobacco cans and making horrible noises!"

By the time he was ten, his mother attempted to channel his musical energies. First, it was singing in the local church. "I don't know why she decided on the church choir. She wanted me to do something respectable."

Herself a pianist who played classical music, she sent him off for piano lessons. This was at about ten or eleven, and he tolerated the instrument for a couple of years. But young Jeff had his own ideas about his musical education. Made to practice for two hours a day on the grand piano in the front room, eventually he demonstrated his disgust by ripping one of the black keys off. "My mother got the idea then that I wasn't too keen on it!" Instead, he made it clear where his preferences lay by getting hold of a snare drum so he could play along with the music he liked—his dad's jazz records. It was the start of a lifetime's love affair with the drums.

"I used to fool around with a snare drum and brushes, just to try to get behind the record. There was this song, I forget what it was called. It was a trad jazz thing with a trumpet playing and the snare just going along. I just knew exactly what the drummer was doing, and I practiced and practiced until you couldn't really tell that I was playing along with it."

There were plenty of musical influences in the family, one of them an uncle who passionately loved classical music but loathed the jazz and pop on the radio.

"I remember he bought an MG sports car that had a radio in it. And before the engine was even cool, he ripped the radio out and threw it in the dustbin. But he was fanatical about music and taught me how to play his cello because he caught me messing around with it one day. He showed me all the fingering, although I couldn't come to terms with the bow. So I started playing the upright bass and loved that."

The same thing happened when he had violin lessons with that same uncle: again he felt more comfortable plucking with his right hand. "I remember messing around on a violin and I couldn't stand the thought of bowing instead of touching the strings. There was a frustration because the bow was getting in the way. And when you're a kid, I suppose you just want to get at the strings and pull them—some sort of built-in, natural thing. It was more fun."

So, more fortunate than many, he had an early familiarity with the world of music which would soon become his universe. And doubtless, in that indefinable way that children soak up influences, the exceptional skills he later developed must have owed something to his brief experience of formal training. Beck's feel for sweeping legato phrasing, so evident in the intensity of his melodic ballad style, may even echo his uncle's early teaching on two of the most expressive of stringed instruments.

Today he claims to have no particular knowledge of music theory. Like so many virtuoso performers, it's from playing music—not studying—that he has become its master.

It's difficult for parents, of course, when their fond hopes for their offspring veer into unwelcome directions. But Beck is eternally grateful for that strong musical background. "My dad was a Fats Waller fanatic. He used to play Art Tatum stuff. When you're seven or eight years old and you hear that coming out of the same piano that you kick and bash every day—that did it for me. I thank that guy forever and a day because he made me realize what music could do for me. It had nothing to do with the *guitar*, it was just hearing this sound wafting out of the music."

And when twanging rock 'n' roll became his overriding passion, at least his early experiments weren't totally discouraged.

"My parents both couldn't stand what I was doing. They thought rock 'n' roll guitars were grating and metallic. . . . But I think my mom started to realize there was something. Even though the noise was unbearable, I think she realized there was something there. But the *guitar*—when you wanted your son to play piano and impress all the neighbors with Rachmaninov, and all you got was Chuck Berry!"

JEFF'S SCHOOL YEARS came at a time when popular music, and the youth culture to which it gave voice, underwent an earth-shattering transformation.

In Britain, the revolution started in the mid '50s, after long years of "moon-June" love ballads and perky "Get Happy" whistle-along tunes. Still steeped in the 1940s, BBC radio play was dominated by middle-of-the-road light music, American-style swing, and the occasional mild excursion into trad jazz. LP records and 45s had only recently supplanted the breakable 78 rpm variety, and if anyone in the family bought them, it was mom and dad.

On to this placid scene in 1955 suddenly burst a frenzy of sound from the other side of the Atlantic, as Bill Haley and his Comets assaulted the airwaves with hammering sax, slapback bass, and frantic solo guitar. It was rough, raving, and hit you between the eyes. It fired you up to dance, to dare, to double-dare. All at once there was a new species of record-buying public—British teenagers were crazy for rock 'n' roll.

In the United States, it was the same story. Rebellion was the youth cult, delivered to eager cinema audiences by angry young heroes like James Dean and Marlon Brando. But when rock 'n' roll hysteria broke out, the new teen revolution represented something more insidious: it threatened the very fabric of a society still steeped in racial prejudice.

When American teenagers listened to Haley's frenetic "Rock Around the Clock" and "Shake, Rattle and Roll," what they were hearing were up-tempo white versions of gritty black rhythm and blues. Stigmatized as "race music," R&B was the post-war urban incarnation of earthy negro blues. Though sanitized for popular consumption, Haley's songs plainly tapped into forbidden roots of a music that was allowed no part in mainstream white entertainment.

R&B had injected a pulsating, driving back-beat into the old blues forms, defiantly celebrating or disconsolately bemoaning the black man's experience of big-city life. Frequently accompanied by bottleneck guitar, aggressively amplified, it throbbed with an urgent undercurrent that spoke of raw emotions and often open sexuality.

The term "rock 'n' roll" itself came from a black expression for sex of a particularly enthusiastic nature. Disc jockey Alan Freed took up the cry in his radio shows by pounding on his desk in time to the music and yelling, "Rock 'n' roll, everybody!" Freed had long been a dangerous radical with his devotion to R&B, programming black music for white listeners in segregated Cleveland, Ohio. Now he latched on to the new sound and promoted it energetically.

With R&B's small guitar-and-rhythm lineup augmented by dance band instrumentation, and its beat wildly pumped up in speed and volume, the new rock 'n' roll blasted the ears of American youth with a no-holds-barred explosion.

And what was worse, nobody could stay still when they listened to it. Kids trying to dance in the aisles at concerts were chased back to their seats by police, with fights and scuffles the inevitable result. An entire generation of parents, teachers, and civic leaders went into panic mode and demanded to have it banned, condemning the wild sexual gyrations induced by rock 'n' roll's insidious jungle rhythms: "It appeals to the base in man, it brings out animalism and vulgarity."

In Britain, without that frisson of forbidden black roots, Bill Haley's effect was to grip young people in the fever of a new dance music craze. The sounds were exciting and the beat was infectious. And you loved it all the more because your mom and dad hated it—especially since it often left a trail of trashed theaters and dance halls.

Particularly expert in the art of wrecking were the teddy boy gangs, who affected a post-austerity fashion statement of narrow drainpipe trousers and long, velvet-collared drape jackets echoing the Edwardian era, fetchingly set off by Day-Glo socks and crêpe-soled suede shoes, their hairstyles sporting pompadours and heavy sideburns. Not all teddy boys were perpetrators of mob violence, of course, but the one thing they all had in common was their tribal allegiance to rock 'n' roll and the energetic, uninhibited, partner-twirling dance it gave rise to.

Haley's rock 'n' roll, however, with its well-drilled instrumentation, didn't immediately catch on with Britain's embryonic music makers. During those postwar years of deprivation, the chosen do-it-yourself medium for an entire generation of grubby-kneed schoolboys (including, notably, Hank Marvin, John Lennon, and Rod Stewart) was skiffle: American country blues, mountain ditties, and songs from the Old West played after the manner of the depression years, when all you had were comb and paper, washboard, tea chest bass, and an empty suitcase which you thumped with a kitchen brush.

Lonnie Donegan's "Rock Island Line" was a monster British hit in 1956, and kids immediately started forming backyard skiffle groups with home-made instruments. (To afford shop-bought instruments was a sign of middle-class affluence, or of resort to the new practice of buying on credit, the dreaded "never-never," which your parents regarded with deep suspicion.) Instantly accessible, skiffle was the catalyst that got them playing instead of just listening, and it led to an incredible blossoming of homegrown music-making.

Back in the mid 1950s, the universal haunt of underage kids was the coffee bar, where they could congregate and play their jukebox favorites. Some coffee bars had their own scene going, with groups playing live music, like in the basement at London's famous 2Is in the heart of Soho. Tommy Steele and Cliff Richard both started there, and Hank Marvin, later to lead the immortal Shadows, was a resident from its early days. There was also a kid called Mickie Most who worked the Coca-Cola machine, of whom we shall hear more in later chapters.

THEN SOMETHING AMAZING happened. In 1956, Elvis Presley's hit recordings started arriving on the other side of the Atlantic. They brought a new era that kicked Britain's young skifflers in a totally different direction.

Almost single-handedly, Elvis popularized a new style that his guitarist, Scotty Moore, described as "hillbilly cat": a mix that drew on Merle Travis–Chet Atkins type country guitar styles, underpinned by bluesy rhythms with throbbing bass lines. When Elvis took it into the charts, it became known as rockabilly.

To this speeded-up bluegrass/negro music was added an aggressive rocking edge and hefty doses of barefaced raunch. Presley, steeped in the country music of the South, was heavily influenced by the blues and black musicians. As well as mingling their styles in his songs, he even affected the colorful, snazzy outfits of the black street hipsters of Memphis, Tennessee. An explosive combination, it marked him as a target of instant disapproval—and as a trend-setting rebellious role model for the young.

His successes like "Heartbreak Hotel," "Hound Dog," and "All Shook Up" added a further individual dimension. Incoherent and raw, they spoke for all the sexual energies and pent-up longings of a new generation, out to stamp their own mark on the messed up world they inherited. These were personal statements by someone their own age, with an attitude, a presence, and a language never heard before.

In Britain, the effect was electrifying. Soon, with more Stateside stars to emulate—like Buddy Holly, Carl Perkins, Gene Vincent, and Eddie Cochran—rudimentary instrumental techniques improved by leaps and bounds. Especially influential was the punchy, nimble-fingered energy of guitar instrumentalists like Presley's Scotty Moore and Vincent's Cliff Gallup. Skiffle in Britain soon gave way to rockabilly and white-boy rock 'n' roll, just as country music had done in the United States.

THOSE INTOXICATING SOUNDS of flying fingers on the guitar were integral to the magic of rock 'n' roll. Instead of just a background instrument, the guitar had now become the all-important counterstatement to the vocal line.

Soon it was phenomenally popular. But not merely the traditional acoustic guitar; it was above all the *electric* guitar, whose infinitely flexible range of signals had yet to be fully explored. These signals, though transmitted by pickups, came essentially from the direct human pressure of fingers on strings, allowing all the expressiveness of individual touch and tone.

Efficient electromagnetic pickups on acoustic guitars had been around since the 1930s, amplifying the guitar's modest volume so as to be heard within a band, or simply to compete with the noise and hassle of a club or barroom blues session. The embryonic Rickenbacker company started fitting pickups to Spanish models around 1933, but the solid-body guitar, with no sound box at all, came into its own with '50s music, designed specifically to be heard on the radio and jukebox.

Of course, solid-body electrics became widespread only when sophisticated amplifiers were available. American manufacturer Leo Fender started making amps with built-in speakers in 1948, and developed his Esquire/Broadcaster guitar design soon afterwards; the two-pickup Broadcaster, rechristened the Telecaster in 1951, was the first commercially successful (Spanish style) solid-body. A much derided "plank," mass produced and functional, it had a cutaway recess in the body where it joined the neck to allow the fingers easier reach to the upper frets.

Essentially, the solid-body was developed to eliminate the hum and distortion which plagued electrified hollow-bodies. Les Paul was an innovator in this as in so many other electric guitar developments: he was already experimenting in the late '30s and early '40s, when his first electric solid-body—the Log—was handmade for him at the Epiphone factory. In 1952, the Gibson company brought out its first Les Paul solid with Paul's endorsement: a beautifully made instrument with a carved top body and single cutaway.

Then, in 1954, Fender introduced a guitar that was destined to dominate solid-bodies for decades to come: the revolutionary Stratocaster. It was the first commercial model to incorporate a device called a tremolo arm—known ever afterwards as the whammy bar—which, because of its pitch-bending effect, should properly be called a vibrato arm. With its double cutaway design, allowing the thumb just as much movement up the neck as the fingers, the Strat also sported an exciting futuristic look with two projecting horns in place of the old rounded Spanish shape.

All three of these early designs produced instruments with wonderful tonal qualities that are still sought after today. And all three, with their very different sound and feel, have been weapons of choice for Jeff Beck at different points in his career. But the Strat has remained his overall favorite.

WHEN BECK AND his contemporaries were falling in love with rock 'n' roll, its early guitar wizards were virtually anonymous. But soon they found out who the guitar players were, even if the singer was meant to be the star of the show. Scotty Moore was an early idol of Keith Richards, who describes his solo on Presley's "I'm Left, You're Right, She's Gone" as the most exciting thing ever recorded. "I could never work out how he played it, and I still can't. It's such a wonderful thing that I almost don't *want* to know."

Beck shares a similar sense of awe. "It was this amazing explosion of rock 'n' roll, right in my face. It was this nonsensical guitar sound that got me. All I was exposed to here was sort of playtime radio—[*Workers Playtime*]—a sort of lunchtime factory music they used to play. Then something happened: I tuned into this station called Radio Luxemburg. It was just fading and cross-fading and flanging. You couldn't hear a bloody note! Then one glorious cascade of electric guitar notes would come out and it was like tuning into a God somewhere. It was all helped along by my older sister; when I was twelve and she was sixteen she had these records. She used to wrap them up and hide them, and I used to dig them out when she'd gone out."

When Beck discovered that the singer on the record didn't actually play the guitar, he was incensed: "I made it a point to find out the name of the guy who was responsible for the guitar work. In those days, album info was nothing. You find me an early Elvis recording that says Scotty Moore on guitar and Bill Black on bass! That upset me to the point of learning the guitar style, adopting it. And once I got over the first rung of the ladder, of learning a part of 'Hound Dog,' I realized I was better than Elvis because I was doing something he couldn't do!"

But Cliff Gallup, the original guitarist with Gene Vincent & the Blue Caps, was the ultimate, and a lifelong influence on Beck's career. Gallup's stint with the group was a brief one, lasting just seven months from April to October 1956. During that time he recorded 35 songs, including Vincent's biggest hit, "Be-Bop-A-Lula."

"Cliff Gallup is the most unsung hero of rock 'n' roll guitar," Beck maintains.

"Those solos on those Vincent records—you cannot get any better than that. Go out and get all the early Vincent recordings. His voice is so animal-like. 'Cat Man' and 'Cruisin'' and 'Pink Thunderbird' are all so amazingly street rock 'n' roll."

A scratch backing group of local musicians, most of the Blue Caps had day jobs (Gallup was a plumber), but they were among the top country music players on the local Virginia circuit. Gallup was a true rockabilly guitarist of the early school, with more country and even jazz and bebop influences than blues—very little string bending, lots of slapback echo—with incredible dexterity and an aggressively rocking, exuberant sound.

With Gene Vincent a hot chart success, they hit the road from June of 1956. Which was fine for the 21-year-old hell-raising Vincent, who seemed to have boundless energy for girl chasing and hotel room trashing, despite constant pain from a leg damaged in a motorcycle accident. But the life took a tremendous toll on the group's more home-loving members. Thirty-three-year-old Cliff Gallup left at the end of September, as the band prepared to fly to Hollywood for a cameo appearance in the film *The Girl Can't Help It*.

Gallup had by then played on all their singles, together with their first album, Bluejean Bop. So, after they finished the filming, he agreed to record album number two: *Gene Vincent and the Blue Caps*. It was completed in just four days—every track recorded live—and he then retired to become a rockabilly legend. Beck declares it was these two albums that set his soul on fire to start playing guitar: it was the most raucous, frightening stuff he'd ever heard.

"He would do accents, you know, jabbing, and building into a riff, and then picking out the individual notes. He was no lazy-ass! And then he would just hit you into left field with some ridiculous run. Plus, when I discovered Gallup, he was the first guitarist playing with a real bright sound, using tremolo and stuff like that, in such an organ-like way. It was such an orchestral sound, all these big fat chords which I'd never heard before. The desire to make sounds like Cliff Gallup took hold of me and would never let go. Every solo he played was a blast of energy that helped me through my dreadful school days."

It was the following year—1957—that Elvis Presley, with the help of Scotty Moore, charted in Britain with no fewer than 13 songs. Gene Vincent acquired another brilliant guitarist, Johnny Meeks, made yet more classic recordings, and continued his rock 'n' roll rampage.

Early that same year, 12-year-old Jeff Beck was transfixed by seeing *The Girl Can't Help It,* a freewheeling music flick that also featured performances by Eddie Cochran and Little Richard, and in which the Vincent gang gave a sensational performance of "Be-Bop-A-Lula."

"That was what completely did my head in. I mean, it was enough to have the records at that time, but to actually go and see the Blue Caps and everything in living color—it was just too much! There was Elvis, sure, but Vincent was a street guy. A real guy, but very shy. And I was really withdrawn and shy myself back then, and I remember wishing that I was just four or five years older, and I could have been beating on his door for a job."

It was seeing this movie that made Beck want his own guitar. For a while he plunked away on a friend's zither, and next came the inevitable "cigar-box" guitar, which he put together from (literally) the tops of cigar boxes. "I painted the frets on and for machine heads I used a straightforward nut and bolt. Oh yes, and because I didn't know how many strings a guitar should have, I only put five on! Eventually I decided I wanted a proper guitar, so I went round all the shops just picking up leaflets and living in a sort of make-believe world where I could buy any of them.'"

But in the '50s, a guitar for a preteen kid was simply out of the question. "Absolutely. It was the money involved, you see." So, with great determination, he tried his hand at building his own, a hollow-body which he made out of plywood, carefully measuring the dimensions and steaming the sides into shape. He bought the wood, cut out the shape, and glued the whole thing together.

He based this effort on a guitar borrowed from a friend at school—the first one Jeff had ever got hold of: "This horrible cowboy-type guitar with black paint all over it." He was smitten immediately, and couldn't put it down. "A beaten-up old acoustic thing. It had about one string, but that's all I needed—one string was plenty for me to grapple with..Then that broke, and where were we gonna get another from? I didn't know." This was in the days when sixpence a week—or perhaps a shilling—was the kind of pocket money you could expect as a kid. And with a set of new strings running at ten shillings, they seemed completely out of reach. So he simply restrung it with some piano wire he used for flying model airplanes, oblivious to the fact that the strings were all the same thickness.

Nevertheless, Jeff was hooked—and that borrowed guitar was what led him to build his own. His plywood model had a hopelessly elongated neck and was impossibly heavy. He'd used a pretty thick gauge of plywood throughout, making his hollow-body equivalent in weight to about six electric guitars! "It was about fourteen feet long and ridiculously out of proportion, but it was a start. It was a good thing to get hold of, and wield about, and that's where it all started really, with that one guitar. I used to prop it up in an armchair and just look at it more than play it, because I loved the way guitars looked.

"I ended up having a row with my old man over something and he tossed it out into the garden and busted it. This was before I knew about solid guitars. When I saw a Fender like Buddy Holly's, I thought, 'That can't be hollow, it's got to be a solid chunk of wood.' So I drew pictures, scaled them up from photographs, and built a new guitar, a solid guitar. But the neck was still a couple of miles long!"

Using the Stratocaster shape, which he'd seen on an album cover, he had the basic guitar made for him for about £5 (around $20 in those days). "It was 'orrible. This bloke made me a guitar that looked like half a pine tree. It had about four hundred frets and about four-foot cutaways . . . but it looked great."

Jeff finished the job in his workshop at school, making his own frets with bits of wood and wire. It was playable, but he didn't know anything about the neck scale. He just put the frets on wherever he thought they should go. With no formal training on guitar, he found his own way around as best he could: "I couldn't tell a middle C from a B flat. That guitar of mine was diabolical. It was in tune around the E register, and when you got up the fretboard to A it was recognizable as an A, but when you reached C it was way out of tune. It was really good therapy, because you'd ping around and you'd know that the 12th fret was supposed to be the same as the open string, only an octave higher, and I'd pull notes to bring it into tune—and that's how I got into bending strings."

The toughest problem was how to get hold of a pickup, which would cost an astronomical £2. "I had so little money, and that was the thing I wanted to do so much," he told Steve Rosen in *Guitar Player*. So he swiped one from his local music store.

"I whipped one of these pickups right out of the shop. Oh boy, I couldn't have cared if I'd got thrown in jail for six months, I had my pickup. And there was a little hole cut in the guitar that had been waiting for that pickup. And it just slipped in there with two screws and, boy, I was the king! I used to deliberately carry my guitar around without a case so everyone could see what it looked like. I used to stick it on my back and ride a bicycle. I could see then that it just wasn't a fly-by-night thing, because the expressions on people's faces when they saw this weird guitar, that was something! It was bright yellow with these wires and knobs on it; people just freaked out."

In that same school workshop he even went so far as to make an amp/speaker construction: "There was a straightforward 30-watt unit, but the speaker cabinet was about 15ft x 1ft and was packed with different speakers!"

A thing of that size wasn't welcome at home, so all he could do was plug into a radio. "It sounded rotten, and there was no level at all. It was barely audible if you kept your ear right up against the speaker. But that was enough for me to feel, 'Hey, I'm on the radio!'"

Jeff's parents hated what he was doing. His mom especially, with her love of piano, was absolutely horrified. "Wasting my life away on this instrument. But she didn't know. She didn't know. You had to learn to play piano and do a little sonata when your aunts came around. And we'd all have cucumber sandwiches and tea . . . she wanted to be proud of me doing *that*. But it was not to be. Maybe it was being born in the war that had something to do with it. The explosions, the fire and the mess and everything. All the people going crazy. Perhaps that's rubbed off on me a bit, in that I didn't wanna be peaceful and play beautiful music. So I suppose that has a lot to do with what I play now, kind of manic and disjointed."

Jeff Beck gave his first public performance, with his homemade guitar, in nearby Carshalton Park at the tender age of fourteen. "I'd refused to play on the back of a float that was part of something like a May Day parade—even then I wanted things my own way. And I wanted an audience, so I teamed up with this other guy, who sang 'Be-Bop-A-Lula' or something, and I just played a few notes in the background."

But, thanks to a report in the local newspaper, word soon got around about that gig: "I couldn't find a bass player, so this art student came along. He still had his duffle coat on and he didn't have a bass, he had a cello and it looked ridiculous! He was six foot three and he played this cello like an upright bass. I said, 'Put it on a chair, put it on a chair . . . ' We got through half a number before we folded up and couldn't remember the rest of it, and we got off the stage. The phone never stopped ringing! My mom said, 'What's been going on? There've been floods of phone calls.' And we'd only played half a number! We put it down to a technical breakdown."

Beck never took formal guitar lessons, although, thinking he ought to do the accepted thing, he did go for one session with a teacher on the Spanish guitar. But the effort was useless. "He knew less than I did," he recalls. "He didn't even have the barré chords right."

So his yellow Beckocaster was the instrument on which he first taught himself to play, copying the American legends he heard in his teenage sister's record collection. He reckoned this guitar served him well for a couple of years, but all the while he couldn't resist looking around for something better. The height of his desires was a gleaming white Fender Telecaster, tantalizingly out of reach in the music shop window.

"I was a snot-rag 14-year-old kid, and they wouldn't let me try it until I brought my dad. So finally, one Saturday, I've got it in my hands, and as I'm running over riffs by Scotty Moore, people are stopping to listen." But money remained tight, and it was a long time before he ever had one to call his own.

NO MATTER HOW limited his parents' means, they were determined to see their children with a good education. Jeff was sent to a private school until age eleven, then to Sutton East Secondary Modern School in Greyhound Road; there his talent for art was developed in a special two-year junior art school stream that groomed many successful young artists for college. But his taste for noisy rock 'n' roll was severely frowned upon and he soon became an out-and-out rebel. Asked to paint a still life, he would defiantly turn in pictures of guitars.

Losing himself in his personal world of music was the only antidote. "It was just so exciting to come home from school and not have to worry about being told off. All of a sudden you had this magic thing called a record that could take all your blues away. You could play it over and over again and just get high on it. Then you felt like going out with your friends and talking about it. You made a point of finding out who was interested in music."

Those fellow enthusiasts were few and far between. With no one at school who shared his passion, he was isolated and on the defensive at every turn.

"At school I didn't have anybody that I could talk to, they were all snobby. The joke was, I never had television. There would be all these rich people with TV, and in frustration I had to ask them what Elvis was like. Because he was on TV, everybody would be talking about him. All I had was this scratchy old record. But at least I could understand the musical side of it and the guitar work going on— those people didn't. They just talked about Elvis's wiggling hips."

Happily his isolation was not to last forever. Eventually he teamed up with one particular friend who was equally crazy for his kind of music, whose parents weren't against helping the boys financially. So Jeff was lucky enough to share more of those treasured records from the United States. Soon there were European tours by American stars like Buddy Holly, which fueled Jeff's desire to become a musician even further.

Nowadays, Beck himself is all too familiar with the trials of life on the road; so he acknowledges a heartfelt debt to those early stars who went out and got in touch with their audiences.

"I hate the idea that one has to go away and live unnaturally and all that," he told *Guitar Player* magazine. "But having said that, if it hadn't been for Buddy Holly coming over and playing for us at Croydon in the 1950s . . . He made the effort. I used to think the guy would just disappear into a castle somewhere in the middle of the sky—but the next night he was in Edmonton, Cook's Ferry or whatever. I saw Buddy Holly live, and it was the best thing I've ever seen."

Holly's British tour was in March 1958, and Jeff saw him at the Davies Theatre, Croydon: "It was so great. Coming out of that theater, I just couldn't see anything. I'd walk under buses and not care. I was so overawed by him. I'll never forget it as long as I live. He came on with a little Fender amp, a Strat, and his trio. That was it; all I had to hear was 'That'll Be the Day' and I was floating for six weeks." This classic Holly number was the first tune Jeff had ever learned to play. From the moment he heard it, the record was never off the turntable. "I learned the beginning of that and impressed everybody at school. That's all I could play, though, just the beginning. It fascinated me because it sounded like a honky-tonk piano-type lick, but it was just a single note guitar thing. The notes were rolling into one another. I love that. I'm not sure what it is, but that stuff is just as explosive now as it was the first time."

As he got better, he moved on to more adventurous solos, like those of Ricky Nelson's guitarist James Burton, learning them by putting the needle back again and again and slowing the record down. The first solos he learned were "My Babe" and "It's Late," then "Twenty-Flight Rock" by Eddie Cochran.

With the aid of his pal's record collection, he steeped himself in all the greats you never got to hear on British radio. Soon he was getting more advanced, and started teaching himself fingerpicking in the style of Chet Atkins. "Country fingerpicking style, that's what interested me the most—that so much could be done with a six-stringed instrument. You could accompany yourself, play the melody *and* the solo like Chet Atkins. I used to sit and marvel at those guys. It was this chordal thing that was going on. Bass line, counterpoint? How the hell? And when I heard Merle Travis, I almost gave up. I just thought, 'Oh no, this can't happen. This was not done on one guitar by one person.' . . . You know, I was brought up on the right stuff!"

IT WAS EARLY 1960 before Beck witnessed the legendary Gene Vincent in person. Unhappily for his hopes of seeing Gallup or Meeks, the Blue Caps had already disbanded by then—but Vincent was enough. "Gene was so dynamic, it was frightening. He'd throw his good leg over the mike, slide across the piano, just dynamite. He was the most experimental, wild . . . I mean, some of that stuff holds up even today. Futuristic style. Wild, ridiculous runs all over the place. These are just my schoolboy heroes."

He was fortunate indeed to have seen both Vincent and Holly play live at the apex of their all-too-brief careers. It is now rock 'n' roll history that touring cost Buddy Holly his life—he died in an airplane crash in February 1959, together with Ritchie Valens and the Big Bopper. Gene Vincent was also a touring casualty, when he was injured in the 1960 auto accident in England that killed his friend Eddie Cochran.

But although Vincent's reception in England helped to revive an ailing career, his tearaway image, garbed in sinister black leather, didn't find much favor among the conservative British of suburbia. They preferred the less threatening teen idols who were crooning their way to popularity, leaving the rock 'n' roll greats to languish in obscurity. Even the cellar rockers like Tommy Steele, Marty Wilde and the early Cliff Richard had given way to smooth, pseudo-American heartthrobs like Vince Eager and Mark Wynter. Jeff Beck was devastated.

"I reckon on December 31, 1959, somebody pulled the big 'off' switch for rock 'n' roll. It was finished for me. A certain section of it died right there. Everybody was looking for Johnny this and V-neck sweaters and the respectable boy next door crap. That wasn't the way I wanted to hear it. There was such a difference between the U.S. and England. There was some law that said the English people are only allowed to play covers. It upset me, because I wanted the real thing. I wanted to see the guys who played the original 'Bluejean Bop' in early '56. They never came over here, and I felt really cheated. Scotty Moore never came with Elvis. I felt really bitter about not seeing them."

Even while he was still at school, Jeff was already in several little local pickup bands where all they did was play covers of the current chart favorites. "You had to wear a suit, you know? I hated that, even then. You couldn't get a gig unless you looked like the Shadows or the Ventures. Thank God there's no film of that! I wore pointed white shoes, a blue suit, and a handkerchief sticking out of the pocket. I wore a bleached pompadour, like Brian Setzer. I have a picture of it somewhere; there's all of us guitarists down on our knees mimicking the playing and the drummer is sitting there smiling and holding his stick in one hand."

In the late summer of 1960, desperate to keep the rockabilly flame alive, he decided to try his luck with a package that was touring Britain in the wake of the revived interest in Gene Vincent. Mounted by promoter Bob Potter, it featured a number of singers in the Vincent mold, including a strikingly close look-alike named Cal Danger. Plucking up courage to approach Potter, Jeff auditioned under the name of Jeff Mason and nailed the lead guitar slot in the Bandits, a rock 'n' roll instrumental group from the Hampshire area that backed the singers on the tour.

One of these singers was Kerry Rapid (real name Alan Hope), who remembers first meeting Jeff, a spotty-faced youngster, in the back of a tour bus in 1960. "The reason Jeff and I hit it off was that I knew a lot of Vincent's rarer material: Jeff was a 'gallupin' Cliff Gallup freak. I don't recall him being around for long, but he certainly played the Aldershot Palais and the Agincourt Ballroom in Camberley, Surrey. The one gig he definitely won't forget is the Newark Corn Exchange in Nottinghamshire, when the whole evening ended in one massive fight. We all unplugged our equipment and made a hasty exit left of stage."

Meanwhile, amidst all these musical excursions, the time had come for Jeff to leave school and think about his future. An art college training was the obvious choice, and he certainly had the right talent. So on 19 September 1960 he enrolled for a two-year fine art course at the Wimbledon School of Art.

As it happened, art colleges all over Britain soon began a brisk turnover in the honorable trade of turning out rock musicians. Countless embryonic bands started out as informal art school groups, using classrooms and locker rooms for after-hours practice.

As Jeff reflects—only half jokingly—"It was an excuse to not work. You got a grant and you would dress up in silly clothes, you didn't have to answer to anybody. You could walk around with a van Gogh under your arm, some paint brushes, and a Miles Davis album—those were the tools."

That album, moreover, was probably borrowed. It was like a pot of gold to find a whole new set of cronies with records to supplement your meager supply. Today it takes an effort to visualize the handicaps that beset young would-be musicians around the year 1960, especially those in England, endeavoring to master American guitar styles light-years away from their source. Remember, the audio cassette hadn't yet been invented, so you had no chance to record anything unless you had rare access to a reel-to-reel machine.

BY THIS TIME Beck had acquired his first shop-bought guitar for £25, a Japanese Guyatone in bird's-eye curly maple (the LG-50, as used by players like Hank Marvin). "I'll always remember that Guyatone because it had a big toggle switch, and that was the business. It looked like it'd be more at home at a railway station. I made a case for the guitar, but I didn't allow for the switch. I was about ⅛ of an inch out. I put the guitar in the case, slammed the lid down, and pressed the switch right through the plastic. So I stuck it back together with Araldite and went off to a gig. Stood at the bus stop and the guitar case fell over and did it again! Did the gig and it was all right, went home, plugged in and it just buzzed. So I stuck it back together again, painted it black . . . chopped it in and got a Burns."

With memories clouded by the mists of time, Beck's recollections may be a little off the mark. In fact it's likely to have been the Burns, with its protruding three-way lever switch, that enjoyed his Araldite attentions. Described by Beck as a "Tri-Sonic" with three pickups, this was probably the Vibra Artiste which came out in 1960, a popular upgrade from the Guyatone. It was while playing the Burns that Beck made the next significant move in his career, which involved approaching a band that had quite a following in the local area: they were called the Deltones.

"That was the hot item around our way. I used to see this van with 'Deltones' written on it, and I loved the name, and they also had pink jackets, which I thought was great. Then I was asked to go down to see them, and this guy called Ian Duncan, who was fabulous, was leaving them, and I thought, 'My God, how am I going to fill his shoes?' He said, 'Look, I'll bugger off for a cup of tea, so you have a play and see how you get on,' and from that moment on, I realized there was a job for me there, because I was playing the solos off pat—but that was what they wanted, solos like the record. If they'd asked what else I could play, I'd have been finished. . . . So I was knocked out, skipping home, and they said, 'You're playing at Putney Ballroom.' It was great. You never forget moments like that, turning up in a Dormobile and getting all the gear out."

The Deltones had metamorphosed from a skiffle group, the Discord Skifflers, into a pop group with the arrival of their boyish new lead singer, Derek (Del) Burchell—rechristened Johnny Del by the group's manager, Roger Jarvie—who had a nice line in Cliff Richard songs like "Living Doll." So they'd switched to successful covers of the chart-topping Cliff, featuring on lead guitar "a little left-handed genius named Ian Duncan," as Jarvie describes him. Their previous gigs around the jazz clubs gradually gave way to regular spots at dance halls like the Wimbledon Palais, Hammersmith Palais, Park Lane Ballroom, and Tonbridge Dance Club; they even auditioned for BBC radio's *Saturday Club* and financed their own private disc.

Beck's chance came when Duncan accepted a job as backing guitar for a new young singer, the brother of one of Britain's already rising popsters, Eden Kane; the young singer in question was Peter Sarstedt. The Deltones knew Beck as one of the regulars in their audience, but the idea of auditioning him was another proposition altogether—the lad was an art school student of sixteen, and the rest of the band members were in their early twenties. But they had nobody else lining up for the job, so one Thursday night they asked him along to a rehearsal in Croydon at Bowaters' Canteen on Purley Way.

Beck appeared with a long cardboard box under his arm, leading the skeptical Roger Jarvie to wonder what kind of junk lay inside. "Then he opened it," Jarvie continues, "and took out an instrument that made all the rest of our equipment look ready for the scrap yard: the most beautiful red and gold Burns London guitar. And when he started playing we simply froze in disbelief—he was magic."

Beck's condition for joining the group was they had to take his school friend John Owen on rhythm guitar, but no one was going to argue about that. Initially he was quite proud of his three-pickup Burns—"it really bellowed"—but it didn't last for long. "About that time my mate [we may assume this was Owen] bought a Telecaster. £107 it cost him. It was a beauty, and I was stuck with this bloody Burns thing. So while I was in the group he played the Burns and I played the Tele." From other Beck recollections it seems likely that Owen's choice of instrument was guided to a considerable extent by his mate's self-interest.

However, this arrangement didn't last long either. After swapping the Burns for a Hofner Futurama, John Owen evidently decided to reclaim his Telecaster. Beck, penniless as usual, found himself saddled with the Futurama, which he describes as disgusting: "It looked like a Fender Strat. It had a lot of rocker switches on it that were useless. You'd strum one chord and they'd all go into the middle position and turn off. So you were standing there plunking away with no sound coming out. The vibrato arm was a disgrace to technology. It didn't go up or down; it was just rigid."

Owen's Telecaster was not an uncommon sight in those days, but the Strat was far more exotic: Beck first laid eyes on one in a Charing Cross Road music shop. "I was with a guy from the Deltones—we'd skipped off school and got the bus up to Victoria. From the top of the bus I said, '*I have seen the light!*' and went bowling down the stairs knocking the conductor out of the way, jumped off the bus and ran across the road. There was a sunburst Strat in the window. I thought, 'This is *it*!' We went in and the guy in the shop knew we didn't have the money, but he let us play on it, and it was like being on a cloud—we didn't come down for ages."

Not long afterwards, Jarvie recalls being summoned to see Jeff's parents, who wanted some kind of assurance of the group's earning power: Beck was about to buy his own Strat on credit and had asked his mother to guarantee the loan. In a rare 1961 photograph of the Deltones, reproduced in the booklet to the *Beckology* boxed set, Jeff can be seen sporting his very first sunburst Strat.

Having worked so hard to learn all those Cliff Gallup solos, young Jeff had been itching to play his rockabilly licks. But although the Deltones didn't mind featuring a few of the old songs, their audiences weren't really interested.

"The real numbers they wanted to hear were the ones they could buy in the shops, the ones they were hearing in jukeboxes at the time. They liked 'Peter Gunn' or 'Sweet Little Sixteen.' Those things were happening at the time, whereas what we're talking about was four years earlier. Four years back in the '50s was like 400 years! I thought, 'Why fight it?' So I was naturally lured away from that, even though it was pulling at my heartstrings to leave it behind. I would just go home and play it and wonder why nobody loved it."

Another disappointment was his experience at art school. Although it had its compensations—and Beck remains an accomplished painter in oils today—he saw quickly enough that it held no future for him. Given his ready success with the Bandits and the Deltones, he soon realized music held out better prospects than trying to make it as an artist: "If I'd stayed I'd probably be designing cornflakes packages." He left on 22 May 1961 "to pursue a musical career," as noted in the art school's records.

"I thought, a couple of years, I'll learn to paint and make a living at it. But you saw people from previous years who'd left and they were coming back in rags, still couldn't get a job. I was cast aside by all the teachers as a complete failure: I was nothing more than a banjo-twanger!"

Not yet seventeen, Beck had already left home and got a foothold in the music business. "Within a year I'd made more money and got more recognition doing that. . . . One of these days I'd like to go back and say, 'Hey! Good job I didn't listen to you, isn't it?'"

2 Rebirth of the Blues

AS THE '50S MOVED towards the end of the decade, the United States took on the aura of a promised land. Unlike postwar Britain, it enjoyed the fruits of victory without the wholesale devastation: a land where being a teenager meant having cash to spend on the latest clothes and the records you heard on a wealth of radio stations, where automobiles were easily acquired and gasoline was plentiful, while British kids were riding around on bicycles wearing cheap, dreary hand-me-downs, and being virtually ignored by the BBC.

But rock 'n' roll was still highly suspect—many saw it as the devil's music—and feelings ran high when American youngsters reached the stage of embracing full-blooded black rock 'n' rollers in the pop charts along with their white idols. It was only thanks to groundbreakers like DJ/promoter Alan Freed that audiences were able to attend shows where black and white played side by side on the same concert bill.

Headline black acts included the deliciously outrageous Chuck Berry, along with Little Richard of the ever more demented scream, and Bo Diddley with his amazing stage act and identifying riff of "shave-and-a-haircut—two-bits."

As a brilliantly inventive singer/writer/guitarist, Chuck Berry's influence was fundamental in shaping rock 'n' roll. His guitar combined the twang of country and the bent blue notes of R&B, together with a biting-edged tone that was as in-your-face as his insolent grin, duckwalk and crisp, sassy lyrics.

And he was not only capturing audiences in America. Berry was another of Jeff Beck's major influences: "'Sweet Little Sixteen' was what got me going on him—it was just the driving music, not so much the separate guitar playing but the block sound that made me jump up and down."

But even more far-reaching was a new revelation that opened the eyes of many young Britons, when they started delving deeper to discover authentic R&B and blues.

In the United States, R&B charts and country charts existed alongside the world-recognized pop charts. Chuck Berry and Little Richard hit the '50s rock 'n' roll boom and quickly made it in the wider world of pop, but countless others never made the crossover at all. And outside even the R&B charts there were dozens more supreme artists known only to minority audiences—bluesmen from

Chicago and Memphis like Muddy Waters, Big Bill Broonzy, Howlin' Wolf, John Lee Hooker and Memphis Slim—who were masters of vocal delivery and gut-wrenchingly intense guitar.

Many first came to notice through two sets of brothers: the Chess brothers, who started the small Chess label in Chicago, and the Ertegun brothers, who founded the equally small Atlantic label. Through their efforts, and those of even more obscure record companies, a host of blues giants were taped in studios, empty clubs, YMCAs, and ordinary living rooms.

If music like this was rarely heard on mainstream U.S. radio, it was totally absent from the airwaves in Britain. As Beck observes: "We were starved for that. Talk about censorship. You'd be lucky to hear any black music on the radio here in the '50s and '60s unless you tuned in to a foreign station."

A few of those blues legends actually visited Britain during the '50s, at the behest of Chris Barber and his band. Barber was virtually unique in his passionate support of American "roots" music, and even though his band was mainly trad jazz, he always found a special place in his shows for skiffle, country blues, and R&B. Still, it was rare for news of these visitors to reach the ears of any but the initiated. Their recordings could only be had as imports from the jazz record shops in London's Charing Cross Road, on Chess, Atlantic, and more exotic labels such as Sue, Okeh, Imperial, and Delmark.

One such invitee was the great Muddy Waters, from Chicago's South Side, who played the first raucous, gutsy electric guitar anyone in Britain had ever witnessed in the flesh. Young Brian Jones, who later formed the Rolling Stones, was at London's Marquee Club that night in 1958 and it had a profound effect on him. An inveterate experimenter, he immediately switched to electric guitar and taught himself to play like Muddy Waters. Among his other accomplishments was slide guitar in the style of Elmore James, a technique virtually unknown in Britain then.

Ahmet Ertegun, head of Atlantic Records, later commented: "White Southerners had heard these black singers all their lives, but for the British it was something new and exciting. The Southerners would say, 'What's new about these guys? Nigger music, man.' But Jagger, Pete Townshend, McCartney, Lennon, were all intellectual appreciators of this foreign form—in a sense they were appreciating something the Americans did not value. The Brits took it much more seriously and were trying to be authentic in reproducing the music they loved."

Jeff Beck had already gone through rockabilly, country, folk, and big-band jazz by the time he first started investigating the blues. He cited Ian "Stu" Stewart, the brilliant pianist who helped Brian Jones get the Rolling Stones together, as the person who originally turned him on to Chicago blues and bottleneck guitar with the aid of a limitless record collection.

"That was the whole applecart being upset. We were suited and tied and ready to go, with pointy shoes, and then that comes along and you don't want the suit and the shoes anymore. You want to be ragged. There was a whole rumble of this stuff coming over. It was so crude and lovable and accessible. There was no way you could not like it if you were a dirty boy. I opted for that, because I didn't want to be on TV and polished and put in a slot. That was rebellious."

So Beck absorbed as much as he could: "My interest in blues started when the Chicago blues albums began to reach England. I grabbed them. Muddy Waters, Buddy Guy . . . I think they're just great. There's a special way the guitars sound: sort of tinny and rough. The Chicago sound—it's like nothing else. I was listening to Big Bill Broonzy trying to accompany himself, and I loved that thumping crudeness and the stomping foot. It's the kind of guitar playing that sounded crude only until you tried to play it—you know what I mean?

"Then I went backwards—I went back into the deep South, the blues, Cajun music. And I used to just listen to singles by the most completely off the wall guys you've never heard of. Just to try to get an extra lick or an extra tonal something."

Later, he recalled, there was a landmark blues album that influenced him profoundly. It was a Chicago club recording, *Folk Festival of the Blues*, featuring Buddy Guy's band with artists like Howlin' Wolf, Sonny Boy Williamson, and Muddy Waters. "I would have loved to play with Muddy. Try to get that lurch. Nobody phrases like him. They can't—it's that full-bodied hippo voice that he's got."

One of the most important events for Beck was seeing Howlin' Wolf and Buddy Guy perform in 1963. But it was Buddy Guy who made the greatest impression: "It was the total manic abandon in Buddy's solos. They broke all boundaries. I just thought, this is more like it! Also, his solos weren't restricted to a three-minute pop format; they were long and really developed."

Guy's all-out extrovert style instilled in the young Beck a sense of try-anything fearlessness. Guy's own adolescent hero was Eddie "Guitar Slim" Jones, whose raw, superamplified guitar laid down new directions in electric blues, and whose showmanship drew frequent later comparisons with Jimi Hendrix. Almost twenty years before Hendrix, Slim was playing guitar behind his head, barrelling into the audience at the end of a 350-foot cord, and generally earning the title of the performin'est bluesman that ever was. Slim died at the age of 32, leaving very few recordings, but Buddy Guy was one of those who drew on his flamboyant style. Guy would slap his strings with a handkerchief or a drumstick, or begin his sets from inside the men's room, all the while shaking up the house with his wild multi-fret bends and piercing, string-snapping attack.

Jeff Beck inherited that same abandon, together with Guy's readiness to go for broke and risk screwing up. "That's the personality coming out," says Beck. "Somebody who was more reserved couldn't bear the thought of a screw-up. Actually, I can't bear the thought of it, but I do it anyhow!"

UNTIL THIS TIME, there was one tiny sect in London heroically dedicated to playing nothing but the blues, and its leading light was the engaging and cultured Alexis Korner. Korner's Blues Incorporated was a constantly fluctuating caucus of musicians who, after years of occasional stints, started a residency in 1962 at their own small club in Ealing, West London. Thanks to the redoubtable Chris Barber, they soon obtained a regular Thursday night gig at the Marquee Club, at that time owned by Barber's National Jazz League.

Korner's band acted as a launchpad for an amazing number of early blues exponents, including vocalist Long John Baldry, bass guitarist Jack Bruce, drummer Ginger Baker, Graham Bond on organ, Cyril Davies on harmonica (who would later branch out with his own band, the All Stars), and four of the original Rolling Stones.

Aside from Korner's club, there were precious few regular spots where a blues enthusiast could go to listen or blow with like-minded musicians. But later that year a new blues club got started, which was destined to be the birthplace of two of the most successful British R&B outfits of that decade. This was Giorgio Gomelsky's Crawdaddy Club in Richmond, Surrey.

A true cosmopolitan, Gomelsky was a White Russian who had lived in Switzerland, Italy, and Germany, and had long been involved in the London jazz scene with Barber. After encountering the blues and traveling with bluesmen, Gomelsky had set up his own Piccadilly Blues Club; but now it had closed and he was in need of another venue.

Knowing the landlord of the Station Hotel in Richmond, Gomelsky begged the use of his back room for a regular Sunday night blues spot. One of the first groups he booked—reluctantly, as a fill-in—was the Rolling Stones: Brian Jones, Mick Jagger, Keith Richards, Bill Wyman, Stu Stewart, and Charlie Watts. Under Jones's leadership, the Stones were blues/R&B purists whom Gomelsky had previously found distinctly unimpressive. But this night it all came together, principally thanks to the tight-knit input of drummer Charlie Watts, who had just been persuaded to throw in his lot with the band.

The ragged trio of Jones, Jagger, and Richards had been hanging out for a year, jamming now and then in local clubs but getting virtually no paid work. For the whole of that time they'd played and practiced together, living cheek-by-jowl in stark squalor on the edge of starvation, with nothing else to do but perfect their individual techniques and scheme how to hustle their next meal.

The Stones managed to make an impact that night in Richmond, even though they played their blues like bluesmen, seated in a semicircle. They became a big attraction at the Crawdaddy, and Gomelsky became their de facto manager. The relationship was, however, very informal, and he never tried to put them under contract: "It was always a *partnership*," he insisted. "I used to divide the door receipts from each Sunday equally with them. I kept telling them, 'Wait. Get strong, so that you can handle all of it yourselves and don't have to ask anyone for anything. Don't run the risk of someone walking in here and taking you over.'"

A celebrated eccentric and dilettante, Gomelsky had many creative interests. These included film work, and while discussing a possible project with the newly famous Beatles, he invited them to see the Stones at the Crawdaddy. The lads from Liverpool, already on the road to stardom, were vastly impressed by this unknown R&B group that performed the kind of music they themselves had been devoted to when they started out. An instant rapport was set up, which would be influential in getting the Stones started on their recording career.

Giorgio was continually trying to get press exposure for his protégés, and in April 1963 his efforts paid off. An article in *Record Mirror* extolled the Stones as "destined to be the biggest group in the R&B scene." And, as a direct result, a brash nineteen-year-old by the name of Andrew Loog Oldham walked in and signed them to an exclusive contract while Gomelsky was in Switzerland at his father's funeral. The first thing Oldham did was eliminate Stu Stewart from their stage act: with his bluff features and lantern jaw, his image wasn't "hip" enough.

SINCE THE BEATLES have now made an appearance in our narrative, let us take time out to briefly examine their impact on the music industry at the time when Jeff Beck was standing on the threshold of fame.

It's almost impossible to overstate the Beatles' influence in those early years. Led by John Lennon, the tearaway kid who went through all the rebellious phases from teddy boy hooligan to arty beatnik, the group had been gigging since about 1957 in various incarnations. From their early beginnings in skiffle, they picked up on the vibrancy of Elvis Presley and rockabilly, but soon turned to the genuine black R&B of stars like Chuck Berry. This music, imbued with Liverpool street-toughness and art-school bohemianism, emerged as their own style of "beat" music.

Fired by Allen Ginsburg's poetry and Jack Kerouac's *On the Road* philosophy, the beat generation had a more coherent and self-assured view of life than the mixed-up rebel without a cause of the mid '50s: kicking out conformity to stale, superficial values, and ditching materialism in favor of rootless wanderings in search of self-realization.

The beatnik was as much a public enemy as the erstwhile teddy boy, and Lennon's anarchic group adopted a name that defiantly identified them with the beat movement. From stints in the Hamburg lowlife clubs they returned to Liverpool with searing, raving rip-offs of Chuck Berry, Carl Perkins and Little Richard that engendered a fire in the bellies of their devoted Cavern Club followers; such a fire as the blues-dedicated Rolling Stones had never dreamed of (but very soon would).

It was exquisitely ironic, therefore, that the purist Stones would come to epitomize the great rock rebellion just when the rebellious Beatles—"groomed for stardom" by their new manager, Brian Epstein—had been thoroughly toned down, their black leathers exchanged for matching band suits and their unruly hairstyles coaxed into bouncy, shiny mop-tops.

They knew it was a cop-out, of course. But the rewards were immediate and tangible. And what group of provincial twenty-year-olds could have resisted what seemed like a small price for instant fame and fortune?

At the time of the first Beatles-Stones meeting, in 1963, the Beatles had developed from a great bunch of Liverpool rockers into a national hit group writing hugely commercial material: raw and raving enough for the youth market, catchy and foot-tapping enough for mass appeal. It was exactly the right combination to boost them to global fame, and it was destined to turn the tables—sensationally—on Britain's poor-relation status vis-à-vis the United States.

By now, rock 'n' roll was becoming a sadly discredited term anyway. A strangely complaisant Elvis had been drafted into army service, and at KWK Radio in St Louis, an entire week was devoted to smashing rock 'n' roll records on the air.

The big U.S. record labels had ousted their more adventurous independent rivals (and Alan Freed with them) as a result of the great payola witch-hunt, a carefully orchestrated exposure operation from which even the Mafia could learn a few tips, and no doubt did. In their place, the market was saturated with clean-cut, coyly posturing teen songsters delivering nonstop schlock, to the great relief of American matrons, while giants like Chuck Berry and Jerry Lee Lewis were gleefully hounded from the public stage on dubious morality charges.

A number of other great rock 'n' rollers had died, either literally or figuratively, with Elvis leading the headlong lemming rush to be an "all-round family entertainer." He emerged from the U.S. Army to sing—yes—nonstop schlock, and to star in a series of cretinous movies over which, in deference to his once sublime pre-eminence, we shall draw a discreet veil.

The only other innovation of the time was a succession of dance crazes, notably the Twist, which had nothing to recommend them musically. They did, however, represent two significant departures. They were the first of the new free-form dances in which no bodily contact was made. And they heralded the phenomenon of teenage modes and manners gradually infiltrating, and eventually dominating, the entire social mainstream.

The world was ready, almost holding its breath, for the Beatles to arrive. And they scattered all before them with a sound that was unique. Unique, that is, until the music industry discovered what it considered to be the Beatles formula. Whereupon, in imitation of the Fab Four, a legion of instantly forgettable groups were quickly foisted onto the affluent youth market in a kind effort to relieve teenagers of the wads of money in their pockets.

THE '60S IN BRITAIN had ushered in a boom in spending power on the part of the young, who found themselves able, at last, to catch up with their American cousins. A variety of jobs beckoned them in the expanding economy, and an even greater variety of consumer goods targeted their three main concerns: music, clothes, and dating.

Their elders and betters were stunned by this reversal in the natural order of things, which had hitherto dictated that all your life you must scrimp and save to have a bit of money to spend in your old age. Heavens, these upstarts had the money while they were still young enough to enjoy it! What's more, the invention of the birth control pill meant they could indulge in sex whenever they wanted, which seemed to be all the time. Everyone knew the natural order decreed that you exercised sexual restraint while you were at the peak of your powers, in order to reap the rewards of permissible sex after you were married—when, between being kept awake all night by the kids and slaving all day to support them, you were too exhausted anyway. Which was only right and proper.

A mind-boggling assortment of fads were adopted by the young, whose massive economic power dictated ever-changing fashion: the clothes you bought, the clubs you frequented, the dances you did, the pills you popped, all immediately disposable in favor of the next craze.

It must have been quite a jolt for the diehard adherents of blues and R&B to find their music, so long languishing in obscurity, was suddenly in vogue with the all-powerful youth market. In particular it was adopted by vast sectors of the mods, the self-styled fashion trendsetters of the day with their severely razored hair, stark white faces, high-button Ivy League suits, and Lambretta motor scooters. (Their antithesis was manifested in the cult of the rocker, booted and studded in grubby leathers, whose ethic was sworn devotion to authentic rock 'n' roll, motorbikes, and scrapping with mods on Bank Holiday beaches.)

At the clubs in the South of England where mods and students gathered, their cult heroes were the rough-hewn modernists of the genre, more raw and experimental when they played their blues, more wild and propulsive when they stomped out their R&B. One of the top haunts outside of London, which had a magic atmosphere and a huge assortment of bars, was a cavernous old dance hall in the Eel Pie Island Hotel at Twickenham (literally a tiny island on the River Thames, you reached it via an old wooden footbridge over the water). There was also the Crawdaddy, of course, and the Ricky Tick clubs at Windsor, Kingston, and West Wickham, as well as innumerable back rooms in local pubs.

These places were often frequented around 1962 by a young Eric Clapton, already a serious student of the blues whose career at Kingston College of Art had been cut short in favor of jamming on guitar. By early 1963 he was playing semi-professionally but sporadically.

At about the same time a young blond-haired vocalist/harmonica player named Keith Relf teamed with guitar player Paul Samwell-Smith to form the Metropolitan Blues Quartet, which then dropped two members and acquired three others to become the five-piece blues/R&B group the Yardbirds. The name, adopted from the writings of Jack Kerouac, referred to the hobos who hung around railway yards and "rode the rails." From small beginnings in the pubs and clubs of Richmond, they were the next group to come under Giorgio Gomelsky's wing.

In September, the Rolling Stones were booked on a package tour: a golden opportunity for the Yardbirds to approach Gomelsky about a slot at the Crawdaddy.

Chris Dreja recalls: "We'd only been going about six weeks, but Paul and Keith decided it was worth a try and they invited him down to see us rehearse. He loved us and took us on the spot. That was a real breakthrough: we had a major venue to play. But can you imagine what it was like to follow the Stones?"

The Yardbirds' lead guitar at the time was sixteen-year-old Tony "Top" Topham, who shortly afterwards was forced by parental pressure to return to his studies. So in October 1963, Relf invited the unknown Eric Clapton to take his place. The first classic lineup of the group was thus established, with Paul Samwell-Smith firmly relegated to bass at Clapton's insistence, Chris Dreja handling rhythm guitar, and Jim McCarty as drummer. And this time Giorgio Gomelsky, doubtless a wiser man after his last experience, signed them to a management contract.

Gomelsky always seemed a larger-than-life character to his protégés. As Jim McCarty remembers, "He drove a silver Lancia—he was mad about old Italian sports cars—and he spoke several languages; he seemed an incredibly worldly figure. He adopted an almost parental role with us and saw himself as the sixth member of the band. Most managers of the time were really sharp business types, whereas Giorgio was one of the first creative and humanitarian ones. Even if he was a disaster in other areas, he was the best thing that could have happened to us at the time."

Gomelsky proceeded to do an excellent job of shaping the Yardbirds' early career, starting with a tour backing Sonny Boy Williamson, who was in Europe with the American Blues Festival package. It was a dream come true for the boys from Surrey, whose duties included cutting a live album with Williamson in December.

The LP was not released at the time, however. It was held back for several years in the U.K. and only appeared in 1966, long after Clapton had left the group. By the time of its release, Clapton had perfected a superb guitar technique that was to single him out as one of Britain's foremost blues exponents; one can only imagine his reaction on hearing again those enthusiastic but unformed guitar sounds on the Williamson album, recorded at a time when he was serving an early apprenticeship.

Clapton later reflected that British musicians in the early '60s held an exceedingly romantic image of the blues. "The love affair, the obsession with the blues was reinforced by the fact that it was so inaccessible. And I belonged to this incredibly exclusive club—whose members included Keith and Mick and Peter Green and people like that—who had, like, a mission. We were crusaders in a way, and that was a great, secure feeling for a person of my type, who came from a very nowhere sort of place, to have somewhere really worthwhile to go.

"And the Yardbirds liked to listen to 'Five Long Years' by Eddie Boyd. We thought something like [Bo Diddley's] 'I'm a Man' was pretty commercial, because we were all into Jesse Fuller or Furry Lewis. Those records were gold dust to us. We were country blues fanatics—but to play, we had to have records to emulate that had drums and bass and guitars, so they had to be R&B records."

For the Yardbirds 1964 was a breakthrough year with residencies that included the Marquee Club, now a storming R&B venue, together with months of one-night stands. On 28 February they played at the first British Rhythm & Blues Festival at the Birmingham Town Hall.

They signed a recording contract with Columbia, producing two singles—the first Billy Boy Arnold's "I Wish You Would," and the second Don & Bob's R&B standard "Good Morning Little Schoolgirl," which reached number 44 in the charts.

A live album, recorded in March at the Marquee, would be released in December as *Five Live Yardbirds*. This showcased a style of playing they'd cemented even before Clapton joined them, which was to extend their numbers with sudden changes in tempo and volume, building to a gradual climax and adding a coda in which the group improvised wildly at top volume, bringing their cheering fans to their feet—a "rave-up" that had become their trademark.

Their sound was a pile-driving, two-fisted R&B with Keith Relf's harp and hard-edged, somewhat nasal vocalizing very much to the fore, to which Eric Clapton's increasingly compelling solos often served as a welcome antithesis. Clapton soon built up a devoted following for whom his masterly guitar work was the main attraction.

The Yardbirds finally ended their busy year as the opening act on the Beatles Christmas Show at the Hammersmith Odeon, West London. But by now things were not going at all to Clapton's taste. Blues and R&B seemed to be taking second place to pop shows and package tours, and he felt out of place in the commercialized direction they were taking.

When the time came to select titles for their third single, opinions were sharply divided. Clapton suggested "Your One and Only Man," an Otis Redding title, but he was overruled and the song chosen was the chart-oriented "For Your Love," written by Graham Gouldman (who would achieve fame in the '70s with 10CC).

The song also presented new opportunities for the kind of interesting instrumentation the Beatles were introducing on their records. The group decided to feature a harpsichord on the intro, punctuated with the sound of eerily decaying bongos. Yardbirds fans were somewhat taken aback by this new departure, but it had the desired effect: released at the beginning of March 1965, it reached an impressive number three position in the national charts.* In June it made number six in the United States.

Clapton hated the song, especially since there was no lead guitar and they expected him to reproduce the harpsichord sound onstage with a twelve-string. Declaring he wanted his music to be taken more seriously, he announced his

*The chart positions quoted in this book are the ones most generally accepted: Billboard charts in the United States, and GRR publications in the UK. However, many music industry journals ran their own charts in the 1960s, and on several of them the Yardbirds' singles scored higher placings than are mentioned here, including number one slots.

intention to leave the Yardbirds only a matter of days before the single was released. A month later he was invited to join John Mayall's Bluesbreakers, one of the leading club-based outfits that concentrated on authentic blues.

The Yardbirds now had to enlist a replacement for Clapton, with two heavy responsibilities: promoting what promised to be their first hit single, and stepping into the hallowed shoes of a guitarist who was rapidly becoming a cult figure.

3 Five Yardbirds

BY 1965, JEFF BECK'S career had taken some varied turns. He had continued gigging with the Deltones until they split up (probably about the summer of 1961) when Del Burchell, their vocalist, moved on to front another group. Known as the Crescents, this new group operated around the West London area—the Boathouse at Kew Bridge, the Airport Bowl at Heathrow, etc.—and for a while Beck was persuaded to play Shadows-style guitar again. The young Beck's later description of his "first professional appearance" may have referred to his debut with them in Tunbridge Wells. While playing with the Crescents he cut what was almost certainly his first record, a demo of one of the Deltones' best loved songs, "Wedding Bells." Roger Jarvie remembers that it was recorded as a single for one of the major labels, but was never given a commercial release.

Cash was, as always, a weighty problem, so Beck started on a number of stopgap jobs to earn some money. Over the next couple of years they included a spot of carpentry, painting and decorating, a stint driving a tractor on a golf course, and doing fuller's earth deliveries. "I was sweeping roads and delivering milk," he joked later.

More to his liking was his job at a body shop, earning around £10 a week. Here he learned body work and became proficient at the demanding art of spray painting—skills that he's used ever since in his passion for building and reworking hot rods.

Somewhere along the line it's clear a certain disillusion with music had set in. "I was still trying to find out what the hell I should be doing. Nothing much was happening, because a lot of soppy pop records were coming out, and nobody wanted to be a part of that. There was just no position for a guitarist like me, no way I could get off on it."

So his next move was to sell his Stratocaster and buy a car instead. But not before he'd repainted it and tampered disastrously with the wiring. The handsome sunburst had first been painted red, and then repainted white.

"I'd seen a Gene Vincent LP cover with white Fender Strats being held by his group. I thought I'd try and get their sound out of mine, so I painted it white and then set to work on the electrics. That was a big mistake! I just couldn't get the sound right no matter what I did, so I threw it off the end of my bed one night in a rage. It cracked, of course, down the back where the neck meets the body. I decided to sell it and jack the whole thing in. I'd always wanted a car. For a time I was happy just to drive around, but after a while I felt like playing again and joined another group as lead guitarist. I didn't have a guitar of my own, so another of the blokes let me use his Fender Telecaster." (Even so, whether his own or borrowed, Beck never seems to have been without a guitar in the interim. Reports have him playing a "grubby old white Watkins," a British design catering principally to the beginners market.)

The group in question may have been the Nightshift, his first regular R&B group, which seems to have been formed in 1962 or early 1963—by which time he'd fallen in with Stu Stewart of the Rolling Stones and his indoctrination into blues and R&B was well under way. Around the same time he also came under the spell of Patricia Brown from nearby Crawley; they would marry in July 1963. A pretty brunette with long hair and a talent for dress-making, Pat didn't seem to mind that fashion was the last thing Jeff had any use for. His style, in fact, was distinctly bohemian. Much like the Jagger-Richards partnership of the time, his devotion to the blues meant a rejection of all that was safe and conventional: of middle-class aspirations, of comfortable white music. The despair of his parents, his graceless ways and scruffy clothes even earned notoriety among his friends.

A loner from way back, Beck had drifted from group to group until settling into the Nightshift. He'd hear that a certain R&B outfit needed a lead guitar and would wander in without speaking to anyone, set up his amp, and plug in. They'd usually be taken with him and ask him to come back, which he might or might not do. Then he'd be off somewhere else again.

An irregular contact at this time was vocalist Phil Somerville, an old crony of Beck's from his junior art school. Somerville formed a group, Brian Howard & the Silhouettes, and Beck played guitar on a few of their gigs. Later, when Somerville moved to 'Im & the Uvvers, he put the word out for Beck to stand in for their lead guitarist, who had upped and left. Beck agreed, rehearsed a couple of times, and strolled into the Foresters Hall at Epsom in time for the fourth number of their set. Somerville knew better than to remonstrate with the wayward Beck, just as he knew better than to comment on his down-at-heel appearance and unkempt, overgrown hair.

"He was an amazing bloke—he'd come to a gig and he'd be filthy. He'd have been working on a bike or something and his hands would be covered in oil and grease. He'd have smudges on his face and his hair would be stuck together with oil. . . . But when I chatted with him about music, his knowledge was extra-ordinary for someone so young. It was quite literally all self-taught, from old records and stuff like that. He created that magical talent just from within himself."

After eight or nine gigs Beck lost interest in the Uvvers, and a flurry of other short-lived liaisons ensued. We may suppose it was around the turn of 1962-63 that the Nightshift came into being, and Beck seems to have been a founding member, together with a drummer mate by the name of Dave Elvidge. A full-blooded R&B group, the Nightshift started playing regularly at Eel Pie Island and some of London's leading club venues like the 100 Club; Phil Somerville recalls they once headlined a bill with the Rolling Stones opening for them.

After this promising start, the Nightshift went into the studio to record two singles for the Piccadilly label. The titles were "Stormy Monday" backed with "That's My Story," an early Tim Rice composition; and "Corrina Corrina," B-side title unknown.

By now Beck was pretty well known on the circuit, and offers were coming his way. In an eerie parallel of Eric Clapton's career at around the same time, he found himself approached to join Tom McGuinness' group the Roosters, which was just getting serious and looking for a guitarist. After Beck said no, the job was taken by Clapton.

"Although I considered it seriously, I finally blew the Roosters out. And then I had a request to play with John Mayall, but I didn't know anything about him. I was in a guitar shop in Charing Cross Road when I heard his name mentioned, and I asked who he was and whether he was any good; and one of the guitar salesmen was saying, 'He's the guv'nor, you'd better see him,' but I never did get around to it."

Once again Beck had passed on a band that later featured Eric Clapton. John Mayall made repeated telephone calls trying to track him down, but if this was, as we may suppose, sometime around spring 1963, then Mayall hadn't yet made his reputation on the London scene and scarcely had more to offer than the Nightshift, with its recording contract and regular R&B gigs.

When Beck made his next significant move, probably around late summer/autumn of 1963, he had perhaps come to realize that the recording career with Piccadilly was not about to become reality after all: both the Nightshift singles had been shelved. They would eventually appear in 1965, at a time when, ironically, their release was probably the last thing he wanted.

HIS CHOICE WAS to join the Tridents, a thriving group from the Chiswick area who played regularly around Richmond, Kingston, and Twickenham: "They were really my scene because they were playing flat-out R&B, like Jimmy Reed stuff, and we supercharged it all up and made it really rocky. I got off on that, even though it was only twelve-bar blues."

The Tridents were John Lucas (rhythm guitar/vocals/harp), Paul Lucas (bass/vocals), and Ray Cook (drums). Their most recent lead guitarist, Mickey Jopp, was an excellent player but reluctant to take the plunge and go professional, so they invited Beck to join them. (Paul Lucas remembers he jumped at the offer: "I wondered how long it would take you to ask me!")

Beck recalls: "I'd been screaming to be recognized, and I finally found this little R&B band which I thought was great. I helped build them up. We had a guy who used to play the harmonica like Little Walter, an unbelievable blues player. And a little drummer who was seventeen or eighteen or something. They had no image whatsoever. I remember the drummer had hair three feet long that used to hang over the snare drum. And the other two guys in the band were brothers who had short, nondescript hairstyles. But we played very good authentic blues."

Beck was impressed enough with the Tridents to want to stay put, which he did for a year and a half, although oddly enough during this time he was photographed playing with the Nightshift again when the group appeared at the 4th National Jazz & Blues Festival in Richmond, Surrey, in August 1964—perhaps filling in for this one gig.

Now indulging his growing mastery of his medium, he was constantly finding new inspirations. He perfected his slide technique, for example, by emulating Chicagoan Earl Hooker, one of whose recordings—"You Shook Me"—led to a later famous Beck cover version.

But without a doubt it was wild-man Buddy Guy who was his major influence. Wildness soon became his hallmark as he explored his extraordinary taste for innovation, wringing more and more amazing sounds from his off-white Telecaster—a guitar on which bassist Paul Lucas specially rewired the pickups for him. (This was probably the borrowed guitar which Beck recalls he bought eventually.)

The style he evolved was a personal amalgam of everything that fired his musical imagination. Right from his earliest days he'd been profoundly affected by the genius of Les Paul, and would practice Les Paul runs for hours so he had them down perfectly. Playing with jazz-style wizardry in the Charlie Christian idiom, Paul notched up 11 number-one hits with his elegant brand of swing-influenced pop, and by the late '40s had opened new vistas for the electric guitar with the technical effects he created: sound boxes, tape echo, speed shifts, and multiple overdubbing.

Beck remembers: "Les was at his peak during an era of great melody, all those lovely chords, so he had a whole ocean of stuff. Then he'd go bananas with all his effects, showers of notes and whatnot. I wanted to get those atmospherics. I was just as unrestricted, in a way, as Les because our music was a wide open sea of emptiness where I could do what I wanted."

Another potent influence was the rich, glowing soul music that appeared in the early '60s, full of awakening black pride and optimism. Solomon Burke, Otis Redding, and vocal groups like the Impressions with Curtis Mayfield. The never-ending flow of inventive, tuneful Motown hits. And the superb Memphis funk of Booker T & the MGs—best remembered for "Green Onions," which made a lasting impact on Beck—and of Rufus Thomas ("The Dog"), which meta-morphosed into the blue-beat craze. It all added up to a wonderful new fund of black music that was positively inspirational.

RIK GUNNELL, one of the leading bookers of R&B groups, started advertising the Tridents in February 1964. Already they were regulars in the West End of London, packing out the 100 Club on Oxford Street, whose agency also advertised them, and playing the famous all-nighters at Studio 51. ("Nobody had any bread or homes, they all came for shelter and music—and they got it.") Soon, with a

Beck rejoins the Nightshift for the 4th National Jazz & Blues Festival, Richmond, August 1964 (L-R Jeff Beck, Brian Wiles).

residency at Eel Pie Island on Sunday or Wednesday every week, they were at the height of their considerable popularity.

"At Eel Pie Island down in Twickenham, which I expect most of the old looners will remember, I used to just play amid a wash of beer and smelly cigarettes. We used to have a really good time . . . and then all of a sudden people started turning up in droves." According to Arthur Chisholm, who ran Eel Pie, they would regularly attract crowds of around 1,000 at their gigs—leading to a handsome fee increase from £25 to £40 a night. Once, when they supported Jesse Fuller, a record 1,500 people packed the place like sardines.

By now Beck was unleashing some seriously anarchic guitar. "I remember de-tuning the low E and A strings and just whining the hell out of 'em, making ridiculous noises, and everyone went berserk. There wasn't an ounce of musical sense to it, but they loved it because it was different."

Most revolutionary in his arsenal of ridiculous noises was the controlled use of feedback, that ear-splitting screech caused by the amplified signal being picked up by the instrument. Even before joining the Tridents Beck had learned it could be tamed and harnessed for his own nefarious purposes.

"I had a terrible home-made amplifier. If I turned it up to get more volume, it would squeak and make hideous noises. It was a monster which I rewired and nailed together. People would come round and say how great it sounded but it was just awful. That's when I discovered distortion and feedback—so I bought a better amplifier and refined the weird noises."

In the ensuing years, claims and counterclaims ran rife as to who actually invented this "playing" of feedback, one of the leading contenders being his contemporary Pete Townshend who was also one of guitar's early anarchists. Beck has usually tried to stay out of the firing line, but he's made it clear that he, at least, never heard anyone previously using feedback that way. "I had been experimenting with feedback since at least 1960," he told *Guitar World* in 1999. And he perfected it to an amazing degree.

"I started fooling with feedback because we began playing larger gigs where we couldn't be heard. In the end I just got berserk. . . . I thought, 'Wow, that whistle's controllable; it's coming from the string.' So I'd just bend the note around the feedback. The more I got into it, the more I found I could control it. I started finding the resonant points on the neck where it came in best. I loved it because it was a most peculiar sound that contrasted wildly with a plucked string, this round, trombone-like noise coming from nowhere."

One night in 1964, when the BBC recorded the Tridents at the Island, the sound engineer was so destroyed by the noises coming from Beck's guitar that he came rushing down, headphones still dangling around his neck, to find out what the heck was going on!

John Platt, in his magazine *Comstock Lode*, reported that people who saw Beck with the Tridents reckoned his playing was better with them—and wilder—than at any other time. The group was even featured in a song titled "Richmond," recorded by Andy Roberts and released on a sampler LP, *Clogs*, on the Peg label around 1972. The words recall: "Remember the nights on the Island / Newcastle Ale on the grass / Jeff on stage with the Tridents / Talkin' 'bout the past, my love / Talkin' 'bout the past." (Cloud Cuckoo Songs Ltd.)

PLAYING WITH THE TRIDENTS was a fantastic experience during those years, when the whole scene had an incomparable vibe—and there he was, plonk in the center of it all.

"Yeah, that was really good," he remembers. "I felt like I was part of something back then. All the groups knew each other by name and everybody'd be watching and stealing each other's licks. You really felt as if you were *in* on something. The only trouble was that I found myself being encircled a bit too much by the blues. That's all that was going on in England at the time. And if a group suddenly tried to go off on a tangent, everyone would laugh and say, 'Ayyy, come on, stop all that crap. Play some proper blues.'"

The Lucas brothers, mainstay of the Tridents, 1964/5 (L Paul, bass/vocals, R John, rhythm guitar/vocals).

A taste of that era can be heard on three previously unreleased Tridents tracks, which the Lucas brothers—who still play professionally—provided to Gregg Geller for the 1991 three-CD retrospective *Beckology*. Two of these, recorded in 1963 or early 1964, were the old blues standard "Trouble in Mind," featuring Beck on bottleneck guitar, and the group's self-penned "Wandering Man Blues." They were actually the B-sides of two demo discs they'd produced in their search for the ever-elusive recording contract, the A-sides being, respectively, Louisiana Red's "Keep Your Hands Off My Woman" and another Tridents composition, "That Noise."

Beck retains only the vaguest memories of the latter demo: "I couldn't believe it when I heard it back—it sounded really great to me, and I thought, 'That's it, we've done it!' And of course it probably never went any further than [the agent's] office. I can't really remember what the songs were, but I think one was like a half-assed blues thing with the words changed, which wasn't a very good thing to put out, and the B-side was just us jamming."

But Matt Resnicoff, reviewing the *Beckology* set for *Musician* magazine, singled out the Tridents recordings for particular praise: "One moment he's supple and twisting, by the next pure caterwaul. Jeff Beck, barely out of his teens, was a class act—in a class by himself."

The third Tridents cut, Bo Diddley's "Nursery Rhyme," was recorded live at Eel Pie Island in April 1964. Replete with feedback and atonal dissonances, it captures the wild malevolent snarls of Beck's stage freakouts in those heady days of experiment in sound, long before guitar anarchy became a rock way of life.

"The amplifiers would feed back anyway, but to use it was a good way of getting out of it. It would start whistling and singing, then you found that you could probably handle it, and make quite an interesting trumpeting noise with it—and with an echo all sorts of mysteries started to happen and it would sound really bizarre."

Beck's echo unit with the Tridents was a Baby Binson—a unit that Alan Hope (Kerry Rapid) remembers him using when he was with the Bandits—which worked on the magnetic drum principle. But Beck also owned a tape unit, a Klempf Echolette, which he rigged to produce a myriad of different effects: "It had alternate delays. I knew how to hot rod the sounds without actually touching a soldering iron to it. It was an advanced little box for the time, but it broke down a lot at gigs. There'd be a temperature change, and the tape would snap halfway through the first number, and all my tricks would be gone! I used to have half-second, quarter-second and eighth-second delays built in, and I could let it build and build and build. I'd play a note, and then before the echo would come back on tape I'd play another note—and on and on."

Trident Paul Lucas recalls there were people who actually doubted Beck's ability to play some of his runs without using echo: "So one night at Eel Pie we took along an old Spanish acoustic guitar, which he played in front of a mike with no effects at all. His prowess earned him a tremendous ovation from the audience."

John Lucas also remembers the noises Beck would wring from his first fuzz-box, built for him in 1963 by brother Paul, a true electronics wizard: a ground-breaking unit for its time, the fuzz reproduced the effect of valve (tube) distortion in an overdriven amp, but at controllable volumes. "It made an incredible, fat sax-like sound which was amazing—we really should have patented that fuzz!

"The way we played together was really tight," John recalls. "We didn't do much rehearsing because we just picked up on each other as we went along. I remember when we'd do 'Jeff's Boogie' and he would decide to put in a quote from 'In the Mood' or something—all he had to do was look up at me and I'd know. We'd just go straight into it, with me playing off him, whatever it was. Those tracks on *Beckology* weren't the best of the Tridents by any means: Paul has a collection of tapes and some of them are much better—better quality too— more typical of what we used to do."

To quote Gregg Geller, himself a longtime Beck fan, "It's astonishing what Jeff was up to prior to being in the Yardbirds. His work in the Yardbirds has been cited quite rightly as the beginning of a lot of what we call rock guitar playing; and here he is, a year before, doing all that—and sometimes more."

Though Jeff was self-deprecating in his recollections, "Wandering Man Blues" is a miniature gem despite the inevitable deficiencies in sound quality. Thanks to *Beckology* we are again able to hear Beck, after an interval of more than thirty years, as he lays down an eminently satisfying 12-bar blues, with a bang-on-the-nail solo that begs comparison with the later Eric Clapton. In fact, his fluency of touch easily rivals what his contemporary was doing at the time— witness the Sonny Boy Williamson/Yardbirds tapes—which this writer can confirm from many a Clapton gig in those days.

Beck also deftly handles the vocals on this track, which John Lucas remem-bers was not an uncommon event: "He could sing blues really well, it's a pity he never developed that side of his voice." But Beck was always a victim of his own

100 Club Calendar
SEPTEMBER

All sessions 7.30 p.m. until 11.0 p.m.

Tuesday	1st	The Pretty Things Brian Knight's Blues By Six
Wednesday	2nd	WEDNESDAY NIGHT BEAT SESSION Duffy Power and the Fentones Brian Something and the Whatsits
Thursday	3rd	The Graham Bond Organisation The King B Four
Monday	7th	The Birds The Blues By Night
Tuesday	8th	The Pretty Things Brian Knight's Blues By Six
Wednesday	9th	WEDNESDAY NIGHT BEAT SESSION The Kinks Danny and the Torinos
Thursday	10th	The Graham Bond Organisation The King B Four
Monday	14th	The Birds The Blues By Night
Tuesday	15th	The Art Woods Brian Knight's Blues By Six
Wednesday	16th	WEDNESDAY NIGHT BEAT SESSION Peter Jay and the Jaywalkers Ray Dell and the Deacons
Thursday	17th	The Tridents The King B Four
Monday	21st	The Birds Brian Knight's Blues By Six
Tuesday	22nd	The Art Woods Brian Knight's Blues By Six
Wednesday	23rd	WEDNESDAY NIGHT BEAT SESSION John Lee and the Ground Hogs The Heebie Jeebies
Thursday	24th	The Graham Bond Organisation The King B Four
Monday	28th	The Birds Brian Knight's Blues By Six
Tuesday	29th	The Tridents and Brian Knight's Blues By Six
Wednesday	30th	WEDNESDAY NIGHT BEAT SESSION The Honeycombs The Forerunners

This programme is subject to alteration

100 Club Program advertising the Tridents, 1964.

exacting standards, and never put in the groundwork to develop that vocal instrument of which he maintained a crushingly low opinion. Had he done so, and had he too followed a similar career as bluesman, we'd probably be hearing Beck sing today as often as we hear Clapton.

AMERICAN BLUES AND rockabilly were a love the teenage Beck had shared with another Surrey schoolkid, Jimmy Page. Just a few months older, Page grew up in Epsom, not far from Beck's home in the South West suburbs of London. He had started the guitar quite late—only when he was fifteen—and hadn't been playing long when the two had their first encounter through Jeff's sister, Annetta.

"Pagey's name was being bandied around my house a lot, because my sister went to [Ewell Technical College], Epsom, where he went, and she kept telling me I should meet this guy—'You gotta meet Jimmy, this weird thin guy playing a weird-shaped guitar like yours.' She was laughing at me all the time I was the only one, but as soon as she saw someone else, she urged me to meet him. We went over on the bus to see him, and he just knocked me out straightaway, because he was far more into it than I was."

Page also vividly remembered that first meeting: "He came round to my house with a home-made guitar and played the James Burton solo from Ricky Nelson's 'My Babe' and we were immediately like blood brothers." As Page responded with his own fluent Burton licks, an instant friendship was formed.

Soon, evenings and weekends found them together in each other's houses, listening to records and trading licks. Page's mother, who fortunately enjoyed his music, bought him a tape recorder so he could convert the front room into a studio, complete with assorted instruments and a drum kit. They did a lot of jamming, even making home recordings together. And the lasting bond that was forged as teenagers would prove to have a far-reaching influence on the destinies of both guitarists.

Jimmy Page left school in 1959 to start gigging with local groups around the Surrey area. In fact, before they ever met, Beck had seen him at the very same fairgrounds where he himself used to make his eager weekend forays on fame.

"Page was sort of raving around with a big Gretsch Country Gentleman," he told Steven Rosen in *Guitar World*. "It looked big on him because he was such a shrimp—all you saw was this guitar being wielded by a pipe-cleaner man. He used to play really fiery sort of fast stuff, but nobody was listening, nobody wanted to hear him. He wasn't playing funky at all, it was just sort of 'Hava Nagila': terrible, but it was impressive!"

In 1961 Page was invited to join Neil Christian & the Crusaders. Though they had no hit records, they were a big draw around the club circuit, and his brilliant guitar work and showy stage gymnastics made him the band's main attraction. But by the following year he was thoroughly burnt out by life on the road and suffering repeated illnesses; despite an offer from Cyril Davies, he decided to give up touring and go to art school. He still kept on gigging locally, and one night, playing with an interval group at the Marquee, he was spotted and invited to do some sessions. By 1964 he was in high demand as one of London's most sought-after session guitarists.

Jimmy and Jeff had progressed to the blues together, and often spent time listening to records and working out ideas. Curiously enough, Page suggested his pal when Neil Christian was auditioning guitarists for a later incarnation of the Crusaders. But Beck was not destined to join the Christian band: "The only mistake I ever made," Christian said years later.

The two friends also jammed with members of other groups on the scene, including the Rolling Stones. One such jam took place at Eel Pie Island in May 1964, when the participants were Bill Wyman on bass, Stu Stewart on keyboards, a couple of Stewart's friends on drums and harmonica, plus Beck and Page on guitars. "Nobody knew we were going," Stewart said, "and we had a marvellous evening just playing the sort of music we all like." Confined to the sidelines with the Stones, Stewart also enjoyed flexing his muscles onstage at gigs with the Tridents, which he rated as a fine authentic blues band.

Another jam was actually taped at the time, and unintentionally produced recordings that survive to this day. It happened about a week after Christmas 1964, after an unreleased studio session with Jimmy Page producing and Glyn Johns as engineer, which had Beck augmenting ex-members of the Cyril Davies R&B All Stars, including pianist Nicky Hopkins. Hopkins, whose destiny would also become entwined with Beck's, had recently emerged from a long stay in the hospital: it was their first meeting. The tracks that survive include "Chuckles," an up-tempo boogie shuffle, and "Steelin'," a slide guitar workout predating Beck's "Steeled Blues," both released in 1968. Sadly unreleased was the first ever recording of "Jeff's Boogie," which would become his most famous personal showpiece.

The recordings were variously packaged, much against the wishes of all concerned, with extracts from another jam the following year involving Jimmy Page and Eric Clapton. Page, under contract to Andrew Oldham's Immediate label, was pressured into handing over all these tapes on the pretext that Immediate had rights to them.

By 1964 Beck was already getting session work through his pal; Page would bring him in when anything suitable came up—"Whenever they needed a rock 'n' roll guitar break, I'd play it." Ritchie Blackmore remembered the impression he made: "He was really good, even though he couldn't read at all. He was using the Telecaster and echoes and God knows what else. Jeff was the guy who would come along and people would go, 'Christ, who's he?' Nobody had actually done that kind of bending of notes before, not as much as Jeff had done it. He was the first I ever heard play like that."

Later, in *Guitar Player*, Ritchie added, "I remember saying to Jeff after a take, 'What was your name again? I've never heard of you.' I meant it as a compliment, like, 'Where have you been?' He said, 'The Tridents.' I saw him a few years later, when he was very big, and he said to me, 'What was your name again? Never heard of you!'"

Beck didn't keep track of what was recorded or released, so a definitive discography of his recordings will never be available. However, everything that has been checked as far as possible, including sessions, appears in the discography section at the end of this book. Those that we know about include the forgettable "Rinky Dink"/"Java" with the Johnny Howard Band, a combo in which he occasionally played guitar; and a session with his old pals the Crescents, now backing singer Phil Ryan, on the songs "Mary Don't You Weep"/"Yes I Will."

Another product from this period was his lead guitar on "Dracula's Daughter" for the Savages, the constantly varying backing group fronted by the amazing top-hatted Screaming Lord Sutch. Sutch's long and irrepressible career (sadly curtailed by a too-early death) included regularly standing for election to Britain's Parliament on ever more whimsical party platforms. On the B-side, "Come Back Baby," Beck is heard giving his fuzzbox an early outing on record. Plus there was another of those forgettable singles, "I'm Not Running Away"/"So Sweet" with an outfit calling itself Fitz and Startz, which may have included Paul Young.

The start of 1965 saw Beck on sessions for "Yesterday Man" with Chris Andrews, coupled with "Too Bad You Don't Want Me." "Yesterday Man" enjoyed Top Three chart success in England and went gold in Germany.

IT WAS SHORTLY afterwards that the Jimmy Page connection came back into play again, this time with what would prove to be a pivotal role. In March 1965, when Eric Clapton finally quit the Yardbirds, the group was searching for a top-line replacement. The obvious choice—indeed the only guitarist they knew who could fit the bill—was Jimmy Page.

When Giorgio Gomelsky approached him, with an offer of about £25 ($70) a week, Page was not impressed. He was already averaging £80 a week as a session king and knew it could more than double in the very near future. However, Jeff Beck now had a considerable reputation with the Tridents, and was a known name around the session circuit. Page recommended they try Beck instead. "I don't know why," says the modest Beck. "There were plenty of other guitarists at the time. It came as a surprise—you know, it was a big favor."

"One night, when I was playing with the Tridents at the 100 Club, Giorgio and his sidekick Hamish Grimes came down and dragged me off after the set. I was all sweaty, had hair down to my ankles. They said, 'You're coming with us. . . You're gonna be in a top fucking band. Be at this address tomorrow.' It was the Marquee Club. When I turned up, there was a Yardbirds van outside. 'Let's go!' I thought. There were other guys auditioning, but I think they knew I was gonna be the one." A few licks of Matt Murphy and Buddy Guy were all it took: twenty or so hopefuls lined up outside were quickly sent on their way.

That first encounter was something of a culture shock all round. Beck showed up with scruffy hair falling over his ears and eyes, wearing oil-stained jeans that looked as if he'd just emerged from under a car (which no doubt he had). His appearance stunned the sprucely turned-out Yardbirds enough to send him straight off for a haircut and new clothes. Described by one reporter as "a very straight and serious crowd," the four blues scholars had played together for the best part of two years and seemed a tightly-knit, somewhat exclusive little clique.

Beck remembers: "I didn't like them when I first met them. They didn't say 'Hi' or anything. They were pissed off that Eric had left, they thought that the whole Yardbirds sound had gone. That was the impression I got. They said, 'Can you play blues?' I said, 'What—slow blues? Chicago blues?' They said, 'Anything.' So I honked around. They said to get rid of the echo . . . you don't use an echo in Chicago blues. Yeah, that's just what they said!"

All he knew of the Yardbirds so far was solid, workmanlike R&B. He privately considered the Tridents to be a better group: more earthy, more real. What's more, at Eel Pie Island they had regularly outdrawn the crowds pulled in by the Yardbirds at the Crawdaddy. He'd even had misgivings on the night they hoiked him out of the 100 Club, although they seemed to regard his acceptance as a foregone conclusion: "Like, 'This is it—you can't get much better than this.' And I was really hurt they didn't make any reference to the fact that we'd just stormed the place!"

Inevitably there were regrets at leaving the guys he'd paid his dues with for so long. "After all the things that we went through, scrambling up and down the country, it would've been nice to see that band make it. But we just couldn't. I had to do a really dirty trick on them when the Yardbirds offered me that job. Just as we were drawing audiences in the South London clubs, I had to leave. Why I did it I'll never know, because the Yardbirds didn't mean anything to me. I think the real reason was because the Yardbirds appeared to have good management, and seemed to be going places."

Although Beck's recollections point to being so broke he couldn't even afford guitar strings, in fact the Tridents were averaging up to £30 a week per member, at a time when £10 a week was considered a living wage. So probably it wasn't just money that swung his decision: now age 20, with a wife whose ambitions centered on a house in the country, an Alsatian dog, and a horse of her own to complete the picture, more likely he sensed security and better prospects.

An item long in doubt that can now be laid to rest, thanks to Paul Lucas' personal diary, is the date Beck actually left the Tridents: this was on Tuesday 2 March 1965. He debuted with the Yardbirds—and Eric Clapton officially left—on 5 March, the very release date of the offending single "For Your Love." Beck would remain with them for nearly two years, leading them to the peak of their popularity in Britain, Europe, and the United States.

Of his four new colleagues, he found Chris Dreja and Jim McCarty were fairly easygoing types, but they weren't the prime movers behind the group: its driving force was the odd partnership of Paul Samwell-Smith and Keith Relf. Samwell-Smith was the intellectual one, the self-described "social misfit," stiff and distant and highly strung. And Relf was the sensitive, unpredictable type, an acute asthma sufferer who was inclined to get into a state emotionally and physically. In the end it was drummer Jim McCarty that Beck palled up with most often. "We had this sort of comedy duo routine and I just crack up laughing when I think about him. When we meet it's just as if no water passed under the bridge at all."

Beck's first gig with the Yardbirds was a sizeable concert at the Fairfield Halls in Croydon, a Radio Caroline Show where the group was second on the bill to the Moody Blues.

Next Monday, 8 March, they were due at their favorite residency, the Marquee Club. This would be the acid test—Beck's initiation to their club set, when he would have to play the entire Yardbirds repertoire. They gave him the *Five Live Yardbirds* album to learn the songs and he had to get them down in a matter of days. Nevertheless, as Beck recalled, they blew the place apart.

"I had to learn about fifteen bloody songs in four days because they had such tight schedules; and I was quite frightened, to put it politely. It was a do or die thing really, but I played 'Jeff's Boogie' and got a ten-minute ovation for it, so that was great, and it just nailed it all together for me."

Right after that they started the rounds of TV, radio, and nonstop gigs promoting "For Your Love," on which Beck played electric 12-string. His first TV appearances were on 18 March in Granada's *Scene at 6:30* and BBC's *Top of the Pops*, followed by Rediffusion's essential *Ready, Steady, Go!* on the 19th.

Meanwhile, the recording of a new EP was announced for mid-March, although it's not known whether this took place. The earliest recording this writer can confirm was a month later at London's Advision Studios, around 13 April. Whatever the actual date, it would produce the first blueprint for their follow-up single, another Gouldman song: "Heart Full of Soul."

On the B-side was a Beck slide solo, "Steeled Blues," intended to showcase their new guitar ace in the same way they had showcased Clapton with "Got to Hurry" on the flip side of "For Your Love." Clapton's instrumental had been recorded in 20 minutes, and "Steeled Blues" received about the same amount of attention. Beck: "We cut the B-side first to warm up and get the balance. Two takes, boom, that was it."

After the harpsichord on their first hit single, the Yardbirds decided to capitalize on a reputation for using unusual instruments: for "Heart Full of Soul" it would be a sitar and tabla. Beck was still very much a newcomer, and scarcely felt reassured when, late as always, he turned up to find two Indian musicians there. "I was thinking, 'I've just joined, and already they're getting these other guys.'"

However, the sessions didn't go too well. The classically trained Indians had their own concept of counting time and bars (measures), totally different from the Western approach. "They couldn't understand the timing," Beck explains, "which was 4/4. They were playing all over the place. When they'd gone, I had the riff going through my head and I just picked out the notes playing octaves on the middle G string. By bending the notes slightly off key, it sounded like a sitar. I used the fuzz just to dirty up the amp."

Although fuzztone had been known to insiders for some time, it was still highly unorthodox as a studio effect. Beck had been using homemade fuzz-boxes for some years: after the unit custom-built by Trident Paul Lucas, he had a later one made by Roger Mayer, whose company still designs effects today. Jimmy Page had actually commissioned the first unit that Mayer produced, and as luck would have it, Page was in the studio at the time of the sitar recordings, so Beck was able to borrow his fuzz.

The guys were impressed by Beck's impromptu soundalike, and quickly booked another session, where the famous Beck solo was laid down—this time using his own unit, a recently acquired Sola Sound Tone Bender. "I think it came free with a packet of cornflakes," said Beck, who, surprisingly, still has it in his collection. "We did one take, it sounded outrageous. They rushed that out, and

Photo: Hamish

The Yardbirds' first EP release with their new lead guitarist, August 1965. (L-R Chris Dreja, Jim McCarty, Jeff Beck, Paul Samwell-Smith, Keith Relf).

the rest was a rollercoaster ride." (Sola Sound later claimed that its Tone Bender was the first ever foot switch-type effects box commercially produced, and that it was used for the first time by Jeff Beck on "Heart Full of Soul.")

"Heart Full of Soul," which went straight to number two on its release in June, unleashed the first onslaught of that heavy distortion which had long been intrinsic to Beck's fiercely individual sound. Preceding by several months songs like the Stones' "Satisfaction" and the Beatles' "Taxman," it was the first significant hit single built around the kind of angrily buzzing guitar riff that soon made the foot-switch distortion unit essential rock hardware.

Those exotic Eastern sounds were equally revolutionary in early 1965, especially for a supposedly R&B group like the Yardbirds. But it would not be long before a growing taste for the East cast an incense-laden spell on the '60s. Curiously enough, George Harrison, later to become a serious student of the sitar, had a first-hand introduction to the instrument as a result of "Heart Full of Soul," thanks to the ubiquitous Jimmy Page.

Page, who had traveled in India, already owned one of the few sitars in England, and when he happened to drop into the Yardbirds session that day, he offered to buy the Indian player's instrument on the spot. A little later he played it for Harrison, who was blown away by the sound; not only did it feature in the soundtrack of the new Beatles movie *Help!*, but soon afterwards Harrison recorded the famous double-tracked sitar on "Norwegian Wood," released on the album *Rubber Soul* in December that year.

But it was Jeff Beck, with his instinctive feel for the sitar's timbre and intonation, who first reproduced it with his magic guitar trick, which, though legend would place it immediately after the aborted sessions with the Indian gentlemen, probably took place at a rerecording shortly afterwards. And he continued with the Yardbirds to bring more Eastern sounds and scales to rock music.

Working at Advision on various April dates, they finished laying down the new single by the 20th together with three numbers for their promised EP. These were the Vibrations' "My Girl Sloopy," Mose Allison's "I'm Not Talking," and "I Ain't Done Wrong," written by Relf. "Although a bit rough on the edges," said Giorgio Gomelsky, "his playing on these tracks is full of passion and intensity. His sense of rhythmic accents, big 'tearing' chords and long sustained single notes added a whole new dimension to the band's sound." Released as *Five Yardbirds* in August, it remained in the EP charts for several months and reached a high of number two.

Encouraged by the Yardbirds' eagerness to experiment, Beck was thankful to discover they were not blinkered blues addicts. "I knew they wanted to break away from the standard blues thing. When I had both feet in the door, and it closed behind me, I started putting a little pressure on, saying, 'Why don't we do this?' It was the first time in my life where I felt secure because I had a job—which meant that I could get away from home, and they'd take care of the bills."

Country houses would come later, but his Yardbirds success at least made it possible to move into a flat of his own in Balham, with Pat and his beloved Afghan hound, Kehm Karahn (better known as Pudding).

The band could hardly have realized how quickly a live firebrand like Beck, with his tougher sound and blistering technique, would ignite them to flashpoint. Starting with "Heart Full of Soul," four of their five Beck singles charted consecutively in Britain's Top Ten and America's Top Twenty.

Ex-Yardbird Paul Samwell-Smith recalls Beck's amazing impact on the group: "He brought us a different style of guitar playing. I think Eric's was very melodic and fluid and quite intelligent. Jeff was much more from the body, from lower down. It's lovely; I slightly prefer Jeff's playing. His influence began to show itself when he relaxed and expanded. . . . I can't believe that we were lucky enough to land on our feet by finding Jeff."

4 The End of the Beginning

JEFF BECK WAS NOW tasting the first fruits of commercial success—the recognition on one hand, and the relentless pace on the other. "The tours were four or five weeks of England, just up and down, up and down. The first time we were on *Top of the Pops* [the van] was still quite clean when we parked it outside the BBC TV studio in Manchester. When we came out it was smothered in lipstick—the windows, the windshield, everything plastered with girls' names and phone numbers. I thought, 'This is great! Not only am I enjoying the shit out of what I'm doing, but I get fame as well.'

"So we did one TV show and I raced home to tell my mom, and the people next door cutting their hedges said, 'Saw you on the telly, very good.' They were the same people who, up to this point, were yelling for me to turn it down all the time. All of a sudden, I was somebody. It was a mind-blowing experience."

On 30 April they were off on a Kinks package tour, during which Beck met the Walker Brothers—the three Americans Scott Engel, John Maus, and Gary Leeds. The encounter would lead to a change of guitar allegiance. When he'd joined the Yardbirds he was still using his Tridents-era Telecaster, a '59 model with a rosewood fretboard. But on 20 June, when the Yardbirds supported the Beatles for a single date in Paris, he managed to leave it behind. Lost without his own guitar, it seems he owned no replacement, and on some Yardbirds dates he was seen with the unusual red Tele that Eric Clapton left behind—perhaps a temporary stand-in at the time of the loss.

Prompted perhaps by this incident, it was around this time that Beck acquired John Maus' '54 maple-neck Fender Esquire, which he'd greatly admired when he saw Maus playing it.

The Esquire was well battered by the time he bought it for about $60 or $70, and Maus had shaved the back and sides to give it the comfortable contoured body of a Strat. Beck's own modification was to swap the white pickguard (scratchplate) for a black phenolic one. "Because it had a blond neck and a black scratchplate, it was just one of the most sought-after guitars in England," he told Steven Rosen in *Guitar Player*. "All the guitar freaks would go, 'Hey,' and they'd all be putting on the black scratchplates, but didn't have the blond neck to go with it. And I had the blond neck; I was the cat's whiskers again."

It seems Beck managed to retrieve his original Telecaster, but the Esquire remained his favorite instrument; we may even speculate that the Esquire's black pickguard was cannibalized from the Tele, which reappeared later with a white one.

With "Heart Full of Soul" reaching number nine in the U.S., they now had the opportunity to sample the other side of the Atlantic. Delayed by work permit problems, they left on 2 September, but their visas didn't give permission for performing live, and all they managed were a few shows in Oklahoma, Arizona, Tennessee and Arkansas. Radio and TV dates like *Shindig, Hullabaloo,* and Dick Clark's *Where the Action Is* had to be repeatedly rescheduled.

Beck also found there were other ways in which his expectations were disappointed. As the home of his greatest idols, he thought America would be the place to see them all; but everyone was into Beatles music. "I couldn't even get sense out of people about where Muddy Waters played. And we'd just been playing most of his stuff, in some disguise or other. It was a shock with them living in Chicago and not knowing who he was. I realized that I was part of a very fast-moving train. It was totally weird. Where was the rock 'n' roll, the greased-back sideburns? Where was Elvis and Chuck Berry? All of a sudden we realized we were the people that were happening, not them. Us spotty oiks from England carried a lot more weight than those guys. . . . I wanted to see the real thing—Jerry Lee. I wanted to see Little Richard sing 'Lucille.' I wanted to be in the front row, I wanted to see my face in his boot."

But at least there was no disappointment when it came to recording. On this trip the group managed to fulfill long cherished dreams of cutting tracks at their twin Meccas: Sam Phillips' legendary Sun Studios in Memphis, and Chess Records in Chicago.

Beck says the late-night session at Sun Studios was incredible: "We started at ten and we cut four or five songs, including 'The Train Kept A-Rollin'.' I was in heaven listening to the playbacks on the same speakers that 'Hound Dog' came out of. That was enough for me."

Loving the old rockabilly numbers as he did, it was Beck's idea to introduce the group to Johnny Burnette's "The Train Kept A-Rollin'," a longtime personal favorite. The Yardbirds' propulsive, power-driven version, however, deviated radically from the original. Beck: "I could go into great detail about my disapproval of that. I'm afraid things were very screwed up in those days. They just heard me play the riff, and they loved it and made up their version of it. We didn't bother to make any references to the original record." Although it was never put out as a single, the Yardbirds' recording plucked the old Rock & Roll Trio number from obscurity and turned it into a classic among classics.

Then it was on to the hallowed halls of Chess, with recording sessions arranged to coincide with one of their few live shows, at the Arie Crown

Beck as fashion icon: a publicity shoot featuring outfits from a leading Carnaby Street boutique, arranged by the author in summer 1965.

Theater, on a double-bill with the Hollies. At Chess, appropriately enough, they laid down their own version of Bo Diddley's "I'm a Man": "We heard the playback and just went berserk. The bass drum was shaking the foundations of the building. We weren't playing that loud, but the engineer did Muddy Waters and Chuck Berry stuff, so he knew how to get that."

Beck's radical guitar was directly inspired by Bo Diddley's unique style, mixing wild rhythmic patterns and frantic washboard-style scratching. "'I'm a Man' was supposed to be orgasmic music. If you listen to it in that sexual tone, you understand the song was like reaching a whole climax. In fact, before I joined, the Yardbirds had this reputation for doing climactic music, where it would start off soft, build up and go completely crazy, explode into rhythm. I loved doing that. It was so animal, and so simple."

· That first U.S. visit was unforgettable for all the band, and equally so for the few Stateside listeners who were treated to the Jeff Beck sound and style: the most inventive, outlandish electric guitar they had heard till then. Even Sam Phillips was impressed.

One of the high spots was their exposure to the West Coast during their off days—an incredible experience for them all, and an absolute revelation for Beck.

Saturated as he was in the American rock 'n' roll mythos, for him the U.S. was a cornucopia of soft-top T-birds and pink Cadillacs, powerful V8 Chevrolets and Chevy-powered hot rods. Seeing his first Ford rods began a lifelong love affair with those preposterous little prewar coupes and roadsters with blown engines and multiple carburetors, beefed up and stripped down and customized and chopped and chromed. As a paint-shop expert himself, he could almost taste their mouthwatering finishes, sizzling in classic hot rod red, or bursting with eye-grabbing orange and yellow flames that promised explosive performance underneath the hood.

"We got to California and there they were. It would be T-buckets, 1923 Model Ts, going along all chromed. It was exactly what I remembered from the early '50s movies. And then I got curious about what they did to them to make them so outrageous, because a Model T didn't look like this with flames and chrome and Jag rear ends. Then, gradually, you start looking into the magazines and seeing where the shows and swap meets are . . ."

Three years after that West Coast visit he began his own collection, starting with a black '32 Ford which he bought in January 1968.

While the other Yardbirds were slow to throw off their British inhibitions, the supposedly reticent Beck lost no time embracing the heady delights that California had to offer. Always a great one for the ladies, with whom his sullen, rough-boy-lost looks made him a favorite, it was here that he met and fell for a stunning California starlet, actress and model Mary Hughes. Hughes had appeared in several of the famous Hollywood bikini beach movies of the '60s with Frankie Avalon and Annette Funicello. His new American girlfriend would soon become as great a passion as his growing obsession with hot rods, a combination that resulted in an irresistible attachment to the West Coast.

"The epitome of Hollywood semi-stardom" was how Chris Dreja described Mary Hughes. "It was Jeff's first introduction to a beautiful, available woman like he'd never seen before. When he joined us he was in the throes of ending this dull and morbid marriage. . . . What was interesting was that Jeff was a lot less inhibited than we were." Just for the hell of it, Beck ordered himself a color TV and a Corvette Stingray—for the week. "For him it was a total explosion, and he had no qualms about climbing in there and soaking himself in it."

It took time to get to know Beck in those days: often silent and circumspect, he was adept at surrounding himself with an impermeable outer layer, a Beck defence against uneasy situations, and a weapon used with unerring effect whenever he suspected hype. But he was far from introverted.

At ease and on his own terms, he could be wild and outrageous and unpredictable, both personally and musically, with a hip-shooting humor and a wicked sense of the ridiculous, and full of challenging ideas that gave scant regard to convention.

Indeed it was Beck's safety-be-damned iconoclasm, which he brought to everything he did, that helped break the comfortable guitar mold the Americans had grown used to. In contrast to their ultra-modern Jazzmasters, Beck's 11-year-old Esquire, with its single pickup, must have raised quite a few eyebrows—as did the way he ferociously wielded the instrument, lunging and brandishing it like a weapon.

For the rest of his hardware, the AC30s had by now been replaced by two 100-watt amps and a pair of 4x12 speakers, and his Tone Bender fuzzbox retired in favor of one he designed himself; that was all he used. The effects he got were supplied by his own powers of invention. Always experimenting to add new dimensions to the group's sound, Beck reveled in cranking out traffic noises, Klaxons, sirens, wheel-spins, a multitude of bomb blasts, and pure electronic phantasmagoria. Often he would end a number with the guitar leaned against the amp, endlessly shrieking its feedback while he wandered off to regard it from a distance with baleful eye or wolfish grin.

Jimi Hendrix was just one of the many who took due note of Beck's guitar pyrotechnics during his Yardbird days: the massive volume, feedback and distortion, the oriental influences, and even Beck's party trick of soloing—especially in "I'm a Man"—with the guitar behind his head.

AFTER THE HIGH of their U.S. trip, it was back home to plug the October release of their new single, the double A-side "Still I'm Sad"/"Evil Hearted You," which made its way to number three. "Still I'm Sad" was another brave group experiment, re-creating the haunting plainsong and striking modal tonalities of medieval Gregorian chant.

Meanwhile, Eric Clapton's devoted followers were delighted to see their hero, now the leading attraction with John Mayall's Bluesbreakers, playing the music that was his single great allegiance. The proclamation "Clapton is God" began to appear on walls in clubs and London Underground stations. Other guitar aficionados would equally travel miles to hear Jeff Beck's brand of feral experimentalism. Though the "guitar hero" was as yet an unknown breed, his status with the chart-topping Yardbirds had become precisely that. In the 1965 year-end poll of *Beat Instrumental* magazine, he would place second to Hank Marvin in the Best Guitarist category; twelve months later his name would top the poll. Inevitably, a degree of fan rivalry built up.

"That's the British for you: they always have to have a king of the castle! When Eric and I were around Wardour Street and the Marquee, it was like, 'Oh, you gotta see Beck.' 'Nah, you gotta see Clapton.' Y'know, all that jiggling for position. At that time, the Yardbirds were totally a pop experimental band who just touched on some blues. Mainly it was rock 'n' roll injected with some experimental psychedelia: wild solos right smack in the middle of a pop song—that was our game."

But the time was fast approaching when tastes would sharply divide between groups who played commercial "pop"—fodder for teenagers and dance halls—and those who played the more heavyweight "rock." The Yardbirds tended to have a foot in both camps, and lacked the clearly defined image that press and public liked to respond to. There was no coherent line to explain their musical ideas, or why each new record sounded different from the last.

Left to their own devices, they seemed to cultivate an anti-image. Certainly the individual members were not inclined to see themselves as "rock stars." Only afterwards did they realize what a seminal influence they had on generations of rock musicians to follow, scores of whom grew up immersed in the Yardbirds' unique synthesis of sound-pictures, blues-rock, and psychedelia.

Maybe they might have kept their edge had they benefited from some development of their individual talents. Giorgio Gomelsky was actually thinking along these lines, and separate solo recordings were part of the plan; but only Keith Relf ever got as far as releasing a solo single.

With fame came ever increasing pressures, without any sense of controlling their own destiny. Indeed, Beck had the least control of all, since at least the others were directors of Yardbirds Ltd, whereas he was merely a salaried employee. Morale inevitably suffered, their tolerance of each other was sorely tested, and the eventual result was disintegration.

This was yet to happen as they took off in December for their second tour of the United States, a six-week marathon with plenty of live shows this time, spread over at least 12 different states. After an initial half-dozen shows they were allowed a few days respite in Chicago, where it is almost certain the group revisited Chess Studios and laid down the classic "Shapes of Things." Although some recollections place this recording back in September (and the song also received finishing touches the following January at RCA's Los Angeles Studios), nevertheless it is most likely the initial session took place at Chess on 21 December 1965. It would be their most celebrated single, with a monumental fuzz-drenched solo on Beck's Esquire that presaged the age of heavy blues-rock that would soon follow (and was widely held to have inspired Paul McCartney's guitar solo in "Taxman").

Still heavily into Indian sounds, Beck was finding the guitar frustrating because it wouldn't bend far enough. "So I was given this song with a break in the middle that changed rhythm completely, and told to go mad with it. The thrill of being in a Chicago studio was enough. But also the frustration of being there and not being able to play like Buddy Guy . . . I just went crazy. That solo was all done on one string, the G. It was all done in two hours."

The way they worked was completely off the cuff: "We'd jam, Keith'd rush off and write some lyrics in the toilet—it was exactly like that. 'After four verses, let's go into this raga thing.' I kept changing guitar sounds all the way through. So we did two or three takes of my guitars and blended them all together. But the solo on 'Shapes of Things' was pretty honest up until that feedback note that comes in over it. If I did nothing else, that was the best single."

Back on the road throughout the Christmas season, the Yardbirds found themselves celebrating the New Year in chilly Seattle, Washington, prior to a two-week stint in sun-drenched California. Their best reception of the tour was at a four-night engagement in the Hullabaloo Club on Hollywood's Sunset Strip, where they got an excellent sound and played to houses of 1,200 every night.

Beck's best memories of the Yardbirds dated from this tour. "As far as the Yardbirds go, my musical utopia was back in early '66—before all the hang-ups. We were all on the threshold of this new thing. The Yardbirds were the very first psychedelic band, really, just an experimental psychedelic crazy bunch of loonies from England. That's the strongest thing we had, this underground thing. You couldn't buy it in the shops, you couldn't go and see it on TV. You had to be there."

Their last ten days in the States included a memorable week in New York where, being the leading British attraction around town, they found themselves adopted by the local in-crowd of the day, led by the Andy Warhol set, who made sure they were seen with them at restaurants and clubs. The East Coast groupie scene was also out in force, offering enticements more alluring— and more awesomely imaginative—than their pallid English counterparts. Jim McCarty particularly recalls, among such close encounters, "three lovely black groupies" who entertained them in New York. Of yet another caliber was the inevitable accolade from Chicago's Plaster Casters, whose mission was to immortalize, in their chosen medium, that feature of a rock star's anatomy which would never grace the cement outside Grauman's Chinese Theatre. In their book *Yardbirds,* Dreja and McCarty were prepared only to speculate as to which of their number accepted such immortalization. Needless to say, the speculative names did not include their own.

On their return at the end of January, they found that Giorgio Gomelsky had unaccountably booked them for Italy's poppy San Remo Song Festival. The entry rules required them to record covers of a pair of trite Italian songs, the A-side an out-of-character ballad, "Questa Volta." Beck was disgusted and flatly refused to do it, although he did agree to contribute to the B-side, "Pafff . . . Bum" (a spaghetti "My Girl Sloopy"). Under pressure, he relented enough to play the A-side onstage at the actual contest—in black tie and dinner jacket, no less.

Back home after this incongruous jaunt, the group needed to get back to recording again. In March they entered Advision to continue work on their much-delayed album project, which rejoiced in Gomelsky's title, *A Yardbirds' Eye View of Beat.* But the album would never be finished. It was aborted, quite simply, because the Yardbirds decided they wanted a new manager. About a dozen tracks were preserved from the sessions, release of which Gomelsky later authorized in various compilations.

A number of problems had accumulated in the two and a half years of Giorgio Gomelsky's management, and inappropriate excursions to pop festivals were only a minor annoyance when compared with the glaring fact that, for all their chart success, the band had very little cash to show for it.

Their choice of replacement was a young go-getter by the name of Simon Napier-Bell, who had started in pop management by teaming up a black girl/white boy vocal duo, Diane Ferraz and Nicky Scott. Gomelsky was duly ousted, and Napier-Bell took over. On the financial side, there was immediate improvement when he got them a £25,000 advance against royalties from Columbia—their first ever advance from their record label.

However, not all the group members were content with his overall management. Where Gomelsky had erred by being over-involved, Napier-Bell erred in the opposite direction. At a time when the pressures were building up, this was not the approach the five stressed-out lads needed.

Meanwhile, their date book kept them on the move. A Continental tour started with a headlining slot on 1 April in *Ready, Steady, Allez-Oops!* from the Locomotive in the Moulin Rouge, Paris. But by now the pace was really getting to Beck and the following night, at a show in Marseilles, he collapsed, fell down three flights of stone stairs, and had to be rushed to the hospital. Meningitis was suspected, and Beck fans on both sides of the Atlantic waited anxiously to know whether he would pull through the life-threatening illness.

Beck remained hospitalized for some days while the Yardbirds considered an emergency replacement, but thankfully he was fit enough to fly back home the following week. It wasn't meningitis; in fact, he'd suffered a nervous breakdown. And to make matters worse, his tonsils were infected so badly he couldn't speak.

Two months of complete rest were immediately ordered, and a tonsillectomy was scheduled for early May. But with the group's commitments, there was no chance for either remedy. As a result of neglect, his health got steadily worse for the rest of the year.

"Shapes of Things" had been released in February, and now a new single was needed. On 19/20 April, he found himself back at Advision Studios, where "Over Under Sideways Down" was recorded; and once again Jeff Beck came up with some fiercely original sounds. His schizoid contribution to this number comprised a distorted guitar hook in Eastern vein, reminiscent of manic, skirling, Moroccan dance, overdubbed against a contrasting boogie-style walking bass, also played by Beck, that smacks you as soon as you hear the track. Rock 'n' roll meets psychedelia.

Next it was time to lay down a new album to replace the aborted sessions. Amazingly, it was the Yardbirds' first studio LP—and the only one with Jeff Beck on lead after he had notched up well over a year with them. With Advision booked at the beginning of June, the group proceeded to lay down six new titles plus reworkings of four from the Gomelsky sessions. The A- and B-sides of their latest single were added to make up the 12 tracks of the LP, simply titled *Yardbirds* (perhaps better known by its nickname, *Roger the Engineer,* in honor of Advision's Roger Cameron, whose caricature by Dreja decorates the sleeve).

Paul Samwell-Smith, as co-producer, expressed his growing disenchantment. "We have five days to do this LP, writing all the numbers ourselves. If we could only have the studio for a month it would be fantastic. Instead we have to rush all over the world."

Their method entailed recording the basic tracks without any lead guitar; then Beck was called in to overdub whatever embellishments he saw fit. It may have been a nod towards his state of health, but it also avoided the mounting tension while Beck waited endlessly for them to map out their writing ideas. "I would sit around twiddling my fingers in anger waiting for my chance to get in and rip it in half. And they used to watch the flame build and build till I couldn't really take it. And then we'd all laugh and have a drink afterwards."

It wasn't a unique way of recording for those days: Brian Jones would often be called in at a late stage to add his touches of instrumental magic to the Rolling Stones' records. But it didn't serve to integrate either Jones or Beck into the creative process, nor into the togetherness that was shared by the rest of the group. In both cases they also outshone the other four in terms of musicianship, adding fuel to talk of mounting egocentricity. As Jim McCarty quipped in the liner notes for the album: "It's been said that Jeff Beck is one of the leading guitarists in the country—and I'm inclined to agree with him."

Released in July, *Yardbirds* reached a very healthy number 20 in the U.K. charts. Gene Santoro summarizes it admirably in his liner notes for *Beckology*: "By the time they recorded the landmark *Yardbirds* . . . they'd forged a new musical synthesis of Eastern sounds, jazz, blues, rock, and noise. The rave-up section of 'Lost Woman' rides out on a recurring feedback-and-whistle cloud of power chords; the first section of 'The Nazz Are Blue' solo closes out with a single sustained note spiralling into feedback—and this before Jimi Hendrix's revolutionary *Are You Experienced*. All told, *Yardbirds* is a primer of the Jeff Beck Sound, and was studied as closely as any primer by both the guitarists of San Francisco's Summer of Love bands and the embryonic heavy metallists of the late '60s."

The Jeff Beck Sound of those *Yardbirds* sessions introduced something else that was studied with interest: his latest choice of guitar. This was a 1959 Gibson Les Paul Sunburst, which he'd found (probably in February/March) through a contact at Selmer's music store in Charing Cross Road, London. He acquired it for the price of about £175—less than $500.

Eric Clapton now played a Sunburst with the Bluesbreakers, and Beck was impressed by the tone as soon as he heard it. In fact, since Gibson had discontinued the design in 1960, the two Brits were among those who rescued its career—it would soon become highly sought-after by blues-rock guitarists for its rich, earthy sound.

BY THE END of the album sessions, everyone's tolerance seemed to have suffered a serious breakdown. It came to a head on 18 June when they played for the annual Oxford University Ball. The show turned into disaster.

Keith Relf, juiced up on drink and infuriated when he couldn't raise a glance from the upper-crust students, decided to go for the jugular. He blew raspberries at the crowd, said, "Fuck you," into the mike, then rolled around onstage and managed to fall into the drums.

The rest of the group removed him bodily and continued with instrumentals. But by that time Paul Samwell-Smith had had enough. Already fed up with the uncivilized life of a band musician, he blew his top and told them he was leaving. He did—and went on to become a producer in his own right with such stars as Carly Simon and Cat Stevens.

To replace him on bass, the Yardbirds recruited that very same Jimmy Page who had passed up the lead guitar slot a year before.

As Page remembers it, he went to the Oxford concert and thought it was "a great anarchistic night"! Backstage afterwards he witnessed Samwell-Smith's walk-out: "I'll play bass if you like," said Page, and that was how it happened. "The studio work got to the point where it wasn't fun," he said. "That's when I pulled out."

Chris Dreja: "Page had been doing sessions for years. He wanted to get out on the road, and I think he saw it as a good opportunity to join a band that was out in the thick of it. And he jumped at the chance. He was prepared to possibly play drums if necessary! Although it wasn't his normal instrument, he was happy to remain on bass. I think he just liked being in the band. He was very sweet and wanted to please. He'd do anything for you until his ego got in the way."

Beck, desperate to inject new life into the band, had for some while been hoping to enlist Page in a dual guitar combination, which he thought would be devastating. As they drove home from the gig that night, he asked Page if he was serious about sitting in on bass. "Sure," Page said, "I'll do it for a few months until you get the situation sorted out."

Jimmy Page made his debut Yardbirds appearance on 21 June 1966 at the Marquee. It mattered little that he was less than proficient on bass, since a plan was already being hatched to have this slot taken over by Dreja, allowing Jimmy and Jeff to share guitar duties. Simon Napier-Bell was against the idea of having another lead guitar: "I told Jeff, 'You're the genius guitarist in the group—to bring in someone as good as you is crazy.' But Beck absolutely insisted."

For Beck there were no two ways about it. He was utterly delighted to have Page on board. To complete his joy, another cherished ambition had recently been fulfilled when he took delivery of a beautiful pale blue Corvette Stingray, replacing the car he'd been driving since his Tridents days—a Mk 1 Ford Zephyr Six sprayed metallic maroon and customized with a continental spare wheel bumper and whitewall tires. The Chevrolet was the model Beck had tried out in California, and he would remain faithful to the marque ever afterwards.

It was about this time that Beck gave Page his valuable 1959 Telecaster, which sported the name "Jeffman" on the back: "He had a Danelectro which he'd sprayed pink or something; he also had a black Les Paul Custom, and I didn't think it sounded very good—which is why I gave him the Fender."

Page used the Tele a lot from then onwards, both with the Yardbirds and with early Led Zeppelin. He had it painted in Day-Glo psychedelia, and added a silver scratchplate to mirror the dazzling reflections of the stage spotlights. Five years later, when he came to lay down the monumental solo for Zeppelin's "Stairway to Heaven," he turned to the treasured Telecaster that Beck had given him.

THE PACE OF success was now taking an increasing toll. Neither Keith Relf nor Jeff Beck had the iron constitution to stand up to night after night of hectic performance on top of booze, smoke, and greasy junk food grabbed on the hoof. Several gigs that summer had to be canceled, and some Beck appearances. And there was also the suspicion that illness wasn't always the cause.

When the Yardbirds recorded the two sides of their next single, it was Page who played guitar; Beck came in later to overdub the surrealistic "Happenings Ten Years Time Ago" together with the B-side, "Psycho Daisies," on which they inveigled him to sing by including a mention of Mary Hughes in the words.

"I think they were playing live without me, and Pagey was taking over on lead and enjoying every minute of it, but I was brewing up these weird solos in the studio that he didn't know about. When you look back, 'Happenings Ten Years Time Ago' reflects quite accurately the confusion of the '60s. There was an accident in it—we simulated a car crash or something in the middle—and it was just a chaotic record."

That middle section also had Beck's spoken voice, supposedly a "man in the street," maniacally blathering in the background: "Pop group are yer? Why yer all gotta wear long 'air? Betcha pullin' the crumpet aren't yer . . ." The voice actually mimicked a guy at the VD clinic in Hammersmith, who would say things like, "You playin' in Chicago tonight then are yer?" before carrying out an examination. With wailing police sirens and a thunderous explosion, it was the most off-the-wall thing they'd ever done, but it was scarcely Top Ten material. It reached number 30 in the U.S., and a miserable 43 in the U.K.

Because of Beck's enormous popularity, he was noticeably being given more prominence, and earlier that year Simon Napier-Bell had promised to deliver on Giorgio Gomelsky's offer of a solo album.

A track that would have provided superb material was Beck's personal tour de force, "Jeff's Boogie," released as the B-side of "Over Under Sideways Down." This had long been in his repertoire in the time-honored tradition of the instrumental showpiece, with a genealogy that started with Chuck Berry's "Guitar Boogie" and went back to Arthur Smith's "Guitar Boogie" of the 1930s, taking in Les Paul on the way. Les Paul provides clear inspiration for Beck's dazzling little opus, which captures his mentor's agile swing with amazing assurance and dexterity. But there's a good helping of his other mentor, Cliff Gallup, in there as well—for example, in the cascades of pull-off triplets, a signature Beckism.

Stevie Ray Vaughan remembered how everyone was so blown away by Beck's licks on this number that they used it for guitar-slinging battles to see who could do them the fastest: "Everybody would play 'Jeff's Boogie.' You'd play it part of the way, then double-time it and double-time it again. Chuck Berry's version was a lot more tame, but Jeff Beck took it and it had wild guitars and echo and the whole bit."

Always prone to an impish touch of humor, Beck at one point interpolates a set of parlor-clock chimes, but goes one further by playing them as harmonics: natural overtones which are produced by stopping the string lightly without pressing it to the fretboard, a technique that requires considerable skill to produce a clear and bell-like tone. Long exploited in classical and jazz guitar—and a favorite Les Paul device—few rock guitarists in the '60s would have even considered trying to use them melodically. What was even more impressive was to hear Beck play the instrumental live in the Yardbirds' set, when he rattled off all those runs and effects with stunning fluency.

There were other specially arranged sessions intended for Beck's solo project, and plans for him to handle vocals on several songs. Sadly, however, it went the way of so many other missed opportunities—no such album ever materialized.

Whether Beck's continuing health problems were real or at times merely excuses, on 27 July he suffered another severe infection of the tonsils that he should have had removed. It delayed the Yardbirds' departure on their third U.S. tour, for which they eventually left on 4 August with Beck still not 100 percent fit. Soon they were back on the road with a five-week trek that started in Minneapolis and ended in Honolulu.

One of Beck's greatest assets, his musical unpredictability, was now being echoed more and more in his temperament. Always mercurial and emotional, he found himself increasingly singled out to embody the group's progressive, experimental image. Indeed, some concert promoters billed his name larger than the rest. It was a situation he would grapple with for the rest of his career: required to be brilliant, in the full glare of the spotlight, rather than sharing the load with a team of equals. Beck was not equipped to take it all on his shoulders and perform at a constant pitch of inventiveness.

"They placed a really high demand of creativity on me," he explains. "I just had to keep delving to the bottom of my bag to see what I could come up with. I had to keep on trying to impress them with my playing all the time. I was pretty unbalanced when I joined the group. I was 20, which is pretty young to be marched off from rags to riches, and it took me by surprise. I got really sort of messed up."

The nonstop tour eventually took them to California, where their first date was a memorable gig at the Casino Ballroom, Catalina Island. Two days later, on 25 August, they were due to play the Carousel Ballroom in San Francisco; but Beck missed the date. By now his throat was swollen and raw, aggravated by all the climatic changes of moving from place to place. This time there was no putting off the operation.

With Mary Hughes on hand to soothe his brow, he underwent emergency treatment while the tonsils were still infected, recuperating afterwards at Hughes' Hollywood apartment. It meant missing the rest of the tour, but it was the only thing to do. By now his system was overtaxed by all the hazards, mental and physical, of life on the rock star road. As he put it: "I had this throat thing come on—inflamed tonsils—and what with inflamed brain, inflamed tonsils, inflamed cock and everything else . . ."

Chris Dreja found himself switched to bass at short notice while Jimmy Page stepped into the spotlight, conjuring up bizarre psychedelic swirls of sounds as mesmerizing as the Carousel's freaky light show.

With Beck's encouragement, Page now regularly started to alternate his bass duties with those of second lead. On their return, the two spent hours rehearsing at Page's Victorian boathouse on the Thames, playing in unison or harmony until they got the most exciting, fevered, dueling solos and climaxes.

Beck: "I really wanted Jim Page on lead guitar with me because I knew it would sound sensational. We had fun. I remember doing some really nice jobs with Page. We were probably the closest two friends that could ever be, although there was this amazing rivalry. He's such an old right fox, y'know, underneath all that. But I never felt that we were the same styles—I never, ever worried about that."

This revolutionary double guitar lineup was characterized by some journalists as the Golden Age of the group, but in truth the partnership was short-lived. "I think it could have been really dangerous for both of us had it gone on," Beck says. "Page and myself together was like a complete amalgamation of sexual anticipation and utter schizophrenic tendencies."

Page: "It was good. Unfortunately there is very little of it that was recorded, but for the amount of time that it was working, it was really fabulous. It could have led to so many good things, except that there was a personality conflict within the group that wasn't coming from Beck and me, and that's why things started to bubble up." Most of it came from Keith Relf, in fact, who resented any focus being diverted from himself. "Keith always had this thing of being overshadowed by Jeff and that, which was nonsense."

With no letup in the pace, they were on the road again in September with a Rolling Stones 66 tour which included Ike & Tina Turner. Beck already loved Tina's "River Deep, Mountain High," which had been number three in the U.K. charts that June. Mick Jagger and the Stones were so crazy about it that they asked for her on their tour. The sight of this beautiful, wild woman with legs right up to her armpits, shimmying and shaking along with the miniskirted Ikettes behind her, was a fantastic turn-on for the audience. It assured her of a devoted following in Britain ever afterwards.

It also introduced Tina Turner to Jeff Beck, as she remembered in her book,

I, Tina: "I was in the dressing room and I heard somebody playing guitar—and were they ever playing it! I followed the sound out into the hallway, and I came to this other dressing room, and there was Jeff Beck, just sitting there, playing . . . Jeez, you should have heard him. I couldn't believe it. Ike said: 'Man, these guys can play over here!'"

But it wasn't a good tour for the Yardbirds. Somehow, with the hyped-up atmosphere, the dual lead partnership got out of hand: the two started engaging in some fiercely competitive guitar action. Beck was described as trying to blow Page off stage while, according to Simon Napier-Bell, Page deliberately upstaged Beck.

Also compounding the general disgruntlement was the press reaction. The Yardbirds and their fans felt they wiped the floor with the Stones, their hugely amplified twin guitars creating a barrage of sound that had the audience stomping and shouting for more. But all they got from the press was a terse mention—and in *New Musical Express*, a put-down recommending that Jeff Beck "cut out the gymnastics with his guitar."

It was a snub that Beck felt keenly, and he snubbed the press right back. He was widely reported as petulant and unapproachable, acquiring a notoriety that spread like wildfire. But at that time he was used to the press describing him as one of Britain's finest, most creative guitarists. He felt like he was riding the crest of a wave, which indeed he was. Beck admits he notched up quite a reputation for arrogance: "I really became a jerk—I was a jerk for quite a few years. I used to think I was it all the time. And there's usually someone around the corner who's better, y'know."

SOME TIME EARLIER that year, the Yardbirds had been invited to appear in a movie: the new Michelangelo Antonioni art film *Blow-Up*, starring David Hemmings, Vanessa Redgrave, and Sarah Miles, with Hemmings as the trendy photographer who dispassionately observes Swinging London and its world of models, drugs, and parties.

Shot at Elstree Studios, the film portrayed the group against a faithful replication of Windsor's Ricky Tick club. Supposedly furious at an equipment failure, a snarling Beck—sporting white pants several sizes too small for even his slender frame—slams his guitar into a Vox AC30, stomps on the instrument, and tears off the neck with sinister relish. He then throws the shattered remains into the crowd, which descends like a pack of jackals to snatch up the pieces.

It was the Who, with Pete Townshend's nihilistic guitar-smashing act, that Antonioni originally wanted, and Beck was totally aghast when the maestro directed him to demolish his prized Les Paul. "I had a fit. I said, 'Wait a minute, that's Townshend's thing.' I didn't mind playing a very wild number with lots of violence in it, lots of chords, smashing away, but I didn't actually want to destroy the guitar . . . so I smashed up a cheap old $35 model."

The model in question was a Hofner semiacoustic—of which they had a

Mid-1966, the new Yardbirds lineup with Jimmy Page appears on Britain's trendy TV pop show *Ready, Steady, Go!*

daily delivery brought to the studio while the rep stood happily by and watched them reduced to matchwood! But Antonioni himself was difficult to please. Beck remembers: "You never got the feeling anything was right with him. He'd take the thing 20 times over, and you *knew* it wasn't any different, that you did exactly the same motion, breaking guitar after guitar. I still have a scar where one of the strings sliced my finger. He said, 'I want you to *rip* the neck *off*,' and of course the string was still on it."

In preparation for the film, while the Stones tour was still in progress, Beck had been given some of these "disposable" guitars to practice his demolition act. So he decided to pull a stunt on the tour's compere, Long John Baldry. Pointing to one of them, he said it was a valuable instrument loaned to him by a girl who'd been in an accident and couldn't play anymore . . . and then he marched over, grabbed the thing by the neck, and smashed it to pieces under Baldry's horrified nose!

In the movie, Antonioni wanted them to pull out all the stops with their most electrifying number, but he rejected their showstopping "Smokestack Lightning." Their solution was to use "The Train Kept A-Rollin'," so they rewrote the lyrics and gave it a new title, "Stroll On." The soundtrack was laid down earlier, and they mimed to it when they came to do the filming on 12-14 October: in the film and on the soundtrack Dreja played bass, with Page on his Telecaster sharing guitar duties with Beck, their third and final recording together as Yardbirds.

Always the anti-hero, Beck was ambivalent about it all. He hated the idea of adopting the rock-star pose. "It was like you played movie star for four days. They pick you up in a limo and take you along there and . . . oh, it was embarrassing. What was *really* embarrassing was in the canteen where they had breaks for meals. There'd be all these extras and half of them went to the same school that I did; somehow there was about six or seven from Wimbledon Art School, and they're all giving me the raspberry and making rude gestures—crazy jealous, you know—'Look at 'im, fucking guitar player.'"

Destruction, as a deliberate piece of theater, was a tempting route to follow. Though Beck never could bring himself to smash guitars in the Townshend mode, he began to find release by using them to ram and butt the sound equipment. Already he had no qualms about kicking his amp offstage any time it let him down, and of course such letdowns weren't unusual in those days.

"The electronic equipment just wasn't up to the sounds that I had in my head. It was an endless battle to get my feelings across. You'd get to a gig and find a PA that was virtually nonexistent. We'd play a big ice rink with a few thousand people on hand and room for ten thousand more, and it was really frightening. I used to fly into rages and tantrums—I had a terrible temper then—and purposely play all the wrong notes and bend them in complete contempt of the whole situation."

Drummer Jim McCarty recognized the nature of the problem: "We really expected quite a bit from him. We leaned on him so much. It was always unpredictable what he'd do, he was obviously very wound up onstage. Sometimes he just seemed to turn into something else. It was almost like a monster movie. He just transformed."

BY LATE OCTOBER the group was on the other side of the Atlantic again. After initial dates on the West Coast, next up was a Dick Clark Caravan of Stars tour starting on the 29th in Dallas, Texas. If anything could drive you mad it was traveling 600 miles a day, cooped up in a bus with no air-conditioning, with an improbable mix of popsters like Bryan Hyland, Sam the Sham & the Pharaohs, Gary Lewis & the Playboys. A lot of the audiences weren't into the Yardbirds' music and couldn't understand it. For Beck, already drained of any enthusiasm for touring, it proved to be the last straw.

Dick Clark had started his Caravan of Stars back in 1959; pretty soon the bus was leased for 52 weeks a year, playing 14 shows a week with up to 17 acts on the bill. Things had moved on by the mid '60s, but it remained a horrendous schedule, gigs being lined up with no heed to distances or conditions. Jim McCarty reckoned they averaged four hours of sleep a night. Reaching a pitch of high energy at every show, and traveling like nomads in between, you had only an empty motel room to look forward to at journey's end. And—love them or hate them—always the same four guys at your side.

As Beck explains, "About that time people realized that there was huge box office to be dealt with, and the business people didn't bother to cultivate the groups, to say: 'There's some real talent here, let's sit down and think about this.' It was just a question of, 'How many records can we make, how many gigs can we play, how many tickets can we sell,' and they just burned the groups out."

Jimmy Page found it utterly exhausting: "It was the worst tour I've ever done as far as fatigue is concerned; it was living on a bus, driving hundreds of miles, doing double gigs every day. We didn't know where we were or what we were doing."

He remembers the state that Beck had reached by then: "I was doing what I was supposed to, while something totally different would be coming from Jeff. That was all right for improvisation, but there were other parts where it just did not work. Jeff had discipline occasionally, in that when he's on, he's probably the best there is. But at that time he had no respect for the audiences. When I joined the band, he supposedly wasn't going to walk off anymore. Well, he did a couple of times."

Already on the previous tour Beck had found conditions intolerable—one night he literally chucked a malfunctioning amp out of a window. Beck: "We were playing in this unbelievable place, packed solid, with the ceiling onstage just above our heads. And the air-conditioning had gone. So I had one of my tantrums. It was 140 degrees, unbearable heat, and the amp was crackling and then the heat just blew it up. It was a Vox I think, and I just tossed the whole thing out the window. The power amp had a fixed cannon socket, so it wouldn't pull out, and it was only that which prevented it from hitting this passerby underneath. The amp was swinging above his head."

Now, incredibly, the Dick Clark tour was even worse. The crunch came one night which was almost certainly in Texas*: "I felt like I'd die if I stayed another day. I broke down in the bedroom and told Jimmy I was out of there. It was awful, because I had to shove all the duties on to him the same bloody night."

Beck was plainly suffering from exhaustion and well set for another breakdown. Still treated as an outsider after nearly two years and allowed no say in group policy, his relationship with Keith Relf had reached such a crisis that on his last night, after a snide remark from Relf, he nearly brained the singer with his guitar.

Jimmy Page recalls: "I walked into our dressing room, where Jeff was holding his guitar over his head, about to bring it down on Keith. But he smashed it on the floor instead."

A legend quickly grew up around this incident, to the effect that Beck kicked over his amps, destroyed his guitar, and walked offstage. It's a good story, and indeed there were tour members who claimed to have seen it happen. However, the Jimmy Page version is the only one supported by members of the Yardbirds. Beck later showed the (thankfully repaired) Les Paul to a columnist for *Hit Parader,* pointing out how it had been shattered into four or five pieces—"This is where the Yardbirds career ended for me."

If he'd had enough of the Yardbirds, they had equally had enough of him. Beck went off to nurse his resentment in California with Mary Hughes, and when the rest of the group arrived they told him he could go. With a sense of

Beck reportedly departed from Corpus Christi Airport on 31 October 1966.

enormous relief he departed the Yardbirds, although for a while he maintained the fiction that he was just taking a break. The parting, "by mutual consent," was officially announced on 30 November as being due to persistent ill health.

"I don't regret leaving," he said later. "The management was the real reason that group broke up. We could have been enormous. We were limited by bad management, and the gigs were wrongly chosen. . . . I would have liked to see them develop a bit more, that's the regret I had, but physically I couldn't wait to get out of that band."

As if to prove the point, Simon Napier-Bell hammered a far more significant nail into the Yardbirds' waiting coffin: he brought in "popcorn king" Mickie Most of RAK Productions, as their producer.

At the same time he turned them over to a new manager, Peter Grant, with a warning to watch Jimmy Page. Page was a troublemaker, he said, asking too many questions about where all the money was going. But Grant was already a pal of Page's from way back, so he asked him how he'd managed to acquire such a reputation: "Troublemaker!" said Page, "You're dead right. We did *Blow-Up*, four weeks with the Rolling Stones, and an American tour, and all we got was £112 each."

LOOKING BACK MANY years later, Beck confessed himself puzzled over the now-defunct group's continued following when its entire duration—spanning Clapton, Beck, and Page—was a matter of only a few years. It wasn't as if they were together for a decade, he said. But of course it was not the longevity of the Yardbirds that made them so unique and so influential; it was the genius of their three exceptional guitar talents. Long before Jimi Hendrix and Cream, the Yardbirds were the first band to gain fame for the extraordinary instrumental prowess of their lead guitarists.

Jim McCarty had this to say about Jeff Beck's 21 months with the group: "The great thing about Jeff was, because we relied on him to fill up the sound, he developed a lot of his futuristic ideas. I still think he's the greatest rock guitarist there is, and he's still got a lot of very far-reaching ideas. But he's a complex character, isn't he? I mean, he plays from his heart all the time, and it takes quite a lot out of him. I know that he's spent periods where he hasn't even got out of bed because he's been so low. But he's come back, and he's playing rock 'n' roll again, which I think is great."

Chris Dreja adds: "We all feel, I think, that the period Jeff spent with the band was the most creative. His scope of inventiveness was probably the widest of the three, and coupled with his emotional qualities it made him my favorite to play with. See, Jeff can play very aggressive stuff that's not like brain damage because there's an emotional quality about it that's extremely pleasant, even when it's high-powered. That's something that's in the soul, and it gives his playing a durable quality."

Sixties Psychedelia

ANYONE WHO WAS there during the extraordinary years from 1966 through 1969 will look back on them as an unforgettable kaleidoscope of music, fashion, color, protest, and rebellion, offering open defiance to tired, outmoded patterns of thought and behavior.

Young girls shocked convention by sporting high boots and scandalously abbreviated miniskirts, while young men became peacocks with bright, braided, Edwardian toy-soldier uniforms, or ruffled satin shirts with high-collar, velvet Regency jackets.

Hair was a statement—over your ears, over your eyes, over your collar—and not merely a fashion statement. A generation of distraught parents felt much as the aging film star Tallulah Bankhead did, when visiting a friend with a particularly shaggy-haired son. "We just don't know what to make of him," said his despairing mother. "How about a nice rug?" Miss Bankhead suggested.

The Rolling Stones, always anti-establishment, adopted the ultimate long-haired image and came to represent everything in the way of irreverence, vulgarity, bravado, sexual come-on, and drug experimentation.

Even the Beatles, formerly beloved by parents, ceased to be inviolate as soon as they outgrew their cheeky, boyish image and entered the world of experiment. Did "Lucy in the Sky with Diamonds" really refer to LSD? Was there a hidden message in the run-out groove?

While debate centered on such pressing issues, the young had other concerns: the cold war, the nuclear arms race, death in Vietnam, starvation in Biafra. For some, the new reality was active rebellion—burning draft cards and occupying campuses in the U.S., or taking to the streets like the Paris students in 1968. For others, it was a passive statement of dropping out and adopting alternative values.

When psychedelia arrived along with LSD—new enough to be, for a while, legal—mind expansion became the latest game. Paul McCartney arranged funding of full-page advertisements in *The Times* advocating legalization of marijuana, and went so far as to admit he had taken LSD. "It opened my eyes," he said. "We only use one-tenth of our brains. Just think what we could accomplish if we could tap that hidden part."

Free and easy sex was another feature of the times, now that the contraceptive pill was here and AIDS had not yet made its ghastly appearance. Nothing better characterized the unacceptable face of sexuality than the rampant groupie phenomenon, that overheated coterie who not only made themselves available but actively scalp-hunted rock stars. The combustible mix of sex and drugs, and their association with rock, came to dominate the overriding perception of the '60s youth culture.

Soon the dream of a new world populated by beautiful people was no more. Partly because it was harried out of existence, its heroes tainted, its publications, clubs, and meeting places systematically closed down. Partly because cynicism set in, with the realization that no unstructured movement could prevail against the massed ranks of authority. And partly because of the ever-increasing heedless use of drugs, especially the new and unpredictable LSD.

Sadly, in the closing years of the decade, drug use that was no longer recreational but literally life-threatening pervaded a growing number of the top names in rock.

Brian Jones, unbalanced and easily unhinged by drugs and alcohol, was hounded beyond the brink by those who latched onto him as a vulnerable target. Though his death by drowning in July 1969 was not directly drug-induced, he was widely held to have been helped to his grave, as a spoiled and arrogant young lord of rock, by hands that were motivated by malice and envy.

It was a chilling portent of the forces that could so easily be unleashed, and would rise again for the Rolling Stones at their open-air concert at Altamont, California, in the last month of the last year of the '60s. Given at the very home of those flower children who had inspired the movement for peace and love, the Altamont free festival sparked off such violence and bloodshed, with a toxic mixture of bad acid, worse facilities, and brutal crowd control by the resident Hells Angels, that the Stones were lucky to escape unharmed.

ALTHOUGH SO MANY of his contemporaries turned to the plentiful dope that was always available, or sought inspiration in more destructive pharmaceuticals, Jeff Beck didn't get off on the fashionable drugs of the day. He always said he got freaked out enough on simply playing guitar. Which was more than true. As a newspaper report once commented, "With all that supercharged energy and explosive creativity, Jeff Beck doesn't play like he's on drugs; he plays like he *is* one."

Beck needed no other rush than the endless excitement of shattering musical boundaries—and perhaps the occasional amplifier—in a world where anything was possible. "I miss the absolute abandon and the musical lunacy that you can't get away with so much nowadays," he says. "But I didn't care much for the drugs side of it. I wanted people to hear us when they were sober. Maybe we sounded a lot better in the condition they were in! But I never took anything. I was like a vigilante. I mean, I was whiffing . . . it was passive smoking. You couldn't help that, unless you went on with a mask and a respirator!"

But music was still circumscribed within the three-minute format demanded by the pop charts; and Beck, like Eric Clapton before him, felt hemmed in by the incessant commercial pressures. His departure from the Yardbirds was a symptom not merely of stress but also of a fundamental need for change.

Clapton had already reached his personal crossroads earlier that year. Not that he suffered the same pressures: quite the opposite, in fact. His stint with John Mayall had been personally and musically fulfilling, and the band had released an excellent album with Clapton prominent in the credits. But he began to feel he'd gone as far as he could go with a conventional blues band. He was, in fact, a big fish in a small pond.

As the Bluesbreakers album reached number six in the charts, he made a decision which caused a momentous shift in his career. Teaming up with Jack Bruce on bass and Ginger Baker on drums, he formed the first of rock's supergroups, Cream, with the intention of concentrating on modern blues injected with the jazz/blues energy of Bruce and Baker.

Ginger Baker was a jazz/blues drummer of extravagant talent and unpredictable Irish temperament, while bassman Jack Bruce had studied at the Royal Scottish Academy of Music before starting a distinguished jazz and blues career.

The project of getting together with Clapton was originally Baker's idea. Clapton, who had enjoyed a strong rapport with Bruce when he played briefly with the Bluesbreakers, immediately suggested adding him to form a trio. Perhaps Clapton was unaware of how deep-rooted was the long conflict between the two fiery Celts, who'd played and fought together in the Graham Bond Organisation the previous year. Or perhaps he was simply, misguidedly, optimistic.

Though there was still plenty of time-honored blues in the new trio's repertoire, they soon found their music taking off in a direction and style of its own—characterized by pounding volume, crunching distortion, and heavy fuzztone (Bruce being one of the few bassists who employed such effects), with extended improvisations that took them right outside the accepted three-minute sound bite. Eventually they reached self-indulgent lengths of 15 minutes and more at a stretch, depending on the muse of the moment. But their fans on both sides of the Atlantic loved it, and Cream's U.S. tours of 1967 and 1968 assured them of gigantic international status.

Sadly, the peace and love of the '60s never permeated the members of Cream, and eventually all three found it impossible to maintain a reasonable relationship. Just over two years after forming, at the height of their success, they resolved to call it a day. Mounting a farewell tour that encompassed both Britain and the United States, they played for the last time at an emotional Albert Hall concert on 26 November 1968.

MORE THAN ANY other music of the day, it was the amazing sounds of Jimi Hendrix that most surely characterized the groundbreaking new dimensions of the declining decade.

Hendrix burst on the scene in Britain in late 1966, and literally redefined the art and language of electric guitar. His was a stardom that scaled the greatest heights, only to be snuffed out after four brief years, during which its incandescent flame provided a beacon for every guitarist who would follow.

A ferocious conjurer of magic and atmosphere, Hendrix held audiences in thrall as he wove his spells with throbbing, snarling, soaring, juddering, screeching, wildly inhuman sounds . . . delivered from a guitar that he used equally as love object and sex object, to be caressed to ecstasy or humped to a climax, its strings gnawed with his teeth or fingered as it lay across his shoulders . . . eventually to be flung aside, trampled and howling, its protests finally consigned to a funeral pyre as he set light to it and watched it burn, leaving a smoking ruin lamented only by the tortured whining of amplifiers.

Hendrix's success in England was almost instantaneous. Late 1966 was the precise moment when London was a nexus around which the rest of the world was happy to gravitate. And London was ready to be taken by storm.

Raised in poverty, which he'd escaped only by signing on as a U.S. paratrooper, Hendrix at 24 had led a man's life far longer than the ex-art school dropouts who populated most of the British rock scene. And with this challenging macho maturity he combined a fashionably rail-thin, gawkily elegant physical presence, draped with outrageous garb and festooned with scarves, the whole topped by the wildest of electric Afro hair.

But Hendrix was more than just a colorful stage performer: he was a superb musician and songwriter, and an electronic painter of sound pictures par excellence. As a lefty, he would play a standard Strat flipped over and restrung; but he was equally proficient with right- or left-handed instruments, restrung or untouched. He just sounded the same whichever way he played.

Like many before him, and many since, Jimi Hendrix became a victim of his public persona—the drugged-out showman superstud in whom the musician inside became little more than a fellow traveler. With the world at his feet, he was increasingly torn between the public's demand for more of what they'd had before, and his own desire to somehow create the music he alone could hear in his head.

Hendrix died as a result of barbiturate intoxication in September 1970, at the age of 27. A decade later, Jeff Beck still felt the loss: "I'm still really sad about his not being here, because I need somebody around that I can believe in. I don't believe in anybody else."

Asked how he felt on first seeing Hendrix perform, "I was embarrassed," was Beck's reply. "Because I thought, 'God, that should be me up there.' I just hadn't had the guts to come out and do it so flamboyantly, really. I'm just too withdrawn a character to do that. I bitterly regret not having exploited my style a bit more, because there was a lot of stuff he did actually get from me, which he admitted—the Yardbirds stuff, with the freaking out and feedback and all . . . some of the little licks he did came from the Yardbirds records. That was a compliment; I could never thank him enough for doing that."

Beck's personal reminiscences of Hendrix are plentiful, and always tinged with regret: "We could never enjoy a real close friendship because of what we did. He and I were both after the wild guitar playing. I liked Jimi best when we didn't talk guitars. Like when we used to go out. It was just sadness that we couldn't nurture the friendship a bit more. In those days life was just totally crazy. He would be off in a 24-hours-a-day lifestyle, and I couldn't keep up with it. I had to have my sleep. He was a boogier—a club here, a club there—and he'd be jamming till five in the morning. My lifestyle was never destined to be like that, so I just had to say, 'Adios, Jim, I gotta go to bed!' I felt very amateurish alongside him, because he lived and breathed it. I'm not in love with the guitar as much as Jimi was."

And jamming with Hendrix? "Well . . . it was awful! [*Laughs*] The first time, I felt like a peanut, like a fucking hole would have opened up and swallowed me. The thing that puts it right is the fact that there's a genuine love Jimi had for my style as well. Which I couldn't believe. Then I realized that Jimi was not a messiah; he was a very genuine, dyed-in-the-wool, music-loving person. He didn't give a damn about the reputation, the showbiz razzmatazz. All that he was interested in were the licks and what you were feeling like . . . he wasn't out to blow you off the stage at all."

But Beck was there to see Hendrix's playing suffer as a result of the intense pressures on him. "Playing live to people expecting miracles every night was just too much for him, really. I could see him going down as a result of it. And then, unfortunately, the worst happened. It's a bloody shame there was nobody around to make sure it didn't. He was just riding on a high, constantly, and that can't go on forever. It's one of the saddest losses in rock 'n' roll guitar history, because who knows what he'd be doing now?

"I often think of him when I'm playing," he says. "Maybe he's smiling up there."

DURING THE SECOND HALF of 1966, when Cream and Jimi Hendrix were about to blaze into glory, Jeff Beck was busy with the Yardbirds and the commercial slog of touring. Only after he left did he take note of the Hendrix phenomenon. Now he realized that for him the London scene had subtly changed—perhaps more so than it had for other guitarists.

"Once the Hendrix era came along, I had a very hard time doing what I'd always done because Hendrix had started doing it. I thought, rather than be a follower, I'd rather not play for a while. He was like a big explosion that flattened everything, left nothing standing."

If Beck's own plans had come to fruition, however, he would by then have been in a position to challenge both Hendrix and Cream. Before either had appeared on the scene, he'd already put together a group that promised a whole new dimension in progressive rock. And had it survived, it would certainly have changed the course of rock history.

It was some time in May of 1966 that the personnel for this potential supergroup got together at a hurriedly arranged recording session. Those present were Beck playing lead on his Gibson Les Paul, Jimmy Page on an electric 12-string, two leading session players—John Paul Jones on bass and Nicky Hopkins on piano—and the madcap Keith Moon on drums.

For Beck, the cornerstone of the group was to have been Moon: he had the wildest personality and the most vicious drum sound, both of which endeared him mightily to Beck. "I didn't really like the Who then; they were annoying me because they had my drummer! I thought of cutting a track with Keith, so we rang him up, expecting to get the blank. But he said, 'Yeah, I'll be there tomorrow,' and he turned up!"

Simon Napier-Bell came in initially to produce, at the time when Yardbirds members were trying out solo projects. Jimmy Page then ended up in the producer's box because Napier-Bell simply disappeared and left them to it.

This lineup set to work on a number of recordings, which produced just one release: the landmark "Beck's Bolero."

"The session started at ten and we were done by twelve," as Beck remembers it. "I wanted to see that band come out of there cemented with that one record. But Keith obviously couldn't do it because of the Who, although he led us to believe he was leaving them, probably just to make the Who jealous. And John Paul Jones was a fabulous bass player. It was the obvious solution, going with that band. But it never happened."

Though "Beck's Bolero" is the sole surviving track, there were certainly others laid down which time has deprived us of the chance to hear. Uncharacteristically, for someone who dislikes raking over the past, Beck himself has remarked that he hopes someone may one day unearth those missing tapes.

In fact, the planned lineup for that recording might have been even more intriguing. Bassist John Entwistle, like Keith Moon, was unhappy with the Who and had been scheduled to join them for the session; it was only when Entwistle failed to arrive that John Paul Jones was brought in instead.

"That was probably the first Led Zeppelin band—not with that name, but that kind of music. Page and I wanted to form a group with Moon and Entwistle; then Page and the two guys from the Who were gonna form a group and call it Led Zeppelin. I wanted to release 'Bolero' as a single aside from the Yardbirds material. We kept that track in the can until after I left the group."

Beck describes how they set it up: "We'd arranged a session with Keith Moon in secret, just to see what would happen. But we had to have something to play in the studio because Keith only had a limited time—he could only give us like three hours before his roadies would start looking for him. So I went over to Jim's house a few days before the session, and he was strumming away on this 12-string Fender electric that had a really big sound. It was the sound of that Fender 12-string that really inspired the melody.

"I know I'm going to get screamed at because in some articles he says he wrote it. And I don't care what he says, I invented that melody, such as it is. This is what it was: he hit these Amaj7 chords and the Em7 chords, and I just started playing over the top of it. We agreed that we would go in and get Moonie to play a bolero rhythm with it. That's where it came from.

"We sat down in his front room," Beck remembers, "and he was sitting on the arm of a chair and started playing that Ravel rhythm. And I just played the melody, then I went home and worked out the other [up-tempo] beat."

As a matter of record, Jimmy Page does equally insist he wrote the song ("wrote it, played on it, produced it"), and indeed it is credited to Page. But, to be realistic, it was obviously a collaboration.

Anchored by the insistent bolero rhythm, "Beck's Bolero" features a chromatically wandering tune embellished by an astonishing range of mind-blowing effects—described by writer Gene Santoro as "a kind of shriekback tip of the hat to Ravel shot through with insane slide guitar slashings and billowing feedback." ("The phasing was Jimmy's idea," Beck recalls. "I played a load of waffle and he reversed it.")

The song is a classic early showcase for the benchmark Beck legato technique, delivered with a vengefully bone-shivering intensity of tone; and it remains a favorite of his from his entire recording career. It's also memorable for a priceless moment when Keith Moon destroys the studio miking setup for his drums: "Moon smashed a $250 microphone while we were doing that session, by just hitting it with a stick. Halfway through 'Bolero' you can hear Moonie screaming. He hit the mic and smashed it off, so all you can hear from then on is cymbals!

"Moon was pretty pissed off at the Who at that time, but he still had to turn up at the studio with dark glasses so that nobody recognized him. He got out of the cab at IBC Studios in Langham Place wearing dark glasses and a Russian cossack hat, so that nobody could see him being naughty with another session. I'm sure that would have been the first Led Zeppelin if Moonie had been able to join, but nothing really took off."

"That lineup could have been Led Zeppelin," Page acknowledged to Steven Rosen in *Guitar World,* "even though the name came later*. . . . And the singer was either going to be Steve Marriott [Small Faces] or Stevie Winwood. In the end it came to Marriott and he was contacted. And the reply came back from his office like, 'How would you like to have a group with no fingers, boys?' Or words to that effect."

It's interesting to note that Mike Bloomfield recalled "Beck's Bolero" having a significant impact on Jimi Hendrix, who named it among his favorite tracks: "He learned to apply melodic ideas to permanent sustain, tied in with feedback, from the Yardbirds and other English groups. I think he even mentioned 'Beck's Bolero.' Jimi had been fooling with feedback, but when he heard the Yardbirds he

*Keith, though he never became a member of the group, was responsible for Led Zeppelin's name. There was a piece of old stage jargon that he used as something of a catchphrase—"it went down like a lead Zeppelin"—an alternative to "like a lead balloon." Since it referred to an act that bombed with the audience, Jimmy Page adopted it in a mood of fate-challenging black humour. The change of spelling to "Led," of course, was to avoid mispronunciation.

realized its immense potential. He was listening for such things, and I believe he heard them on the English records, particularly by the Yardbirds and Jeff Beck. He was very modest. He never said he took feedback further than the Yardbirds. He said, 'I fool with it, and what I'm doing now is the fruits of my fooling around.'"

Jimi Hendrix also personally told Jeff Beck that he used some of "Happenings Ten Years Time Ago" for his song "Stone Free"—a number that Beck would later choose to cover on a Hendrix tribute album.

Whether the suits won out in the end, or whether Keith Moon simply came to his senses, the short-lived Led Whobirds soon joined the annals of bands-that-might-have-been. Moon returned to the ranks of the Who, and John Paul Jones reverted, for a while, to his work as a studio session musician.

Jimmy Page continued with the Yardbirds for a last desultory 18 months after Beck's departure, but by then they had lost their cutting edge and were on their way to oblivion. When they eventually split, he teamed up with John Paul Jones to fulfill the promise of those IBC sessions, and in the formation of Led Zeppelin created a group that owed a debt, in more ways than one, to the vision of Jeff Beck.

6 A Momentary Lapse . . .

WHILE CREAM AND JIMI HENDRIX were just beginning to hit pay dirt at the end of 1966, Jeff Beck had returned home, still haunted by the ordeals of touring and far from well after his breakdown in America. It was now he made a move that he would seriously regret: he signed a contract, a month after officially leaving the Yardbirds, with the group's soon-to-be producer, Mickie Most (whom we first met working the Coke machine in Soho's 2Is coffee bar). Beck was to be comanaged by Simon Napier-Bell and Peter Grant, with Most in charge of record production. Beck: "It was a fabulous contract that guaranteed I wouldn't get anything, no matter what!"

Born Michael Hayes, Most adopted his new name in the '50s on forming a singing duo with Alex Murray (later producer of such recordings as "Go Now" by the Moody Blues), calling themselves the Most Brothers and appearing on occasional British package tours. During the early '60s, Mickie Most had moved for a while to South Africa where he had a band called the Playboys and was known for his ersatz Buddy Holly act. He racked up a number of local hits on the Rave and Gallo labels singing covers of Stateside releases, one of them the Crickets' "Think It Over" ("I was like the Elvis of South Africa"). But his talents as a performer were, to put it kindly, limited: "Most's presence was pretty ridiculous," according to *Rolling Stone*. "A plump figure leaping about, falling on the stage, all the while shrieking in a laughably inadequate voice."

Failing to take London by storm on his return, he turned to record production—and hit a lucky streak first off with the Animals; their second session, recorded in the space of half an hour, produced the chart topping "House of the Rising Sun." By 1967 he was a full-time manager as well as producer, handling groups like the Animals and Herman's Hermits, and churning out a succession of mainstream pop hits. When he brought his talents to bear on the Yardbirds, the result would be a sudden shift to strings and pop arrangements.

Before Mickie Most had made his baleful mark on the Yardbirds, however, he seemed to Beck the kind of finger-on-the-pulse hustler who could kick-start his new career. But Most's plans for Beck could scarcely have been farther from his own personal aim, which was to form another band and start playing the kind of music that let his wide-ranging talents roam free. Beck soon found himself being pushed in an entirely opposite direction. Disregarding the "guitar hero" success of Eric Clapton and Jimi Hendrix, not to mention Beck's own status as the Yardbirds' star guitarist, Most hauled his protégé into the studio in January 1967 to cut a pop record. His idea was to make Beck a singer.

"He said, 'I know what you should be doing.' He also had a very binding contract on me. I had no artistic influence at all; everything was to be done per his direction. I thought, 'Okay, make me a big star.' And he nearly finished my career with that one record, 'Hi Ho Silver Lining.' He didn't even want a guitar part on it. 'All that wah-wah-wah, forget it,' he said. 'You're going to perform on television doing this song, whether you like it or not.'"

Written by Scott English and Larry Weiss, "Hi Ho Silver Lining" was a deceptively jaunty sing-along ditty with an acerbic lyric somewhat after the style of the Kinks, with their neatly turned observations on Swinging London and its ultra trend-conscious habitués. "You're everywhere and nowhere baby," the words begin, "That's where you're at," which Beck delivers with steel glinting behind the smile.

In fact a band called the Attack brought out their own version just a few days before the Beck release in March. But they were immediately eclipsed by Beck's powerful riffs and heavily distorted solo, backed up by a chugging beat that was infectious from the first moment.

Beck has since variously described it as "a pain in the ass" and "a ball and chain round my ankle."

"I didn't like the song—it was ghastly, stupid. But it's still a mega-success all around England: they play it at the end of discos, turn it off halfway through and everyone sings along."

Most was right about the song's potential. Despite its being wholly out of keeping with anything Jeff Beck could have conceivably wanted to record, this first solo single gave Beck a hit when he needed it. It reached number 14 in Britain in April 1967 and remained in the Top 50 for 14 weeks, during which time he became quite a regular on the BBC TV show *Top of the Pops* (it was subsequently reissued twice, in 1972 and 1982, with further chart success).

"Silver Lining" was coupled with "Beck's Bolero" on the B-side, for which the production was (typically) claimed by Mickie Most—entirely ignoring any credit to Jimmy Page or Simon Napier-Bell. "Talk about being naïve," was Napier-Bell's comment; "I just said, 'What the hell, I don't need it.' I didn't, really—but that track became a rock milestone."

Inevitably, Beck the hard rocker was unhappy with the line of trade that Most envisaged for him. With hindsight, it's likely his disenchantment with "Silver Lining" was also aggravated by the less-than-perfectly-overdubbed guitar solo. This was one of the first ever double-tracked solos in rock, but he was never given the time to nail it accurately.

"That double-tracked guitar solo, where everything is slightly off, sounds like two guys playing? I was actually trying to get it right but couldn't, because I had all these little inflections in the first take that I couldn't copy. 'That'll do,' Mickie said—he was one of those guys who always said that: 'Next. We've got Suzi Quatro coming in.'"

However, even before this, Beck had already begun planning a new band. It would be called, with typical simplicity, the Jeff Beck Group. And it would cut new ground with a style of ultra heavy rock that would one day earn the title of embryonic heavy metal.

First to come on board was a certain unknown vocalist with an amazing, raw-edged blues-shout voice. His name was Rod Stewart.

Stewart had long paid his dues in a number of bands on vocals and harmonica, among them Jimmy Powell & the Dimensions and Long John Baldry's Hoochie Coochie Men. Beck had heard him with Baldry when the band was re-formed into Steampacket under Giorgio Gomelsky's management, taking in Brian Auger (organ) and Mickey Waller (drums).

When Steampacket split in May 1966, Stewart moved to a new group, Shotgun Express, whose changing lineup included Mick Fleetwood on drums and, for a while, Peter Green on guitar, together with Dave Ambrose on bass. But by the end of the year the group's fortunes were languishing.

As Jeff Beck remembers it, "One very slack night at the Cromwellian, there was one guy there ploughing into some food and getting drunk on his own: Rod Stewart. He didn't even look at me, so I went over to see what was happening. He was really drunk. So I asked him whether he was still playing with Steampacket*; I'd seen him with them, and he was outrageous.

"He said, 'No, I'm not gonna stay with them.' So I said, 'If you ever want to put a band together . . .' He said, 'You're joking.' I said, 'No.'

"He said, 'You ring me tomorrow. I'll leave Steampacket.' So I rang him and that was it." For some reason they met up in one of London's museums—a war museum, as Beck recalls—and walked around without looking at any of the exhibits, deep in their plans to set up a blues/rock band.

It now remained to fill the slots for bass and drums. Rehearsals were held in January at a place in London's Goodge Street, where former Shadow Jet Harris was the first candidate on bass. Viv Prince (ex-drummer of the Pretty Things) was tried out at the same time, but this combination quickly folded.

Guitarist Ron Wood—later to lend his talents to the Rolling Stones—was the next permanent recruit. Ron had been playing in the short-lived Santa Barbara Machine Head, and before that with modest success in the Birds, which included Kim Gardner (Creation, AGD and Badger). A friend of Beck's ever since his Tridents days, Woody had once sat in on harmonica with the Yardbirds when Keith Relf was sick. He had actually been asked to join them when Beck left, but very sensibly turned the idea down. Instead, he rang Beck.

Wood and Stewart, who had met a couple of times already (most recently in 1966 when Woody had played on a Rod Stewart solo session, "Come Home Baby," produced by Mick Jagger), hit it off immediately. Soon they would be thick

---

* *For Steampacket read* Shotgun Express.

as thieves, hanging out, drinking together, and sometimes driving the others mad with their farcical sense of humor. Beck never got that close to either of them, but musically there was alchemy between the trio; they would form the nucleus of the first Jeff Beck Group, which lasted from January 1967 to August 1969.

The music papers, always eager to report on Beck, were avid to hear of his new plans. And not all of them shared the "bad boy" view. *Hit Parader* described him as one of the most talented faces on the British scene; the Yardbirds were simply a group he was too good for.

"It's a funny business, I accept that," Beck commented, "but then people just don't accept my reasons for leaving. As far as I'm concerned, I can split from 20,000 groups if I want to. If a person's not happy with a job, he leaves."

But though he wasn't looking for immediate raving success, he admitted it would be tough to find himself playing small clubs again without the recognition he'd enjoyed of late. "That's something that would bring anybody down, but you have to get used to it," he said. "I'm accepting this. All you can do is entertain, and the one that does it the best is the winner."

If Beck had decided to take the philosophical view, he would soon find it sorely tested. In the typical rush and tumble of the times, he suddenly found himself urged to get the personnel of the band decided when Mickie Most's cohort Peter Grant called him in February, while he was vacationing in Brussels, to say he had been squeezed on to a tour with Roy Orbison and the Small Faces—due to start in a week's time.

Some quick thinking by Beck produced Ray Cook, his erstwhile drummer with the Tridents, who was pressed into service on his old mate's first JBG outing. The lineup was completed by the simple expedient of asking Woody to switch to bass. Less than confident as second lead backing up the mighty Beck, he was happy to make the move.

In his book *The Works,* Ron Wood tells how he acquired the instrument for the job: "I went round to a music store called Sound City and stole a bass, because I didn't have the money to make the payments. Five or six years later, when I was in the Faces, I went there and told them, 'I'm the guy who stole your Fender Jazz bass and I've come here to pay you.' They were delighted."

With only a week's notice, by the time Beck finally got the hasty setup together, they had not much more than a day of rehearsal. And it must have set a record for short-lived groups, as their opening with the tour was disastrous. They played just one date, on 3 March at the Finsbury Park Astoria, and pulled out that same night. As Rod Stewart told it to Tim Ewbank and Stafford Hildred (*Rod Stewart: A Biography*), the story goes like this:

"We all walked on stage in our band uniform. We all had white jackets and Jeff had a different one because he was the leader of the group. We got through one number and the electric went off. Somebody had pulled the plug. We immediately blamed the Small Faces. I always blamed Mac [keyboard player Ian McLagen] for doing it, or instructing someone to do it, because he thought we

Early rehearsals of the first Jeff Beck Group, February/March 1967 (L-R Ray Cook on drums, Beck on Gibson Les Paul #1, Ron Wood on bass).

might steal the show. Beck decided this was the end of the show, he wasn't going to stand any more and walked off stage.

"I remember I wasn't too pleased because I looked down and saw I hadn't done my flies up. We'd been on stage for one and a half minutes and the curtain came down and nearly knocked Woody over because it was so hefty. I caught him and he knocked it into me and we sort of did a dance off the stage. We still had to find someone to take the blame. In the end we made the drummer take the blame."

"He just froze completely and couldn't play," Rod told *ZigZag* magazine, "so he had to go. I don't know what happened to him . . . it was a real shame, actually, because his old man had bought him a brand new drum kit for the tour, and he was sacked the first day. Very sad."

Within a short while Beck had replaced Ray Cook with Mickey Waller, probably just to hold the fort since Waller had a major tour lined up with the Walker Brothers at the end of March. A graduate of John Mayall's Bluesbreakers, Waller had a pedigree that went back through Steampacket to the Brian Auger Trinity and the Cyril Davies R&B All Stars.

This new lineup seems to have been first heard on BBC Radio's *Saturday Club* on 18 March, recorded on 7 March, despite the BBC's annals noting the ousted

Ray Cook as the drummer (they also wrongly dated it as 10 March). Things were in such a state of flux that they probably weren't informed of any personnel beyond Beck, Stewart, and Wood, which may explain why the press announced "the Jeff Beck Trio" for the broadcast.

The radio show featured some brilliant guitar from Beck, which went a long way towards salvaging his shattered reputation. Interviewed by Brian Matthew during the program, Beck remarked: "I've completely re-formed the group and added another couple of members." Waller was one, of course; the other was probably a new bass player, since Wood's switch of instruments was evidently regarded as a stopgap. That being the case, he was likely referring to Dave Ambrose, Rod Stewart's former colleague from Shotgun Express, who was added to the lineup at about this time.

Mickey Waller's temporary tenure on drums came to an end in late March, whereupon Rod Coombes (later of Juicy Lucy, Stealers Wheel and the Strawbs) entered the fray. Coombes lasted scarcely longer than Ray Cook. But he survived long enough to appear on 11 April, together with Ambrose, in the group's impressive debut at the Marquee—still one of London's leading music scenes—where the five-man JBG had an audience of over 1,000.

The bewildering game of musical drumstools eventually came to an end in mid-April, when stability was achieved with the arrival of Aynsley Dunbar. Already one of the leading drummers on the scene, Dunbar had played with a host of blues bands including the Mojos and the Bluesbreakers.

Around the same time, Dave Ambrose disappeared (later to reappear with Brian Auger), and Beck reinstated the four-piece format with Wood permanently shifted to bass. "Jeff used to just let me go," he said, "because he knew that I was nice enough to stop playing guitar. He could've got a few bass players, mind you, but they weren't very inventive." (One aspect of Woody's inventiveness was to play through a 200-watt Marshall, making him easily the loudest bass on the circuit.)

Bookings were mostly clubs and ballrooms during those first few months, with occasional TV exposure for "Hi Ho Silver Lining," which Beck performed with mounting reluctance. But clubs and ballrooms were what they wanted, rather than another ghastly package tour, and the provincial wastelands were alleviated by regular gigs at the Marquee where audiences got heavily into the group's visceral sound.

On 2 July they performed on the same bill as Cream and John Mayall's Bluesbreakers on the prestigious stage of London's Saville Theatre—a venue that Beatles manager Brian Epstein had recently taken over for a sellout series of Sunday rock concerts showcasing some of the most glittering talents in the industry.

Flower power was all the rage, and their outfits were nothing if not flamboyant. For the weekly music paper *Disc,* trendy pop columnist Penny Valentine was there to record the scene for posterity: "A bit more togetherness would have helped Jeff Beck on Sunday, in his green floppy hat and fur coat,

Jeff Beck on the cover of *Beat Instrumental*, August 1967. Jeff was a regular columnist for several months from summer 1966.

into cutting a single that was the worst lapse of an illustrious career: a sugary instrumental arrangement, with orchestra and female choir, of the banal Eurovision Song Contest tune "Love Is Blue" (on which Beck overdubbed bass as well as lead). Released in February 1968, it provided another modest chart success, reaching number 23 despite a performance so malevolently pedestrian that the scowl on Beck's face is almost audible.

A stipulation of his contract was that he had to play the songs Mickie Most provided or approved of, and at the time he could come up with no alternative that suited Most's chart-oriented ideas. "Mickie Most, let me tell you, all he wants to do is make hit records," Beck told *ZigZag*, "and all I want to do is play my music. When 'Love Is Blue' was recorded, he was terribly difficult to work with— he really let me know who was the boss."

The effects for Beck were far reaching and even today remain a thorn in his side. His fans were dumbstruck by his release of the Paul Mauriat number, and even more so by the maestro's performance, in which they detected passages of (heaven forbid!) questionable intonation. Later he confessed he'd made an effort to send up the piece, but the joke had misfired: "People who knew my playing were so blind they couldn't see the humor in it. They deserved to be offended!"

Though sales of the record were useful when it was a battle even to pay the rent, it was scarcely likely to enhance the reputation of his struggling group. Once more the single's saving grace was the B-side, a slow blues, "I've Been Drinking," which put Stewart's gravelly vocals in front for the first time with the JBG.

Through the auspices of Mickie Most—by now known privately to Beck as Mickie Mouse—he was finding himself pushed in all sorts of unlikely directions. First he was to star in a couple of B movies about life on the road; then there was the suggestion of a separate solo (guitar) career, recording a concerto and giving concerts backed by an orchestra, no less; there was even a curious move to rename the group Jeff Beck's Million Dollar Bash.

Small wonder that at one point, early in the group's existence, Beck considered packing in the whole music thing. A career in photographic modeling briefly caught his fancy—sparked, perhaps, by experiences in his Yardbird days, when he'd done some moody Carnaby Street shots and found himself pursued by an artist who was fixated on painting him: "His face is like craggy summits and windy places; a wild animal struggling to be free . . ."

Beck: "We had a very rough time then. We had no money at all, to the point where I was borrowing just to buy food. I'm talking serious poverty. It was heartbreaking to think how much we were doing musically and how little we were getting over."

IN THE SPRING of 1968 the JBG was still touring consistently, if not lucratively, and during April the group played a brief series of dates in Switzerland, Denmark, Sweden, and France. The following month it was time to get down to recording an album at last, which in Mickie Most's terms meant six-hour sessions spread over as few days as possible. They took place on 14, 15, 16 and 25 May. For material, the group basically used a collection of songs that had been in their repertoire for the best part of a year. The result was their debut album, *Truth*.

Recorded at Abbey Road studios, the minimal studio time might have led one to expect an album of little consequence. Instead, it was to produce a landmark in the world of rock, showcasing Beck's brilliant guitar in a dazzling variety of moods and styles, proving once and for all his range and mastery of his medium.

Certainly the limited time must have concentrated the mind wonderfully, leading to that rarest of phenomena, a virtually first-take situation with all the spontaneity of live performance.

Mickie Most was unconvinced of the group's potential for success and had little to do with the production (which doubtless benefited the result): "Technically he probably doesn't know one reel of tape from another," was Beck's

Jeff Beck Group, 1967: the group that took the USA by storm (L-R Mickey Waller, Jeff Beck, Rod Stewart, Ron Wood).

acid comment. "He was yachting in Cannes and just generally swanking about the place. All he was interested in was hit singles; he was still in the chewing gum market."

Concurrently in Olympic Studios was another act from Most's stable, the folksy singer/songwriter/guitarist Donovan; Beck would sometimes go over after JBG sessions to lay down some guitar tracks on Donovan's *Hurdy Gurdy Man*.

It was a happy association, so the following year brought more work with Donovan, this time featuring the entire Jeff Beck Group (incidentally giving rise to unwelcome speculation of a permanent link-up). Among the numbers recorded at their sessions in May 1969 was the single "Barabajagal," backed with "Trudi." Unusual for Donovan, with its jazzy style and Latin beat, "Barabajagal" would be his last hit single, reaching number 12 in Britain. A few other titles were produced with the JBG at the same session: "Homesickness," which was included on the later album *HMS Donovan,* and two that were never released, "Suffer Little Children" and "The Stromberg Twins" (recalling Beck's mania for hot rods).

Turning the calendar back briefly, Jeff Beck had already contributed his talents to a few other sessions. The first was in 1967 when he played on the B-side, "But She's Mine," of a single by one of Simon Napier-Bell's groups, John's Children—probably his first recorded performance after leaving the Yardbirds.

His second guitar outing on someone else's record was another B-side, this time for John Walker (né Maus) of the Walker Brothers, who had sold Beck his Fender Esquire. "I See Love in You" was the name of the song, but Walker's solo effort was doomed to sink without a trace.

Soon afterwards, in early 1968, there came a similar invitation from Peter Asher to sit in on a single with Paul Jones, previously Manfred Mann's star vocalist, who was also looking to start a solo career. Asher was already part of the pop duo Peter & Gordon, and was branching out into production; he was also the brother of Paul McCartney's current girlfriend, Jane Asher, which did his ambitions no harm at all. An impressive list of session men was lined up for the recording, including McCartney on drums, Nicky Hopkins on keyboards, and Paul Samwell-Smith on bass.

The A-side, "And the Sun Will Shine" by the Bee Gees, had very little of Beck; the most interesting song guitar-wise was the B-side, "The Dog Presides," written by Jones himself, where Beck contributes some bluesy, driving leads and funky fills.

Asked about his hardware for the session, Beck recalled it was very likely a Les Paul/Marshall combination. With the JBG live he was using two 200-watt amps (with the Yardbirds he had used 100-watts), and his preference for Marshalls went naturally with the Les Paul, a combination pioneered by Eric Clapton. Beck would stay with these British-made amps for many more years.

He is also known to have co-produced the song "Utterly Simple," with Dave Mason of Traffic, for the Yorkshire group Smoke. Written by Mason, the song was briefly released as a single and then withdrawn. It can now be found on the CD *Smoke—The Best of Sugar Man,* released in Germany on the Repertoire label.

Beck enjoyed doing these brief appearances, and there followed a career-long proclivity for sitting in on other people's recordings. Sometimes his contributions were even uncredited, which certainly doesn't make life easy for the discographer, and readers are cordially invited to suggest amendments or additions to this book's discography.

Beck himself is inclined to go glassy-eyed when asked about obscure sessions, but doubtless the lack of hassle and pressure yielded some thoroughly enjoyable moments over the years, enhancing the recorded output of a wide variety of talents from the little-known Upp and Dorian Passante to the world famous Stevie Wonder, Mick Jagger and Tina Turner.

ALTHOUGH BECK WAS signed to Columbia in England, Mickie Most was unable to get an immediate release for the Jeff Beck Group's first album. Perhaps he didn't try too hard.

By now things were not all smooth sailing within the group, and this was another area where Beck was not given sound managerial guidance. In the spring of 1968, on Most's advice, he fired Ron Wood—the first of a series of firings and rehirings, the precise details of which have become irretrievably blurred in the memories of all concerned.

This first occasion seems to have been in March, whereupon Woody went and joined his ex-colleague Kim Gardner in the almost-successful band Creation. With Wood on guitar, they recorded three singles and took off on a tour of Germany, but within three months Creation had sadly folded.

Without Ron Wood for the JBG's European tour in April/early May, bass duties were taken by John "Junior" Woods from the group Tomorrow, now in the doldrums after guitarist Steve Howe had moved to Yes. But Ron Wood rejoined for the sessions on *Truth,* and his return happily coincided with the break they had been waiting and praying for. It came when they got their chance to capture the altogether more receptive audiences on the other side of the Atlantic.

This was entirely thanks to Mickie Most's enterprising partner Peter Grant, who had bought out Simon Napier-Bell's interest and taken the JBG under his wing. A seasoned ex-roadie who had a good deal more street sense than the "popcorn king," Grant would later steer Led Zeppelin on the path to glory.

"We were literally down on our last crumb," says Beck. "We had nothing left. But Peter Grant was smart enough to see there was an underground scene happening, where bands were making it without being seen on the surface—newspapers, records, none of that. So he said, 'I'm gonna put you out there.' It was a last-ditch thing, to keep the band going. So we rehearsed. We had just one set of good clothes that had to last us the whole tour."

Their triumphant opening was at New York's Fillmore East on 14-15 June, where they played to a 3,000 strong audience that was there to see the Grateful Dead as top of the bill. The JBG had initially been booked as the headlining act, but the promoters brought in the Dead as an afterthought to ensure a better gate.

"We played two numbers in a segue to open," Beck recalls. "Finished with a big RRRAR-RHHHH. Rod came out from behind the amps—he sang from offstage—in a mackintosh and a hat, ready to go home. I said, 'I think you can take 'em off: they liked it.'"

Indeed they did. In fact they couldn't believe their ears or eyes when Jeff Beck made his entrance, bare-chested and shaggy-haired, clad in jeans and white suspenders.

The group had a horrendously daunting start, following a band called the Seventh Sons who were literally booed off stage in the middle of their act. As Beck launched into their opening steamer, "I Ain't Superstitious," the tension got to Rod Stewart in a big way and not a sound would come from his throat! In England he had rarely sung in front of more than 800 or so. But the audience went ape for the snarling Beck guitar, and by the end of the set they'd done multiple encores and the crowd was still yelling for more. Following the Jeff Beck Group, the Grateful Dead—famous for never-ending, all-night sets—could only fit in half an hour.

The next day, the *New York Times* printed a rave review under the headline "Jeff Beck Group cheered in debut." Robert Shelton was full of praise for "Beck's wild and visionary guitar" and went on to declare: "The British group up-staged, for one listener at least, the featured performers, the Grateful Dead."

Beck: "It said, 'Beck and Stewart were playing like two angels with a Pinter script.' Wow! I'll never forget that magic night in New York, the warmth that came from the audience."

Wood: "That appearance at the Fillmore East is what built the Beck Group's reputation. They Xeroxed the write-up Robert Shelton gave us and bang, the rest of the country was intrigued."

Their high-powered sound and potent command of blues-inspired rock soon became a sensation with American crowds, garnering glowing press acclaim which included comments like "Devastating . . . unbelievable . . . they didn't come on as though they were playing for money, but like they were playing for people." Beck himself was described as one of the finest guitarists on either side of the Atlantic.

With their soaring popularity, Stewart began to lose his painful awkwardness onstage, and Beck also let loose with the kinds of crowd-pleasing tricks he'd kept to a minimum at home—twirling the guitar above his head, for example, or grating the strings against any unlikely object within range.

Another payoff from Fillmore East came when the hard grafting Peter Grant telegraphed the *New York Times* review to the president of Epic Records. It resulted in a U.S. deal with Epic, guaranteeing them the major label release they needed in the States. Beck has remained with Epic ever since, and has recorded for the label longer than any other artist.

Their following activities included the Daytop Music Festival, Staten Island (a free festival at which Beck jumped up and joined Jimi Hendrix for a jam), and from 18 June a week's residency at New York's leading club venue, the Scene. This led to some legendary jams, with Eric Clapton appearing on one occasion, and Jimi Hendrix dropping in almost every night: "He used to come towards the end of our set. He would just get up on stage; it was so good. No one else could have done it. You would've said, 'Hey, look, man, once is enough.' But with Jimi you felt part of something massive, history."

Their U.S. bookings extended through July into August, convincing them they had moved into the major league at last. They included 2,000 and 3,000 seater halls like the Grande Ballroom in Detroit, and at the end of July the huge West Coast venues: six nights at Bill Graham's Fillmore West (the old Carousel Ballroom) in San Francisco, during which they supported one of Jeff's top favorite acts, Sly & the Family Stone; and four nights at the massive Shrine Auditorium in Los Angeles, where their farewell concerts on 2 and 3 August proved a high point when they shared the bill with the great Albert King.

THEIR TRIUMPH IN the U.S. was staggering, almost unbelievable. The British music press described them as pulling record business equaling that of Jimi Hendrix and the Doors. And all of this without an album release: amazingly, the American public only got its first dose of *Truth* in August when the group was on its way back to England. The album shot to number 15, setting the seal on their phenomenal success.

Truth was a raw, kick-ass celebration of the heaviest rock and proto-metal yet committed to vinyl, with Beck's lightning licks—now clean, now brutishly distorted—perfectly complemented by Stewart's pile-driving sandpaper voice. Wood's bass playing on the album ranks among the best work he's ever done.

A masterpiece of guitar versatility, Beck's playing was an object lesson in frightening technique and fiendishly manipulated sound. In the words of *Guitar World*'s John Swenson, it "easily outpaced what Clapton and Page were doing at the time."

"*Truth* is the mightiest album he's ever made," Steven Rosen declared in *Record Review*. "It has made any guitarist who ever heard it cringe with jealousy"—adding that "Let Me Love You," "I Ain't Superstitious," and "Rock My Plimsoul" contained the most precise and pulverizing solos to be found anywhere. In fact, the version of "Rock My Plimsoul" is different from the earlier single, and contains some amazing stereo imaging that predates by a long way the famous Jimmy Page passages in "Heartbreaker."

A number that would remain in Beck's repertoire for a good many years was "Blues De Luxe." His unpredictable solo, built around the tensions of the bent flatted fifth on which it starts, and exploring a wealth of subtle cross rhythms and bruising tonal effects, is regarded by many as featuring his best blues licks ever. Though you get the impression this track is taken from a live set, the background audience was actually added by Beck. Always ready for devilment, he'd found the effects tape in the studio and decided to overdub it for a lark.

From the album's very first track, you knew you were in for trouble: a version of the Yardbirds' "Shapes of Things" drenched in guttural malevolence.

"We had a great sound," Beck explains, "but nobody'd written anything. Rod wrote folk songs then, which wouldn't really have worked out for us. So he suggested 'Shapes.' I said, 'Let's slow it down and make it dirty and evil.'"

This was the way the whole album was constructed. For the most part the material consisted of covers, twisted almost beyond recognition by mind-blowing arrangements . . . except that as "arrangements" they were mainly spur-of-the-moment affairs. "We just used to play and somebody would say, 'Nah, that ain't right, play this, or play that!'"

Some unusual numbers come in for highly irreverent treatment, including the Tim Rose single "Morning Dew." Introduced, at Stewart's instigation, by a certified genuine bagpipe lament, the innocuous little song is delivered with an undercurrent of sinister foreboding. There's an even more unnerving version of "Ol' Man River" as a duet for voice and timpani (Keith Moon's guest appearance on percussion being credited to "You Know Who"), with contributions from John Paul Jones on Hammond organ and Beck playing bass as well as slide guitar.

The set also features less unlikely tunes, including two Willie Dixon blues standards. One of them is the Howlin' Wolf classic that slayed them at the Fillmore East, "I Ain't Superstitious," on which Beck achieves some seriously offensive noises—screaming, sighing, groaning, barking—with unusual use of wah-wah accentuated by delay. Years later, guitarist Steve Morse would name this track as containing his favorite licks of all time. "More or less an excuse for being flash on guitar," was Beck's wry comment on the sleeve—and for unleashing the Beck humor as well, with wah-wah effects like cats meowing.

The other Willie Dixon number became an anthem for the JBG. "You Shook Me" was a monumental performance that ended on a groan of guttural feedback as Beck jabbed his guitar into the amp. "Last note of song is my guitar being sick," he observed in the sleeve notes.

For "Shapes of Things," Beck went further with his experiments in weirdness: "I got a Sho-Bud steel guitar and messed around with it. We were always messing around with other instruments to see how they'd work." But his main guitar for the album was the '59 Les Paul Sunburst from Yardbirds days, with a Colorsound Tonebender effects box coming into play occasionally. His arsenal still included the '54 Esquire, plus a recently acquired Telecaster set up with super light gauge strings. Later that year the much abused Sunburst suffered the added indignity of being stripped of its body finish, in emulation of a pale guitar he'd admired in a 1950s book.

Another off-the-wall idea was contributed by engineer Ken Scott, who stashed Beck's speakers in cupboards to get that amazing muffled, distorted sound—but still maintaining sharp definition between all the instruments. The album was actually recorded at very low levels so that listeners would be forced to play it at maximum volume—with Beck recommending it as "background music if you have the vicar over for tea." (Once let loose on album notes, Beck's lunacy makes for entertaining reading.)

In complete contrast, *Truth* also includes a brief 100-second interlude of Beck unplugged, with a rare and delicious solo on the traditional "Greensleeves" played unaccompanied on Mickie Most's Martin D-18 acoustic. Added as a last-minute filler, it wasn't a performance he was particularly proud of ("plinking and plunking and playing bad notes"), but most listeners will disagree.

It's almost impossible to overstate the importance of *Truth,* both for Beck, now that he had the freedom to develop his own style and ideas, and for the direction of rock music as a whole, which was suddenly kicked into a whole new gear. Its influence was nothing short of radical.

Beck comments: "Listen to some of the *Truth* things, and the framework for other things, ballads, blues-based stuff, and heavy metal was there. I felt like me then. I had more control over the record. The ideas were all mine, the arrangements. We had that feeling, plugging in in the studio, that wouldn't have been any different to the feeling plugging in at a pub or club somewhere. We'd just go blasting away for four hours and come back and listen to the whole thing."

This was a magical period for Beck that he looked back on with great fondness, especially for the camaraderie among the leading guitarists of the day. "There weren't too many people doing what we were doing. There was a half dozen of us in a sort of circle around the London area, keeping tabs on one another. You were more interested in what the others had to say, not outdoing one another. You wanted them to fail, but you would have died if they had. I miss that badly. I would like one place to go where I could just settle down in a club where there are some great players playing."

THE YARDBIRDS, MEANWHILE, had finally come to the end of the road that summer. Jimmy Page was keen to keep going, but Keith Relf and Jim McCarty were into other kinds of music, and Chris Dreja wanted to move into photography. Unhappily, Relf's career, after forming Renaissance, was suddenly cut short in 1976 when he died from electrocution while playing his guitar at home.

After the group split up, Page took on the project of fulfilling a Yardbirds tour of Scandinavia in September. But with no enthusiasm from the rest of the guys, he decided to launch an entirely new lineup. Originally billed as the New Yardbirds, they soon emerged under a different name: Led Zeppelin.

John Paul Jones, a long-standing session crony, was an obvious choice for bass, and on vocals Page recruited an unknown Robert Plant from Birmingham, whose bizarre style somehow struck a resonant chord. Drummer John Bonham, an old buddy of Plant's from previous groups, was persuaded away from Tim Rose's band to become a key performer in the Zeppelin circus, which then proceeded to shake the world for the next decade and longer.

The new group's first album was released at the beginning of 1969 and soon stormed up the U.S. charts. On hearing it, however, it was impossible to overlook its obvious similarity to the JBG's material; Beck's reaction was to be "stunned, shocked, annoyed, flattered and just a bit miffed by the whole thing."

A particular shock was Zeppelin's version of "You Shook Me," which was distressingly similar to that on the Beck LP. Page had played Beck the demo before the album was released, and Beck said his heart just sank when he heard it. "I looked at him and said, 'Jim—what . . .?' and the tears were coming out with anger. I thought, 'This is a piss-take, it's got to be'—I mean, there's *Truth* still spinning on everybody's turntable. . . . Then I realized it was serious."

Jimmy Page claimed to have been innocent of any attempt to rip them off: "You've got to understand that Beck and I came from the same sort of roots. If you've got things you enjoy, then you want to do them—to the horrifying point where we'd done our first LP with 'You Shook Me,' and then I heard he'd done 'You Shook Me' on *Truth*. I was terrified because I thought they'd be the same. But I hadn't even known he'd done it, and he hadn't known that we had."

Sadly, however, a gulf began to widen between the two one-time friends. Both Beck and Stewart had vivid memories of Jimmy Page traveling around with their U.S. tour that summer, when he'd obviously listened to all their material. When Led Zeppelin took form, reflecting much of the heavy style that made his own group so successful, Beck felt it was a product of Page's very astute business brain. He'd spotted a winning formula, and produced an even more marketable version. "They had a better looking lead singer, for a start; he had golden, curly locks and a bare chest and the girls fell in love with him," Beck says. "They also had Bonzo on drums creating all sorts of pandemonium. It was a much better package than I had, so obviously they did better."

Indeed they had to be something altogether exceptional to eclipse what the

JBG had become as a live act. Even the album *Truth* conveys nowhere near the full effect of just how amazing they were; in fact the Jeff Beck Group was rated by John Swenson of *Guitar World* as a better band onstage than Led Zeppelin ever was. "Their live shows were beyond belief, far in advance of what was for the time a pretty awesome recorded sound. Beck's fertile imagination and crazed improvisational daring ensured that no song sounded the same from one show to the next."

Writer Gene Santoro comments thus: "Though Led Zeppelin's debut album is usually cited as the opening blast of heavy metal, *Truth,* along with some of Beck's Yardbirds sides, is clearly where Page copped his ideas about how to thicken and mutilate sound. That first Beck Group made some of the most molten, barbed, downright funny noises of all time—and helped spawn Page's paler-sounding, more studio-bound group in the process."

True, one man's influence may be another man's rip-off. But in the end music is an eclectic art and development doesn't happen in a vacuum. *Musician* magazine perhaps summarized it most accurately in its "Hundred Greatest Guitarists" feature with the observation: "Led Zeppelin became the template for riff-rock and metal, but Page . . . never displaced his former co-Yardbird Beck as the main memorable guitar force of [the '60s] era."

"In Four Days
We Nailed It Together"

WITH *TRUTH* YET TO BE released in England, the Jeff Beck Group returned home for a few weeks in August-September '68 to consolidate the band's U.S. success.

On 10 August they played at the Eighth National Jazz & Blues Festival at Sunbury, an event which marked their first public outing with a pianist. This was Nicky Hopkins of "Beck's Bolero" fame, who also sat in on "Blues De Luxe" and "Morning Dew" for *Truth*. A top session keyboard player at the time, Hopkins had in fact been asked to join Led Zeppelin, but turned down the offer (and more money) and instead called Jeff Beck to suggest joining his outfit. He became a permanent member two months later on the Beck Group's tour of the United States.

The reporter for *New Musical Express* was mightily impressed with Beck's playing at Sunbury, commenting that he sounded like Chet Atkins—a compliment that Beck must have been pleased to hear. "There is no doubt," he went on, "that this group have come back from the States with a harder sound and a much more together act—particularly enjoyable is the vocal-guitar play between Beck and Stewart."

In September the JBG was to be heard on BBC radio, where the group premiered a funky new instrumental titled "Mother's Old Rice Pudding." It would later appear as "Rice Pudding," in substantially rearranged form, on their follow-up album and quickly became a classic. (Jimi Hendrix quoted it at the end of "In from the Storm" on his *Cry of Love* album.) One of the few rock pieces to successfully explore the genre of expanded composition, this would be a huge psychedelic/funk tour de force on their upcoming U.S. tour. But first they did a brief tour of Sweden and Denmark in early October.

On 4 October came the much delayed U.K. release of *Truth*. All the music press except *NME* gave it enthusiastic reviews, and *Disc* awarded it four stars and an accolade of "outstanding"; but for some reason the album stiffed in England and never made the charts. A major factor was the lack of airplay, with John Peel virtually the only DJ to feature it on BBC radio. And it was singularly bad timing to have their first LP released when they were out of the country touring.

If the guys were disappointed by its British showing, they had good news to greet them in the United States: as they arrived to headline on 11 October at Chicago's 'Lectric Theater it peaked at number 15, with sales of over a quarter-million. Soon after their arrival, a promotional film of "Shapes of Things" was shot, providing a rare visual record of the late '68 era JBG.

At this point in time Mickie Most, who had no idea of the huge underground scene in the U.S., decided to make his first visit to see them. "Mickie was completely out of touch," Beck says. "It wasn't until halfway through a tour that he came over and saw for himself—that there were monster venues to be played, that it wasn't like ten people in a sleazy club!"

This was one of the few times that Most made himself useful, when Beck suffered a devastating blow. His stripped Les Paul, which he'd left lying on top of a Marshall amp, was badly damaged when a roadie dropped it, breaking the neck and headstock. Beck carried a spare Telecaster, but it suffered from tuning problems and was usually left in the case, so he was in bad shape without his main instrument. Mickie Most was pressed into service lining up guitar dealers, one of whom sold Beck a stripped '54 maple-neck Stratocaster that he was photographed playing at the Tea Party in Boston on 22–24 October.

But he didn't switch to the Strat completely. Rick Nielsen, before his Cheap Trick days, happened to be standing there at the very moment the Gibson was dropped, and found himself bearing the bad news to Beck backstage. As an avid collector, he had accumulated a number of guitars, and impulsively offered to bring over a few. Some days later he got a call asking him to fly to Philadelphia—all expenses paid. Beck was playing at the Electric Factory on 24–25 October, and it was there, right before the show, that Nielsen let him have a fine Les Paul Sunburst for $350.

Beck immediately took it onstage, and stayed up jamming with Nielsen all night at the hotel afterwards. In descriptions, he remembers it as "very bright and beautiful," with a chunky neck that he loved to death, and it would become his favorite Les Paul of all time. Rick Nielsen recalls that, although not of the highest grade, the body did have a very nice flame; compared to the featureless wood grain of Beck's 1966 acquisition, its attractive tiger stripe was very pleasing. This is almost certainly the Les Paul first photographed in November 1968, which had a humbucker with black bobbins at the bridge and a "zebra" (one black, one cream) at the neck. Nielsen cannot be 100 percent sure after all these years, especially as his guitar still had pickup covers on, and it also—interestingly—sported an added Bigsby vibrato arm. These, of course, would be easy enough for Beck to remove.

But Jeff Beck's bad luck wasn't over. His original Les Paul fell victim to a repair job that must give him nightmares to this day. It was sent to a repair guy in Memphis who not only substituted "this revolting skinny neck," but switched the pickups as well. Beck didn't realize this when it arrived complete with pickup covers, but when he came to play in Michigan it started feeding back like crazy. They took the covers off and saw that the guy had taken out the prized PAFs and put new Gibsons in!

Jeff Beck (with "zebra" Les Paul recently acquired from Rick Nielsen) at the Shrine Exposition Hall, November 1968.

A few years later this ill-fated guitar was knocked over and damaged yet again (Beck: "The young lady was surgically removed") and this time the repairer lavished it with inlays: the headstock—which might, in fact, have been a wholesale replacement—was embellished with a lily design and the motif "The Gibson" in the logo style of Gibson's earliest guitars, plus the initials "J.B." were inlaid on the fretboard. Beck was not amused, and by the mid '70s that first Sunburst had been permanently retired.

The tour pressed on, and in November they arrived to take California by storm, breaking all box office records at the Shrine Exposition Hall with sellout crowds of 7,000 on the 29th and 30th. Although they could have stayed on endlessly, they finished on a high note, headlining on 5-8 December at the Fillmore West. They wanted to be home for Christmas.

A curious spin-off from the Shrine involved the leading clique of local groupies known as Girls Together Outrageously (the GTOs), whose talents contributed generously to LA's reputation as groupie paradise. Minor celebrities in their own right, their members rejoiced in names such as Miss Pamela, Miss Mercy, and Cinderella, with tastes in entertaining itinerant musicians that ran to occasional chastisement with whips.

Backstage after the opening show, the girls this time had more in mind than Beck's much lauded prowess in the sack. "We want you to play on our album," they told him, and then revealed that their producer was the exquisitely eccentric Frank Zappa—an old acquaintance of Beck's from long before. With Rod Stewart and Nicky Hopkins in tow, they took him off to a session that produced three cuts on the GTOs' ensuing album, *Permanent Damage*. Bizarre though it was (in more ways than one), Beck still managed to produce some vintage noises: check out a brief but riveting slide solo on the track "Shock Treatment."

BACK HOME IN DECEMBER, the JBG appeared at the Middle Earth Club, which was based at the Roundhouse, London's foremost rock scene, a converted railway building in Chalk Farm. On 14 January they played at their old haunt the Marquee, to glowing reviews, and this was followed by a gig in Surrey on 5 February. But the United States wanted them back as soon as possible: their bookings were due to start on 14 February with two nights at the Fillmore East.

By now, however, Beck was again dissatisfied with the JBG's drum sound. He knew he needed a bigger, heavier sound to compete with what was going down in America. So, heedless of consequences, he fired Mickey Waller on the very eve of the tour. At the same time, he had one of his periodic bust-ups with Ron Wood and decided that Wood too had to go. "Their playing had deteriorated," Beck was reported to have said.

The U.S. dates were rescheduled to start from 28 February, with Waller replaced by Tony Newman, who had the right credentials from his playing with Sounds Incorporated; in place of Wood the group now featured one Douglas Blake on bass. Blake, a New Zealander who played with Junior Walker & the All Stars, lasted just two gigs (Worcester, Massachusetts, on 28 February, and Alexandria, Virginia, on 1 March) before Beck thought better of his decision. Several transatlantic calls and an increase in wages persuaded Woody to rejoin, and he was rushed over to complete the tour. From then on he was seriously on the lookout for another group to join.

Inevitably these hirings and firings scarcely served to enhance the group's cohesion. There now seemed to be a constant feeling of discontent. Rod Stewart was so tight with Woody that he made it obvious he was disgusted at his pal's treatment. Beck, he thought, was "very jealous" of himself and Ron Wood: "We had a sense of humor unto ourselves. And we never let anybody join in with us. Especially Beck. It got to him after a while."

Within a few weeks of starting the U.S. tour, Beck's health was also under strain. Suddenly the press announced that he'd collapsed after a concert in Minneapolis on 23 March. To add to the group's troubles, they found they were playing some venues where they had already been exposed in recent months and their once packed-out audiences were falling off. What they needed was another album of new material.

Beck: "We were touring the States for a second time on the strength of *Truth*, and we weren't selling any tickets. Partly it was our fault, not having any new product. Also, the world was ready for the Jeff Beck Group in a way much bigger than I had imagined. I suddenly realized I had to go home and do something about it. So in four days we nailed together *Beck-Ola*."

To fit in recordings meant canceling tour dates right into May, among them Bill Graham's Fillmore West. It wasn't something Graham easily forgot. Writing off an estimated $250,000 in gross receipts—and a sizeable chunk of American goodwill—they flew back to London on 24 March 1969.

"We cut the tour short, went back home and straight to the studio. We did *Beck-Ola* in about two weeks: four days for the tracks, a week for the over-dubs and mixing. That whole album was pretty well dreamt up on the spot. I didn't know what I was gonna do in the morning at breakfast."

"It was made in desperation to get product out," he said later. "We just got *vicious* on it, because we were all in bad moods, and it came out quite wild."

Beck was again responsible for the arrangements on the album, worked out around that unique guitar/voice combination with Stewart. With only seven tracks, it showed signs of a hurried compromise—especially since they had announced earlier there would be six new songs and six old songs reworked. In the end there were five group originals and two well-known standards.

Ron Wood, who with Rod Stewart contributed most to writing the original material, was quite up-front about how they operated. "Jeff liked to have that input. He knew who he liked and who his influences were, but he couldn't utilize—steal from—them to make another song. Whereas Rod and I would say, 'Oh well, take the bit where the Temptations do this and Booker T does that . . .' The Meters, Gladys Knight, James Brown . . . Rod always idolized Sam Cooke."

Produced at Kingsway Recorders in London, once more under the eye of Mickie Most, *Beck-Ola* was widely held to be one of the best albums of the year, although it didn't quite live up to the high promise of *Truth*. Their special popularity in America sent it to number 15 in the U.S. charts; in the United Kingdom, with a September release, they were pleased to see it reach 39.

Though Beck was still devoted to the Rick Nielsen Sunburst, he'd begun more and more to substitute the '54 Stratocaster, which was a hardier touring instrument and easier to repair; this was the guitar he used for *Beck-Ola*. He described it to guitar expert Tony Bacon as "an original '54 that's been stripped to the bare wood . . . but it's not an important guitar." (Recognizable by the missing pickguard corner on the lower horn, this Strat was still in use in 1977, but by then it had acquired a "CBS Seventies" bullet truss-rod neck system and rosewood fretboard.)

His effects included a wah-wah, Colorsound Tonebender and Booster, and Echoplex delay unit; and not to be overlooked was that built-in effect of the Strat itself—the instrument's vibrato arm. Old memories of his days as a 16-year-old must have flooded back when he took up the Fender after nearly ten years, and there's a noticeable glee in his liberal use of whammy throughout.

Beck-Ola acquired its title because Peter Grant used to call him "Beckola," after the Rockola jukeboxes. Mickie Most then suggested adding *Cosa Nostra:* "It suits you," he said, "it suits the band's music, it's evil and it's a great title for an album." But the record company didn't like the name at all, so they put it in smaller letters, which is understandable, considering that Cosa Nostra—literally "our thing"—is an alternative name for the Sicilian Mafia.

Probably the high spot of the album is the instrumental "Rice Pudding," which exhibits some of Beck's best slide work, ranging from metal blues licks to introspective explorations, and demonstrating fine cohesive interplay between the players.

Apart from two Elvis Presley songs, the remaining material consists of self-penned riff- and blues-laden hard rock workouts, noticeably light on content and heavy on volume. Phrases used to describe it have included "flawed but dynamically intense" and "one of the rawest albums you may ever hear." Even the Presley numbers are subjected to ordeal by fire, and "All Shook Up" gets such scorching mutilation that it scarcely earns the Presley/Blackwell composer credit on the album. As Gene Santoro says: "Two chunks of Presley gold, 'All Shook Up' and 'Jailhouse Rock,' get rudely blasted into new shapes as Beck's multitracked guitars screech and wail over Wood's galloping bass to hedge Stewart's sandpaper vocals."

Innovation it didn't lack, but discipline it did, and the album's production was particularly poor. A firmer hand at the controls wouldn't have gone amiss. But Mickie Most, who was used to recording straight pop with artists like Donovan and Lulu, simply didn't understand how to cope with heavy rock.

"Without a doubt the dumbest thing I ever did was signing up with Mickie Most," Beck said later. "There was just nothing right about it. It was expensive both emotionally and financially; he just didn't know who we were or what we could do. He just wanted to send us out there to do it."

THEIR BRIEF STINT in London over, they resumed their U.S. dates with gigs on 2–3 May headlining at the Fillmore East, where Joe Cocker joined them onstage.

The good news was their *Beck-Ola* material was wowing American audiences. The bad news was they would soon find the album suffering a number of delays, including problems with the cover, and eventually it wasn't released until the end of June, which meant that, despite having new material, they didn't have the album to promote it. Ron Wood: "It was still a great show; the Grande Ballroom with foot-long hot dogs. We did all those 2,000–3,000 seaters, the Kinetic Playground, Boston Tea Party, Fillmore East and West . . . though those two [Beck and Stewart] had more of a thing of not talking to each other. I got on so well with Rod that I joined in the fun as well, but I wouldn't let it go too far because I respected Jeff's more or less purist approach to being a great manipulator of his guitar."

The situation wasn't improved when Rod Stewart was continually mistaken for the "Jeff Beck" of the group's title, which ceased to amuse at quite an early stage. Beck would glower furiously when even executives from their own record label would slap Stewart on the back and say, "Great show, Jeff!"—and compliment him on the "good guitar player" he had in his band. With Stewart's newfound confidence, and his long held ambitions to be a solo singer, he was finding it increasingly irksome to be overshadowed by the group's guitarist. Years later, Beck admitted it would have been more comfortable for Stewart if they'd changed the name to a band name.

In his book *The Works*, Ron Wood recalled that their management created a lot of the tensions: "They treated me and Rod and the rest of the guys like second-class citizens, both musically and financially. . . . Jeff stayed at the Hilton while me and Rod crammed into one room at the Gorham Hotel. We were so desperate at times that we'd go down to the Automat to steal eggs. That's how we lived. But the Gorham was actually the place to be. Cream, Sly Stone, Hendrix, we met 'em all whenever we stayed there."

As June arrived, there were more signs of strain. By now Wood, Beck and Stewart were long-standing sparring partners, and tended to avert trouble by avoiding each other's company. It was the group's newer members who tipped the balance towards its eventual disintegration.

First it was Nicky Hopkins who gave vent to dissatisfaction over the group's financial and managerial arrangements, citing in his complaints both Mickie Most and the road management, as well as Jeff Beck. "Then," as Woody recalls, "there was that final drummer with the group, Tony Newman—a *real* businessman—[*mimics*] 'You mean you're being paid what? Mickie Most is doing *what*? You need somebody to get organized.' And on and on."

Financially they were convinced there was something seriously amiss, and Beck's latest purchase of a radical hot rod roadster in Boston, at a cost of £1,000, only served to fan the flames. Ron Wood: "Jeff was kind of thrown into it from a number of different ways, like accountant, record producer, manager, and so on, and they were all trying to single him out in different ways."

But Beck was no more in control than they were. "None of the guys got their money," he told *Crawdaddy* in 1973, "and I can't even go into the full discussion of that because I still don't know the whole story. In fact I'm still waiting to see the accounts dating from 1968 through 1970. They were just saying, 'Hey look, we're selling out, we're doing 6,000 people at the gate, getting $8,000 or $9,000 a gig.' That was the most we'd ever earned, and they just wanted to know where the hell this money was going to. Of course I got the rap for it. We *were* getting ripped off . . . fleeced."

Nicky Hopkins' resentment had been voiced loudest and longest, and at the beginning of June the pianist found himself on the retirement list. Later he claimed to have quit, adding that Beck was "totally unsuited to be leading a successful band"—which may well be true, since it isn't every 25-year-old guitarist who is blessed with managerial skills. When the tour proceeded it was without Hopkins, who no doubt regretted missing his Led Zeppelin opportunity. He had still kept up his lucrative session work, so having played for Quicksilver Messenger Service he joined them full-time that summer. Later he contributed to innumerable session recordings for luminaries such as the Rolling Stones.

From mid-May to the end of June there was a break in the U.S. tour, during which Rod Stewart started his first solo album with Mercury. In London, Stewart and Wood met up with the Small Faces, whose lead guitarist/singer, Steve Marriott, had quit the previous month, and it was agreed Woody would join as Marriott's replacement on guitar. Thinking of his pal for the vocal slot, he persuaded Stewart to do a couple of gigs with the band—billed discreetly as Quiet Melon—at a Cambridge University Ball and a Surrey college.

However, the Jeff Beck Group still had a tour to complete, including a prestigious headlining appearance at the Newport Jazz Festival. With Stewart still thinking over the Small Faces idea, he and Wood returned to fulfill the remaining U.S. dates, which started in New York State on 2 July. At a memorable music festival in Central Park, Beck inserted a snatch of "The Star Spangled Banner" as a little ditty at the end of a song. Six weeks later Jimi Hendrix would stun the crowds at Woodstock with his own sensational rendering.

Then on 13 July they played a concert that would prove to be a turning point for everyone involved. It was at the Singer Bowl in Queens, New York, where the Jeff Beck Group and Ten Years After were support acts on the Vanilla Fudge tour, which was also attended by members of Led Zeppelin although they weren't on the bill. The Beck Group's rowdy encore of "Jailhouse Rock" occasioned a drunken invasion from backstage that resulted in what history has dubbed the "nine man jam," including Jimmy Page, Robert Plant, and John Bonham, during which Bonzo started pounding out "The Stripper" while removing his clothing piece by piece.

"It was one of those riotous sorts of day," Beck recalls, "everyone's energy level was 100 percent and we were throwing things at each other onstage. I threw a mug of orange juice at Alvin Lee and it stuck all over his guitar. It was just one of those animal things. Three English groups at the same place has to add up to trouble!"

Rod Stewart: "The stage was full of people—we were doing 'Jailhouse Rock' and it was fucking incredible. I finished the whole thing by shoving a mike stand up John Bonham's ass and he got arrested, the cops pulled him off and I ran away . . . we were all pissed out of our heads. And the Vanilla Fudge couldn't follow it."

The audience actually began leaving at the end of the jam, and during the Fudge's set, when Vince Martell took a solo, there were even a few boos. They were so demoralized that by the end of the evening they'd decided to split up.

The Fudge had scored a huge hit with their high-decibel fuzz-ridden mutation of the Supremes' "You Keep Me Hanging On," dominated by Carmine Appice's thunderous drums and Tim Bogert's reverberating bass. Beck had seen them at a London concert in '67 and was totally knocked out. So he was even

As the Jeff Beck Group starts to disintegrate, Led Zeppelin arrives. Jeff Beck and Robert Plant meet onstage in the notorious "nine man jam," July 1969.

more knocked out when Bogert and Appice called him after the Singer Bowl extravaganza and suggested getting together: "'We wondered if you might need a bass player and drummer,' they said. I nearly fainted on the floor."

By now the writing was clearly on the wall for the JBG. Beck himself recognized he wasn't the easiest person to get along with during this period. "I used to buy all that stuff about how great I was and how great my guitar playing was. Everyone goes through an ego trip." Plus, of course, it was not only Beck who had one eye on his ego and the other on a more congenial future. During that last tour both Rod Stewart and Ron Wood were simply marking time.

Although Stewart had the option to remain as vocalist, Bogert and Appice completely turned him off. But Beck was more prepared to listen. His interest was rooted in their storming funk/soul sound, a direction he had been trying to import into the JBG. Looking to the future, he agreed to meet with them to sort out the complicated contractual situation. This would be Beck's shot at the "supergroup" league, and he wasn't about to miss it.

The JBG played its final few shows at the end of July, one of them in Massachusetts, where Beck openly had a major skirmish with Stewart. The group's last date was probably at the Grande Ballroom, Detroit on 26 July, from which a private tape survives to prove just how brilliantly a spark can flare before it dies. But morale was in tatters, and Beck put an end to the band by canceling the rest of the tour, consisting of at least half a dozen shows, of which one was to be at Woodstock, the gigantic outdoor festival on the weekend of 15 August 1969.

"I deliberately broke the group up before Woodstock," Beck says. "I didn't want it to be preserved. Even though we were playing really well, the vibes in the band were totally shredded. So I figured, 'It's only one gig.' Of course, it was the biggest gig ever. But I couldn't face it. I didn't have any control over the PA, anything. I couldn't have stood failure."

Rod Stewart subsequently suggested that Woodstock might have been the group's breakthrough into the real big time. But Beck in retrospect felt that disbanding it was maybe the best thing he ever did: "I would have been labeled forever as a '60s psychedelic act much like, I hate to say it, Ten Years After." And, he reflected, it also left him with something of a reputation. "There was a big neon sign over my head saying 'Unreliable Motherfucker' [*laughs*]. For a while, people wanted my grandmother for a hostage before they'd let me do anything!" (Promoter Bill Graham was one of them: he insisted on a deposit from Beck on all dates from 1969 onwards.)

BACK IN ENGLAND AGAIN, the meeting with Bogert and Appice took place in September when the two came over from the U.S. But fate decided to take a hand, and the group was not to be—or not yet, at least. The only collaboration that would materialize at all during the '60s was a brief recording with the Fudge for a Coca-Cola TV commercial ("a funky thing," according to Beck), which he made one afternoon that July in New York when guitarist Martell fell ill.

The event that torpedoed all their plans was Beck's sudden hospitalization due to a near-fatal motor accident.

Booked to fly to the U.S. on Monday 3 November, it was on the previous morning (not 5 November, as frequently cited) that Beck's passion for hot rods led to disaster. His beloved 1923 Ford T-bucket blew a tire while he was driving through Maidstone near his home in Kent, colliding with a small Morris. "It wasn't the speed. The front tire blew completely out. With a transverse front spring, I didn't stand an earthly [chance]. And with cross-ply tires, it was like I was on ice. I just went straight across the road and hit this other guy. He broke his knee."

Beck, who was thrown out onto the road, racked up a list of injuries including damage to his back, a four-inch skull fracture, facial lacerations, dental injuries, and a broken nose. (The scarred and recontoured Beck proboscis still attests to this accident today.) Suffering from a concussion, he was kept under close observation for 48 hours, whereupon they were ready to discharge him ("as long as you're not bleeding from the ears, they'll let you go home!"). It was only when Beck insisted his back was killing him that further X-rays revealed tissue damage in the spinal area, necessitating three more weeks in the hospital lying on a board.

Afterwards he was on painkillers and out of commission for several months, and although he made light of it to friends, it was an anxious time before he was back in shape again. Doctors told him it could take up to five years to recover completely; as it turned out, they were not exaggerating.

To this day he prefers not to tempt fate on that anniversary: "The same day when I was eleven years old I was hit by a car while riding my bicycle and squashed up against a wall. So I don't go out on that date. If you've got anything planned you'd better tell me about it, because I'm not going out!"

In fact the four-inch split in his head actually joined up with the previous fracture he'd sustained as a kid. Fortunately it wasn't so bad as to need a steel plate, but in Beck's words, "my head's in bad shape." For years he was plagued with fatigue, recurrent headaches, and an inability to concentrate.

Tim Bogert and Carmine Appice were on tenterhooks all this while, waiting in New York. They even had a name for the new group—Cactus—but after three months, with no sign of Beck getting back in action, they formed a different Cactus with two other guys as a four-man heavy blues boogie band.

Rod Stewart, meanwhile, had decided to join Ron Wood in the Small Faces. Although they weren't huge, they were a seasoned British group with some chart standing, and had a rocking, balls-to-the-wall live act that frequently dissolved into hilarious chaos. After the turmoil of the JBG, the prospect offered some of the good times they'd been sorely missing. The new group became simply the Faces, staying together for some six years on and off, while Stewart continued to make recordings on his own. It was during this time that his solo career finally took off in earnest. From 1971 he started topping the charts with a succession of blockbusting albums and singles . . . and never looked back.

During the years after their breakup, the press regularly sought out Beck and Stewart as a source of good copy—recriminations, accusations, malice. Stewart would badmouth Beck; Beck would complain about Stewart badmouthing him.

To *ZigZag* magazine in 1971 Stewart commented, "I've said so many nasty things about Beck, and yet they're fucking true." Nevertheless, only a couple of pages earlier he had conveniently twisted facts to claim his involvement with Beck came about through sympathy: "We thought we'd better help him out. I mean, for a guitar player like that to come out with a thing like 'Hi Ho Silver Lining'—it was a crime."

In *Rolling Stone* the following year it was Beck's turn to respond: "He's a pop star and I'm a rock 'n' roll guitarist. We're absolutely not in the same room, y'know. No singer ever likes playing second fiddle to a lead guitarist. It must have been at the back of his mind that he wanted to be a solo artist and I didn't want to stop him. Except that I didn't expect him to turn around and run me down in every interview . . . seeing that when I met him he was sitting in a bar and didn't have any work. That really bugged me."

Happily, the antagonism didn't last. By early 1974 they had patched up old wounds at a reunion jam that also involved Woody on drums and Mick Jagger on piano. More recently, Stewart publicly paid tribute to those early days. At the Brits Awards ceremony in 1993, on receiving his Lifetime Achievement award, he said: "I'd like to thank Jeff Beck—I first went to the States with Jeff Beck and if it hadn't been for Jeff, who broadened my horizons, I would never have got a look in in the States."

And Beck had this to say of his association with Stewart: "Those were magic days. I just knew [Rod] had a freak voice. He is a freak; nobody can sing like that. They're just copies. He's the prototype."

Even more affecting was his comment in a *Vox* magazine interview of 1993: "You see, I've had the best singer in the world. I had Rod. It's hard to come to terms with any other singer who doesn't have that incredible grit. I was completely spoiled. You don't realize how good it was until you try someone else and they're all trying to sound like Rod."

8 Into the Unknown

THE START OF 1970 found Jeff Beck just out of the hospital, with the members of his once successful group now dispersed, and without any clear idea of where to go from here.

At least he now enjoyed some stability at home, thanks to the present lady in his life, the beautiful English model Celia Hammond. With Beck's long-defunct marriage officially laid to rest in 1968, they had been together since about that time (Celia's face had been the subject for the *Truth* album cover) and would enjoy a happy partnership for nearly eighteen years.

Their comfortable home was a country cottage in Egerton, Kent, dating from around the year 1500 and reflecting Beck's love for the gracious, mellowed antiquity of old houses. He took a particular delight in the architecture of that ancient seafaring county, rich in cottages built from old ships' timbers—Hansel and Gretel country, he called it.

With grounds of ten acres, it also afforded plenty of room for their many animal friends: Jeff's two dogs (Pudding had been joined by a basset hound, Ethel Floon, donated by Jimi Hendrix), plus eighteen cats that Celia had made it her mission to save.

Robert Brinton from *Disc*, interviewing Beck in their homey kitchen, noted these once-unwanted waifs clambering over every surface. "In the words of the song, Jeff's place is not a house, it's a home," he commented: an aspect of Beck that provides an important key to the man.

Brinton continued: "Surrounded by woodland, tall trees which shield it completely from the road, the house is compact and perfectly lived in. Like the structure, the inside literally breathes with age; nearly all the furnishings are antique or worn remnants from earlier this century—even the radio playing constantly in the kitchen must have been nearly 20 years old."

A love of animals was something that Jeff and Celia shared, and both had lent their weight to the growing campaign against the wanton slaughter of seals for fur. Celia's stand in refusing to model real furs led Donovan, a kindred spirit, to write "Celia of the Seals" about her. With her commitment to protecting animals, it was inevitable that her philosophy embraced vegetarianism; and at Celia's instigation Jeff made the decision to cease using animals as food.

For the Jeff Beck who had long loved his Indian curries, Sunday roasts, and good old British fry-ups, the idea was a bit radical. "She said, 'You're not eating meat any more,'" he told journalist Douglas Noble. "I went, nonchalantly, 'Oh, right!' I actually put my sausages in the bin! And I thought, 'Well, let's see. If I die in a couple of weeks, then I die. If I feel shitty, I'll start eating meat again.' Then I realized what a fool I'd been eating meat at all: because, you know, you can't just carve animals up—it's not necessary."

He also came to realize it conferred more benefits than were at first apparent. The uncontrolled outbursts, both physical and emotional, were gradually becoming fewer: "Being vegetarian slows you, stops the animal aggression a bit. But it also opens another door, of self-control. You can accept a lot more criticism without losing your temper. When I ate meat I was much more aggressive. After about eight months of not eating meat I found I went more for the throat on the guitar [*laughs*] than other people's throats."

Though life had scarcely been smooth sailing with the Jeff Beck Group, it did represent an important slice of time when he had created and consolidated something. Now, as the '60s became the '70s, disintegration appeared all around. The Yardbirds had split and the Beatles were about to. Cream was no more, and Eric Clapton's Blind Faith was also in its death throes. The Hendrix Experience had disbanded and Jimi was no longer dominating the scene in Britain; the shock of his death would come later that year. Only Jimmy Page seemed to have hit on a formula where the band was musically coherent and the members managed to live with each other's egos. And now they had a clear field to operate in.

As Beck began his slow recovery, it was the worst kind of torture to have glimpsed a new start with Tim Bogert and Carmine Appice only to see it snatched from under his nose. He was out of action, depressed, sick and in pain . . . but worst of all, he was stranded.

THE YEAR WHICH brought the '60s to a close had seen Britain stay awake one long summer night, on 20 July, to witness men walking on the moon; it was the year when "Space Oddity," released that month, rocketed David Bowie to the stars.

Art rock had arrived, encompassing all that was avant-garde in music, art, mime, dance, and multimedia happenings. Embraced by Bowie with his Beckenham Arts Lab, it launched him on a succession of dazzling presentations: *Ziggy Stardust*, his archetypal doomed rock messiah, and *Diamond Dogs*, his bleak Orwellian vision of ultraurban breakdown. But if art rock was the face of Bowie's coin, the obverse, glam rock, soon brought devaluation with tack and tarnished glitter.

Pink Floyd spearheaded the cult for sci-fi, outer-space, inner-mind fantasy, while Deep Purple engaged in ambitious maneuvers with London orchestras. Out on a different limb, John Lennon departed on his wanderings with performance art person Yoko Ono. Even the Who made forays into art rock with "rock operas" *Tommy* and *Quadrophenia*.

More radical influences appeared in black music from that extraordinary human dynamo named James Brown. Enlisting the guitar talents of Jimmy Nolan, Brown transmuted soul and R&B into irresistible, high-energy funk. But perhaps the most revolutionary influence came from Sly & the Family Stone. With masterpieces like "Dance to the Music" and "I Want to Take You Higher," their big sound took the sweet soul vocal tradition, laced it with gutsy R&B, and injected rock instrumental wildness.

Meanwhile, a major new movement among jazzmen had been going on: jazz was becoming influenced by the advances made in rock. Melding jazz improvisation with rock and dance beats, Miles Davis' *Bitches Brew* of 1969 was the first of the jazz crossover albums, appearing in the U.S. pop charts at a phenomenal number 35.

British guitarist John McLaughlin, a Miles collaborator, started his Mahavishnu Orchestra in 1971, showcasing the gifted guitarist's jazz-inflected virtuosic solos. Jazz-rock and jazz-funk soon became an important new direction in rock, epitomized by bands like Santana, Chicago, and Blood, Sweat & Tears. And among those who would be drawn to the new feel for jazz was Jeff Beck.

THIS, THEN, WAS the backdrop against which Beck hesitantly returned to action in the spring of 1970. The accident had slowed him down dramatically, and for four or five months he could scarcely handle the idea of playing again. "I got less and less interested in going back on the road and facing the hassle of trying to find musicians. I didn't have anyone there to organize."

Bassman Noel Redding, from the Hendrix Experience, was a long-standing pal who lent sterling support during Beck's months of recovery, and even cut some tapes with him around February, but they both knew Redding's other commitments prevented a permanent liaison.

At least Beck had his hot rods to keep him sane: during his enforced retirement he was reportedly working on a "Little Deuce Coupe," a custom '32 Ford coupe with a 350 Chevy engine. But eventually it got to the point where he picked up the guitar and couldn't play a note. This was seriously frightening. "You can't force yourself. If the feeling isn't good and strong, you can't really make it happen. What finally happened was that one day I got tired of wondering what I would play like if I started playing again, and so I got myself a drummer."

Beck's choice was fellow hot rod enthusiast Cozy Powell, recently the high-octane propulsion unit behind the Ace Kefford Stand and Big Bertha. After traveling all over the country in a fruitless quest, he'd resorted to holding auditions—and was amazed to find 20 or 30 guys lined up at the rehearsal rooms. But Peter Grant sent a message saying he must be sure to listen to Cozy Powell.

Powell takes up the tale: "All these other guys were tapping away at this little Hayman drum kit that was there. I brought my Ludwig kit down—the old red double bass drum kit—and set it up right in front of him. When it was my turn I thought, 'I'm just going to go for it; and if I don't get the job, at least I will have left my mark.' A drummer has got to be in charge of the band, so I just started one of the tunes, and he put the guitar down halfway through and said, 'You've got the job.'"

"Straightaway there was this understanding, telepathy thing," said Beck. "It just felt so good playing with Cozy, because we both dug the same things."

Once the two had found each other, however, any permanent candidates to add to the lineup were extremely thin on the ground. Beck tried out dozens of bassists between March and May. And now he was impatient not merely to get his fingers back in action, but to find a whole new sound.

More than a year earlier he'd told *Hit Parader* he was thinking about moving into other types of music. "But I don't know what. I just feel a softer thing coming over me. . . . It's my nature, at the moment, to play hard. I'm very tense, and when I play hard it relaxes me. I expect, though, as I get older I'll become more harmless!"

One of his lasting obsessions had always been the "Motown sound." A masterful blend of caressing soul, finger-snapping pop, rousing gospel, and punchy arrangements, it was crafted by a team of brilliant musicians and a stable of great performers: the Supremes, the Temptations, Stevie Wonder, Marvin Gaye, Smokey Robinson, and a dozen more.

If he hadn't exactly gone harmless, a somewhat mellower Beck seemed to be surfacing: weary of electric blues-rock, his tastes had turned to the funky black music coming out of the United States. Now his idea was to take himself to the Motown Studios, check out the black music scene, and try out a Beck version of the Motown magic.

"I wanted to get some vicious Motown stuff, with melodic bass lines and lyrical chord changes, and still have my style laced with it. I was getting bored with 12-bar blues and also bored with playing simple rock 'n' roll. I wanted to do something else."

By the end of May, with Beck and Powell still in splendid isolation, the dynamic duo decided to go it alone. For their pilgrimage to Motown they would work with the label's staff musicians, who they knew were just superb, and they might even pick up a permanent bass player. So they flew to Detroit (with Mickie Most accompanying them as producer) with hopes of recording an album's worth of instrumental tracks. Along with the Motown brass section there was also on hand the great James Jamerson, whose wonderful bass lines contributed so much to all the classic Motown recordings.

As Beck recounted in an interview for *Crawdaddy*: "I thought it would be a nice breaking-in period. I didn't have to face loads of people, I just went along with the rest of them and I had about five tunes I wanted to cut. The head of A&R came down and said, 'What kind of stuff do you want to do?' I said, 'Just simple R&B tunes. I wanna use Jamerson on bass, Cozy on drums, and make a customized kind of music, a combination of heavy rock 'n' roll guitar with a bit of R&B feel, mixed with Motown funky bass lines, stuff like that.'"

And this was precisely where they ran into trouble: they had brought no music with them. Mickie Most, the all-knowing producer, hadn't thought it necessary. "Mickie Most was in charge and he didn't get the material together. He thought we'd go over there and write something. Those guys were laughing at us, saying 'Where's your songs?' We didn't have any."

Like most musicians who played in groups, Beck was used to working out concepts on the spot in the studio. "I went straight in and started laying these chords on them, and they didn't want to know. They all wanted the notes written down. It totally blew the illusion that they were all in there playing. I think one guy did all the arrangements. Oh dear, what a rude awakening. It was a totally unfulfilled thing, the welding of Motown with my style of blues."

The worst of the embarrassment was Beck's encounter with Jamerson, whose work he revered so highly. Some of the Motown lineup felt these no-account Britishers gave themselves too many airs, and Jamerson had little time for long-haired white rock musicians.

There were a few other problems they had to contend with besides. "Let me put it this way," Beck remarked to Gene Santoro. "We went to Motown to get the Motown sound. The first thing Cozy does is remove the Motown drum kit and put his own in. Jamerson said, 'You want the Motown sound? You've just taken it out.'"

Eventually the only thing to do was regard the sessions as an experiment. Cozy Powell, who like Beck still has copies of the tapes, recalls about seven or eight tracks being cut—covers of old hits by groups like the Four Tops and the Temptations, plus Stevie Wonder's "I Got to Have a Song," and the beautiful "I Can't Give Back the Love I Feel for You" by Simpson/Ashford/Holland.

But the odyssey had produced the germ of a future sound, and versions of the latter two songs would resurface in a later recording. Although the "Motown album" itself was shelved, it did create a couple of records of a different kind: they were the first outsiders ever to do sessions at Hitsville USA, and these very tapes were the last ever recorded in the old Motown Studios.

OF COURSE, AS the year went on, there were managerial urgings to get Beck moving again. A brief notion of linking up with Curtis Mayfield raised his hopes when he was invited to play with the admired godfather of Chicago soul, now split from the Impressions and heading for a more frenetic sound. But Beck had to veto the plan as soon as they got together, realizing Mayfield was into a black/white agenda more political than he could handle.

At the other extreme was an oddly assorted venture, doubtless viewed as good box office at the time. This was an attempt to sign up our hero as guitarist-in-residence with superstar-in-waiting Elton John.

John had an impressive music pedigree: a piano scholar at the age of eleven, and blues-rock performer with John Baldry's Bluesology at the age of fourteen. After establishing his solo credentials at the end of the '60s, he was well on his way to a career as a celebrated international caricature. Not the most obvious teaming for Beck, but John was putting together a band for a U.S. tour and Beck had already expressed interest in playing with him. He was also given to understand there might be an opening for Cozy Powell.

"We did actually get together and play," Beck recalls. "It was a town hall somewhere in Haverstock Hill. I turned up late and he gave me a terrible roasting. My car had broken down or something, and then I found myself playing lead guitar with a band that was completely formed. I thought I'd have to wear a suit next. It didn't work out."

Interviewed for *ZigZag*, Elton John revealed he had early misgivings that Beck might want to turn his outfit into a "wailing guitar group," but seemed pleasantly surprised by how well he fit in. His misgivings then resurged when Beck suggested bringing in Cozy Powell instead of drummer Nigel Olsson. With the United States beckoning, where John was unknown and Beck was a star attraction, he suspected a dastardly plot to take over the band "and go touring the States on his reputation." A meeting ensued, and they agreed to part company. "I think he's a really great guy," John concluded, "as well as being an incredible guitarist, but I told him no and that was it."

Almost a year would pass between the Motown jaunt and Jeff Beck's next group, and in the interim his guitar would be heard in a few more session recordings. The first was the 1970 release of an album recorded the previous year with his old friend Lord Sutch, with a lineup of guests like Jimmy Page, John Bonham, Noel Redding, and Nicky Hopkins. It was a project that Beck promptly forgot all about, and was later startled to see materialize as *Screaming Lord Sutch and Heavy Friends*—"although I don't know why, because I volunteered and I must have known what I was doing. I vaguely remember recording it, in some sleazy studio up a side alley!"

Another brief digression was a "jam" to which he was invited one late and well-oiled night in early 1970 at a hall in New York's Madison Square Garden. Three years later he discovered the whole thing had been taped, unknown to him, and released on a double album titled *Music from Free Creek*. Beck would find himself billed as A N Other, in company with a host of star guests including Eric Clapton in the guise of King Cool. *Music from Ripoffsville*, he called it.

Late in 1970, a Yardbirds reunion (of all things) was mooted, with a putative date set in December for a Roundhouse appearance. It's doubtful whether Beck would have gone along with the plan, but the idea was scuppered anyway by Keith Relf's firm refusal. Nevertheless, Beck agreed to contribute some typically blazing guitar to a project featuring Relf and his sister Jane, together with Jim McCarty, who were cutting a one-off single under the group name the Holy Smoke. Beck joined his old mates for the A-side, "If You've Got a Little Love to Give," originally written by McCarty for Dave Clark of Dave Clark Five fame.

Since the subject of ex-colleagues has arisen, we might mention here that in November 1970 Rod Stewart and the Faces released a single titled "Had Me a Real Good Time," of which the title of the B-side instrumental, "Rear Wheel Skid," was rumored to be a derisive reference to Beck's 1969 auto accident.

IT WAS NOT until April 1971 that Beck came back firing on all cylinders with a prototype version of the Jeff Beck Group 2. Aside from Cozy Powell, the members seemed hastily assembled, an anxious reaction to what he described as a bad complex after his accident. "It quietens you right down, gives you a nasty fright.

In rehearsal, April 1971, when the second Jeff Beck Group was being formed with Alex Ligertwood on vocals.

I began to realize I'd turn into a vegetable if I didn't watch it. A fractured skull can fuck up a lot of things."

His first move was to recruit a bass player. After months of searching on both sides of the Atlantic, he finally settled on Clive Chaman, a Trinidadian who was currently rehearsing right under his nose in London with Cat Stevens. Given the choice, Chaman opted to go with Beck.

A singer was also found at home in London. Alex Ligertwood, described in one press report as having a "bashed-in Glasgow face," had previously been the vocalist for a number of obscure groups, including the Glasgow-based Quintones, the Senate, and the Primitives. Beck himself didn't know where Ligertwood came from—he just appeared one day at rehearsal.

Ligertwood explains that, returning from a stint in Italy, he heard from singer Maggie Bell that Jeff Beck was auditioning bass players and went along to try his luck. "I went down to the audition and Clive Chaman was there, so I immediately switched to vocals!"

To complete the lineup, Beck recruited keyboardist Max Middleton, who would prove to be his most valuable find. Beck had suddenly stopped rehearsals one day and declared he needed a piano, so Chaman suggested Middleton, a buddy of his from a group named Flare. The 20-year-old Middleton was a classical pianist who had been playing professionally in the clubs for only about six months. His strong jazz orientation exactly suited Beck's growing interest in that direction.

At the end of April, the newly assembled band went into Island Studios in London to lay down some tracks with producer Jimmy Miller (Rolling Stones, Traffic). Everyone in the group loved the sound, but for some reason the record company didn't like Alex Ligertwood. As a result the vocalist was asked to leave. "I feel really terrible about that time," Beck reflected. "I realized I'd wasted a fortune trying to get him to sound right and had to kick him out, which must have disappointed him a lot." (Actually, within a month Ligertwood had joined Brian Auger's Oblivion Express, and later became a mainstay with Santana.)

Meanwhile, turmoil was mounting with RAK. Mickie Most was thoroughly displeased at Beck's latest musical direction, and Beck was discontented with Most's negotiations for a new recording contract and plans for touring as early as June. Anxious to extricate himself and gain more personal control, Beck engaged a new ally in the person of Ernest Chapman, a shrewd London lawyer and staunch friend who has remained his business manager ever since. Chapman's first move was to go straight to his record label and have all future royalties sent to Beck (hitherto they had been going to Mickie Most).

Feelings were getting heated by the time the Island sessions were aborted, and the tapes were appropriated by Most, never again to see the light of day. As *Rolling Stone* reported in June: "A growing animosity seems to be developing between Beck and his managers, RAK. Beck, unhappy with the new record contracts being drawn up, flew to America to negotiate privately with Columbia. RAK, unhappy that Beck was doing things behind their backs, and having already paid for the studio time, confiscated the tapes." In fact, Most was believed to have used underhanded tactics to repossess them.

From June 1971 the creative direction of his career—for good or ill—rested firmly in Jeff Beck's hands. By the end of the year, Mickie Most had ridden into the sunset with a percentage of the new album which would be recorded that summer. Interestingly, despite the feud with Most, Beck's amicable relationship with Peter Grant remained unaffected.

In July the group finally materialized in its permanent form, fronted by a new vocalist, Bob Tench (ex Gass, another one-time colleague of Clive Chaman and fellow Trinidadian), who combined with Chaman to push the lineup in the direction Beck wanted: earthy black funk. This, plus the jazz-inflected input of Max Middleton, was significant for the new Beck Group sound.

Their first record was *Rough and Ready*, which Epic advertised with the headline "While Jeff Beck was away, his music took over the world." It continued: "Jeff Beck dropped out of the music scene for a while. . . During the time he was gone, the music he was famous for became the biggest music around."

The second Jeff Beck Group in the studio, 1972 (L-R Max Middleton, Clive Chaman, Cozy Powell, Jeff Beck, Bob Tench).

But Beck by now wasn't interested in the music he was famous for. He was off on a new tack, declaring that ever since the accident he couldn't relate to anything he'd done before. "I don't know what it was, but I didn't want to sound like me any more."

Sure enough, what came out was very different. Produced by Beck himself, *Rough and Ready*'s uneasy mix of grungy funk with shifting, progressive jazz inflections marked it as reaching into unexplored territory. The scarcity of good tunes didn't help either, and Beck's spaced-out licks seemed too often sidelined to a supporting role, although the melodic and expressive "New Ways Train Train" went a long way towards redressing both deficiencies.

At this time he was still fond of using the stripped and battered '54 Strat from the *Beck-Ola* days, but he preferred a Les Paul for studio work. As well as a Colorsound Tonebender to dirty up the sound, there's wah-wah on "Got the Feeling," and on "Jody" there's an unusually heavy use of echo with nearly half a second of delay on one of the solos.

Altogether the album's atmosphere seems rather like some late night club gig, with Bob Tench's smoke-filled vocals well suited to the thick, meandering instrumental textures. The musicianship of the group is evident, but *Rough and Ready* is a difficult album to love, as Beck has himself confirmed, with material that is more downbeat and less accessible than any other Beck recording. An added problem—with a new group, a new deal with Epic, and a new producer (himself)—was the pressure to come up with something brilliant. "Even the title was inspired by the music that was going on—it was about the most tough and frustrating period of my life. I couldn't enjoy it, because people were breathing down my neck so heavily to say 'What's he doing, is it good, is it bad?'"

Still plagued by headaches and an inability to concentrate, Beck lacked the patience to spend hours working on production. "Often I'd fall into the trap of sitting there with beers and booze and falling asleep at the desk," he confessed. This is perhaps why, though the sound seemed great in the studio, he was unhappy when he heard the master—it didn't jump out and grab you like he wanted.

Mac Garry, in a *ZigZag* article welcoming the release of the album ("I really have missed Jeff Beck"), reflected that he was already one of the truly legendary figures of rock. "Beck is usually depicted as either the amazing guitarist whose brilliance wiped out any competition, or the irritated bandleader racked by moodiness and indecision. To the current rock audience he is a name floating around in search of a reputation, though his new album and new band, which is doing a brief American tour this autumn, may change some of that."

After completing the album at Island in July 1971, the group debuted at a few European dates, of which the first was on 22 August at Turku, Finland. They then embarked on their October/November tour of the States, where *Rough and Ready* was well reviewed in *Rolling Stone* and charted at number 46. A modest showing, but reasonable in view of its new and unfamiliar style, coupled with the two-year gap since Beck's last release. Given his own dissatisfaction with the album, he was not surprised when it failed to dent the British charts. It was very popular in Germany, however, where it sold up a storm.

THE NEW YEAR brought plans for a second album. Beck's follow-up idea was to try again for a Stateside sound: the tight soul/funk groove of the Stax label bands, like his favorite, Booker T & the MGs.

With throbbingly intense vocalists like Wilson Pickett and Otis Redding, and anchored by a full, fat drum sound, the Stax hits were mostly underpinned by the same group of studio musicians. Initially known as the Mar-Keys, they later subdivided into the horn section (the Memphis Horns) and the rhythm section (the MGs). Steve Cropper led the MGs on guitar, a mix of black and white musicians who became legendary for a sound that was laid-back, punchy, and supremely economical.

For ultimate authenticity, Cropper was enlisted to produce the album, and in January 1972 the Jeff Beck Group decamped to TMI Studios in the Stax hometown of Memphis. Now they had the task of marrying two different extremes: the pulsating, high-output Beck and the tight, disciplined Cropper. "I had anticipated the final product to be my own personal ideal of what a group should sound like—a Stax drum sound with a fat bass and really cooking guitar." But Beck afterwards felt the marriage didn't work too well: "Overall we probably got as energetic a record from Stephen as he's ever produced. He's so laid-back, it's hard to sneak any craziness past him!

"I wanted to play like Booker T & the MGs," he explained, "but we had the totally wrong impression of their music because it was always played loud. They recorded it soft. I mean, look what happened to 'Going Down' when we did it. But honestly I didn't know what I was doing; I was walking around with headaches all the time."

The resulting album was the snappily titled *Jeff Beck Group*, known as the "orange album" from the single orange pictured on the cover. In places pure electric funk, in others jazz-tinged bluesy soul, it varies in quality from amazing to near-miss; but it contains a lot of 24-carat gold and allows everyone plenty of room to solo. Despite Beck's reservations about "Going Down," his guitar is heard to devastating effect in his personal imprint of the Don Nix blues classic, a number that always gets pile-driving treatment whenever he performs it live.

To quote Brad Tolinski in *Guitar World*, "On the highly underrated *Jeff Beck Group* the guitarist began fusing blues, jazz and rock and stumbled upon something strange and new in the process—a bizarre interplanetary future music. Just listen to Beck's screaming Strat declare fullscale war on the blues classic 'Going Down,' demolishing the song's simple I-IV-V structure in a burst of chromatic octaves."

Beck's comment on that freakout treatment: "That's just me going nuts. . . . Some people have asked me if I ever laugh at the humor in my solos, and I tell them no, mostly I just break out in a sweat!"

If it was the precise, chunky Memphis rhythm-section feel they were after, then some of the tracks (notably "Ice Cream Cakes" and "Glad All Over") capture it excellently. But the restraint of the Stax sound often disappears elsewhere under Cozy Powell's cymbal-crashing percussion and Max Middleton's thumping piano. Beck's guitar contributions are superb, providing brilliant contrasts from down-home funk to lunatic, howling leads, with deft little touches in the fills that send you rushing back to listen again.

"At the time, everybody was jumping about it," Beck recalls, "until *Rolling Stone* said that it was a large piece of junk. It was a pretty good record with some nice things on it, but once again it was lacking in concept and direction and strong sound, which were all vital ingredients it needed."

The album is particularly memorable for two standout instrumental tracks: "I Can't Give Back the Love I Feel for You," and the haunting "Definitely Maybe," penned for Beck by Max Middleton, which gives full rein to his supreme (and hitherto seldom exploited) gifts for lyrical melody. His use of wah-wah is again noticeable on this album, and he even goes so far as to double-track it on "Definitely Maybe."

Promoting the album on television, it was this classy instrumental that Beck would vouchsafe to his bemused viewers—quite a change from their usual camped-up fare of Elton John in outsize Day-Glo glasses and Rod Stewart in leopard-print leggings. But despite a three-week tour in Britain (Beck's first for three years), ending with an impressive concert at the Roundhouse on 19 March, reaction to the album at home was the same as for its predecessor. Although well reviewed by Chris Welch in *Melody Maker*, *NME*'s headline read "Beck doesn't make it."

In the U.S. it was quite a different matter. With a release coinciding with their April/May tour, the "orange album" sold almost as well as Beck's 1968/69 outings, charting at number 19. "Some people in the States like that album a lot," he commented later, "which makes me feel better about it, but for my part I wish I hadn't gone through with it, and waited until I got the right guys."

In the end, he came to regard the group as more or less an interim working band. He was happy with their playing, but not the musical direction. "I was caught up in a great horrible carnival of clashing musics at that time. I was confused—it was a terrible feeling of insecurity."

As a showcase for his varying inclinations of the time, it clearly indicated that Beck was now (literally) calling the tune. The problem was that he was always changing it. Sometimes it was full-on heavy hardware rock with Cozy; sometimes jazzy chords and riffs with Max; and sometimes soul/funk grooves with Bob and Clive. Cozy, who was furious enough one time during recordings to smash his hand into a wall (it was the hand that broke) recalled Beck being pretty difficult to work with: "He couldn't ever decide which style of music he was going to pursue. It was like that all the time."

Their audiences were similarly perplexed, and touring produced some mixed receptions. At a gig in Birmingham they were greeted by tremendous applause, but after the first three numbers there was a desperate stony silence.

American audiences, according to *Circus* magazine, expected what Beck called his old, vicious rock 'n' roll: "They couldn't cope with the subtle, laid-back soul and blues mixture he offered. And Beck soon realized there were too many different elements pulling against each other. As a result, at a critical point in his career, Jeff lost interest in the band. He fell asleep practicing. He forgot things from day to day, and occasionally he failed to show up at a concert."

"There was always a reasonable explanation," John Swenson commented in *Crawdaddy*, "but the combined effect served to reinforce the man's mystique—Beck is known as being erratic, unstable, hard to get along with. Fed by these reports I expected a fire-breathing monster when I finally managed to talk with Beck. I was more than surprised to find him to be a quiet, soft-spoken musician who was willing to discuss himself critically, who seemed to disparage his past achievements. In fact, one of the points Beck kept emphasizing was that he really had no desire for stardom. 'So you never wanted to be a big star?' I pressed. His denials seemed unlikely; one remembered that *image*. Beck searched for words. 'Oh . . . I didn't directly steer clear of it; but at the same time I wasn't looking for it.'"

AT THE END of May, at the precise moment of recording their next single, Beck put an end to his latest group. "I just felt we'd reached as high as we were ever going to go," he says. "Unfortunately it took us a long time to see we weren't compatible. There was always this strange sort of feeling—like everyone was trying too hard to get along, being ultra polite about everything the whole time, instead of talking about what was actually on their minds."

But friendships, apparently, were not entirely broken. Both Tench and Middleton reappeared to work with Beck again, and he retained close ties with Cozy Powell, who, until his untimely death in 1998, contributed his distinctive talents to a succession of seriously heavy outfits, including Rainbow, Michael Schenker, Whitesnake, and Black Sabbath.

At the historic Electric Lady recordings with Stevie Wonder, June 1972 (L-R Stevie Wonder, Jeff Beck, Cozy Powell).

Earlier in May, shortly before the breakup, Beck was disaffected enough to confess to the people at Epic that he was pretty bored with music in general, especially his own music. Asked what might get him going again, what material he'd really like to do, impulsively he mentioned his huge admiration for Stevie Wonder. And that remark gave rise to a far-reaching set of consequences.

In Beck's words: "Somebody at Epic told Stevie that I love the shit out of him, and asked him if he could maybe write a song for me. Forget it—I was 20 feet tall at that." The project discussed was for Beck to guest on Stevie Wonder's new album, while Wonder would write and record a song with the group, to be released as a single under their joint names. Beck's tracks on Stevie Wonder's *Talking Book*, recorded at Electric Lady Studios, included "Lookin' for Another Pure Love" and "Tuesday Heartbreak," although the album when released included him only on the former title.

Stevie Wonder at the time had reached a stalemate in his career and perhaps felt the collaboration with Jeff Beck would help revive it. He also badly needed a hit because he had recently turned 21 and was desperate to renegotiate his Motown contract to gain more artistic control.

"So I did a couple of tracks on *Talking Book*, which went down very well; he liked what I did. Then it was his job to write us a song. One day I was sitting at the drum kit, which I love to play when nobody's around, doing this beat. Stevie came kinda boogying into the studio: 'Don't stop.' 'Ah, c'mon, Stevie, I can't play the drums.' Then the lick came out: 'Superstition.' That was my song, in return for *Talking Book*. I thought, 'He's given me the riff of the century.' We played a version that he quickly put down."

At that point, however, Wonder suddenly realized he'd hit gold. "He said, 'Hold the session, I'm paying for it from right now,' went out and jotted some lyrics down. So he took our quickie demo to Motown and got his contract."

Of course, once the Motown bosses heard it, "Superstition" had to be a Stevie Wonder song. He recorded his own version and added it to the *Talking Book* album, which went to number three in the United States and proved to be the breakthrough he needed.

Jeff Beck, meanwhile, simply let the song slip through his fingers. It was during the JBG's sessions for "Superstition" (or "Don't Be Superstitious" as the title went originally) that the group's breakup was precipitated. Cozy Powell recalled the moment in an interview for *Modern Drummer*. "We were cutting a single with Stevie Wonder and there was a big argument in the control room. Our bass player had a go at Jeff in front of everybody and, of course, you just didn't do that in front of all the Motown heads—Stevie and all. There was this big argument and Jeff said, 'That's it!' We flew back to London on a Saturday, and on Monday morning a letter came through the post stating, 'You are no longer required' from Jeff's manager, who was also a solicitor."

Powell felt the blowup in the studio merely gave Beck his chance to cut loose: "The whole band was fired because Jeff was going through a bit of a funny period at that time. I've forgiven him since for that. In fact, I was with him just last night . . ."

The disbanding of the group combined with other contractual problems meant that the tapes of those sessions were never released. And although he soon got busy on "Superstition" with a new set of colleagues, Beck failed to grasp the opportunity to release it as a single before Stevie Wonder's version, taken from the album, came out and stormed to number one in the United States in January 1973.

The Motown star obviously didn't know how many hopes had been riding on it; but for Jeff Beck, so sorely in need of hit material, it was a massive disappointment: "That was the right decision but we were gutted, you know, totally. We would have had a monstrous, monstrous hit."

9 The Last Dirty Weekend

IT WAS JUNE 1972, and three long years had passed since Jeff Beck's attempts to hitch up with Tim Bogert and Carmine Appice. Now, suddenly, it seemed the timing was right. Bogert and Appice had gone through various incarnations of Cactus, each one less and less successful, and (was it by chance?) happened to be recording at Electric Lady Studios. In fact, it was widely believed their presence precipitated the JBG2 bust-up. With "Superstition" burning red-hot tire tracks in his mind, Beck invited them to lay down some trial recordings the very next night. Beck, Bogert, and Appice had finally got together.

A lot of people, when they heard about his new associates, were mystified about how Beck would jell with the massive Bogert bass and the pounding, stick-twirling Appice on drums. Musically, however, they claimed they were not so far apart. All three were steeped in soul/R&B and funk: Wilson Pickett, James Brown, all the Stax music, Sly, Joe Tex. The two Fudgers had been fans of Beck since *Truth* and *Beck-Ola*, and Beck had been blown away by the "Shotgun" track on their *Near the Beginning* album. "It was a revelation, particularly Carmine's drumming. I just knew I had to work with that rhythm section."

Beck was also tired of being the whole focus of attraction; he wanted to be part of a team of equals. "I don't want to hog it all the time. I want it there when I want it, to be able to jump and do it. I don't have enough confidence to be a solo artist—I want to be in a group, and if they're playing the sort of stuff that I like to hear, it may just be I *can* be a soloist."

The other great incentive was to put together a "name" group and profit from the combined selling power of its members. Beck was not blind to the phenomenon that was Led Zeppelin, and knew there was a huge market out there which he'd never exploited. Now he figured it was the right moment to head for the big time.

"When the economy started sliding in England," he told *Trouser Press*, "and it looked like I really would have to start worrying, I looked around and I saw that my colleagues were making millions—I don't mean loose change, but millions, real millions—and I would probably wind up in the streets if I didn't work again. That shook me. I woke up again. I saw that they were existing on the nucleus of what I had started doing. I'm not one to blow trumpets, and it's terrible to say it, but that's the way things were."

There was an obvious rapport between Beck, Bogert, and Appice, which seemed to augur well for the band's longevity; not least because they were all hot rod and motorcycle freaks. Not only did they like nothing better than getting up to their elbows in ironmongery, it also relieved the pressures of touring when they could pull in at hot rod meets or make time to go in search of parts. Beck at this time was the owner of three Ford rods—his pride and joy a black and chrome Model T roadster. Conversation at press interviews would often get around to rodding fantasies, like one of Appice's favorite scenarios: "If this band gets as big as we hope to, we may even all drive into gigs in hot rods, put on a little exhibition before the show. Or we'd do all our gigs at a speedway—race around, pull up onstage, get out and rock 'n' roll!"

As another important bonus, his new colleagues were well aware that Beck's head still wasn't right after his crash. Appice was good at cheering him up when he felt low, and between them they could share the load when fatigue or insecurity set in ("He doesn't even *know* when he's playing a blinder," according to Appice).

"My problem," Beck explained, "is that during troubled times I have always been subjected to the moods of the musicians I was playing with. To play well, I had to be in the right company. I feel completely revitalized with these two guys."

To REPLACE THE JBG2 version of "Superstition," recorded originally with Stevie Wonder on clavinet (and, of course, never released), they worked on new versions with takes featuring Beck, Appice and Bogert superimposed over Stevie Wonder's keyboards, with Beck occasionally taking the vocals. Another version brought in an American vocalist by the name of Kim Milford, previously of the *Jesus Christ Superstar* stage show, and came out as a Milford single in Sweden. Unfortunately, as already noted, none of these versions was ever released by BBA. Nor was their taping of "Lose Myself with You," a reworking of "Let Me Love You": this would later be rerecorded for the new group's first album.

It must have seemed almost preordained that Cactus had only a few dates left to fulfill, and Beck had just a handful of European shows before another U.S. tour was due on 1 August. The new lineup would be introduced then. So the Americans flew to London towards the end of July, with enough time for six days of rehearsal after Beck's last gig with JBG2—a box office record-breaker at the Roundhouse on 23 July with Ritchie Blackmore in the audience.

Still under the name of the Jeff Beck Group, they initially started out as a five-piece, with Milford on vocals and Max Middleton on keyboards. But Milford—though he had initially impressed Beck—wasn't a success at all. He looked good and sounded good, but onstage he just came apart.

Starting their three-week tour at the Stanley Theater in Pittsburgh, they gave a great show to a stupendous reception. But there followed a disastrous gig which really sealed Kim Milford's fate. It was at their New York debut at Gaelic Park in

ROLLING STONE

We Call On
Clifford Irving
by Drs. Phyllis
& Eberhard
Kronhausen

William
Burroughs:
Up Clear Creek
with an E-Meter

Lenny
Remembered
By Ralph Gleason

The
Naked Truth:
Jeff Beck's
Back

The ultimate accolade: Beck adorns the cover of *Rolling Stone*, October 1972, on the eve of BBA's first US tour as a trio.

the Bronx, when Milford was described in one review as having "the worst lead singing stage presence I've seen in many a mile." Beck didn't help by showing up late for the gig, and the park curfew cut their resultant set to little more than half an hour. They ended up dodging missiles hurled by the angry and heavily boozed crowd.

"Kim Milford got booed off the stage," Beck recalls. "He was a real pretty boy with long blond hair, and a great guy, but they didn't want to know: they just wanted to see us burn." So Milford was dropped around 8 or 9 August, Bob Tench being quickly drafted in for the rest of a tour that was successful enough to be extended to 17 dates.

Next they were booked to appear in Britain, Holland, Belgium and Germany, and in the interim some new material had to be hastily written. Their set had previously concentrated on selections from the *Rough and Ready* album, plus old standbys like "Shotgun," a reworking of "Plynth," the essential "Jeff's Boogie," and a song by Cactus—"Oleo"—which was a vehicle for Bogert's storming bass solos. A week or so was duly spent writing and rehearsing in the sleepy location of South Molton in rural Devon, where they would return again a year later while preparing their second album.

All this time the volume was getting more and more cranked up, with the music heading towards a thunderous boogie style. It was getting more reminiscent of Cactus, in fact, which in Beck's words was "couldn't-give-a-shit music," and at this point Max Middleton decided it wasn't for him. Bobby Tench hadn't stayed beyond the U.S. tour, and no suitable vocalist could be found. So Beck, Bogert and Appice pressed on as one of the few power trios of rock, with the potential to figure right up there in the major league.

Beck was much happier with the three-piece sound, the sound he'd had with the first Jeff Beck Group. But they were still cautious about changing the name, and they started their European tour in September 1972 as the JBG; it was on the 23rd, at Grangemouth in Scotland, that the name Beck, Bogert and Appice was first unveiled.

Soon they were pulling in packed-out, raving houses at 3,000 seater auditoriums. A second U.S. tour followed in October, now mostly at 4,000–8,000 seat halls, and Beck enjoyed the distinction of seeing himself on the cover of *Rolling Stone*. The audience reaction was mind-boggling: "We were kicking butt," Bogert recalls. "About one out of every three shows was a killer. And the money was great!"

Picking up on the audience vibe, the guys began to enjoy themselves with a bit of clowning around. Beck would receive the time-honored custard pie to the face and feign death on the floor of the stage . . . then, to a roar of approval from the crowd, he would rise up and return the favor by smashing another pie into Appice's bristling beard. At other times Bogert and Appice would grab a couple of towels and go through the pantomime of fanning him down during his red-hot "Jeff's Boogie" solos.

WITHIN THE TIGHT format of three instrumentalists, the group was still able to produce an amazingly full sound, with Beck's ever-working guitar filling in with chords as well as leads. The individuals were able to complement each other, the rhythm section taking their share of solos and at the same time keeping Beck on his toes, pushing him to blast away at his best.

"For the first time in as long as I can remember the excitement is back," he told one reporter. "Now I know I'm really doing what I want to again. In the past I've always worked against other people, but now I've learned to work with them."

Snatching time off to record between tours, from November '72 to January '73 they laid down their powerful debut album, *Beck, Bogert & Appice*. Unhappy

(L-R) Tim Bogert, Carmine Appice and Jeff Beck at the Hollywood Palladium, May 1973.

with the sound produced at a trial recording in England, they rerecorded at various studios in the U.S., mostly at Chess in Chicago, with the aid of production and material by Don Nix (who had penned the classic Beck showcase "Going Down"). Released in April, it reached a peak of number 12 in the United States, Beck's highest album chart showing yet. In Britain it charted in 28th position, also his highest ranking in that country.

A showstopping number on the album is their highly original rendering of Nix's "Black Cat Moan," a stomping, down 'n' dirty Southern rock slide-guitar tour de force with Beck moaning the vocals (for the first time in six years), and a rare example of Beck in full rocking new grass mode. OK, so Beck is not at his strongest on vocals . . . but the quality of singing is not always what matters, as many an illustrious career has shown. The special dimension of the human voice is the pleasure that counts, a pleasure granted to Beck's listeners only occasionally. When it comes, let's welcome and enjoy it.

Released as a single, "Black Cat Moan" was coupled with "Livin' Alone" as the B-side, also taken from the album. The intro for this song, with its excursive rhythmic treatment, has been compared to the celebrated intro of Buddy Guy's classic "Wee Wee Baby," which uses an unpredictable rhythmic structure to lead into the number. Eric Clapton cited Jeff Beck as one of the few people who could touch on this kind of original idea and then use his inventiveness to go beyond it. "It's such a random start—no one seems to know how it's going to go. And Jeff's got that down, so that it sounds positive and rambling at the same time."

Various friends contributed to the album, including Pete French and Duane Hitchings from Cactus. On "Sweet Sweet Surrender" they had help from members of Three Dog Night—Jimmy Greenspoon on piano and Danny Hutton to boost their vocals—but this only highlighted one of BBA's major problems: their vocal sounds failed to measure up to their blistering instrumental power. "Their whinings and thin voicings on the BBA album make it almost impossible to listen to," was *Record Review*'s biting verdict. "Only on 'Lady' are they bearable, and this is only because Beck wipes out any memory of off-key singing with an eccentric solo break." "Lady" is in fact an object lesson throughout in Beck's ferocious guitar work, whether in its hard-edged riffing, snarling leads, or bruising power chords.

One of the tracks was a new, superbly heavy version of "Superstition," recorded almost as an afterthought since by now Stevie Wonder had made it a hit for himself. But it was already a blockbuster in their stage set and earned a well-deserved place on the album. It was never released as a single except in Japan (in May 1973), but it remained indelibly associated with BBA.

Opinions on the album are usually extreme: some people hate it, others love its raw, pounding energy and drive. One critic gave it four stars and headlined it as "unbelievably brilliant." Comparing the band to Cream, he went on: "They have that same sensitive grasp of pure, controlled power, but somehow there's a greater consistency and spontaneity about them—live and on album." Another said: "Beck and his new band have moved out of the blues. All Beck fans who have been disheartened lately should give this new LP a chance." And, of course, let us not forget its number 12 position in the U.S. charts.

The album, however, doesn't accurately reflect just how heavy they were. We can tell by BBA's live performances—and by the track "Superstition"—that their trademark was a gritty Gorilla Sludge blues-funk-with-distortion that rocked the joint. But the sanitized production lacks depth and filters out too much of the sludge. In stark contrast to the storming funk-metal onslaught of the instrumental arrangements, most of the vocals are very forward and trebly in the mix, leaving us with overtones of blue-eyed '70s soul and even occasional Cream-like harmonizations; in particular, Beck's vocals on "Black Cat Moan" are buried and need more presence. And the guitar on many tracks has far less prominence than the thudding bass.

Carmine Appice's explanation is that Beck gave the tapes to Don Nix to take to Memphis for the final mix, telling him: "Make Timmy and Carmine sound good. They're angels." So Nix did exactly that—mixed down Beck's guitar while playing up the rhythm section.

In February 1973 the group got ready for a massive touring schedule. It was around this time that Ralph Baker first joined them. Replacing Clive Coulson (who had lately written himself into history with the Led Zeppelin juggernaut), Baker became Beck's permanent road manager/personal manager/friend and confidant, and has remained so to this day.

Touring opened with a string of dates in British clubs and colleges, and on the 16th they played a memorable show at the Sundown Theatre in Edmonton, where Rod Stewart was among those cheering in the front row. The sensation of the night was Beck's encore when he roared back onstage, amid clouds of dry ice . . . at the wheel of one of his hot rods.

A hell-for-leather North American tour followed from 28 March to 8 May, plus a triumphant visit to Japan, where they had a tumultuous reception. The hectic schedule was completed with more dates in Europe before they were due back in the U.S. again.

Beck had started the group using his stripped '54 Strat, then moved to a recently acquired white 1970/71 Strat with a rosewood fretboard; but on the 1973 tours he now relied on a Gibson Les Paul, just as Eric Clapton had done when competing with the other powerful players in Cream. He still took the Strat and used it when he could, but it was simply not up to BBA's massive levels of volume and distortion.

The Gibson was a rare 1954 Goldtop which, according to Beck's recollections, he'd bought in 1972 during the last U.S. tour of JBG2 when his beautiful tiger-stripe Sunburst was stolen. He'd even gone so far as to advertise for a Les Paul in an American newspaper, and flew down to Memphis to buy the Goldtop for $500 from the Strings & Things instrument store (Strings & Things recalls the purchase taking place later, in January 1973). The guitar had already been refinished, but he decided to refinish it again in a very dark brown color—almost black—which he describes as "ox-blood." He also replaced the original single-coil pickups with PAF humbuckers. This would become his most famous Les Paul, synonymous with the Jeff Beck sound of the mid '70s.

On tour he was using Sunn tops with columns of Univox speakers lining the stage. Asked about other hardware, he expressed dislike of most custom-built guitar gadgets. But there was one never-to-be-forgotten effect that Beck first adopted at this time: his intriguing "talking guitar." Known to BBA as The Bag, it was an electro-acoustic device with which he could modulate the guitar sound using his mouth.

The sound was something he'd remembered from a children's record, *Sparky's Magic Piano*, which was popular a generation earlier—a memory prompted by Stevie Wonder who had his clavinet rigged to reproduce the same effect. The story had a Disneyesque scenario where the piano came to life and magically talked to Sparky, the reluctant little boy who hated to practice his scales (though Sparky was too well-behaved to rip the black keys off!).

Similar effects had been used previously by Iron Butterfly's guitarist Mike Pinera, and before him by pedal-steel players Pete Drake and Bill West. In fact Joe Walsh, who used it later himself, was given the device by West, and suggests that he was the original inventor. We will leave Beck to describe how his version worked.

"It was a horn driver encased in one of those Mexican drinking-bottle bags. Instead of having the horn deliver the sound, it was unscrewed, and we put a piece of plastic piping in the little round threaded hole where the horn used to go. The whole thing was encased in foam rubber to keep the sound in and drive it up the tube. So the extension leading from the amp used this as an amplifier.

"You put the tube in your mouth, and form a voice box where you mold the sound by the shape of your oral cavity. You don't sing at all. Then it comes over a mic to be reamplified. People were quite amazed."

Peter Frampton became famous for employing the same effect in later years, and it was even utilized by Kiss—though by then Beck had wisely sidelined it before it could become stale. "I dropped it because it's only a trick or a toy, and I didn't want to be labeled as the guy that makes that funny noise with the tube in his mouth. It's a mind-blowing sound when you've never heard it before, and it gets people's attention for a few seconds. But if you did that on one tour, you've got to do something else on the next. You can't tell the same jokes every time."

ONE THING THAT surprised him was that he was now playing to concert crowds younger than he'd ever known before, with row upon row of fourteen- and fifteen-year-olds. "Some nights it was really incredible," he marveled. "The energy level was just ridiculous, static electricity in the air even before we got onstage."

Whether as an introduction for new fans, or as a reminder for the old ones, he took to including in his set occasional references to well loved hits from the past. During a medley of "Plynth" and "Shotgun," for example, he would quickly quote the hook from "Heart Full of Soul." "I give 'em a little taste of a number, then go on to another trip."

With this group, however, nothing ever seemed to be smooth sailing for very long. At a gig in October '72 they found themselves playing to a group of fanatics in Hanover, Germany, who took an aversion to the backdrop of enormous flags they used on the stage—a Union Jack and two Stars and Stripes. About a hundred or so political agitators started up a chant, demanding the downfall of the flags and throwing bottles at the stage, eventually demolishing Carmine Appice's drum kit. The situation wasn't helped by Beck's uptight attitude and the behavior of his management and roadies, who, according to one group that was scheduled on the same bill, acted like superstars. Beck: "It was hell—so we just blew the whole thing out. What's the point?"

In November '73 there was another nasty incident at a sellout gig in Paris, when Ralph Baker as chief roadie discovered there was a danger of electrocution with the stage setup. He refused to let them perform, and the cancellation led to near-rioting.

In Japan, by contrast, they could do no wrong. While the heavy trio format was losing its appeal elsewhere, Japan was just getting into it. BBA was absolutely enormous there (Beck still retains a huge and loyal following in that country), and the group's concerts at the Koseinenkin Hall in Osaka in May 1973 were recorded to produce two great live albums. Released in Japan only, *Beck, Bogert, Appice Live in Japan* came out in both double and single LP formats.

A cut from the Osaka recording, a full bore blues-rock mutation of "Black Cat Moan," is included in the retrospective *Beckology* set, which—together with "Blues De Luxe/BBA Boogie," recorded live at London's Rainbow Theatre in

Beck demonstrates "The Bag" with BBA in 1973.

1974—provides an illuminating taste of the powerhouse that was BBA in the flesh.

To quote *Rolling Stone*'s review of one of their concerts, "Beck steps up to the mike, swizzles a tube in his mouth that leads through an airbag into his guitar, and speaks/wah-wahs the opening syllables to Stevie Wonder's 'Superstition.' Bogert and Appice pound in behind him, Beck spits out the tube and leans back, his right arm the swoop of a hawk, his left raking strings to bend them out of all proportion to reality, speed-shifting, the force of acceleration howling back on itself in a continuous circular channel.

"Jeff has dropped the flashes of subtle virtuosity and sense of humor which characterized his stage presence in [his last group], and at the Forum seemed content to play at his most hammeringly insane, interspersing the madcap violence with lines as internally coherent as they were deadly true. In terms of richness, I thought, he hasn't sounded this good since the first Jeff Beck Group."

The reviewer noted, however, that with one or two exceptions their songs were weak and repetitious. Which was something they admitted right from the start—their material was in dire need of strengthening. Both Stevie Wonder and Sly Stone were writers they were hoping to enlist, but these efforts came to nothing.

There were also more serious shortcomings that couldn't be fixed merely by injecting new material. One of them was BBA's lack of a strong vocal presence. Tim Bogert and Carmine Appice were manfully filling in with singing roles, as they did previously with the Fudge, but now they were carrying the bulk of the vocals as well as playing. The result was simply not up to what was needed for a top-line band—"they fall far short of competent vocalists," as one reviewer accurately put it.

There were also signs of tension starting up between Beck and Bogert. As Appice explained, "Tim is such a great bass player that after a few months into a new band he just starts to go wild and play those amazing solos." But his solos were not the basic problem. What Beck couldn't tolerate was Bogert busily playing all over his own leads. "Whenever a guitar solo came up," Appice recalled, "Timmy would go after Jeff, and he'd end up right up his ass." Beck approached Appice one day and asked, "Does Timmy ever just play the bottom groove?" But the drummer knew Bogert of old: "What you hear is what you get!" he replied.

Though he wanted to play with the best, Jeff Beck hadn't bargained for being upstaged all the time, and it soon affected his mood and performance. Later, after the group broke up, he reflected: "Tim was so impossible, a total nutter, a fabulous player. But we just couldn't harness that energy."

These were just some of the problems that would never be resolved. In their year and a half of existence they built up a good-time rocking boogie act that cornered an audience all its own. But it was a welding of talents and temperaments too diverse for a lasting bond. Like a doomed love affair, starting at fever pitch with no thought for tomorrow, it was too hot not to cool down.

As A FOOTNOTE, at around this time Beck made a surprise guest appearance at the famous "retirement" night of David Bowie's *Spiders from Mars* world tour, mounted at London's Hammersmith Odeon on 3 July 1973. Beck's appearance was arranged by Bowie as a birthday treat for his guitarist, Mick Ronson, who idolized Beck's playing and had always longed to play with him onstage.

Beck was sent a mysterious note from Bowie, enclosing tickets and asking him to be at the show. Called up for the encores, he joined the band on "Jean Genie" and "Love Me Do" (Bowie supplying the harmonica part). A second encore, "Around and Around," also featured Beck on his magic voice tube.

The surprise appearance entailed even more of a surprise for Beck when he learned that the show had been filmed for cinema and TV. This was something he hadn't expected, and frankly he didn't feel he had performed too well (as anyone connected with filming will know, playing to camera is very different from playing to an audience). There was also the fact that the *Spiders from Mars* show was less a conventional rock concert than a musical set piece showcasing Bowie as Ziggy Stardust, in which Beck felt his presence was rather incongruous.

Given the option, he decided to exclude his appearances and they were duly edited out of the film and the official live album. Nevertheless, the first two numbers were shown on U.S. television and the third one was broadcast in Europe, an embarrassing situation for all concerned.

Beck was left with a strange memento of the occasion when he was given a weird rag doll by Bowie and Ronson which they said resembled him. An odd gift, but one that he kept ever afterwards. He also attended Bowie's retirement party at the Café Royal the following night, where the guests included Mick and Bianca Jagger, Ringo Starr, Paul McCartney, Keith Moon, Lulu, Cat Stevens, Lou Reed, Barbra Streisand, Britt Ekland, Tony Curtis, Elliot Gould, Ryan O'Neal, Peter Cook, and Dudley Moore, with music supplied by Dr. John—surely one of the most glittering rock events of the decade.

AFTER JAPAN IN May, and a trek around Europe in June, BBA now had a whole lot more U.S. dates to fulfill in July; but by this time Beck was all toured out. He had simply been on the road too long. He was also weary of the continual competition with Bogert in terms of volume and soloing, and after half a dozen shows he simply vanished back to England, supposedly summoned home by a personal emergency. "We woke up at the hotel one day," said Bogert, "and Jeff was just gone!"

It was mainly thanks to Appice and his freewheeling, anything-goes attitude that BBA didn't fall apart at that juncture. The end of the group may have been looming already, but Beck didn't feel that way just yet: he told the guys all he needed was a rest. In less than a month he was on the telephone asking the two Statesiders to come over and record a follow-up album. The plan was to work in England, allowing him to spend more time at home with Celia and their growing menagerie: as well as Beck's Afghan hound, Pudding, and his Alsatian, Joe, this now ran to several assorted mongrels and around thirty rescued cats.

The two Americans had recently bought new homes on their side of the Atlantic, and in Beck's terms it was perfectly natural that they should live in the U.S. and he in Britain: "I've no aim to move permanently to America; luckily we're in a position where we can afford to lead separate lives when we're not working."

So, after some preproduction rehearsals at their Devon hideaway, it was at Apple Studios in September of 1973 that they eventually gathered to make their next recording. Dissatisfied with Apple, they very soon moved their efforts to a bewildering number of other locations in an attempt to bed down the sound they needed: the right color on the drums, the right texture on the bass. But the project seemed doomed all along, and despite herculean efforts, it was fated never to see the light of day.

In late September they were recording at De Lane Lea, attempting to do their own production. But by this time they sorely needed a fresh influence from outside. With various producers being considered or unsuccessfully tried, like Mick Ronson and Jeffrey Haskell (previously Cactus and J Geils), they joked that they were even considering bringing back Mickie Most.

Their next move was to Escape Studios, close to Beck's home in the Kent countryside. Recording continued through October, but they remained displeased with the results so far and decided to take time off in November.

The numbers they worked on are listed in this book's discography and included the pile-driving instrumental "Jizz Whizz," which is featured in the *Beckology* set. Moody and full of spiky time-changes—another sign of Beck's interest in jazz-influenced rock—it was actually inspired by Bogert's indignant reaction to a prank of Appice's when the drummer crashed a cymbal just as Bogert stuck his head into a malfunctioning speaker.

As well as "Jizz Whizz," their live sets at the time are known to have included "Prayin'," "Solid Lifter," "Satisfied," "All in Your Mind," "Laughalong," and "Get Ready Your Lovemaker's Coming Home."

Bogert, who now described himself as "resigned to being the hired bass player," had his own problems to contend with: "Jeff plays how his mood strikes him and he's a man of a million moods. He's a Cancerian—always goes sideways, never knowing what his real motives are."

December brought renewed attempts when they moved to London's CBS Studios to try to salvage the project. This time they teamed engineer Andy Johns with producer Jimmy Miller, who had worked on the early JBG2 sessions. Beck had been impressed by their work with Led Zeppelin, and progress was now made in leaps and bounds.

In the new year Beck went into Island Studios, ready to mix the tracks they had; but fate took a hand before the tapes could be completed. Britain was seized by the devastating energy crisis of winter 1973-74, the effects of which led to a three-day working week. Like many other small operations, the recording studios were shut down. Beck still has the unfinished tapes hidden away, but cannot be persuaded to permit their release.

PRESSURE HAD BEEN MOUNTING meanwhile for a tour of the U.K., where they had last hit the stage in autumn '72. In September 1973 they found time for a music festival held at London's Crystal Palace, but disasters kept intervening to prevent anything more. First Bogert broke his foot in a motorcycle accident, then Appice and Bogert were both sick, Carmine with pneumonia and Tim with a bad stomach ailment.

Eventually, strung out and not in the best of humor, they reunited in January 1974 for the much-postponed tour. But Appice got sick once more—this time with flu and a temperature of 103—and their opening dates in Scotland had to be canceled. After an intensive two weeks, the tour climaxed with two celebrated shows on 26 January at London's Rainbow Theatre, of which the early performance was broadcast on 9 September 1974 on the syndicated U.S. radio program *Rock around the World*.

Tensions were at their peak during the Rainbow concerts. Beck was impatient with BBA's endless repetitive boogies and was already aching to do something different on his own; while Bogert, whose turn it was now to suffer his own bout of pneumonia, couldn't wait to get home to the States. Tempers flared between the shows, and Bogert took a hard swing at Beck which landed him on the floor. But the show had to go on, and that night's concert produced some fine performances from Beck, notably his beautifully phrased slide solo on "Livin' Alone," and a bending emotional workout on "Laughin' Lady."

A couple more desultory dates followed in Scotland to replace the canceled shows, but BBA had reached the end of the line. Returning to their respective homes, they never appeared together again. But it wasn't by any means an official breakup, and later that spring Beck got a transatlantic call from Appice at four in the morning: "Hey, Beckola, got a surprise for you—Sly Stone's here. Man, things are jumping—we've got Sly and he's going to sing and help produce our albums."

Beck was a major fan of Sly & the Family Stone, especially of guitarist Freddie Stone. Suddenly he was optimistic: "It all seemed like the end of a bad run of trouble."

But the genius who had captured the world of both white and black (and in the process made himself a small fortune) was now a raddled, unpredictable eccentric whose music proclaimed the biting edge of uncompromising black testimony. "I went out to Sausalito and saw the bay and a few boats, counted a few bricks in the Holiday Inn wall. But nothing much happened—except that I wasted two weeks and realized I wasn't a negro, and didn't want to be part of all that black power thing."

A few recordings were made with Sly, reportedly under bizarre circumstances, which are evidenced by Beck's account of their first encounter. He went into Sly's studio and waited hours for him to make an appearance, until eventually the great man emerged from sleep out of a room at the back. "Hey, Jeff, come back here man," he commanded. Motioning to a couple of guitars he said: "Play something—anything," and plugged in his bass. Jeff duly sat down, and with the tape running they jammed for a couple of hours. Then Sly simply disappeared. Beck never knew what became of the tape—all he came away with was a bill for $25.

From that moment the group just drifted apart, the official end announced in May 1974. Part of the problem was simple geography, aggravated by Beck and the two Americans having separate managers. They were both positive thinking managers, he said, but tugging in opposite directions.

Though Beck had hailed BBA as his "dream band," eventually it became clear it had lost all cohesion. In Bogert's words, "BBA isn't really what I call a band—it's the three of us playing as a unit but completely individually. It's not, 'Well, I'll try to outdo you' . . . it's 'I'm going to really let loose and if you don't keep up—too bad!'"

Beck: "I always wanted to see what it'd be like to play with a drummer who used two bass drums, and a bass player who really got it on. I have to have that bottom, I love strong, powerful bass, and I can't play unless my trousers are flapping with the noise. Your feet can feel it through the stage."

Unfortunately he hadn't bargained for what it did to his ears. In later years he paid a high price for being subjected to such prodigious levels. "BBA was uncreative and self-indulgent," was his summing up. "They thrived on excess and overplaying. If you could zero in on the energy, you got the goods— otherwise it was a cacophonous, nasty, horrible noise. That's the reason I couldn't go on with it—the noise was hurting me so much. When we weren't fighting we were playing slush: I was doing a bottle of Smirnoff a day just to survive it all."

"I wanted to do something very badly," he told *Creem* magazine, "there was a magnetism pulling me in that direction. I wanted a band that could outdo all of the heavy metal stuff around. I didn't ever think of it as a long-term thing. We just got enough material together for one show and took it from there."

But . . . "I don't repudiate it. It was just kind of a 'dirty weekend group,' you know. And when they were *kicking* they were the hardest fucking white rock group going. Carmine—jeez, there's no rock drummer, except maybe Moonie, who can come close to him in energy. I mean, he *explodes*."

Others were less kind about the merits of his two teammates, and one commentator dismissed them as "two musical fools." But the alliance also drew many accolades: "Today he's found his groove," *Circus* reported in 1973, "stepping back into place as the master wailing guitarist he used to be." "They made most of your heavy groups sound like stale bread soaked in milk," was another comment; "Beck, Bogert & Appice's performance was one that will be remembered when we have all gone to the Great PA System in the sky."

In September 1973, on the strength of one album and a handful of concerts, British *Melody Maker* readers voted BBA "World's Brightest Hope." But the promise was never fulfilled. As Beck observes: "We were just three maniacs, complete and utter maniacs. It went on all day, offstage and onstage. If we'd sat down and thought about it, if somebody had said, 'Look lads, you're going to have ten million-selling albums if you do the right things,' maybe we would have done it. The amazing overspill of talent was there, it was screaming out all over the place. But we needed to work out how it was going to be done."

10 Blowing Solo

AFTER THE DEMISE OF BBA, Jeff Beck retreated to his roots in the south of England for a sorely needed period of reflection: "I just needed some time to wash old things away and conceive new things."

Already he was tempted to give up on the whole group formula and do something entirely on his own. He actually began working on a project during 1973, just using a drum box, rhythm guitar, and overdubbed melodies. "I'll be writing all the material and playing all the instruments," he said at the time. "I want to record it at my leisure, just put it out without any fuss—then hope that people will like and accept it. Everyone seems to get trapped into doing one kind of thing, and I want the album to show there's a lot more influences than some would imagine."

But the idea didn't last, because playing with real people was so much better. Beck was facing a classic Catch 22: he wanted to go his own way, try new things, but he didn't want to do it alone. He needed the support of a team of associates, but that always created problems. The logical course seemed to be a solo career, but he didn't want to stand on his own in the spotlight . . .

Though stardom was there for the taking, he frequently declared he didn't relish the idea. "I just don't want to become super-famous, because it would affect me and slowly eat into me. I just want to ride beneath." Lead guitarist, yes, he wanted that. But guitar god? No, thank you, it wasn't his style. "I don't want to be up [at] the front," he'd said in the days of JBG2. "I want to do two jobs: I want everything my way, but still not be featured, which is very hard."

After BBA he'd also revised his ideas of riding the gravy train: "If I got a hit record it would only mean trouble for me. It would probably elevate me to something that I'm not, something I'm not capable of carrying out. The thought of having millions in the bank is no security to me. The thought of working with good players is security."

Beck's determination to be his own man clearly flew in the face of rockbiz—and audience—expectations. Soon it would become a Beck trademark. He had taken rock the full distance anyway, and now it had little to offer that was new and challenging. By contrast, the emerging world of jazz-rock presented new frontiers to cross, new forms and languages to master. And it admitted instrumentalists in their own right. "I want stuff that enables me to *roast* on the guitar, but roast well, and not have to come out with all the old shit that people expect from me. You can keep up with the times as well as kick ass, you know what I mean?"

Already, in his last months with Tim Bogert and Carmine Appice, he had been turned on to sounds like the Mahavishnu Orchestra; soon his thoughts were far more with this technically advanced style of music than the dated BBA formula. It took a while before he had focused on the right medium—but when he did, it thoroughly surprised everybody.

IF JEFF WAS retrenching and rethinking his true métier, so equally was Eric Clapton. Having formed Cream and Blind Faith, both of which broke up in disarray, by 1970-71 Clapton had resigned the role of guitar hero and found solace in the relative anonymity of larger bands. With Derek & the Dominos he recorded *Layla*, arguably the greatest performance of his career, and then retreated to do battle with his encroaching heroin habit.

When he emerged once more, it was to appear chiefly as a singer playing tasteful guitar in a relaxed, economical country blues style which appealed to a mainstream audience. The frightening brilliance had been left behind, but commercial success was the not unwelcome compensation.

The '70s heralded a period when the cutting edge seemed to disappear from many of rock's former fire-eaters. David Bowie ceased his cataclysmic imaginings and moved on to his *Young Americans* phase. Fleetwood Mac went soft. Paul McCartney sprouted Wings and flapped off to safe havens along the middle of the road.

Jimi Hendrix, Janis Joplin and Jim Morrison had embraced rock's dangerous extremities, and in death would remain forever mythologized in the collective consciousness . . . so where were the next Hendrixes, Joplins and Morrisons of the new decade? In the general bland-out that followed, superstar status was accorded to the Osmonds, the Carpenters, David Cassidy, and ABBA. Soon disco music would become a worldwide infestation, constructed to an endlessly recycled formula of sleek orchestration and monotonously thumping beat.

Stadium rock produced ever more grandiose exponents, among them the monumental Yes, Genesis, Queen and techno-rockers ELP. Love them or hate them, Queen at least partially redeemed the '70s by introducing, in Brian May, a sonic delight for all who love seven-league-boots guitar.

The fashions of the day sank to an egregious tastelessness. As if in retaliation to the '60s casual, frayed and shaggy look, a new fashion arrived with sharp, narrow-waisted suits sporting padded shoulders and ten-inch-wide lapels, worn with flamboyant shirts unbuttoned to display hairy chests clanking with jewelery. Preposterous bell-bottoms and garish platform shoes completed the picture, while middle-of-the-road macho singers led the trend for elaborately coiffed, ear-muffling hairstyles and heavy sideburns, aped by a prematurely aging Elvis Presley with thickening waistline, a multimillionaire parody playing to crimped and pantsuited Las Vegas cabaret crowds.

Small wonder that there emerged, amid the parade of complacent mediocrity, a virulent backlash against all that was middle-class, middle-aged and middle-browed. That backlash became known as punk.

In London there was already an underground rumble from rough-edged, pub-on-the-corner groups whose streetwise songs dealt in the language of reality and wry observation. But punk, when it arrived, caught the industry with its pants down. Originally an import from New York, it all started around 1972 in punk-chic clubs in the Bowery, whence emerged subterranean street-rock groups such as the New York Dolls. Malcolm McLaren was the eminence grise behind its commercial exploitation in Britain. The owner of a Chelsea clothes shop called Sex, McLaren was into the whole New York Dolls cult and had tried managing them before they fell apart. Working in McLaren's shop at the time was one Glen Matlock, who played bass with an amateur group of questionable ability calling themselves the Swankers. Eager to start a punk trend in Britain, McLaren renamed them the Sex Pistols and augmented their lineup with a singer, John Lydon, renamed Johnny Rotten in honor of his teeth.

Outfitted in bondage gear, ripped clothing, and spiky, rat-tailed hair, the Sex Pistols delivered a venomous two fingers to the fat cats who raked in millions purveying comfortably mindless, marketable pap. Often booed off stage and banned by civic authorities, their message was loudly received and understood by the frustrated underclass of kids in Britain's decomposing economy. The truculent movement spread like wildfire, launching a bandwagon of imitators, camp followers, and press/musicbiz hangers-on. Their combined hostility was indiscriminate, but especially poisonous was their loathing of those "boring old farts" who dominated the international music market: the likes of Yes, Rod Stewart, the Stones, Led Zeppelin, and Genesis.

Punk rock was brutish, tasteless and inept; but it belonged back on the streets where the kids wanted it to be. And its legions of spin-offs, eventually leading to new wave, produced several bands that were coherent and musically talented, some of them injecting strong inflections of that other street music, reggae, in many of their songs.

Reggae was indeed the only other genuinely vibrant and exciting mass-market breakthrough of the '70s, brought to Britain and the United States in 1973 by the mighty Bob Marley after his signing with Island Records.

Bob Marley had cut his first single in Jamaica more than ten years earlier, with a style of music that traced its origins to the blue-beat, ska and rock-steady of the early '60s. Emerging full of zest and vitality from Kingston's infamous Trenchtown ghetto, Marley's reggae spoke of love, life, protest, and the rich symbolism of Rasta, the black godhead who would deliver the righteous from the white man's Babylon. His music found an eager new audience, with a sound that lodged unforgettably in the brain.

THE INFLUENCE OF REGGAE was not lost on Jeff Beck by the time he came to put together his next album in late 1974. In planning the project he went back to an old friend and colleague, keyboardist Max Middleton. Middleton was often to be found in an ad hoc Latin-reggae-funk band called Gonzales (along with Bob Tench and Clive Chaman), which featured the cream of the industry's West Indian sidemen and session players. They were seen a lot on the London club scene, where Jeff Beck liked to come and check them out, sometimes sitting in and jamming.

In fact Beck had made recordings with some Gonzales members in July-August that year under the group name Zzebra, including Dave Quincy on saxes, Tommy Eyre on keyboards, John McCoy on bass, Liam Genockey on drums, and Nigerian Loughty Amao on sax and percussion. They recorded a few jams, but nothing came of them (they needed "some decent lyrics and a wailing singer," Jeff opined in an interview). Nevertheless one track, "Put a Light on Me," ended up on Zzebra's album *Panic* which was released the following year.

Although Max Middleton was not involved in Zzebra, he and Beck were already dreaming up ideas for the forthcoming album which would eventually be titled *Blow by Blow*. Working with Middleton had always given him inspiration to branch out and experiment, and the partnership bore fruit right away with the Jamaican feel that came through in a reworking of the Lennon/McCartney song "She's a Woman." After tinkering with various funky treatments, it was Middleton's idea to give it the reggae arrangement that made it one of the album's most popular tracks.

Max Middleton also opened Beck's eyes to a new vocabulary of voicings and chords more usual in jazz contexts. "I went from heavy riff tunes to things that were a bit more classy," Beck elaborated. "Max was always hitting me with nice chords. I'd have to be like a twerp for about two hours while I fumbled around with them. That's what I've always done, though: just opened myself up and said, 'I can't play guitar, but I'll have a go at this.' Being totally honest and open and willing to start from square one. He's incredibly enthusiastic. He draws out something in me that I've been afraid would be there—which is, like, taste. It just could put me out of a job, you know!"

Beck's words could well have been prophetic, since his ideas for the new project veered right into that jazz-rock which had so impressed him of late; and, what's more, it was to be an instrumental album showcasing Jeff Beck as a guitar soloist. All of which represented a monumental volte-face and a considerable risk with his career.

It was also a leap of faith for Beck's label, Epic. Fortunately, Gregg Geller (of *Beckology* fame) was working in A&R for Epic at the time, and he and A&R head honcho Don Ellis encouraged the project at all costs. Their far-sightedness certainly paid off: not only was it an immediate best-seller, but in the words of Steven Rosen in *Record Review*, Beck's playing was "absolutely the most distinguished and disturbingly powerful heard on record in nearly a decade."

Speaking of the influences that led him in this new direction, Beck put it down to hearing John McLaughlin with Miles Davis: "One day I was working on one of my hot rods, in the pissing rain, and I had this transistor radio. And they played the *Jack Johnson* album, and that was it! I put my tools down and said to my old lady: 'I've just heard something that gives me hope.' This long track with this frantic guitar. I thought, 'This is it, now we're talking.'"

For this radically different departure, it was decided that Beck would work with George Martin, the gifted EMI producer who had been fundamental to creating the magic of the Beatles on record. By 1970 he had opened AIR recording studios in London, and had recently been producing the Mahavishnu Orchestra.

Mapping out their first ideas in August, Beck and Middleton initially got together with Carmine Appice, another Mahavishnu fan. But although he recorded four tracks, Appice's input was reluctantly dropped when his manager demanded equal (or larger!) billing in the album credits. So when recording started in earnest the following month, the lineup was completed by two musicians from the Gonzales rhythm section: Phil Chenn on bass and eighteen-year-old Richard Bailey on percussion.

At the start of *Blow by Blow*, Beck had returned to the white Stratocaster he'd been forced to relinquish with BBA. But the piercing Strat was obviously torture for George Martin's ears, and he didn't want to make the poor man suffer. So the trusty ox-blood '54 Les Paul came out of its case, and the Fender was relegated to a supporting role.

With an instrumental format, and aided by the musicianly Martin, Beck was free to explore new textural possibilities; one example was the addition of orchestral atmospherics to "Scatterbrain" and "Diamond Dust." It took a while to reconcile himself to the result, though it was something he wanted to try, and we can thank Martin for the success of the experiment. As Beck says, "He frameworked some pretty simple tunes and made them sound magnificent."

The jazz-oriented "Scatterbrain" is a superb example of this deceptive simplicity, its themes and solos alternating between 9/8, 6/8, and 4/4 time. The harmonic structure goes through constantly shifting chord changes, and Beck delivers guitar solos in varying timbres, sometimes clean, sometimes thick and distorted. Interestingly, "Scatterbrain" was an off-the-cuff arrangement of something Beck was using as a finger exercise. Middleton heard him and put chords to it: "It was all done in a flash," he said.

"Diamond Dust" has an ethereal, music-of-the-spheres quality, evoking scenes of otherworldly existences . . . and again there is that strong jazz feel, with a time signature of 10/8 and delicious chord shifts moving in unexpected directions.

"Freeway Jam," a number that would become a highlight in Beck's live set, is here presented as a high-powered shuffle, with distorted guitar backed by pounding percussion and a rocking bass.

The album's opener is "You Know What I Mean," with a funky black feel and energetic soloing from Beck. This is followed by the reggae workout "She's a Woman," on which Beck's voice tube makes an appearance, described by one reviewer as "nothing short of miraculous—it's like listening to a singer whose words you can't make out for certain, but the sound is so delightful it really doesn't matter."

By contrast, "Constipated Duck" boogies along with Chuck Berry–like double-stopping alternated with twangy guitar and outrageous picking effects. It's a typically Beckian concept, calling to mind not only Berry's patented duckwalk but also Beck's own celebrated Donald Duck voice impersonation!

"AIR Blower," obviously a studio inspiration, starts as a full-on progressive pelter—squealing improvisational guitar and keyboard solos combined with pile-driving percussion—until it suddenly locks wheels and skids into a slow, dreamy 9/8 tempo, ending with Beck's limpid guitar reflections.

The remaining two cuts are Stevie Wonder tunes. "Thelonius," though not in the same league as "Superstition," was Stevie's gift to Beck in 1972. (BBA recorded a version, "The Chant Song," for their unreleased second studio LP.) Here it is rendered as a chunky, funky rocker, with heavy bass riffs and a full catalog of guitar effects including liberal helpings of wah-wah pedal.

And sandwiched in the middle of the album is its high point, the beautiful "Cause We've Ended as Lovers"—an object lesson in Beck's lyrical melodic phrasing. In stating the theme, with its alternating higher and lower responses, he chooses fingerings and effects that constantly exploit the special tonal values of the various strings. Then he gradually extends into increasingly improvisational embellishments, starting with a series of gritty observations that build and subside, never quite reaching a climax, each establishing a plateau from which the next begins.

In an appreciation for *Guitar School*, Wolf Marshall describes the performance as "a masterpiece of interpretation—a personal signature and, in the process, an absolute classic in rock guitar history. Jeff delivers the melody and fashions the improvisations like a jazz saxophonist would, with great subtlety and drama, unflagging attention to dynamics, detailed shadings of tone color, phrasing nuances and contrasts, and a wide range of expression. . . . We know that Stevie wrote the funk standard 'Superstition' for Jeff, but the way Beck plays this one leaves you with the impression that 'Cause We've Ended as Lovers' was crafted for him as well."

Beck: "That was a ready-made song right there. Stevie loved it—I was so proud." He still regards "Cause We've Ended as Lovers" as one of the most beautiful tunes he's ever played. "It was a lyrical song. I soak in the vibe of a song and then lay on what fits best. There are so many sounds in the guitar, without using any effects. As I recall there are no bends in that solo that I didn't do just with my fingers. If I can't make the solo happen without the whammy bar, there's something wrong."

Beck dedicated this track to the superb but little recognized guitarist Roy Buchanan. His own playing reflected Buchanan's style in many ways: in his use of extreme note-stretching and pinched (partial) harmonics,* and in manipulating

---

These are achieved by touching the string with the right hand at the correct place to produce an upper harmonic, and simultaneously striking the string with the pick pinched between the right thumb and another finger.

volume/tone controls to produce almost vocal effects—a favorite Beck technique that lets him attack a note softly and swell into it.

He first saw Buchanan in 1971 on a U.S. television special, and just sat there aghast listening to some of the best playing he'd ever heard. "I played that song with the same sort of vibe that he had. He defied all laws of verse-chorus-verse and just blazed. I had that style already pretty much in my head, that sort of stroking strings and making arpeggiated sort of chords and bending notes at the end. But he actually made it more comfortable for me to play that style. That's really what I learned from him."

A year after *Blow by Blow*, Roy Buchanan returned the compliment by recording "My Friend Jeff" on his own album. "We hadn't spoken two words to each other. That was really amazing."

Equally in keeping with his tribute to Buchanan was the '58 Fender Telecaster he used for the song. This was a modified Tele given to him by pickup craftsman Seymour Duncan, who had been devastated in 1968 when Beck's pickups were switched on his Les Paul Sunburst. Duncan, although he couldn't afford a vintage Gibson, had resolved to give Beck a guitar that would reproduce the special tone he'd lost. In late 1973, when Duncan was working in London, he gave Beck the Telecaster with two specially rewound Gibson PAF humbuckers and an early '60s maple neck refitted with Gibson frets: "He just fell in love with the guitar, and I found out that he recorded "Cause We've Ended as Lovers" with it. He could do the volume and tone control thing on it so well, where on the Les Paul he couldn't. To this day he still uses that guitar for sessions, and I was pretty proud of it."

A matter of days after getting the Tele-Gib, Beck had a surprise for Seymour Duncan: he sent over three of his own guitars and invited him to take his pick. Among them was the '54 Esquire he had played with the Yardbirds, an instrument that Duncan associated with his earliest recollections of the electrifying young guitarist from England; this was his delighted choice, and he treasures it still.

AFTER THE ALBUM was recorded, Beck suddenly had an offer that left him reeling. The Rolling Stones needed a replacement guitarist, and he was invited to take over the slot. Mick Taylor, who had taken the place left empty by Brian Jones in '69, had quit the band suddenly in December '74 declaring that he wanted "a change of scene" and intended to start a solo career. In truth, the non-smoking, non-drinking vegetarian of five years ago was now addicted to heroin. He was quitting before he passed the point of no return.

Still one of the biggest attractions in the world, the Stones could have had their pick from any number of top names. They used their recording sessions in Rotterdam and Munich (for the album that would appear as *Black and Blue*) as an auditioning ground for an illustrious list of guitarists who went over to blow with them. And one day Beck had a message saying, "Can you come to Holland to do some recording?"

Remembering he'd mentioned to Mick Jagger that he would like to play with the Stones—meaning maybe a session or guest appearance—this was what he thought they meant. So he went along to investigate.

Three days later, when the Stones hadn't even got their guitars out, he started to get worried. Unknown to Beck, the guys had simply assumed his arrival signaled his agreement to join the group! At last they started what Beck thought were rehearsals, and now he got even more uneasy. In their usual laid-back style the Stones just sat around with their feet up playing 12-bar blues. "I couldn't handle it, because my mind wasn't into that way of doing things. I was working a million miles an hour in comparison to the way they were."

Still bemused, he joined his old pal Stu Stewart in the bar. "He said, 'I don't know if you realize what's going on, but we're going to be recording.' I said, 'I knew that, let's get on with it.' He said, 'But on top of that, you prat, they want you to play for real, in the Stones.' I thought, 'Oh boy!' Now this is in no way disrespectful to the Stones, because I really like them, but for the next few hours the sudden realization that I might be a Rolling Stone frightened the hell out of me."

As he went on to lay down some experimental tracks, all the time the thought was preying on his mind that he was going to have to say no. Sometimes the tapes were running and sometimes not, so the only surviving evidence of these sessions is to be found on bootlegs. Beck is alleged to be discernible on three tracks: "Black and Blue Jam," with Sonny Rollins on sax and Pete Townshend on backing vocals, of which a remixed version, sans Beck, became "Slave" on the album *Tattoo You*; the ballad "Sexy Night" (aka "Lovely Lady"), with plenty of funky Beck-style guitar; and the more intense funk number "Come on Sugar" (aka "Let's Do It Right").

Wondering how to break the news gently, Beck eventually decided the only solution was to write a note. Essentially it just said, "Sorry lads, I got to go home," Beck recalled with typical wry humor. "We slipped it under their door and ran off. I hated to do it, because Mick's such a lovely guy. They all are."

So Jeff Beck never became a Rolling Stone—to the great disappointment of many of his fans, but to the considerable relief of many others.

The Stones' eventual shortlist was rumored to consist of Wayne Perkins, Harvey Mandel, Rory Gallagher, and Robert A. Johnson; and they had almost made a decision when news came through that the Faces, with Rod Stewart now a megastar, would soon be splitting up. This meant Ron Wood was available.

Woody had by then developed a great individual style and panache with the Faces, and was (even more importantly) tight with Mick Jagger and Keith Richards, and thoroughly liked by all the Stones. From their point of view he would fit in perfectly, though the move scarcely stretched his talents any more than it would have stretched Beck's. But it was clearly written in the stars for Wood—the wheel had turned full circle: because, although he didn't know it, the Stones had originally sought him way back in '69, when he had just started rehearsing with the Faces. Mick Jagger's message never reached him at the time,

At Regis College, Denver, Co., on the *Blow by Blow* tour, June 1975.

although he said he'd have jumped at the chance if it had. So Woody joined their 1975 tour and, once the Faces did eventually split, became an official Rolling Stone.

AT THIS POINT IT should be mentioned that Beck had found time to play on sessions for several other artists in the early '70s. The first was in August 1973 when he sat in with sax player Eddie Harris on his album *E.H. in the U.K.* The Eddie Harris sessions were incredible, he said, especially jamming with guitarist Albert Lee. During the same month he contributed guitar to an album recorded by American singer Dorian Passante (previously of the new York group Sweet Dirt), who was in London forming a new band called Zero. He also did sessions for the solo album *Lane Changer* by Michael Fennelly of the Crabby Appleton

Band, on which Beck played four tracks and sang uncredited backing vocals on "Touch My Soul."

In 1974 he played on the title track of the album *White Lady* released by Badger, the group formed by Tony Kaye of Yes, incorporating Kim Gardner and Roy Dyke of AGD. And then came a project with Pete Brown (best known as Jack Bruce's cowriter in the days of Cream), along with Jack Bruce on the same session, and also Max Middleton. Beck recorded the song "Spend My Nights in Armour," which was originally intended as a single release, but it would be an astonishing 14 years before it eventually saw the light of day on Brown's 1987 album *Before Singing Lessons*.

Looking forward a little, in April 1975 Beck jetted over to the States to tape a TV appearance with ace keyboardist Billy Preston, who had been blown away by Beck after meeting him at the Stones' Rotterdam sessions. Preston flew him in first class, along with Max Middleton, especially for a segment on the *Midnight Special* show hosted by Wolfman Jack. With the lineup completed by Willie Weeks on bass and Ollie Brown on drums, the show was televised in May (incidentally sparking groundless rumors of a Beck/Preston tie-up). The numbers they performed included "You Know What I Mean," a killer take on "Nothing from Nothing," "Them Changes," and Beck's classic "Cause We've Ended as Lovers," during the taping of which the show's producers managed to screw up four takes; Beck wasn't inclined to go through it a fifth time, so the segment was broadcast with Beck's guitar so out of sync that at times he was not even playing on the correct part of the neck!

Also in May came a reunion that went a long way towards repairing the rift which had grown up between Jeff Beck and Jimmy Page. Led Zeppelin brought its massive laser-lit stadium show to Britain for the first time after two years of exile, with a five-night booking at London's 20,000 seater Earls Court Arena. They celebrated the last night with one of their legendary roisterous backstage parties, and Beck stayed until four in the morning.

HE WOULD HAVE little cause to regret fleeing the Rolling Stones once *Blow by Blow* was released in March 1975. In the U.S. it received tremendous FM radio exposure and shot within weeks to a high of number four—a rare achievement for an instrumental recording—and won Beck his first gold disc.* It was his most commercially successful record ever, and has sold over 2,000,000 copies to date. As recently as 1996, *Guitar* magazine placed *Blow by Blow* among its "Top 25 Albums That Shaped Rock Guitar," with an appreciation that ended, "Beck created a style of guitar that could gently swing at the same time as it was cracking your head."

*Blow by Blow *won a gold disc on 8 October 1975 and went platinum on 21 November 1986, as did his follow-up album,* Wired. *The earlier* Truth, Jeff Beck Group *and* BBA *have also since been certified gold.*

As usual, its U.K. reception was less enthusiastic: it failed to chart in Britain, with *NME* complaining that the album was too jazzy, while *Melody Maker* considered it not jazzy enough.

Blow by Blow has since been described as signaling the age of the rock guitar virtuoso, and a string of guitar luminaries, from David Gilmour to Eddie Van Halen to Steve Lukather, would readily subscribe to this. For his own part, Beck's concern was to remain in touch with his rock audiences while stretching his musical boundaries—and theirs: "Rock's an energy, to me. It's more complex now than it was, but it's rock just the same. They're not getting sick of it, but they need to be led some other place, given the opportunity to get into some other things. I suppose I could get a group and go out there and clean up playing 'I Ain't Superstitious' by turning it into nostalgia. But that is nothing new—I've spent half my life trying to get out of ruts."

The triumph of the album was hastily followed up in April with a three-month tour of the United States, plus August dates in Japan. Needing seasoned road musicians with more attack onstage, Beck reluctantly passed over Bailey and Chenn in favor of Bernard "Pretty" Purdie, the powerful drummer from the Aretha Franklin band ("When he was tuning up, he'd be louder than most guys when they were full blast!"), and the brilliant Wilbur Bascomb on bass, best known for his work with James Brown ("It's really a gas to play in this band," he said. "Me and Purd have been on the road playing sheet music—it's fun to be in a band that relies so much on feeling.").

Their first appearance, a low-key tryout in a pub in London's New Cross, was their only gig in England; and then their U.S. tour erupted. Packaged as a double bill with the avant-garde Mahavishnu Orchestra, the combination was not easily digestible, perhaps, for fans who expected the rock mayhem of BBA concerts. Typically attuned to his audience, Beck made sure he didn't go too far down either road. "It was two extremes: this totally esoteric jazz-rock and this more reasonable sort of music that I was playing. John [McLaughlin]'s stuff was so out . . . I mean, I loved it, but it's much too deep for most people. Funnily enough, people got off more on my stuff than they did on his: they could understand the comparatively simple rhythms. It crosses the gap between white rock and Mahavishnu or jazz-rock. It bridges a lot of gaps."

Soon they were pulling in packed houses, with Beck in top form and playing with a new degree of maturity and consistency. "Possibly the only guitarist in rock worth listening to for up to two hours," was one reviewer's comment.

Although his touring arsenal still included the ox-blood Les Paul, Beck quickly sidelined it in favor of the stripped Strat which he used until a date in Cleveland in May when it started malfunctioning and he threw it down onstage in disgust: a rare outburst for the reconstructed Beck, which was rewarded by the body breaking into three equal pieces. Subsequent reports had him playing a series of white Strats with rosewood necks, at least three of which were successively stolen during the '70s. One of them was a gift from John

McLaughlin—a treasured guitar which he described as "the best white/rosewood Strat ever."

By now he was a confirmed Strat aficionado, as much for the challenge as the tone and response: "It's technically a bitch to get hold of and play—but it comes over well, slices through the atmosphere with the highs."

Still using a 200-watt output, his setup started out with two Marshall tops and two Fender speakers. Then midway through the tour he switched gear, replacing the Fenders with Marshalls: "It was too clear, too virginal sounding—I wanted to get some dirt back into the sound."

Now in the fortunate position of getting any number of free footswitch units to try, he tended to carry a small assortment that included a Colorsound Tonebender and Octave Divider (adding a lower octave), and DeArmond Wawa/Volume Control. But generally the only effects he used were wah-wah plus a specially made preamp power booster, giving instant power, sustain, and distortion.

Touring called for every reserve Beck had at his disposal, since he was virtually on his own fronting an unknown band. "I've always had someone else to share the load with me," he explained. "See, when the group is known as a group and you're not really the star, you can feel a lot more at ease. But I felt that I was stuck right out there. It was a bit unnerving."

Once he was back in full swing, however, the old Beck soon came to the fore again: "The crowd at Avery-Fisher averaged about 16 or 17, but hip, you couldn't fool them. And California! Out there were some 16-year-old chicks who were *beauties*. And I was *playing* . . . oh, you shoulda seen me! Like a spring lamb I was!"

With this being the first all-instrumental Jeff Beck tour, members of the press were avid to know whether he'd given up on the idea of performing with a singer. His answer was he hadn't—he just couldn't find the right one. "I'd be *delighted* to find a singer. I got a bit scared on the tour when I was up front all the time. I suddenly realized that after ten years onstage, for the first time it was just me out there—like Hendrix would be—without Bob or Rod to shake 'is ass and ping-pong the energy. The only ping-pong was between me and the band, and if they were on top of it, it would be great, but finally it was up to me."

AFTER SO MUCH turmoil in the past few years, there must have been times when Beck wanted to pinch himself at the success of *Blow by Blow*. In six weeks it had outsold all his other albums, and at the same time sparked off sales of his back catalog of recordings.

At last he could see his financial horizons widening, and in the summer of 1975 he exchanged his cottage at Egerton for a Tudor manor house set in 80 acres of wooded grounds, deep in the Sussex countryside, at a cost of £110,000 (a handsome price in those days). Dating from 1591, and designed by an architect in the service of Queen Elizabeth I, it was a listed historic building, which placed on Beck the responsibility to keep it maintained to an approved standard.

The house embodied all those things he held most dear. Built in the era of

Jeff Beck jamming with John McLaughlin of the Mahavishnu Orchestra at Winterland, San Francisco, May 1975.

timber frames, inglenook fireplaces, tall chimney stacks, and diamond-pane leaded windows, it was an artifact crafted by the hand of man in an age more in tune with its surroundings. An age when buildings took their shape from hand-hewn beams, settling with time into natural contours that gave pleasure to the human eye; an age devoid of hard, relentless verticals and horizontals.

Describing his "English castle" he said, "I'm fortunate, I have a beautiful house—my own little world, my own little piece of Sussex about 30 minutes by car from where I grew up in Surrey. We just try to keep a bit of English tradition going. It's stupid, really. We're fighting a losing battle. It's fantasy, but I love beautiful things, and I love beautifully made architecture. The way people used to live fascinates me. And I *have* a piece of that. It's three floors and all beamed, and when you walk in the door it's like going back two, three hundred years. It's just an atmosphere that will never be killed. It will always be there."

Autumn brought a second U.S. *Blow by Blow* tour, on a concert bill that couldn't have been more different—sandwiching Beck between Aerosmith and Rod Stewart & the Faces. With his set shortened from one hour to 30 minutes, this tour was much less arduous, and with Stewart and the Faces there was quite a bit of good-natured banter. Occasionally he would deliver a dig at Rod, ending his set by thanking the audience and adding, "You've had enough music for the afternoon—now on with the show!"

Beck also enjoyed the guys in Aerosmith, and has remained friends with them ever since. In fact they would play more dates together the following year, and it was due to Beck that the band produced their celebrated cover of "The Train Kept A-Rollin'."

Since Aerosmith's Joe Perry is a confirmed fan, perhaps this is the moment to quote some of his observations:

"I was heavily influenced by Beck. As far as blues guitar playing goes, Beck is the one. He's still reaching, and his technique still astounds me. He attacks a guitar like it's brand new, every time. I'd pick up one of his guitars, and it would feel like the strings were made of redwood logs—and that'd be after I saw him play so fluidly. Then other times he'd be playing really light strings—same thing. He's so adaptable; he just molds his playing to the guitar. It's hard to say who's the best, because there are so many different styles, but for what he is and what he stands for—and what he means to me—I'd have to say Beck's the best."

11 A Hammer in the Works

BY LATE 1975, when he came to start work on his next album, Jeff Beck had found new inspiration in the synthesizer talents of Czech-born Jan Hammer— better known to latter-day audiences for his *Miami Vice* TV theme, a U.S. number one in 1985.

Hammer's work with the Mahavishnu Orchestra and on Billy Cobham's album *Spectrum* had been a revelation to Beck, helping him through the bad times with BBA. "I had to listen to what was happening and face up to the fact that maybe electronic synthesizers were going to take over. At one point, I honestly felt like giving up. I'd heard enough guitar. The texture of Jan's MiniMoog—I wanted to know all about that, because it was so pure, every phrase was finished off. I learned a hell of a lot from him, to get down to the nuts and bolts of phrasing, hitting where it hurts most."

As usual, he would imbibe all this while working on his cars. "I'd be thinking, 'That was a decent lick there.' There were certain melodic structures to Jan's solos which were just memorable. Jan has a brilliant ear for melody, and that's what makes music. When I found out he had, in fact, learned a lot from me, our friendship got started."

So Hammer came in on what would be Beck's second consecutive instrumental best-seller, *Wired*, also contributing to writing and producing. It proved to be the start of a collaboration that took in his next two albums as well.

After working together, the keyboardist had nothing but admiration for Beck: "He's the only person of his type—which is a genuine '60s rock 'n' roll guitar hero—that actually advanced anywhere beyond the '60s. You take every one of those other guys, from Clapton down to Page and Wood or whatever— they are still sitting where they started, haven't moved one inch. But Jeff has progressed incredibly, because he's open to all kinds of melodic invention."

Starting in October, *Wired* was recorded over an extended period and included a number of different musicians before Jan Hammer came on board in February 1976. Keyboards were contributed by Max Middleton on clavinet and Fender Rhodes, with Jan Hammer lending his presence to four or five of the nine tracks. Bass was taken on by Wilbur Bascomb from the *Blow by Blow* tour, but drummer Bernard Purdie was replaced by Narada Michael Walden (ex-Mahavishnu) on five titles, and Richard Bailey from the previous album was called back for two more.

Once again Beck went to George Martin to produce, with sessions starting at AIR and Trident in London, but Martin's personal involvement came to an end within a few weeks. *Wired* had a harder biting edge than *Blow by Blow*, noticeably more experimental and less structured. This was not by any means a play-it-safe follow-up. "By *Wired* I'd got the power bug back again," Beck explains. "I wanted more vicious power, but with more concise playing—the way Jan plays, that spitfire thing, a million notes but concise. I wanted to take a chance with Mahavishnu-type blasts. I just lost George with that. 'I don't know where the hell you're going,' he'd say."

So Jan Hammer eventually went into the booth to remix most of the tracks, and was entirely responsible for producing his own composition "Blue Wind"—a rampaging Beck/Hammer duel with the two of them playing every instrument.

Much of *Wired* took this direction of virtuosic interplay between the guitarist and his collaborators; but it also went further in re-exploring his rocking roots. If some people were quick to think of it as jazz, Beck would have none of it: "I'm not a jazz guitarist. No way. I consider myself a rock guitarist. If they want to hear jazz they can dig out a multitude of albums and stack them up to the ceiling. But what I'm doing ain't jazz!"

Whatever label you care to give it, Beck's riveting cover of "Goodbye Pork Pie Hat," by the jazz bass supremo Charlie Mingus, was singled out for huge critical acclaim as soon as the album was released in June 1976.

"It's a perfect tune for me. The melody is very simple but the chords are all over the place. The chords are dynamically angular and aggressive, nasty and great. I think what I did was valid. . . . I got a letter from Mingus saying how much he liked it. It blew me away just to know he heard it."

That kind of comment is not unusual from Beck; in conversation, though his sense of self-worth is intact, he's reticent about his own accomplishments. For Beck, the process of creating something in the studio—if he doesn't get it right first time—is often born of anguish, and he's hard on himself because of it. There's a touch of fatalism in there too, a kind of inability to accept that the last piece of brilliance wasn't just a lucky fluke. Beck has always confessed to being entirely at the mercy of his emotions: if there isn't that spark of emotional ignition, then combustion just won't happen.

Still on the subject of "Goodbye Pork Pie Hat," one reviewer pointed out his exceptional use of the Stratocaster on this number, accompanied by the tiny, intimate sounds of the guitar's mechanism: "It is possible on close listening to hear the toggle switch of the guitar moving from position to position, as well as the hum of the amplifiers."

Similarly, on "Blue Wind" you can also hear the perceptible creak of the whammy bar springs; Beck actually wanted to edit out the noise, but Jan Hammer told him he was crazy—"Leave it in, it's cool!"

Of the track "Sophie," Beck remarked "That was fun. What I remember most about that one is the 7/8 time signature. The riff was great because it floated right across, making it accessible to people who would normally have a hard time with the rhythm."

Tapping into the essence of Beck's intensely emotional nature, drummer Michael Walden, who was with the Mahavishnu Orchestra when they toured together, wrote the number "Love Is Green" for him—offering another rare moment of Beck on acoustic guitar, with beautifully reflective, melodic soloing. "He used to psych me out from the side of the stage when my band was doing its set. He'd grab me and say, 'You're just a softie.' I'd say, 'Piss off, I'm not—I'm tough!' He'd tell me I was soft, and that he was going to write me a beautiful melody."

Walden and Beck formed a close and lasting musical relationship which resulted in many informal jams over the years. Beck later played on one title from Walden's *Garden of Love Light* (with Will Lee on bass), and was keen to contribute to further projects, but Walden's hoped-for recording deal didn't materialize.

Of the remaining titles, "Come Dancing" is superb funk, with almost a disco feel, and includes a subtle touch of overdubbed horns. Opening the album at a furious pitch is Max Middleton's "Led Boots," a sideswipe at you-know-who, which combines rhythmically intricate scatting with serious get-down rock 'n' roll. And "Head for Backstage Pass" scats even more wildly, whilst playing with fascinating cross-rhythms. For rhythmic complexity, "Play with Me" is the most remarkable cut on the album, with the insistent jazz beat and even Beck's soaring phrases constantly going across the rhythmic pulse.

Wired didn't quite reach the same dizzy height in the charts as its predecessor, but it too became a million-seller soon after release, earning its gold disc in September and attaining an impressive number 16 in the U.S. (number 38 in the U.K.). Like *Blow by Blow*, sales to date exceed the two million mark, and until Kenny G appeared on the scene, they both represented the highest charting instrumental albums ever recorded.

Another accolade was its nomination for a Grammy Award as Best Pop Instrumental Performance of 1976. And it also won Beck a raft of awards in the 1976 *Guitar Player* Reader's Polls, to add to those won for *Blow by Blow*: Best Overall Guitarist, and a second consecutive award in the categories Best Rock Guitarist and Best Guitar Album. In the jazz oriented *DownBeat* magazine he was voted Rock/Blues Musician of the Year.

Painting with such bold strokes, from a daringly adventurous musical palette, was clear evidence of Beck's determination to produce what he alone wanted—keeping one step ahead of predictability: "You've got to just go through everything, everything. Just go through the mill. Get kicked around, slated for being terrible, you know, just weigh things up."

What's more, he was always ready to step off the treadmill of fame if it got in the way of personal fulfillment. It could scarcely have escaped his notice how the extravagances of fame affected his peers, among whom Mick Jagger and Elton

John found themselves totally divorced from ordinary life. Led Zeppelin's John Paul Jones once said, "It takes me weeks to recover after living like an animal for so long"; and Keith Richards remarked, "It's all you can do to keep yourself going." This was not what Jeff Beck wanted his life to hold in store.

"I don't know what my future plans are going to be," he replied to interview questions. "I think to bring people's emotions out—as would be done in a great play—is my goal, but I want to do it with music and the gut feeling it arouses. Music is the best way of expressing emotions. Everything in the past was playground stuff; now I'm heading for the real thing. I'm not going to grow old wishing I'd done something. That must be the worst killer of all—to know you could've done something that you never did. I know what I want, and I've got to do it."

AS A SIDEBAR to the *Wired* story, Beck invited a band called Upp to join his U.S. tour; Andi Clark from the band had cowritten one of the album's songs, "Head for Backstage Pass." Beck had met them in 1973 and been impressed by the funky white soul group: "Imagine Cobham type funk, but a little bit less complex, with a very spacey Moog player, and a Stylistics voice."

At the time, they were a trio composed of Andi Clark (keyboards), James Copley (drums), and Steven Amazing (bass)—later augmented to a quartet with the addition of David Bunce (guitar).

In September '73 they backed Beck in a *Guitar Workshop* television program on BBC2 titled *Five Faces of Guitar*, hosted by Julian Bream, and featuring John Williams, Paco Peña, John Renbourn, and Barney Kessel. Among his songs were a pre-*Blow by Blow* version of "She's a Woman," and an Upp number, "Get Down in the Dirt." The program was especially memorable for a performance of the famous *Concerto de Aranjuez* by Joaquín Rodrigo, in which the five guitarists each played a short passage—confirming Beck's impressive range as an instrumentalist.

Beck so liked Upp that during August/September that same year he produced and played on their eponymous debut album, eventually released in 1975—the first and last time he has ever produced an outside group—and then appeared on two more songs for their follow-up album *This Way*. (There have been several Upp compilations and rereleases, with varying Beck contributions: please refer to this book's discography for details which have been verified with his management.)

In January 1974 they'd supported BBA on U.K. dates, but this new invitation to open on Beck's *Wired* tour gave them a great chance to appear in the United States. Sadly, they played only a handful of shows, pulling out when their bass player suffered a mental breakdown; subsequently the group disbanded.

Another sad end to a happy relationship occurred with Tommy Bolin's contribution to the same tour. Lately Ritchie Blackmore's replacement in Deep Purple, Bolin's superb work on the album *Spectrum*, with his guitar as counterpoint to Jan Hammer's synthesizer, had opened up avenues of thought for Beck.

Beck with long-time admirer Joe Perry of Aerosmith, on tour in 1976.

The two guitarists had become good friends, and they agreed that Bolin's new road band would back up the Beck/Hammer tour in late 1976. It was after one of these concerts—on 4 December in Miami—that his life was ended by a drug overdose.

UNLIKE *BLOW BY BLOW*, the release of *Wired* was timed to coincide with a mammoth touring schedule, plus a special U.S. compilation album under the wry title *Everything You Always Wanted to Hear by Jeff Beck But Were Afraid to Ask For*.

Faced with the quandary of what backup musicians to use, the answer came in the form of Jan Hammer's own group, which had the advantage of being a cohesive unit already (their album *Oh, Yeah?* was just released). The arrangement was a good solution all round: Beck had a public but no band, and Hammer had a band but no public.

Events started with just one week of rehearsals in April 1976, followed by an unbilled "public dress rehearsal" on 23 May in an Alvin Lee show at London's

Roundhouse (which, to Beck's cynical amusement, set the London press buzzing far more than any scheduled appearance). They then flew to the U.S. for a seven-month tour, during which the explosive Beck/Hammer combination shared bills with such bands as Fleetwood Mac, Journey, Aerosmith, Jefferson Starship, Blue Oyster Cult, and the Doobie Brothers. Although Beck headlined occasionally, the strategy was chiefly to capitalize on guaranteed receipts at the huge stadiums these artists could fill.

Teamed up again with his old pals in Aerosmith, Beck joined them for encores that included "The Train Kept A-Rollin'," which Joe Perry remembered as "one of the highlights—if not *the* highlight—of my career."

For recording the album Beck had leaned heavily on the Stratocaster, now and then turning to the Les Paul on rhythm work for the freshness of a different instrument. Sadly, the McLaughlin Strat had disappeared before touring began: it was stolen in transit when he came to record at Jan Hammer's New York studio, the case arriving empty in a taxi from Kennedy Airport (one hopes there is a special corner of purgatory reserved for guitar thieves!).

Deprived of yet another treasured instrument, he nevertheless seemed happy with a white/rosewood "CBS Seventies" Strat, straight out of the box with no modifications. "It's all in the way you play," he commented. "Like slapping the strings with different degrees of hardness and softness will give you totally different overtones, even on the same note. I could pick up a cheap, £10 guitar and it'd still sound a bit like me, even though it's a piece of rubbish."

He still used Marshall amps, but this time added Univox speakers, and again the booster came in handy "like having a built-in radio in your amplifier: you press the booster and out comes some fellow reading the news, or an entire violin section off the BBC!"

The itinerary was mostly concentrated in North America, followed by New Zealand and Australia, a schedule which lasted into 1977. This suited Beck very well, as it happened, because his rate of earnings by now had pushed him into the "supertax" bracket, under which the iniquitous British tax laws demanded 83 percent in the pound. Since these demands were made retrospectively, and since in the music business you never knew what your earnings were until well after you'd spent them, this meant vast arrears to be paid in subsequent years when you might earn very little (especially if you were Jeff Beck). Until the laws were changed, the only solution was to stay out of the U.K. for at least ten months, save as much as you possibly could, and give it all to the tax man.

On top of that, he felt out of the music scene in England. "It's really sad in London now. There's no electricity any more, not for me anyway. There's no family feeling like there used to be—when you used to know someone who knew someone else, who knew someone else. It used to be fun, but I'm afraid it's gone."

So Beck found himself a house in Los Angeles on Sunset Boulevard, imported his beloved Alsatian, Joe, and proceeded to add to his growing collection of hot rods.

Onstage with keyboard virtuoso Jan Hammer; their various collaborations spanned a period of 20 years.

Basing himself in the United States was the obvious choice: "I'm trying to figure out why I'm more popular there than in England," he told a British reporter. "Americans just seem to accept you more; once you've got good recognition there, the people will follow you. They sniff you out when you're hiding. Whereas over here, if the record's not happening or you don't show, they find someone else to idolize."

Touring with Jan Hammer, however, presented its own problems. Already Hammer's influence was so prominent that many people felt Beck sacrificed too much to the keyboards. His response was simply that he was reluctant to hog all the limelight—a sentiment that Hammer, regrettably, failed to reciprocate when it came to his own role in the partnership.

"What was good about Jan's thing was that whatever shortcomings it had, it still had energy and life in it. But it was redundant from the start, because he had his band and wanted to make himself a star with that band without having me in it. At least he was able to play big, huge arenas with me, where he wouldn't have on his own. So I've done my bit there."

The "shortcomings" Beck referred to so delicately were caused by Hammer's personal stellar aspirations—tongues that were less kind compared him to an ersatz Elton John. But Hammer felt Jeff Beck was huge enough not to have to worry; he didn't realize the guitarist was trying to lay down the blueprint for a long-term thing. Supposed to do just a couple of numbers to get things going, Hammer gradually worked up to as much as forty minutes going totally wild on his portable keyboard, until fans who had come to see Beck lost patience. "Jan was doing half an hour before I went on, and people would start throwing tin cans. I thought, 'If people can throw cans at talent like Jan, I want to get out of this game.' And yet there was that frustration of people not seeing what they paid to see." Eventually a meeting was called to sort things out, followed by the mother and father of a row—but the air was cleared and the tour was able to continue. After that, he said, it was great.

Jan Hammer retained an enormous respect for Beck: "His sound is him, it's the hands, it's how he handles—or manhandles—a guitar. People talk about his ego, but I never really saw his ego at work. Whenever there were troubles, it was more because he wanted so much to be validated and accepted by his peers. Somehow, at certain times in his career, he didn't believe that he was making it, he felt he wanted to be good enough to impress any musician—and he didn't realize he was doing it. So he went through these introspective periods where he felt he had to pull back, even though it meant canceling forty cities and blowing millions of dollars."

Touring with Hammer produced a live album, *Jeff Beck with the Jan Hammer Group Live;* released in March 1977, it reached number 23 in the U.S. Taken from performances at several different venues, Hammer described it as the product of a hundred dates in Canada, America, Australia, and New Zealand. In the opinion of many reviewers, this album is the least essential of any in the Jeff Beck catalog, and in an interview in *Guitar* magazine John Stix referred to it as a big disappointment.

Beck: "Yeah, I know. I never wanted to put that album out, but I was shouted down by the record company. I hated it. I didn't think it was a valid album anyway. All the songs relied on virtuosity, having brilliant solos. That's all we stood for. We were messengers of solos, rather than delivering a really concise piece of music."

That said, the *Live* album at least provides a taste of Beck's stupendous chops, for those (notably in Europe) who missed him at the time, delivered effortlessly with no recourse to studio wizardry. Listen especially to "Full Moon Boogie," and you'll hear guitar work of such complexity it's hard to imagine how he pulled it off live.

On "Sophie" you can also hear the new effect he had introduced during the recordings: a ring modulator, used fleetingly and with typical subtlety, where he hits the note and it rings seconds later. "You'll be playing some phrase, and all of a sudden the noise hits you, even though you actually haven't played any other notes."

The weakest track is the Hammer-dominated "Darkness: Earth in Search of a

With Celia Hammond at CBS Convention Show, July 1978.

Sun," which reviewer Karen Rose rightly suggested should have been the opening cut. "During the tour, it served as Jeff's unannounced entrance. Just pretty synthesizer music again and again, and then a vicious siren of a guitar note as the all-time one jerked forward from stage left and the audience went through instant-freeze shock and then started roaring—for Jeff Beck."

BECK HAD BEEN a tax exile living in the United States since May 1976, and it was not until early 1977 that touring came to an end. New Zealand and Australia were among their last ports of call, the latter especially memorable for the welcome they received when drummer Tony Smith arranged for "a couple of car clubs" to meet them at the airport: their arrival was greeted by a line of vintage hot rods that stretched a mile long!

But by February, Beck had called off any further dates. His urgent priority was to take a well earned rest, and for the next year or so he enjoyed an extended break commuting between England and the United States. By June 1978 he had finally taken root in England again, and later that year another album would start to take shape.

Settled once more in his beloved Sussex home, his immediate concern was to catch up with his hot rod projects. He now had a collection of ten rods, mostly 1930s models, four of which he had left behind in Los Angeles. Among the six Fords in England were his favorite black roadster, a red coupe that he had shipped over and repainted himself, two yellow five-window coupes, one with the legend SuperPro on the nose, and a black five-window coupe with a beautiful flash-and-flames paint job. Soon he was playing host to other collectors, holding hot rod meets at his house.

Between Jeff's pets and Celia's rescued waifs, the menagerie had settled at a total of some 25 cats and four dogs, among them the faithful Joe, who had happily returned with his master to roam again the vast acres of fields and woodlands.

"It's beautiful country—it's *paradise* as far as that goes," he had told *Circus* in 1976. "My folks are dead now, but I've had a lovely lady for about eight years and we get along fine. She stays home and looks after the castle. But I never see anyone, really. People are very reserved, *super* reserved. They're very straight and nice people, but you never get anyone to open out. I like parties—really crazy, zooming parties, but not *stupid*, not wrecking places—just *fun*, you know. And I *love* weird people. I've had some of the best times of my life meeting loony people, and I miss that . . . because I'm a complete lunatic myself."

Of course, music wasn't something he could ignore completely, and he still kept up a modicum of practice. He even had a small studio built at his home, but remarked ruefully that he never used it. "I practice two hours a day, on and off. I don't sit down on a stool for two solid hours and then have a break. When the TV gets boring, which is quite often, I turn the sound down and play without any amplifier. I get exhausted when I play with an amplifier, because sooner or later I start burning up a storm, and then I wish I were on stage!"

Though he'd given himself a rest from touring, Beck sat in on sessions for a few more people during the later 1970s. After *Midnight Special* with Billy Preston, he guested on Preston's 1976 eponymous album and then made soundtrack recordings with Peter Frampton and the Bee Gees on the movie *Sgt Pepper's Lonely Hearts Club Band*. More importantly, he started a collaboration with the brilliant jazz/rock bass player Stanley Clarke. It started with Beck sitting in on two dazzling tracks for Clarke's album *Journey to Love* in 1975, the title track and "Hello Jeff." This was such a success that he contributed to a promo single in 1976—"Life Is Just a Game"—and to two more albums recorded in 1978: *Modern Man* and *I Wanna Play for You*.

Stanley Clarke was impressed by Jeff Beck in many ways: "He's a stylist. I can pick him out anywhere. . . . With Jeff, when he plays, I know it's him; out of all the rock guitar players, he's the most musical."

"The thing I liked most about Jeff," he told *Guitar World*, "was that his music is very much like the way he is as a person, very exciting, pumped-up. When you're around Jeff at his house he's into his cars, kinda laid-back; but once you get close to him and really know him well, you can see that all that is a front—inside he's *wild*. But only on certain occasions, like when you're on tour, do you get to see that, the *real* Jeff. For me it was great to play with him, because I love people who have an over-abundance of energy.

"The real genius of Jeff Beck is that he plays on the fact that he's not a schooled musician, and I think he's one of the few artists that has it really working for him—the things he comes up with are *truly* spontaneous. And the nice thing is that it's put together with the same care that a classical musician would take—the guy knows *exactly* what he wants to do."

Clarke spent some time in England in 1978, and during the summer he and Beck were invited to play at Britain's Knebworth Festival, held annually since 1974 in the impressive natural amphitheatre adjoining the grounds of Knebworth House, one of England's beautiful stately homes. Clarke's drummer Gerry Brown was scheduled to join them, but Brown had to drop out and the appearance never happened.

In November, however, Beck and Clarke teamed up for another project which this time came to fruition. They formed an ad hoc group for a tour of Japan and Europe, with Tony Hymas on keyboards and Simon Phillips on drums. On these dates Beck took an interesting white Stratocaster that he kept in the United States, which had been customized for him by Seymour Duncan. Bought at the Norman Harris guitar shop for $200, it had a rosewood neck dating from 1959 or early 1960 matched to an early '60s body, serial number 56599, with a black pickguard/pickup assembly by Schecter Guitar Research of San Francisco. He also took a rare 1952/53 Esquire with a maple neck and white pickguard, the generous gift of a fan, and the collection was further augmented by his latest interest, a Roland GR-500 guitar synthesizer (he bought two more while he was in Japan).

Curiously, both Phillips and Hymas were second choices for the tour lineup—Phillips instead of Lenny White on drums, and Hymas as an emergency replacement on keyboards for Mike Garson (ex-David Bowie). But as it turned out, the teaming would prove to be an amazingly happy one for Beck. In particular, his almost accidental collaboration with Tony Hymas began a creative musical relationship that would produce inspirational results. Coming from a classically trained background, Hymas' varied career ran the gamut from conducting London's Ballet Rambert to cowriting the theme music for the TV cartoon series *Mister Men*, which Beck would find running insistently through his brain ("Bloody tune—I'm going to do a heavy metal version of that!").

This stunning quartet started out with two weeks in Japan, later taking in Denmark, Norway, France, Holland, Austria, and Spain; but they never played in Britain or the United States.

BY THE TIME their touring finished in July 1979, three years had passed since Beck's last studio album and two since the live release. But the need for a new album hadn't been neglected: Jan Hammer had sent him a cassette the previous year with six or eight tunes on it, some of which were excellent vehicles for Beck, and they had cut several of them in London at sessions during May and October.

However, with the great rapport he had with Tony Hymas, he'd now found himself a new working partner: writing together just seemed to flow instinctively. So Beck and Hymas sat down to complete the much-delayed album.

Thus we find two distinct partnerships apparent on *There and Back*. Hammer is featured on synthesizer for "Too Much to Lose," "You Never Knew," and "Star Cycle," perhaps their best ever collaboration, while Hymas takes on the remainder. Beck decided to handle production, coproducing with Ken Scott, who had so brilliantly engineered *Truth*.

It's on the Tony Hymas sessions that Beck really comes into his own, the outstanding track being the hard-rock oriented "El Becko." Recording with Hymas was done mainly in March 1980 at Abbey Road Studios, and the lineup featured Mo Foster on bass, who was, Beck said, a pleasure to work with. Simon Phillips—by now one of his favorite drummers—was the constant linking factor, superbly holding together both sets.

Nevertheless Beck felt somewhat overawed by this illustrious lineup, and often tried to sneak in his sessions when they weren't looking: "I was surrounded with really hot guys, and it made me a bit nervous. They've been present at some pretty memorable moments, you know. I always worry about that, whether I'm living up to expectations. They may go home that night and go, [*disgustedly*] 'Oh, God.'"

Of "Space Boogie," Beck said it was one of the hardest numbers to get right. "I had about 50 tries at soloing over that, probably because the track was put down with just bass and drums. You really need to be in a mood for that high-speed stuff. You have to be angry, you have to get that kind of naughtiness going, and then let it out. Playing 'Space Boogie' really does the trick if you're feeling a bit annoyed with somebody. I'd have been locked up long ago if I hadn't had a guitar!"

"The Pump," which has since joined the ranks of Beck classics, was described by writer Gene Santoro as "a lovely and at times almost languid ballad with teeth and chops to spare." Both this number and "Star Cycle" would later enjoy rebirths in other media—the latter becoming a television theme, and "The Pump" being used for the soundtrack of the movie *Risky Business*, which saw the debut of a young Tom Cruise before his rise to blue-eyed superstardom.

"The Final Peace" was built from something Tony Hymas started playing at

Stanley Clarke and Jeff Beck captured onstage in Holland, 1978.

Beck's house one day, telling him, "Just listen to these chords and you can blow all over them—but leave it until we get into the studio." So that's exactly what they did, laying it down in a single take.

"It doesn't often happen like that," Beck reflects, "it was just a locked-in mental thing between us. I had no idea what he was playing or what key he was in. I followed him, and he'd pick up from a phrase I'd finished with, and we went on like that." It's since been described as one of the most intriguing instrumentals that Beck has produced.

"'The Final Peace' is some of Beck's most unadulterated, up-front work," *Guitar School* commented, "while 'The Golden Road' builds up to a crescendo not unlike 'Beck's Bolero' some 12 years earlier." Another reviewer thought that "El Becko" had decided strains of *Beck-Ola*'s "Plynth" to it. Indeed, the album seemed to be a summation of the many styles Beck had incorporated into his varied career, including some noticeably more metallic elements.

Released in July 1980, *There and Back* charted at number 38 in Britain, exactly the same placing as his last studio album, *Wired*. In the States it achieved a very satisfying number 21. It was also long overdue on his contract with the long-suffering Epic label. But, as Beck acknowledged, he was lucky enough not to undergo pressure, probably thanks to the success of *Blow by Blow* and *Wired*. "Honestly, I think they'd forgotten I was on the label; when we sent over the master record they were jumping up and down saying how wonderful they always knew I was!"

ON *THERE AND BACK*, Beck was content to use a Strat through virtually the same Marshall amp setup he had with Rod Stewart in the '60s, although reworked by Marshall several times since. "It's amazing—one or two things may have blown up, but it's basically the same thing. In fact, some of the valves—the tubes—have rusted into their sockets and you can't take them out!"

Legendary for the simplicity of his equipment, all he used on the recording was straight guitar. "There might be some double-tracking," he said, "but it's just pure electric guitar. I've got a nice 1954 Fender Stratocaster; it keeps going out of tune but it's got a lovely sound."

The Strat in question was a very special instrument to Beck, a gift from Steve Marriott some three years earlier. He had played it at Marriott's suggestion when he'd gone down to see him at a London recording session, which had turned into a hilarious night of music and booze. Beck loved the guitar for its wonderful sound, and Marriott said, "OK—you can have it."

"He wouldn't have said that if he'd been sober!" Beck joked, but Marriott evidently knew what he was doing, because when Jeff Beck checked with him the next morning, he was insistent that he should keep it. He also gave Beck the history of the guitar. With a serial number of 0062, he told him it was one of the first two dozen Stratocasters ever sold after the first forty had been rejected.

It went through a few changes over the years, the first being a change of neck. Marriott had played it with a Telecaster neck, which Beck replaced with one from a '58 Strat. The pickups, which were original when he received it, unfortunately disappeared later on tour. But he never ceased to love the guitar: "It's got a seasoned ash sunburst body that has cracked due to age and it weighs a ton. It looks just like the Buddy Holly Strat. It's just terrible, but it looks at me and challenges me every day, and I challenge it back. It's difficult to play, it goes out of tune and all that, but when you use it properly it sings to you."

Although there were many glowing reviews of *There and Back*, others had expectations that weren't fulfilled. David Fricke in *Musician* felt that after a gap of three years people expected him to take more drastic steps forward: "In spite of great playing and clever twists, it sounded like the work of a recluse, not an outlaw."

Beck later admitted he was not wholly satisfied either. "If I had the knowledge about recording that I have now, it would not have sounded that way. I would have gone much more edgy. It's so beautifully recorded it sounds tame. But instead of fighting back and putting out another album on a different tangent, I just lost the players and lost the momentum. They wanted to go out and experiment with other bands, which is what they did—I couldn't get them back again.

"But if you look at the gigs we did to back up that album, they were all pretty good. I wanted people to walk out with their jaws on the floor and they did. I needed to back that up with another album, going more commercial and below the belt. But I didn't. I disappeared, prat that I am."

From these and other comments, it seems a note of staleness had already crept in. As it turned out, *There and Back* would be his last excursion into jazz-rock.

It was also the last album on which he used a pick. "I kept dropping it in the '70s from being drunk a bit—a lot!—and in the end I just carried on with my thumb and fingers. One night I realized I'd done half an hour without picking it up—of course I knew the whole audience was waiting for me to do just that, and I thought, 'Sod 'em!'"

As someone who rarely plays conventional rhythm parts, preferring single-note lines and double-stops (and sometimes mind-blowing triple-stop bends), fingerpicking holds no disadvantages for Beck. On the contrary, it gives him greater subtlety and dynamic range, allowing him to use such techniques as pulling the strings back for a percussive snap, or plucking several strings at once for a full, ringing chord.

The year 1980 involved touring extensively with the *There and Back* lineup, starting in the U.S. and going on to Japan. *Creem* magazine covered his New York concert on 12 October, and declared it was a reaffirmation of why Jeff Beck was the supreme guitarist's guitarist.

"Standing at mid-stage, back cocked so that his body resembled a slight S, Beck looked the role of pure and total guitarist. Lean as a rail, his rooster hair hung with the same lazy authority as Keith Richards', his grip on his Fender Stratocaster as assured as Hendrix at his peak . . . investing his latest album with all the passion it needed in his live renditions, and even *singing* a zesty blues in a raw but exuberant voice. A smile on his angular face, Beck winced, then beamed when he hit the magic note or run that tore down the spine. With the pure power of his guitar, the night was Beck's."

Touring also included dates during March 1981 in Britain, where it had been seven years since his last live appearance. "I was very worried beforehand," he said, "but it thrilled me the way the audiences listened. You could hear a pin drop between numbers."

On 10 March, at London's final sellout Hammersmith Odeon show, Beck brought Jimmy Page onstage as a surprise guest. The last time Page had played publicly was the previous July, at Led Zeppelin's last concert in Berlin. Since then, the band had ceased performing after the shock of John Bonham's death from alcohol poisoning. Page was shaken to the core at the loss of the crazy, warmhearted drummer who had shared his life for twelve long years, and had withdrawn from the rock scene.

Beck announced, at the end of the show, that he wanted to introduce "an old school friend." Whereupon Jimmy Page walked on from the wings to join him for a rocking encore of "Going Down." It was a moment of sheer emotion for the two guitarists, who had last performed together publicly more than 14 years ago.

John Swenson's review for *Guitar World* marveled at Beck's "gut-wrenching choruses straight out of his glory days, alternating impossibly beautiful note clusters with sudden explosive forays that sounded like head-on collisions between starships."

Swenson continued: "The man has always insisted on playing his music the way he wanted it—he may have sacrificed some popularity as a result, but the satisfaction he gained in the process more than made up for the loss. There will probably be plenty of good music to come from Beck, but he's already made the contribution of a master. The rest is gravy."

12 Other People's Tunes

WITH THE RELEASE of *There and Back*, Jeff Beck had rounded off the decade having acquired a whole new style and range, a whole new group of musical associates, and a whole new audience. In marked contrast to the Jeff Beck who had ended the '60s as the gutsiest of heavy rockers, in 1978 he'd won a readers' poll for Best Jazz Guitarist in *Playboy* ("I think they must have been confusing me with Joe Beck!").

But Beck is not your average guitar icon. Just when you thought it was safe to hang a label on him, he started turning up in some unexpected places. By the early '80s he had exhausted his enthusiasm for the genre which was now known as jazz-rock fusion; it had, he believed, become discredited. For all that it married different styles to produce new and interesting forms, he felt the result was neither fish nor fowl. Worse than that—each element had detracted from the other to produce a sort of thinking man's Muzak.

"'Fuzak,' Simon Phillips called it. And when I heard him say 'Fuzak,' I went *phtttht*—boxed it up and threw it in a bin."

Admittedly, he felt there was some nice work on those records. And the phase had been good for him in many ways. "I just threw myself to the lions, so to speak, playing with people like Jan [Hammer] and Steve Kindler," he told Brad Tolinski in a *Guitar World* interview. "I was completely outclassed—they knew all the diatonic, pentatonic rubbish and I didn't. It was a humbling experience because I realized they were real musicians and I was just some guy holding a guitar. But I think they liked me because I wasn't chained by all this knowledge."

Tolinski, however, believed that *Blow by Blow* and *Wired* were Beck at his peak. "Though described as 'fusion,' both albums easily rose above most of the pyrotechnical twaddle usually associated with that genre. Like Thelonius Monk, Bob Dylan, Hendrix and a small handful of other musicians, Beck had arrived at a sound and voice so intensely personal that it transcended such generic terms as 'jazz-rock guitarist.' The only way to adequately describe this music is to slap it down and turn up the volume."

But somehow, in all those intervening years, Beck felt he had never recaptured the lasting satisfaction of his early roots. "I didn't like the '60s and '70s, basically. I hated them. Around me were a lot of things I had nothing to do with, like flower power, and *awful* things like flared trousers. The mid '60s were okay because every day was a *hurricane* in the Yardbirds. I just feel that from the late '60s, right up to about '78, I didn't fit in. I felt like a total misfit in music. I always felt [*plays imaginary violin*] I was totally alone."

The only thing that had truly revitalized him in the '70s, he declared, was punk—"which I loved and thought was a smack in the eye for the world. It made things a lot more exciting and insecure. It was getting *very* stodgy. I felt, here comes some trouble!"

FEW WHO DELIVERED that smack in the eye had survived beyond the initial onslaught; but then it wouldn't have been punk had it been otherwise. Of more enduring fabric was new wave, from which source came the Police, infusing attitude and energy with the irresistible rhythm of reggae—a course followed by several two-tone bands that emerged at the time, including UB40 and a bunch of nutters known as Madness.

Meanwhile the home fires of mainstream rock had been kept burning by a few stalwarts who refused to be buried under all the newfangled genres; among them were Bad Company, formed by Paul Rodgers as a heavier successor to Free, and the Irish band Thin Lizzy, which produced two outstanding frontliners in Phil Lynott and Gary Moore. But there was little of rock that had not by then assimilated a host of other influences.

On the hard rock scene, Led Zeppelin had straddled the '70s like a colossus, clearly dictating the direction that seriously heavy rock would take from now onwards.

If those of finer sensibilities couldn't take Zeppelin's bombast and braggadocio, they had only to look at their effect on the music biz environment. Building their supremacy on the giant U.S. stadium circuit, they reversed the status of performing artist as victim, finally dictating every aspect of each engagement including an unheard-of 90/10 box office split. Though their touring schedules might be just as punishing, never again would any leading group endure the cattle-truck treatment or financial shenanigans of the '60s.

At the same time, Led Zeppelin broke free of the constricting format of the single. Their decision to release almost nothing on single marked a significant change towards album buying. Without such a shift, one wonders how and when a mass market would ever have arrived to make the CD a viable format.

The British triumvirate of Zeppelin, Black Sabbath, and Deep Purple ("we're as valid as anything by Beethoven") between them forged the archetypal edifice that would become heavy metal: riff-oriented guitar, cataclysmic vocal performances, thundering bass, and powerhouse drumming, the whole delivered at homicidal volume levels. Few thought the genre would outlast the passing of Zeppelin or the violent personnel upheavals of Sabbath and Purple; but heavy metal proved everybody wrong. The demon guitar cult started by Tony Iommi, Ritchie Blackmore and Jimmy Page found second-generation successors in Ozzy Osbourne's Randy Rhoads and the manic, speed-freak guitar of AC/DC's gloriously demented Angus Young.

Later came the '80s "hair metal" bands like Poison, Warrant, Slaughter, and Mötley Crüe. But none approached the hell-bent suicidal delinquency of Guns N' Roses, echoing the moral illiteracy of punk in a love/hate relationship with their public. And not to be overlooked amid the hype and chaos was the substantial, if erratic, guitar bravura of Slash, a latter-day guitar hero in the classic mold.

From even the smattering of names mentioned here, one thing is strikingly evident: the prominence of rock guitar wizardry marked a conspicuous development. While ten years earlier you could have counted the acknowledged masters on your two hands and had a few fingers to spare, by the start of the '80s there had emerged a wealth of ferocious fretmanship.

It was at the heavy end of the scale that an outrageously brilliant young guitarist appeared whose name would soon be on everyone's lips. In an era when the screaming heavy metal solo had become a derided formula, Eddie Van Halen redefined it as an art form by the dazzling skill and wild emotion of his playing.

It was Van Halen's blistering tour de force "Eruption" on his first album, at the age of 21, that burned every guitarist who heard it. Recorded without overdubs, the dizzying speed of his scale passages and two-handed arpeggios, with the aid of right-hand fingertapping, sent guitarists rushing to the fretboard to work out how the hell he did it. Van Halen was the template for all the maxi-shredders who would follow in the technique-dominated '80s; but, emblazoned though his playing was with technical flash, he was also one hundred percent rooted in pure rock 'n' roll.

Jeff Beck was quick to pay tribute to Van Halen's brilliance, and recognized those roots immediately. Asked what he thought of the current crop of young guns, he replied: "They're all *amazing* really. Eddie Van Halen? Yeah, he's lovely. He's Mr. Rock 'n' Roll—more rock 'n' roll than I will *ever* be!"

Among Beck's former colleagues, Rod Stewart now embraced his purple period as a pop/glam megastar. His singing had matured, yet the person seemed submerged behind the chosen image, descending the scale from good-time adventurer to tacky Hollywood vamp. Meanwhile, Carmine Appice had joined the Stewart roadshow, as had bassist Philip Chenn. Tim Bogert had started his own band, Pieces. And Ronnie Wood was now established as a Rolling Stone ("which is cool but kind of like taking a Civil Service job," as Lester Bangs memorably commented).

Cozy Powell in 1981 had put together his second solo album, *Tilt*, and invited Beck to play (he'd been unavailable for the previous one, *Over the Top*, in 1980). Beck performed on two Jan Hammer songs—"Cat Moves" and "Hot Rock"—which he had featured on tour with Stanley Clarke. His dabblings with guitar synthesizers can also be heard on Cozy Powell's album, though they didn't hold his attention for very long.

Around this time there were other get-togethers with old friends and colleagues. One was in mid 1980 on the Paul Samwell-Smith produced *How Many Ways* by Murray Head, reissued under the title *Voices* (he had earlier contributed to a 1973 Murray Head recording, *Nigel Lived*, but there was no Beck guitar on the album when it was released). And for the Tony Hymas synth-pop group Ph.D. he recorded the song "I Didn't Know," uncredited, on the band's 1983 album *Is It Safe?* It came out as a single in Italy and promptly topped the charts there for seven weeks.

SINCE HIS OWN last album, however, the Jeff Beck profile had remained resolutely low: a conscious decision to keep his head down while punk and heavy metal exploded all around him.

John Paul Jones once said that Beck could have been as big as Zeppelin, "but the man is not consistent enough." The fact was true, but not the underlying assumption: Beck didn't *want* the bigness, nor all the baggage that went with it. He could never box himself in, as he felt Jimmy Page had done: "I don't have to rely on the success of a band—or shaking that off. No one says 'Jeff Beck of so-and-so.' If Jimmy Page leaves Led Zeppelin, it's gonna be 'Jimmy Page, ex-Led Zeppelin guitarist' forever. It'll be twenty years before he can shake off that tag. Even though I do desperately need people to play with, I'm still slowly starting to get a name. By conforming, wearing funny glitter suits, I could probably sell out the place and become a big, huge star. That's not very appealing to me, to be just a commodity."

"I wouldn't swap places with anybody," he said in 1980, "not in the last six years."

Nevertheless, Beck battled with depression after *There and Back* as he entered another hiatus between styles. Not knowing where his next move would take him, he turned to re-explore a lifetime's obsession with the drums. In '81 and '82 he practiced drums daily—but then the guitar was sitting there reproachfully. Unlikely to become a convincing drummer, he realized this was valuable guitar time wasted.

A clue to the five-year gap before his next solo album may be detected in a personal choice to be sparing in his output. "It's an instant death once you start turning out loads of great albums, because you're so near the pinnacle of your career and then you can only go down. I like to just turn out an album when I think I've got enough decent material. If people are around to buy it, then that's all I want."

In the midst of these reveries, Beck was spurred into action by his old mate Eric Clapton. With a friendship that went back fifteen years, they had still appeared publicly together only three times—and all three were jams. The first was one night in 1966 when Clapton had jammed with the Yardbirds at the Marquee Club, and the second was two years later when he'd joined the Jeff Beck Group at the Scene in New York. The last occasion was in May 1980 at the Civic Hall in Guildford, Surrey, on the closing "party" night of Clapton's brief U.K. tour. It was a moment to treasure when Jeff Beck joined Eric Clapton and Albert Lee for a brilliant guitar workout on the song "Ramblin' on My Mind," which the roadies decided to celebrate by spraying the entire band with crazy foam.

Now Clapton suggested an official onstage reunion. He wanted Beck to join him for benefit shows on 9-12 September 1981 for Amnesty International, mounted at London's Theatre Royal, Drury Lane, under the title *The Secret Policeman's Other Ball*.

These Amnesty events had started in the '70s with riotously successful all-star comedy revues, later introducing music into the mixture. The 1981 concerts starred a galaxy of British comedians which included John Cleese, Billy Connolly, and Rowan Atkinson. An equally star-studded roll call of musicians interspersed numbers between the sketches, including Clapton and Beck, Sting, Phil Collins, Donovan, and Bob Geldof. Both an album and a video were released.

Beck and Clapton performed three numbers together in a special set in the middle of the show, as well as jamming on Bob Dylan's "I Shall Be Released" at the end. Clapton took lead on a searing "Crossroads," then Jeff Beck held the theater spellbound with "Cause We've Ended as Lovers," played on his Seymour Duncan Tele-Gib. Finally Beck laid down some pulverizing blues chops as they traded licks on Bobby Bland's classic "Farther Up the Road." "Beck was the more eloquent on this occasion," one reviewer commented. "In fact, Eric's description of Jeff Beck as a gunslinger is very accurate."

WITH THE EXCELLENT sales of his last four albums—two in the Top Twenty and two more in the Top Forty—Jeff Beck was enjoying some of the comforts of success. He seldom emerged in the public eye during this period, but one appearance in early 1981 is worth mentioning.

Judd Lander, a promotions man for Epic, had secured an exclusive interview for Beck to publicize *There and Back* on the well-regarded TV music program *Old Grey Whistle Test*. Having pulled out all the stops to promote his coup, Lander was dismayed when Beck, unpredictable as ever, changed his mind at the last minute. "It wasn't that Jeff had an ego problem," as Lander told *MOJO* magazine; "it was more that he felt uncomfortable being asked questions about himself. He felt his music should do all the talking."

Nevertheless Lander was in a serious fix. "I decided to hatch a plot to retrieve the situation. Armed with a set of bagpipes, I jumped into a limo and sped down to Tunbridge Wells in search of Jeff's hideaway."

On arrival at Beck's "castle," Lander immediately started systematically removing his clothes—much to the consternation of the chauffeur. Equipped with bagpipes and little else, he then marched up the long and winding driveway playing a lament to the tune of "Hi Ho Silver Lining."

A grinning Beck eventually appeared at the door, quickly ushering him in with the immortal greeting, "Who the fuck are you?"

At length, after plenty of lubrication and a lot of waffle on Lander's part, a deal was struck and Beck agreed to do the show. "With minutes to spare, the limo then sped my entourage into Shepperton studios, [where] Jeff was greeted with all the pomp of a royal visitor."

As the live transmission got under way, interviewer Anne Nightingale (and the watching public) would soon learn what that secret deal entailed when an unscheduled wheezing and wailing was heard from the wings. With Beck trying hard to feign surprise, a lone piper marched gravely and ceremoniously in front of the cameras . . . without a stitch of clothing.

March 1983 saw Beck again enjoying himself on TV when he was invited to perform with his schoolboy inspiration, Les Paul, for a new U.S. program, *Rock 'n' Roll Tonight*. The veteran guitarist had been asked to select his own guest for the "superstar jam" segment of the show, and his answer was immediate: Jeff Beck. In Paul's words, "I think the guy plays great, I really do. One of the things that attracted me to him was his consistency, and the second thing was his phrasing. And the heart that he played with. Among all the guitar players that I know of in the rock field, Jeff has more taste and more going for him than any of them."

Recording the show at Perkin's Palace in Pasadena, California, they had fun playing several songs together. One of them was "Chicken Shack Blues," during which, when Jeff Beck unleashed some smoking boogie licks, Les Paul reached over in mock protest and yanked out the plug on his power cord. This set the tone for the rest of the number, with Beck's roadie doing the same to Paul, but both guitarists managed to reconnect and carry on with scarcely a beat missed. There was more slapstick as Beck sauntered over to detune Paul's guitar pegs, then as the duet came to a blazing close, Beck had the final word: he grabbed a moment of extra glory with some unexpected solo runs slipped in after the whole thing had finished.

SUMMERTIME, AS USUAL, offered opportunities for Beck to work on his prized hot rod collection; but as the days grew shorter, he had an interesting proposition to consider. Exactly two years after *The Secret Policeman's Other Ball*, he was invited to do another charity project with Eric Clapton.

Held at the Royal Albert Hall in London, the first night on 20 September was in support of ex-Faces bass man Ronnie Lane and the fund he had helped to set up, Action Research into Multiple Sclerosis—an illness which he was himself fighting. The second night was in aid of The Prince's Trust, the charity established by the Prince of Wales to benefit young people in Britain.

The ARMS concert featured solo sets by Clapton and Beck, plus Andy Fairweather Low and Stevie Winwood. It was even more remarkable for a historic reunion of the two legendary Yardbirds with that third Yardbird lead guitarist, Jimmy Page, who was tempted out of deep seclusion to make the occasion truly memorable.

Armed with a new guitar, a '57 sunburst Strat reissue, Beck came on after the interval: "Vibrant, animated and heroic, he stood out as the show's technical virtuoso," according to *Guitar Player*, as he fluently delivered a compilation of numbers taken from various stages of his career—"Star Cycle," "The Pump," "Led Boots," "Goodbye Pork Pie Hat," and "People Get Ready." Much to everyone's surprise, he even sang his '60s hit, "Hi Ho Silver Lining," with which he was enthusiastically helped by the audience. It had been released a third time the previous year, reaching number 62 in Britain, and it seemed he was now reconciled to people's tremendous fondness for the song. "I've seen the video,

Les Paul trades licks with his favorite student: *Rock 'n' Roll Tonight* TV show, March 1983.

and the audience looks pumped up about it. So I'm not embarrassed by that anymore."

"Star Cycle," from *There and Back*, was also instantly recognized—it was currently the theme for Britian's Channel 4 TV music show *The Tube* ("my sort of 'electro' style seemed to suit that era with computer graphics and digital this and that"). Hosted by ex-Squeeze keyboardist Jools Holland, *The Tube* had a great following and eventually found its way on to MTV.

Jimmy Page followed Beck's set. It was a daunting moment for Page, strung out and playing his first major gig since Led Zeppelin days. Jeff Beck was one of those whose urging got him there.

"The ARMS concert—the first one—was a bit shaky," Beck recalled. "We were all shaky because of all being there on the same stage. At rehearsal I didn't know how Jimmy was going to make it through. But when he got onstage there was a big roar and he was the same old Jimmy Page—magic! He just hovers on the brink of disaster—kind of like Keith Richards." After an emotionally charged instrumental performance of "Stairway to Heaven," the audience erupted as Beck, Clapton and the rest joined Page for "Tulsa Time"—the first time the three ex-Yardbirds had played together in public.

Beck: "The ARMS thing was a great help to me. It was an opportunity to help Ronnie Lane and a cause of the magnitude of ARMS, and a great excuse to get back onstage again. What amazed me was that it was like a huge amateur band that had just been given a contract. What you had was all that talent onstage, everybody hanging their ass out of the window for the world to see, whether they were good, bad or indifferent."

It was such a success that the entire cast, with Winwood replaced by Joe Cocker, agreed to play nine further shows in the United States. This time, Beck and Clapton came on with Page to trade solos in "Stairway to Heaven," and the finale led into Joe Cocker's celebrated version of "With a Little Help from My Friends," with everyone jamming—a song with special significance for Jimmy Page, who had played on Cocker's original 1968 recording. There was yet more nostalgia in New York, when Ronnie Wood joined his former colleague Jeff Beck in the encores. Beck could scarcely believe it when everyone in Madison Square Garden rose to their feet at the end of his set.

Once more the critics gave rave reviews to Beck, many of them agreeing that his was the outstanding guitar performance; Eric Clapton was quoted as saying he was just the warm-up act for the two stars of the show—Beck and Page. To *Guitar Player* he commented that playing with Jeff Beck made him begin to think that Beck was probably the finest guitarist he'd ever seen.

"You can't imagine how that makes me feel," was Beck's reaction when he was told. "For him to say that, it really means a lot. It sort of blows me away. . . . Old Eric—he never seemed to be the slightest bit interested in my style. Judging by that story in *Rolling Stone*, he's been through the mill a few times. I was almost crying when I read it."

All the musicians had invested in filming the Albert Hall concert, which was later released on a video, now discontinued, but there was never an official album (Beck: "Well, you can't put the bootleggers out of business!"). The only commercially available LP was a limited edition of a concert at the Cow Palace in San Francisco, put out by a local radio station. A Cow Palace video was also shot, but contractual problems prevented its release. All that remain available are selections from performances by Beck, Page and Clapton at the Albert Hall, on the MIA video *Rock Legends*.

Backstage at the December concert in New York, guitar manufacturer Grover Jackson arrived to present Jeff Beck with a new three-pickup/Kahler whammy Jackson Soloist, with the result that Beck was impressed enough to add the pink Jackson to his collection of preferred instruments. In fact, he played that night's encore with his new acquisition. Later the company would make two more Soloist models to Beck's specifications, a Fender whammy on one and a Floyd Rose on the other, both in bright orange (to match his tennis shoes). Beck had reached the point of not wanting to take his most prized guitars on the road, and he found the Jackson had the sound and feel of the Strat, with pickups that let it sound like a Gibson Les Paul if he cranked it up. Later he would revert to his all-time favorite Fenders, but for a while the Jackson appealed as a kind of marriage between the two.

Jimmy Page, Joe Cocker, Eric Clapton and Jeff Beck perform "With a Little Help from My Friends": concert in aid of ARMS at Madison Square Garden, December 1983.

There was a reunion, too, with Seymour Duncan, who had some new pickups for his favorite guitarist to try. As he watched Beck casually noodling to himself, Duncan was amazed by his range. "He started playing things I never knew he could play, free jazz and things like that." As a result of Duncan's visit, Beck acquired "an old battered '53 Tele" from the electronics wizard. "Seven hundred bucks—I couldn't care less," he declared. "I picked it up and it felt like I got my old friend back again." It became one of the instruments that Beck would use most frequently, especially when he was playing to himself at home.

THE YEAR 1983 was certainly a time for working with old friends, with no fewer than three such get-togethers being thanks to Carmine Appice, at whose home in Los Angeles Beck was a regular guest. During one of those occasions he joined Stanley Clarke on his new album *Time Exposure*, which was released the following year. Later Beck played with Appice and the rest of Vanilla Fudge on their reunion album, *Mystery*, on which he performed two numbers—billed as "J Toad."

Also in L.A., in 1982, it happened that he bumped into Rod Stewart again (a not-so-accidental meeting also engineered by Carmine Appice). Stewart's greeting was effusive, and by the time Beck returned to California with ARMS the following year, his former partner seemed keen to record something together. "Okay," said Beck, "put your money where your mouth is!" A few nights later, Beck joined the band for an Indian meal. Throwing caution to the winds, and numerous champagne cocktails down his throat, Stewart declared he wanted to do something the very next day.

Beck was stumped; but inspiration struck during a visit to the home studio of an old friend, keyboardist Duane Hitchings. "He had a house guitar. You can imagine what that was like. One string was missing, action about two inches high at the lowest point! I picked it up and the only thing that sounded any good was the D chord. All the other chords were completely off."

The only number he could think of in D was the old Curtis Mayfield song "People Get Ready," originally a hit for the Impressions in 1965. It was a favorite of Beck's, and one that BBA used to perform on their 1972 European tour. Hitchings got the right feel immediately: by some kind of magic it had Rod Stewart stamped all over it. Within minutes Beck had come up with the guitar hook that would be the making of the song. "We took it up to Rod that night. He was on the phone in this glass booth in the house, not interested at all. And then he heard the song coming out and he ran up the stairs, and the next day we cut it in about two hours."

Using his pink Jackson for the recording, Beck remembered the whole thing was over in about two takes: "It was quick, but we had the blueprint. It's a great anthem for people, a great softener. It warms the heart." But although the song worked beautifully, it actually sat gathering dust for two full years before resurfacing on Beck's next album. It would also lead to further excursions with Rod Stewart, as we shall see later.

Meanwhile, only a few months before the ARMS concert which reunited Clapton, Beck and Page, the three other surviving members of the Yardbirds joined up again for a special occasion. This was on 22–23 June for the 20th anniversary celebrations of London's evergreen Marquee Club. Calling themselves Box of Frogs, and adding vocalist John Fiddler (ex-Medicine Head and British Lions), Paul Samwell-Smith, Chris Dreja and Jim McCarty were so enthused by the get-together that they signed to CBS/Epic and went into the studio to record an album. Among the artists they invited to join their sessions was Jeff Beck.

"They sent me a demo tape and I was pleasantly surprised," Beck explained. "They've got just the right guy to replace Keith [Relf]—you couldn't pick up the phone in L.A. and order a more perfect replacement. So I did four tracks on the album."

Described in one report as "Beck's stunning reappearance as a badass rocker," a collection of cooking guitar solos were overdubbed at a farmhouse on Christmas Eve, with his former colleagues making a party out of the occasion. "I just went ahead and did my best for an afternoon. I say an afternoon, but I set up at three and we were working until about eleven at night. And [laughs] half an hour off for a drink. I just love the guys. They're very bright and funny people and it's hard to say no."

Released in Britain as *Back Where I Started*, the album was titled *Box of Frogs* in the United States, where it scored a minor chart success. Aided by some excellent guitar work by Beck, it's a relaxed, very collectable LP of straight-ahead bluesy rock. A follow-up album was later released with Clapton and Page; but the group without its guest performers had no staying power and the reunion project fizzled and died.

WITH ALL THESE activities, it seemed that Beck had now made a decision to get out and about in a way he had never countenanced before. Carmine Appice noticed how he seemed to have mellowed of late: "Jeff's changed a lot. A lot of people used to take his insecurities as being ego trips. But he's come out of his shell somewhat and isn't so insecure as a person. Playing with all these different people on their albums, doing the ARMS concerts—normally he wouldn't do stuff like that."

Though the underlying reason may have been just to keep busy, at least he was working with people who gave him a lot of pleasure. "Why not," was his philosophy, "if they have the tunes?"

Beck's next recording project went straight to the heart of his innermost allegiances. One weekend in March, ex-Led Zeppelin singer Robert Plant got together with Beck and a bunch of other musicians, and the result was a mini album under the name of the Honeydrippers. It also signaled a brief reunion between Robert Plant and Jimmy Page, their first time in the studio together since their Led Zep days.

The laid-back atmosphere and vintage '50s tunes hit just the right note for everyone. Beck's guitar is heard on Ray Charles' "I Got a Woman," and Beck and Page get down to some seriously swinging good-time rock 'n' roll on the big band version of Roy Brown's "Rockin' at Midnight," complete with boogie piano and wailing saxes.

Beck: "I went along there with my guitar in hand, plugged in, and I think we did the whole lot in one afternoon. Nobody knew what was going on, and that's what was so good. We didn't have any more studio time booked, so we just rattled them off. I think we did two takes of each song, no overdubs—it was just one, two, three, four, off we go!"

Issued under the anonymous title of *The Honeydrippers Volume One*, the modest little effort went platinum in December 1984, just three months after its release. The single "Sea of Love" hit number three in the U.S. charts, then "Rockin' at Midnight" reached number 25, to the delight of all concerned.

Also in March of 1984, Jeff Beck joined Stevie Ray Vaughan for the first time onstage at a CBS Records convention in Hawaii. Vaughan had formed an all-star Texas blues revue for the event, and Beck just jumped up and had a play with them: "It was a surprise. I don't think even Stevie Ray knew." It was pretty much a jam for everyone, according to Vaughan. They played about five songs, of which three—"Jeff's Blues," "Hawaiian Eye," and "Lost Cause"—were featured in a TV broadcast of the event.

THE YEAR 1984 was full of star-studded sessions with people whose work he'd always admired, a trend which began with an invitation out of the blue from Tina Turner.

Turner was touring in England and recording an album while she was there, which she was hoping would give her that much-needed breakthrough in her new life as a solo performer. By the time it came to April, she was short of the last couple of titles to complete the set. Her manager Roger Davies called Dire Straits guitarist Mark Knopfler's manager, who suggested "Private Dancer," along with a number called "Steel Claw" by Paul Brady. "Private Dancer" was a song Knopfler had penned for his album *Love over Gold*, but held back because he felt it needed a female singer. Turner was thrilled with the bittersweet torch song, a wonderful vehicle that might have been written especially for her.

It was the day before Mark Knopfler was due to leave for New York, but he quickly laid down a guide vocal track, at the same time offering Turner his band for the recording. Since its lead guitarist was missing, Roger Davies immediately thought of Jeff Beck.

Beck's devotion to Tina Turner was already known to Davies: when she performed at the Venue the previous year, he had bought his own ticket to be sure of the best seat he could get, and loved every minute of her performance.

As he told *Musician* magazine, "When Tina Turner's name came up, I would have bicycled to where she wanted me to play. A long time ago I was asked who would I like to play with most, and I said Ike and Tina Turner. Ever since 'River Deep, Mountain High' that voice was haunting me, how my guitar could fit in with that."

His contribution to the album's title song put the brilliant finishing touches to Knopfler's evocative dance-hall hostess lament. "I love Tina Turner. I did that session in about a half-hour; it was thrilling working with her." Released in July 1984, *Private Dancer* was a landmark for Turner. It went platinum within a month, and sold ten million worldwide.

Beck came up with the guitar sound by using a pair of Roland digital echoes with his Jackson Soloist: "It's a bit heavy metal looking, but it's bloody good. It goes up to high C, which you can scream and it sounds almost like a whistle. That's on the thing called 'Steel Claw,' it's almost beyond human hearing." (Beck's blistering licks on "Steel Claw" are pure combustion—check out the moment when Tina Turner shrieks "Jeff Beck!" as he skyrockets into the first solo.)

"Just seeing someone else's problems on tape, and then seeing the slot that they want me to fill in, gets my mind working at about a hundred miles an hour—because I've got to be quick and I've got to *thrill* them, all in about two or three hours. *That* is a great challenge. I play purely from the heart. It'll either happen or it won't. With Tina I had a fantastic time—we got blasted at the end of the session [*laughs*] and she carved her name on my guitar!"

In *Guitar Player* Beck recounted how he asked for Tina Turner's autograph on his pink Jackson as a permanent souvenir. "She got out this green felt-tip pen, and of course it wouldn't stay on a polished, painted guitar with grease all over it. So she said, 'Do you want it to stay on there for a real long time?' I said, 'Yeah. Write into the woodwork. Go with it.' And she got a knife out of her bag. First of all she started chipping away, trying to make a nice engraved job. I said, 'Never mind that. Just write your name.' She just tore into it and rubbed nail polish on it. I was totally speechless, but very proud."

Amazingly, this was the first time he ever talked to Tina Turner, even though the Yardbirds had toured with her in 1966. "I was too scared," he confessed. "We were shaking in the next dressing room. We were all just boys there, trying to be macho, and then she came on and wiped us all out!"

Asked whether he'd like to work with her again, he clearly would have loved the opportunity—"I was just hoping she'd ask me to form a band or something," he said, only partly tongue in cheek. "I was thinking how great it would be. I would definitely like to do 'Steel Claw' live, just go *nuts* for about twenty minutes!"

Immediately following his recording with Tina Turner, it was Beck's turn to fly to New York for studio work with Nile Rodgers: this was to produce a new album of his own, which we will come to later in our story. While he was there, his guitar was enlisted for another female star from the '60s—Diana Ross—who was working on her album *Swept Away*.

"I was in the studio doing some overdubbing and she came in. We were introduced and she said, 'My God, it's hot in here . . . I mean your music is so hot. Would you come and put some heat on my record one day?' So we went down to Soundworks Studio and I was totally in awe of that golden voice."

Straight after his initial album sessions with Nile Rodgers, Beck was on the move again. This time he flew down to Compass Point Studios in the Bahamas to spend three weeks laying down tracks with Mick Jagger. Ever since the episode when he'd fled from joining the Rolling Stones, Beck always seemed to find himself apologizing each time he met his old friend Stu Stewart. So he told Stewart to tell Jagger he'd be glad to do some guitar for him if ever he wanted. The result was a request to play on Mick Jagger's first solo album, *She's the Boss*.

The Stones had recently left Atlantic and had signed with Columbia instead; and Jagger, with an eye on the heady success of such stars as Elton John, Rod Stewart, David Bowie, and the new young phenomenon Prince, had simultaneously signed a deal to record solo.

Altogether Beck contributed six tracks to *She's the Boss*. Apart from "Just Another Night," for which he used Jagger's Gibson J-300 acoustic, his main guitars were his pink Jackson and a hybrid Telecaster with a '54 body and newer, fairly chunky neck, known to Beck as his "Seymour Duncan Frankenstein." He used the Tele for the main riff throughout "Lucky in Love." And the solo? "The solo has barking noises—that was just a go-crazy Jeff type thing!" For the solo on "Lonely at the Top" he brought out his '50s reissue sunburst Stratocaster.

All the tracks were cut in the studio with a drummer and bass player, playing just like a live band. But Jagger didn't want to tell Jeff Beck what to do, and Beck didn't know what Mick Jagger was looking for: he said they were almost like a pair of old ladies being polite to one another. It was only when they came to "Lonely at the Top" that he really began to reach Jagger ("he wanted some really wild stuff").

"Mick's a very moody guy," Beck recalls. "He would strum chords for about three hours to get into the mood. By that time, I was tired. There's this extra nervous condition I have when I'm not in there for my own stuff; I want to get in there and do it straightaway. I was thinking of his dollar, his time, trying to please him. And he wouldn't show any signs of appreciation or pleasure at what you were doing. 'Oh, yeah, that was all right. Let's call it a day.' You go home and you feel dejected. It was difficult, yeah. Lovely guy, though, super."

But this is again typically self-deprecating. Mick Jagger was so impressed that he asked him back on more recordings a couple of years later: "Jeff was very patient. And very hard working. I went home at like two in the morning and he was still in there. That's not bad."

It was shortly after this that Beck came up with the greatest surprise of the year—a U.S. tour with Rod Stewart.

He'd often had thoughts of how good it would be to work with Stewart singing again like he did in the old days; and with the incredible chemistry on "People Get Ready," he felt almost as if that spirit had been recaptured. "We went into the studio and there was a magic in the air. Everybody stopped what they were doing and came to watch through the glass. I looked up and just saw this forest of faces."

So when Rod Stewart suggested collaborating again, it seemed like a great idea. Beck recorded three numbers in early '84 for Stewart's album *Camouflage*, which included the song "Infatuation," on which Beck delivered some roasting *Beck-Ola*-esque licks with his Jackson Soloist. Released as a single, "Infatuation" reached number 6 in the United States and was promoted with a video on which he was featured splendidly—if briefly—hammering out his lead solo, including a moment where he lifts the guitar to play it behind his head.

Although Beck had high hopes, right from the start things weren't exactly as expected. "I had decent tracks to play on and a producer who liked my playing. Then Rod didn't turn up at the sessions, which upset me, didn't even bother to come and listen to what I was doing."

But Rod Stewart's record company, Warner Brothers, did listen. They liked what they heard, and told Stewart they wanted the pair to tour together. "What was spoken about was a very attractive offer financially, and also I wouldn't have to bear the brunt of headlining a tour, which after not touring for three years— well, it's quite dicey out there, isn't it? So I thought, 'People are going to love this; if it turns out anything like what we're discussing it's going to be great.'"

There was a lot of razzmatazz promoting the tour, which was scheduled to start after the album release in June, covering 70 cities in four months. They did a special for MTV and posed for a bunch of publicity photos. Beck was in buoyant mood on the eve of the tour: "It goes on for four months—can you believe that? Four weeks is long enough for me; it'll be ambulances and stretchers and oxygen! I'll have a spot in the middle of the show. Then I'll finish up with the new tracks from his album, bugger off to get a drink or two, and come back at the end."

But the hard reality was somewhat different. His meager slot consisted of one

Together again—but not for long. Backstage with Rod Stewart on the *Camouflage* tour, mid-1984.

instrumental, "The Pump," introduced by a medley of "Rock My Plimsoul" and "I Ain't Superstitious" with Stewart, and for the rest they were together on "Infatuation," "People Get Ready," "Bad to Me," and "Young Turks."

Beck: "As each day passed and I was out on the road with him, it was painfully obvious we weren't going to come remotely close to what I had in mind. He was doing fifteen or twenty songs before I even came onstage. I was a sideshow. I thought when I came on we were going to go places, blow up a few buildings. But he had no plans for that at all."

"I love his talent," Beck told *Faces* magazine, "and I think he likes the way I play when I really belt it out. I wrongfully assumed that Rod and I would be doing a collective show, y'know? For the people. Here's Rod and Jeff. Jeff's come out from under his car and now he's got the guitar on. But he wanted me to do 'Infatuation' and a couple of other numbers and then go. I was sent packing after about ten or fifteen minutes. It wasn't what I had in mind at all. I'm sorry—it would cripple me if I'd gone on with it."

So Beck stayed with the tour as far as Canada and then quit. He had played only a handful of dates. There were no big fights with Rod Stewart, in fact they indulged in a lot of good-natured onstage badinage, Stewart saying things like, "Jeff's going to give you a taste of his own music now—beware!" And from Beck, obviously alluding to the tender years of Stewart's fans in the audience, "I'm gonna play a tune that's too old for you to remember—it's about three years old!"

By the time he decided to leave, there was real disappointment on Beck's side: "I was just imagining what it could've been like in New York if it was on my terms. People would've gone crazy. They would've been ripping up seats. There would've been lines for ten miles."

They say that onlookers see most of the game, and this was certainly the case when Beck revealed plans of the tour to Keith Altham, a good friend and one of rock's most respected PR men. Altham's comment was: "You must be mad!" And he promptly bet Beck £100 he wouldn't last twelve dates.

It happened that Altham was subsequently asked to take on PR duties, so he flew over to join the tour. He described the scene to Tim Ewbank and Stafford Hildred for their book, *Rod Stewart: A Biography*.

"I went backstage and passed a Number One dressing room which was about the size of a suite in the Waldorf Hotel. It was wall-to-wall with flowers. It looked like a cross between a crematorium and an Interflora shop. Inside there were buckets of champagne everywhere and food piled up on the table.

"The next dressing room was the band's—half the size of Rod's with not so many flowers here, and only one bottle of champagne. Next was the crew's—no flowers and just a bottle of Southern Comfort.

"Right at the end of the corridor was a door with Jeff Beck's name on it. I said, 'Hello, Jeff.' He looked up, and without saying a word he proceeded to write me out a check for £100."

13 Jumpin' Jack

BY THE TIME Jeff Beck came to record his next album, there had been dramatic developments in rock guitar. In the wake of the brilliant Eddie Van Halen, the era of the technical virtuoso had arrived.

Representing just one extreme of the spectrum of shredders, there appeared, after the Dutch-born Van Halen, another European export to the States: Yngwie Malmsteen, that one-man Viking horde who gave new meaning to the word epic.

Inspired by Jimi Hendrix, at the age of nine the Swedish schoolkid was already coating his fingers in Band-Aids to increase his endurance while perfecting a technique that was to become astounding. But hot technique was only a part of the picture. Malmsteen also imported with him some potent influences that suffused his chordal and melodic structures. Spearheading the neoclassical rock movement, his music was redolent of composers like Bach and Beethoven, and violin virtuosi such as Paganini and Kreisler.

Influences derived from classical and archaic music were already present in rock, of course, but in the past they generally went unremarked. Musicians tended to simply absorb influences aurally. It was the new concern with technical proficiency that brought with it a deeper study of music and how it was constructed, delving into the mysteries of modes and scales—Phrygian, pentatonic, harmonic minor and the like—in terms of rock guitar.

It was easy to see how fascination soon led to obsession, which in a way paralleled the extremism at the avant-garde end of fusion that Jeff Beck had observed and eschewed. Asked what he thought of the guitarists of the day, his reply was typically outgoing: "I think they're fabulous," he said. "They just symbolize youth and vigor, energy, power and everything. They should, and they deserve to, have their fingers broken! All those guys are just amazing, dedicated talents. If I had their application I'd be doing a lot better. Unfortunately I don't have that power to apply myself like that. I wander off and do something else."

Yet there was always a reservation as far as Beck was concerned, always that resistance to any one-dimensional stance. "I love it, I think it's the greatest. I mean, those guys like Van Halen are *so* great, but they seem to be stuck in that kind of stuff. Still, he's got the most amazing technique, you've got to take your hat off to him for that: the speed and the frantic element. I could do well to learn from him—some of those tricks he pulls!"

Of course, it was partly Beck's own incendiary, no-holds-barred guitar that had inspired these young bloods in the first place, and he could easily have leapt onto that particular bandwagon. But rock guitar now encompassed the entire gamut from dazzling virtuoso to posturing "big hair" axe-wielder in spandex and chains, and he had a healthy skepticism about joining their ranks. The way he saw it, "I don't want to be fronting a band at a gig full of headbangers and air-guitarists. Those are great guys and they want to get a lot of feeling out of a concert. But I want them to *listen*."

No one, however, could accuse Jeff Beck of taking himself too seriously. When the rock business was brilliantly lampooned in the 1984 movie *This Is Spinal Tap*, he loved every moment of it—especially with the guitarist character Nigel Tufnel being a wickedly identifiable pisstake of Beck himself. "They did steal a bit of my character, didn't they?" he laughed. "You know that one scene at the airport—did you notice that Nigel is reading a hot rod magazine!

"I laughed myself into the ground over Spinal Tap," he declared, "and I recognized some of that power complex, like wanting to turn the volume up to 11." He relished it so much that he couldn't resist guesting on the title track from the group's reunion album of 1992, the resoundingly tasteless *Break Like the Wind*.

THIS IS PERHAPS an appropriate moment to reflect that plenty of other movements and genres had also arrived with the '80s; guitar wizardry in comparison was little more than a sideshow for the initiated.

There was, for example, that African-American cultural revolution known as hip-hop, with its own street language, its baggy trousered fashion, its break dancing and graffiti art—and its radical music, rap. With strutting bravado, clever wordplay and anti-establishment venom, rap took its cue from the streets, exactly as punk had done with white music.

Michael Jackson was just one of the mainstream performers who quickly cottoned on to the happening black scene, injecting relevance into his pop-soul disco act by creating his own version of the image, the style, and the boy-from-the-'hood attitude.

The arrival of the pop video, giving birth in 1981 to the video-dominated MTV, now meant visual style and image were all important, determining what music gained exposure to the public. This was the ideal circumstance for two phenomena of the '80s—prodigy or freak according to taste—that burst upon the scene in the forms of Prince and Madonna.

Both affected a trashy soft-porn imagery, born of punk but aimed at mass-market success; and both saw themselves as visual icons, not only in the pop video but also on the larger canvas of the movie screen. The essential difference between them lay in Prince's multitalented instrumental prowess, probing originality, and bold conceptual sweep; allegations of which Madonna, on the other hand, stood uncontaminated.

In stark contrast, the '80s also saw the arrival of REM and U2, two groups that achieved global superstardom with decidedly fewer pretensions to grandeur,

Never far from a hot rod, Beck poses with a classic from his collection.

relying less on personal glitz and more on the stripped-down message of the music.

But whatever the musical flavor of the month, the zillion-seller of the decade was undoubtedly electro pop: disco, techno, hip-hop, and the impenetrable acid house. The latest electronic fakery had also loaded the recording studio with a myriad of new effects—sampling, sequencing and synthesized sounds, including the superhuman (or subhuman) precision of the drum machine.

So if there was a rising generation of brilliant guitarmanship to exert a pull on Jeff Beck the supreme instrumentalist, there were at the same time commercial pressures in a totally different direction. These pressures made themselves felt when he came to start work on his new album during 1984-85.

His first impulse was to do another all-guitar recording. But the people at Epic, after being kept waiting so long, were looking for chart-oriented product; they dissuaded him in no uncertain terms (which Beck laughingly characterized as having "two Mafia guys beating yer 'ed in and saying, 'You can't do another instrumental album!'").

"I think they've been the most wonderful, *enduring* company," he averred. "They have respect for me, so they haven't pushed me about it. Any other record company would've just potted me away, I think."

Inevitably, against this backdrop, Beck felt he had to listen to his masters and mentors. Their concept was a commercial recording aimed squarely at the charts, produced by the ruling techno/funk guru Nile Rodgers. Beck described it as the biggest risk he'd taken in his career. "Nowadays record companies really want hits on a record more than they ever did," he said. "The tough job is trying to play decent guitar on very pop-oriented stuff. I was looking for something I could put my trademark on."

Rodgers at the time was enjoying an explosion of fame as the producer of such acts as Madonna, Duran Duran, Mick Jagger, and David Bowie, as well as making records of his own with the disco group Chic. His studio time was heavily in demand, but eventually the initial sessions got started in the spring of 1984 at the Power Station in New York City.

Four weeks were spent putting down the guitar solos, and all the time Beck felt like a sideline in the busy man's life. It was a case of snatching moments in between Rodgers' other projects: "With Madonna smoking and boiling and flames coming out everywhere, he couldn't afford to spend much time with me. I was slotted in between two Madonna singles [laughs]. In fact, I think she was still mixing when I was doing my first cuts. She kept coming in, saying, 'How's it going with Nile? When's he gonna be free?' I said, 'He ain't gonna be free until I'm finished! Piss off!'"

Beck ventured into new fields of technology for the album, including the use of a guitar synthesizer for the first time on a recording of his own (a Roland 707 to an Emulator). And what was strangest of all was that he agreed to work with a LinnDrum machine in place of live drums.

"Drum machines—I loathe them," he admitted frankly. "But you have to go with the mainstream for some things. Not having a resident drummer in my band—not even having a resident band—it seemed a lot cheaper and more effective to use a good LinnDrum player. And we got one in Jimmy Bralower: he plays the Linn computer almost like a drum kit."

The first sessions began on 30 April, right after Beck had finished recording *Private Dancer*. The first number to be laid down was a Nile Rodgers song, "Get Workin'," and for a long time the provisional album title also bore the same name—which no doubt suited Beck's wry sense of humor.

Rodgers insisted that Beck should sing on his own album, saying, "This is it. You're gonna be a big star. You're gonna be singing now." Beck, no doubt hearing hollow echoes of Mickie Most, hated the idea ("I wanted to get on with the guitar parts"), but he reluctantly agreed to sing on two numbers—"Get Workin'" and "Night after Night"—using a much warmer vocal timbre in a register lower than usual, which happened to prove rather effective. "I thought, okay, great. I'll give him half an hour of that, and then we'll get him off it and get someone else in."

This someone else would prove to be Jimmy Hall, the ex-Wet Willie vocalist, with whom he had wanted to work for some time. As soon as he heard the Nile Rodgers song "Ambitious," Beck immediately suggested Hall. He was flown in at once and put down the vocals in just three takes.

Techno oriented the album may have been, but there was still room for plenty of Beck's guitar fireworks, and thankfully the recording team made the most of them. On "Ambitious" Beck's driving, raunchy solo was recorded with

Beck with Nile Rodgers working on *Flash*, 1984.

his pink Jackson Soloist with its serious 24-fret neck, which he used for most of the album. The song has a biting, metallic rhythm tone achieved with out-of-phase pickups, and is full of incredible slide effects that aren't actually slide at all but ferocious manipulation of the Jackson's Kahler whammy—"The whammy is my right arm. . . . This guitar has so much movement in the whammy arm, you could almost depress it an octave!"

"This was just amazing," engineer Jason Corsaro commented. "Every time you thought he did the most amazing lick you ever heard, he did it again and again and again. So we really had a hard time choosing the best one."

Corsaro in turn earned appreciation from Beck for getting the guitar so prominent that it literally jumped out of the mix: "Jason is just a guitar freak, and he pushed and pushed until the limits of the studio equipment were reached."

Trying to characterize the outcome of those sessions, the normally articulate Beck seemed to struggle for an adequate description. "A black influence in the rhythmic sense," was how he explained it, "and there's my steely guitar on top. 'Ambitious' is a very black groove. Normally you'd have rhythm chips and maybe some horns on top. But this is wall-to-wall guitar solo, with complete disregard for anything other than going completely mad."

But though Beck delivered on his side of the equation, Rodgers' lightweight material, combined with a formulaic approach to arrangement and production, did the concept little justice.

For "Nighthawks," another Nile Rodgers song, Beck again pulled out the stops in a solo of typically snarling ferocity, giving life to an otherwise undistinguished number. Jimmy Hall handled the vocals once more, as he did also on "Stop, Look and Listen." For this latter track, Beck cranked out some unusual sounds on the first few seconds of the solo break, produced with whammy and harmonics, a combination he was exploring more and more for a unique range of effects.

On "Night after Night" he again used harmonics played with the whammy bar. "Sometimes I keep my hand on it while I play a whole line. In one place I play a descending trill with whammy, and then swoop up with the finger while the string is still sounding."

Later in the solo on "Stop, Look and Listen" he used a fast ascending trill. "That's done by fingertapping with my right-hand index finger," he explained in *Guitar Player*. "I've done that technique a lot. In *Blow by Blow* days and *Wired*, I used to play the whole figure with my two index fingers."

"Are you aware of recent breakthroughs in fingertapping?" interviewer Jas Obrecht asked, referring to the fact that two-handed tapping, which Beck had been doing since the '60s, was now everyone's favorite trick.

"I know that guys are doing it," Beck replied, "because every time you hear a heavy metal record some guy is using it. But I like to just do it on the spur of the moment—[*laughs*]—when I can't think of anything else to do!"

Typically, with his aversion to having a gimmick hung around his neck, Jeff Beck has always used the technique sparingly. "There are times when it sounds outrageously effective," he says. "But when the ear latches on to what's happening, then the trick's out. It's like some guy pulling a rabbit out of a hat: you go, 'Wow!' He does it fifty times—'Okay, *fuck* the rabbit!'"

THOSE INITIAL SESSIONS produced only five usable songs written and produced by Nile Rodgers. Beck felt one of the basic problems was they didn't put enough planning into it.

"We had a half-hour meeting at a hotel in Los Angeles. And of course he had some pressing engagement and we didn't really get down to it. Not that I wanted a wrapped-up concept. But he was convinced that his songwriting and my guitar playing would be enough. It wasn't, though. To be fair to Nile, I was very lazy in the first sessions. I was waiting to be molded by him when I should have been digging in my heels. The frustration built up from one thing to another and I just let loose. Maybe that's the way he wanted it. I got so frustrated I couldn't stand it and I just went crazy. I did that on a couple of tracks [*smiles proudly*]. Doesn't sound too bad."

But Beck was still far short of having an album in the can. Several ideas were started on his own, among them a longer version of the theme from *The Tube* with Doug Wimbish playing bass. In a preview article for *Musician*, columnist David Fricke had obviously managed to hear a tape: he described it as "a mere minute and a half of galloping electro-rock over which Beck solos with all the abandon he can squeeze in." It's disappointing that to this day the theme has never been released.

Another idea he started was strongly Vangelis in style. Looking as he was for further material, it happened that Vangelis was very much in his thoughts at the time.

"At first I had high hopes of covering one of Vangelis' tunes from *Chariots of Fire*, which is still in my opinion a perfect foil for me. I came back to England, met with Vangelis, and he seemed keen to write me a different tune altogether, which pleased me no end. Then his studio blew up and he flew back to Greece, so that never came off. I was left with a three-quarters finished album, if I was lucky. So I sat around and did nothing, waiting for some help."

Doing nothing, in Jeff Beck's terms, actually meant quite the opposite. First there was the trip to the Bahamas to work on Mick Jagger's *She's the Boss*, then the foray into touring with Rod Stewart.

Returning his attention to the incomplete album, he heard the name of Arthur Baker suggested as the producer to finish the job. "I had no idea what he'd done, who he was. But I'm an optimist, so I went to New York. And we came up with three really good songs."

Placing his trust in Arthur Baker, the ruling godfather of dance remix, represented a real leap of faith for Beck, even greater than working with Rodgers. Baker had a string of remixed hit singles to his name including the Cyndi Lauper song "Girls Just Want to Have Fun," and Bruce Springsteen's "Dancing in the Dark." Fortunately his horizons were wider than just techno pop: Baker had made the decision he would do no more remixing for other producers, so when he came in on Beck's project, there was a lot at stake and he gave it everything he had.

Of the Baker songs, Jimmy Hall came back to sing on "Gets Us All in the End," an all-out raver with some wonderfully frenzied Beck aggro. After 30 hell-for-leather takes on the solo, Baker was still looking for that extra mile from Beck. "He didn't want to play any more, he had played so many. I just said, 'I thought you were *Jeff* Beck. C'mon, don't let your fans down.' And that last solo turned out to be the hottest Jeff Beck in over a decade."

It was also something of an uphill task getting Beck to repeat the same riff endlessly in order to achieve the fat guitar sound Baker wanted—quite opposite to his usual method of laying down off-the-cuff guitar lines.

"With the guitar chords I'd say, 'Let's do *bamm-bamm-bamm* 20 times.' It was hard for Jeff, because he'd get bored. He told me that when he plays a solo—and he says it's always been this way—the first 12 bars are great, but after that he gets bored. He'll be going hot for 12, and then on the 13th you know he'll peter out."

Jimmy Hall also did the vocals for "Ecstasy," a nice funky groove allowing Beck to lay down some tasty jazz-style licks, using synthesizer to dial in choir effects. But his hardware on the album was quite conservative: a Pro-Co Rat distortion box, and at various times his Roland Digital Delays. As backup to the Jackson, he also used the Marriott Strat and a stock '58 Telecaster for occasional input.

"Arthur Baker impressed me with the overall power of what was coming out of the studio," Beck summarized. "With the two of them I have a better album than if I'd had just one, for no other reason than they're totally different people. Nile was more into white rock and Arthur was more the groove. Somewhere in that conglomeration of songs there has to be something that hits you, without going radically to the right or left."

To add to the variety, Beck decided to include an instrumental, "You Know, We Know," on which he and Tony Hymas had been working before the album project started. And a welcome addition was that one-off recording of "People Get Ready," which now saw the light of day after lying in record company vaults for nearly two years. "I thought it was too good to leave around and I was going to put it on my album and they said no. Then they said yes. Then I guess they got to like it so much that they insisted Rod put it out as a single, and with the single a video. So that was quickly put together."

In late 1984 it underwent a final remix, with Beck producing and Carmine Appice contributing the wonderful depth of real live drums. Then, in spring 1985, Beck and Stewart got together again for the promo video, which was shot on location near Los Angeles.

Beck later said it was the best thing he'd ever done on video. It has a story line which opens with Rod Stewart penning an ironic note: "Jeff—Why don't you come to L.A. and take up the guitar professionally?" Beck smiles as he reads the letter, then we watch him ride the freight train to meet his old crony, seated on an open cattle truck in cutoff shirt and broken jeans. The guitar in his hands is an Esquire, rather than the Jackson he used on the recording, but the '51 Fender has exactly the right look for the setting. (This historic instrument has been mistakenly described as a Telecaster, but was originally owned by Roy Buchanan, who added a second (neck) pickup. It was said to be borrowed from Seymour Duncan, but in 1996 was offered for sale in Tokyo as a Jeff Beck guitar.)

Filmed in sepia tones to capture the feeling of the dusty Midwest, it includes scenes of Beck surrounded by field hands, and at one point playing the guitar with the help of a little boy on his lap. Rod Stewart waits to greet him as he jumps off at the small country station, and there's a joyful reunion with broad grins on both sides, Stewart throwing his arms around Beck in a huge bear hug.

Beck loved it because it overturned everyone's opinion: "They thought, 'They hate each other,' and then all of a sudden there's the video."

Now a B-side was needed in haste for the single release, which—unusually for Beck—he penned himself in record time. "We needed a quickie to fill up the seven-inch single. They said, 'Quick, quick, quick, we have to have something to go on the other side.' And I wrote it in about ten minutes."

"Back on the Street" had a style unlike anything he'd written before, and was loaded with hit potential. Within the day a singer was found for the lead vocal—Karen Lawrence—with a powerful, raving delivery that takes the song precisely where it needs to go, aided by some seriously mean rocking shred from Beck. It's a great pity that LP buyers were deprived of this track which, as well as "Nighthawks," only appeared on some CD versions.

"People Get Ready" was released in June, but contrary to expectations it was not the huge hit the record label had in mind—although it remains one of Beck's most well-loved songs in the memories of most listeners. It did reasonably well at 48 in the U.S. *Billboard* chart, but (as we have come to expect) in the U.K. neither this single nor any of the others from the album made any chart impression. It would reach number 49, however, on its 1992 rerelease in Britain.

In October 1985, "Ambitious" came out in the U.S., with a promotional video aired on MTV that month. Shot at A&M Chaplin Soundstage in California, the video has Beck playing guitar while a variety of unlikely people are trying out for the part as singer—among them Hervé Villechaise, Rick Moranis, and Donny Osmond. In the audience can be seen Alice Cooper, Madonna, and Dr. Joyce Brothers, with Herb Alpert showing up at the end!

BY THE TIME the album came out, in late June 1985, the title had been changed from *Get Workin'* to *Flash*—which, in the enigmatic words of his manager, Ralph Baker, "in the end seemed more appropriate." It reached number 39 in the U.S. charts—quite an achievement for such an atypical offering, especially since there was no tour to support it, and surprisingly little promotional push from Epic considering it was the label's attempt to tailor Beck for commercial success. If Epic executives hoped for any similar sales in Britain, they were disappointed. The official U.K. chart position was 83, although it appeared in the *NME* chart for one week at a position of 27.

Beck's fans were perhaps nonplussed, but there was plenty of fiery, raving Beck to keep them happy. Jas Obrecht in *Guitar Player* applauded his "ingeniously tearing through the polished neatness with suicide whammy dives, growls, harmonics, and razor-sharp leads." And the gorgeous guitar work on "People Get Ready" was alone worth the price of admission.

But it didn't do what was hoped or expected, Beck admitted. The fact that he sang—under duress—didn't make any difference. "They said I ought to sing in order to get heard [on radio]. No matter how bad the song was, it would enable you to jump over a few bridges, get played. I say balls! I'm a guitarist, not a singer! Why do something that is totally uncomfortable?" Indeed, he felt so embarrassed by the vocals that at one point he said, "If you can't sit in the back of a car when your record comes on without cringing, there's not much point in doing it. You want to be proud and say, 'Turn that shit *up!*'—not 'Turn that shit *down!*'"

There were others, however, who rated the album much more highly. An important song, which merits an honorable mention, is the instrumental "Escape": composed by Jan Hammer and produced by Nile Rodgers and Jeff Beck, it earned Beck a 1985 Grammy Award for Best Rock Instrumental Performance.

"I wondered where it came from," Beck later commented. "There were no rumblings about it, it just came! We realized we needed some serious instrumental stuff to get people going, and Jan had this great track. It's a trick high-tech sounding record—melodically it didn't do much."

True enough, the number itself is unmemorable, and it also boasts a particularly mechanical drum track; Beck's guitar performance alone can be credited for the award. In fact, it was more than a little ironic that the one cut from *Flash* that got widespread recognition was an instrumental.

Critically, *Flash* was poorly received by those who knew Beck's capabilities and were disappointed by what they saw as a techno sellout. "But it wasn't a terrible album," in Beck's opinion, and in the opinion of plenty of others too. "At the time, in '84, the music industry was fiddling about with all that electro-techno stuff, and the stories were coming back to me: 'This is what's happening, you've gotta use drum machines, change your image, get a Mohawk haircut and one trouser leg cut off.' I didn't want to snub that out, because it's stupid to turn a blind eye to what's going on."

And at least it got him away from his image of the late '70s, the abstract jazz-rock kind of thing. "I sensed missed expectations from people coming to my concerts, and I was a bit envious of how the rock bands could hop about instead of standing there concentrating!"

It also prised him out from under his cars and away from his English country retreat, twin obsessions that he hoped it would provide the wherewithal to finance. A restoration of his leaking roof was urgently needed, as he told Jerry McCulley of *BAM* magazine, since the leak presently had him paddling every time he walked to the kitchen.

"It's a major job," the guitarist explained, "because the house is so old that it requires skilled tilers to fix the roof. It's a listed historical building, so I have to do it."

Describing Beck as lean and tanned in jeans and denim vest, McCulley watched fascinated as our hero constructed one of his trademark hand-rolled cigarettes: a minute amount of tobacco in the thinnest cigarette his eyes had ever seen.

Beck: "The first thing I had to do was leave home and not be around my garage too often [*chuckles*]. By cutting off that, going to New York and working with Nile Rodgers, it made me concentrate on the project every day. If I hadn't gone to New York I'd have sat around for another few years!"

Touring was discussed, and Beck spoke of maybe taking in Britain on a tour the following September, but nothing came of that idea. The only live appearances that happened were a tryout at the Greek Theatre in Los Angeles, in April 1986, and a succession of dates for his devoted fans in Japan that June. His touring band consisted of Jimmy Hall, Jan Hammer, Doug Wimbish on bass, and Simon Phillips on drums.

On one of these dates, 1 June at the Prince Hotel, Karuizawa—which was also televised—Beck made a stunning appearance with Carlos Santana, drummer Buddy Miles, and Steve Lukather of Toto, a guitarist he rated as one of the best in the world ("the blur of fingers was unreal!"). He would play again in Japan with Lukather on the same bill some three years later.

BECK SPENT QUITE a bit of time in the United States during this period, and while there he found time to go to a concert from Sting's *Dream of the Blue Turtles* tour.

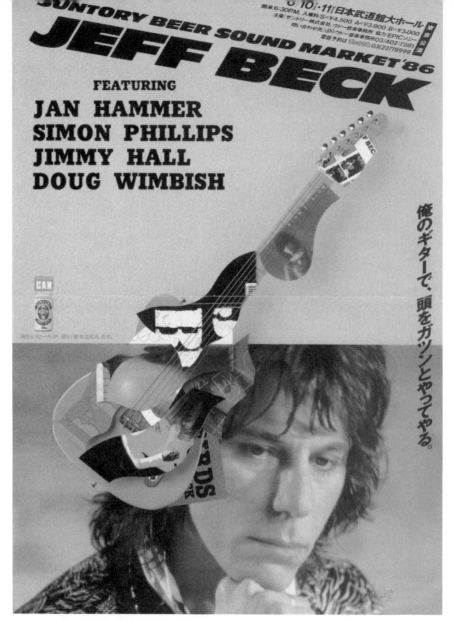

Beck's only tour to support *Flash* was in Japan, June 1986.

He had loved the album, and was interested in Sting's latest musical direction. Sting said to him afterwards, "Why didn't you let me know you were coming? You could have got up and played."

"That's *why* I didn't let you know!" Beck retorted. But Sting was insistent that he come to the next gig. "We'll play the shuffle," he said, "the one you heard tonight."

"I fell for it, of course," says Beck. "I went out and got the album, listened to it, and spent about six hours learning the first shuffle that came up. I turned up at the sound check and said, 'I've learnt it,' played a few lines, and then Sting said, 'No, not *that* one!' Anyway, it was a twelve-bar, so I just jammed along."

The song was "I Been Down so Long," and it was recorded that night with Sting. It was released for a very good cause, in aid of cancer research, on a charity album under the title of *Live! For Life.*

Around this time, in the autumn of 1985, Beck should have been due to start his next album, based on the surefire formula the record company thought it had in *Flash.* Beck had gone along with it on the label's assurances, and lost all heart when the reality turned out to be different. "They told my manager it was cut-and-dried, 'This is going to be a hit; it'll be a big enough hit for Jeff to concentrate on *another* album, and it'll give him that little bit of a boost.' It didn't do that. I was in despair of what had happened to the music industry—just this hopelessness with this endless, powerful corporate cock-up that was moving along at a hundred miles an hour, of which I was no part whatsoever. I just had this feeling that I was wasting my time."

So it was that, lacking inspiration from other sources, Beck began to look back to his roots again. During 1984 he'd taken time out to lay down a delicious recording of the lovely old Santo and Johnny instrumental "Sleep Walk" for the film *Porky's Revenge.* Only a few bars were heard in the movie, but it appeared in full glory on a soundtrack album, together with some other tasty rock 'n' roll covers by his compatriot Dave Edmunds of Rockpile fame (the music was the only touch of class in the entire graceless epic). This obviously sparked off a resonant chord with Beck, and in 1986 it was reported he was to record a rockabilly album produced by Edmunds.

Beck's devotion to the music of his youth had also been rekindled by the brief rockabilly revival that happened in the '80s. He'd loved seeing everybody bopping to Brian Setzer's wonderful Stray Cats when they performed in London (their album *Built for Speed* had also been produced by Dave Edmunds), so he went into the studio with Slim Jim Phantom and Lee Rocker, the Stray Cats' drummer and bass player, and recorded three or four songs.

"I remember the session well," he says. "It was without Brian Setzer. I kind of felt like I was riding a one-wheeled bicycle around the studio [*laughs*]. I think Slim Jim wanted me to be like Jeff Beck, and they wanted to be themselves, and the two things didn't work. It was fun anyway, because we had a good laugh and I got to drive Slim Jim's Corvette."

Still with similar ideas active in his thoughts, Beck was experimenting with a vintage pedal steel guitar ("it looks like you're ironing when you sit down to play it!"), and he even considered a spoof country and western song.

In a *Guitar World* interview in March 1985, yet another side of his musical thinking was revealed when he was asked by Gene Santoro: "If you had a dream project that you could suddenly do, what would it be?"

Beck: "I've often toyed with the idea of doing a rock thing with a full orchestra. I listen to classical music all the time, and I often wish that I was playing somewhere in the beautiful, wide sound that a full orchestra gets. You'd put the guitar where, say, an opera singer would be, so there'd be vast spaces where the guitar would solo, and then would come these huge attacks—very exciting and dramatic stuff. I've laid some groundwork for that kind of thing, actually, made some enquiries with composers, but they're really not talking the same language half the time. I'd have to write the music for it to work, and somehow [*laughs*] I just don't seem to get round to doing that."

Though none of these passing thoughts saw actuality at the time, it was not surprising that in his subsequent album Beck determined to take complete ownership. The time had passed when others would dictate the direction of his music.

AS A BREAK from the busy life of concerts and recordings, it was always Jeff Beck's best therapy to indulge in his passion for hot rods. In 1983/84, in particular, Britain was blessed with long hot summers which provided ideal weather to get outside and do some work. By now he had two fully fitted garage workshops at his Sussex home, large brick buildings with thatched roofs in keeping with the 16th century house, and his collection of rods was steadily growing—mostly '32 and '34 Ford coupes and roadsters.

It was in mid-1985 that he received a request from the American magazine *AutoWeek*, asking if he would tear himself away from his current project long enough to give an interview. They had found out about his addiction and wanted to devote a cover story to Jeff Beck the rodding enthusiast. A date was agreed, and columnist Mike Nickele duly made his way to the Beck estate.

Nickele's article throws a fascinating light on a side of Beck that people don't often see. In fact, the guitarist admitted, a lot of folks thought he was crazy, and others were often annoyed when they found his time taken up by something that made him so inaccessible. But rock 'n' roll, from ZZ Top as far back as Chuck Berry's "Maybellene," has always had a love affair with hot wheels.

"You have to have an inner spirit for it," is Beck's conclusion. "A feeling for speed, glamour and power, and it's in both rock and cars. You see that [*points to a red '34*] coming down the road and it looks amazing. Kind of like watching a good rock 'n' roll group."

But why he devotes himself to these antiques, rather than the latest Italian sports monsters, is an obsession he can't explain. "It's just something that strikes you about an old car, you know. Whether it's a stocker or been rodded out or whatever. It catches your eye so much because there aren't any others around."

Rodding also makes him rely on his own resources and his own creativity. "That's what has Beck hooked," Mike Nickele comments perceptively: "the creative process." He likes driving them. He likes owning them. But most of all, he likes building them.

He has an artist's trained eye for form and symmetry, and confides to Nickele that building the rods may even be an extension of the art he still occasionally practices in oils. One can imagine the gratification he gets from fulfilling two different sides of the complex Beck personality, the artist and the artisan. And then, when his handiwork is finished . . .

"You do get a secret twinge of pride when you're driving it," he says, "but that's not all of it. It's the simplicity, too. . . . You cannot have a more simple vehicle than a hot rod, really. You can make them very complicated with high-tech this that and the other, but basically you're talking about body, frame, engine, wheels."

Beck has half a dozen different rods in varying stages of completion, but right now it's a bright orange '32 Ford convertible—his first fiberglass body. It has the latest stripped down, smoothie look and he's been working on the doors, putting the hinges on the inside so there'll be no sign of them showing. The engine, transmission and suspension will be down to him, and probably the paint job too.

The power plant will be the mighty mouse—the Chevy small-block V8. When it comes to engines, according to Beck, "you're either a Ford guy or a Chevy guy, and I'm a Chevy guy." Witness the 1984 Corvette standing in the drive, and the Blazer in the garage.

Beck now installs independent suspension in his cars. He no longer allows resto-rod hazards like the leaf spring suspension that nearly killed him in '69. And neither does he race. Not that he doesn't enjoy the speed, of course—and the challenge is hard to resist—so he's taken one of his rides to a drag strip where it did the quarter-mile in 14.9 seconds, "two guys up and not even tuned." But gone are the days when he used to scorch around with cronies like Timmy Bogert and Carmine Appice, burning rubber and writing off Corvettes with scarcely a backward glance.

Prophetically, the article discusses certain other hazards that don't involve sitting behind the wheel, some of which will come home to Beck within just a few years. The first being hand injuries while working on the cars. No, it isn't something he worries about. Ralph Baker interpolates: "You really wouldn't be able to do it if you were afraid, would you? Although we've found him on the side of the road with blood pouring out his fingers, on occasion."

Baker also recounts how he's discovered Beck with his head flat down to a 350hp V8, one hand on the carb linkage and the other turning the distributor cap, fine tuning it by ear. "They usually don't have mufflers on them and he's got this bloody thing deafening his ears. It really scares the shit out of me. And it's the same with the guitar volume. . . . But with Jeff, if it sounds good, never mind how it's been achieved, it's good enough."

Asked about the future, Beck isn't too sure if he'll tour with this new album. He doesn't enjoy touring, but it helps with album sales, and he *does* need to fund a new lathe and milling machine.

"The rods are an escape from rock 'n' roll," he reflects. "I have to have an even balance: one has to offset the other. It's a bit uneven at the moment with the cars, I'm so fed up with the music thing." Getting where he wants in music, he feels, involves so many different elements, each one a further link that serves to weaken the chain. With building rods there are fewer links involved. You get the impression that Beck finds the direct, hands-on creative process is much more personally satisfying.

"When I've finished a rod that I've just done right, I like to stand back, look at it and say, 'Yeah—all right.'"

14 Petal to the Metal

A YEAR AFTER *FLASH* was completed, in the spring of 1986, Jeff Beck went into the studio in London. The session would produce a single that was released in the U.K. only: a heavier-than-heavy version of the old Troggs hit "Wild Thing," a standby of his onstage for many a year.

There's been little comment about this recording, which seems to be glossed over as a bit of an aberration, an event of minor significance. More likely, in the view of this author, it is quite the reverse: "Wild Thing" is Beck's personal statement of defiance. Here is an encoded message of two fingers to everyone who wants to harness him, to mold him into conformity. From now on, the message says, I'm in the driver's seat; I'll do things my way.

With distortion cranked up to the endurance threshold and beyond, with straddling power-pumping chords and wave after wave of hellbent climaxes, he throws down the gauntlet to the heavy metal cock-rock brotherhood with a vengeance that sears white hot. "It explodes, right? Totally sonic overload. I wanted to bust back out, Hendrix style."

As if to heave a brick at those who are never satisfied unless he sings, this time it's Beck's own choice to perform the vocal—but using a Vocoder, an electronic device that transforms his voice to an unnatural, insolent snarl. The "Wild Thing" of the song is no match for the wild thing Beck lets loose to sing it.

In this version, the words "I think I love you" are delivered with hard-eyed calculation; "You move me" steams with innuendo; and "Come on, hold me . . . *tight*" makes it plain that in this man's language it's a command, not a request.

Why this sudden blistering eruption? A release of personal frustration, perhaps, too long submerged; conveyed in the language of metal, too long suppressed. We can only guess at the glee of laying it down and kicking butt. Score one big one for the dude with the guitar.

Of course, being Beck, there had to be an element of tongue in cheek. And an overkill cover of a well-worn favorite would carry the right implication: hey, guys, I'm not being serious here. It's just a freakout for my own amusement.

Should there be any doubts, however, about its powerful cathartic role for

Beck, the following disclosure makes it clear that heavy metal still does something for him that nothing else can: "Sometimes I play heavy metal stuff, just for the fun of it, and I just wish that people could see me. But I'd never play it outside my own studio. I just get whipped up into a rage and go down and plug in, dial up a good sound—just to console myself that I can do it, and do it much more *evil* than the guys that are doing it [*laughs*]. And I think, 'Better keep that under wraps.'"

The whole point is that this time it isn't under wraps. This time he wants us to hear it all unleashed, to know that despite the years of maturation and development, a diet of wholesomeness is not his only food. The old lunatic Beck is still alive and dangerous.

A fact known to insiders in the music business was that the Troggs had taped an expletive-undeleted verbal exchange at the end of their '60s recording, which meant that copies of the tape became collectors' items. So at the end of Beck's session, for a lark, he and the engineer reproduced a similar spoken passage mimicking the original voices. Obviously it wasn't heard on the single release, but owners of the *Beckology* set can savor this moment on the "Wild Thing" playout.

Coupled on a 12-inch single with two titles from *Flash*, it was released in July 1986, but failed to make the charts. Probably it wasn't intended to.

EARLIER THAT YEAR Beck had taken to the stage with Eric Clapton and Ronnie Wood once more, when the Rolling Stones held a monster jam session on 23 February at London's 100 Club.

The event was a sad one, mounted in memory of the Stones' pianist, Ian "Stu" Stewart, affectionately known as the sixth Stone. Stewart's death shortly before Christmas of a heart attack, at the age of 47, had caused shock and grief to the innumerable friends who loved him. Beck said his personal farewells in a contribution to the Howlin' Wolf number "Little Red Rooster."

So many people had the fondest memories of Stu Stewart, a member of the Stones from the very first. Dismissed from their stage act, he'd stayed on to contribute his boogie piano from the wings and his calming, commonsense influence to keep the band from falling apart, even in its roughest moments. "I thought *he'd* be the one to hold the shovel, the one to bury all of us," Keith Richards declared, echoing everyone's sentiments. "What a hole he's left—such an obvious gap." Soon afterwards the Rolling Stones faced their greatest crisis when Mick Jagger decided he no longer wanted to tour with them, which effectively broke them up for almost three years.

Jagger was meanwhile planning his second solo outing, *Primitive Cool*, and wanted Jeff Beck's guitar again. In October Beck was summoned to New York, where he added overdubs on most of the album; in fact, there are only a couple of tracks ("Say You Will" and "Party Doll") where his presence is questionable.

Jeff Beck and Mick Jagger recording the video for "Throwaway" at the Country Club in Reseda, Ca., with Terry Bozzio on drums.

A few months earlier Beck had contributed to the B-side, "I'm Ringing," of Mick Jagger's single "Ruthless People" (the A-side taken from the movie of the same name). Whenever they worked together they'd got on really well, so when talk got around to a tour to follow *Primitive Cool*, Beck was enthused with the idea. He thought Jagger intended to put his Stones days behind him and get a new group together, in which Beck would be an active partner.

"I wanted to be in a Rolling Stones Number Two with a tomorrow feel to it, like an experimental Rolling Stones with Jagger singing. And I was sure that's what he wanted. But as time drifted by I realized he was determined to put these old songs on tape the way he wanted them. He wanted to produce and have a very stylized album. I realized I was just slotted in as a guest, studio-type guy."

Scheduled for release in spring 1987, the album was delayed until the following September. It had been something of a disillusionment for Beck, but when they came to record the video for "Throwaway" in October/November (in which Beck appeared) it brought about a meeting that would have far happier consequences.

Jagger needed a drummer for the video, and Beck had heard a lot about Terry Bozzio, the phenomenal American percussionist who had played with Frank Zappa and was currently leading his own band, Missing Persons. He'd wanted to check out the drummer for his own next project, and the idea came to him to suggest Bozzio to Jagger. "Terry came out of the woods straight away, standing there with his drumsticks half an hour later. At the audition he blew my socks off. I grabbed him by the collar and said, 'You're playing with me now, pal.'"

"There I was," Bozzio afterwards recalled, "playing 'Little Red Rooster,' which I used to idolize in front of the hi-fi, with Mick Jagger and Jeff Beck, my other idol from childhood!"

The tour was due to start right afterwards, but by then Jagger had added singers and dancers to the touring band, "turning it into a circus," in the words of one observer. As rehearsals got under way, Beck woke up to the fact that Jagger's idea was to put a big show together where he was the star "and we were all planetary kinds of people"—which meant he had to make a hard decision. "It turned out there were 15 Rolling Stones songs on the set list, and I didn't want to go to Australia and Japan to play a load of Keith Richards licks. That was the worst backing-out of a tour that I've ever done." Jagger was fortunate enough to get Joe Satriani as Beck's replacement.

APART FROM THE Jagger collaborations, Jeff Beck was less visible in guest sessions during '86 and '87; but there was one that he recorded on behalf of Philip Bailey, longtime lead vocalist with Earth, Wind & Fire. He can be heard on Bailey's album *Inside Out*, backing him up on "Back It Up."

In the United States, separated from his lathes and welding gear, Beck usually manages to socialize much more than at home. So it isn't surprising that he was seen at a couple of showbiz parties at New York's Hard Rock Cafe in 1987: the first, also attended by the Kinks, was in March to celebrate the reopening of the Beacon Theater. The second, on 6 June, was the occasion of Les Paul's 72nd birthday, when Beck was practically the only guitarist present who didn't get onstage and jam. The truth was he'd felt so nervous about the prospect that he downed half a dozen margaritas at a Mexican restaurant, then found he was "sort of seeing double!"

On 20 January 1988 he again paid his respects to Les Paul when he inducted the veteran guitarist into the Rock and Roll Hall of Fame with the tribute, "He's given me 33 years of inspiration and good vibes." Later that year he was disappointed at being unable to take part in the subsequent Les Paul TV special; but by then he was fully involved in putting together his latest album in England, and simply couldn't take the time away.

But before moving on to the album project, let us return to November 1987, with Beck getting back to his cars after ducking the Jagger tour. This was when he had a terrible accident which nearly cost him the thumb of his left hand.

"I was in my garage working on the hot rods," he told interviewer Gene Santoro. "I have a deep six-foot pit, an inspection pit; I don't have a cover for it other than these oak planks, which are really heavy. I picked up one of them and pulled it, and the other end went about four feet down into the pit and kicked, pinching my finger up against the chassis. It was just squashed, broke."

The thumb was snapped at the first joint: "I heard it go," he said. "It was so painful I wandered around fainting and sweating—excruciating pain. I went to bed, and the only way I could get to sleep was by downing a whole bottle of whisky. After three hours of deep sleep I must have stretched in my sleep, flexed my hand. I woke up and shot through the ceiling."

The next day he went to the hospital and had it strapped in a splint. "I could still play, because the thumb was poking up vertically when I held the neck; I couldn't bear to wrap it round. I couldn't believe that the broken tip of your finger could be so painful. But your whole body just feels like it's been run over by a truck."

Not only the pain, but also the possible aftermath doesn't bear thinking about. Beck was out of commission for some months, and one of the results was that a session to record with Malcolm McLaren had to be postponed; it was rescheduled for later in 1988. The outcome was two tracks—"House of the Blue Danube" and "Call a Wave"—on McLaren's album *Waltz Darling*, released in July 1989, with Beck making a fleeting appearance in the video.

The unlikely association with the one-time Sex Pistols guru and current techno-freak came about because Beck had loved "Buffalo Gals," McLaren's off-the-wall electro pop offering. "I've always admired him, he's such a nut case. I'm a nut as well, so we get on great."

Unusually for Beck, he made the first approach. "I said, 'What do you think about doing some work together?' And to my amazement he said, 'Yeah, I'd love to.' And it was strange because he sent me all these cassettes of strange and wonderful sort of 1890s music hall music, and surf music and classics and all that. And one thing led to another and I ended up doing the album; I spent about a month on that."

Afterwards, Jeff Beck's "Blue Danube" solo would resurface in the company of four world-famous superheroes: it was used in promos for the *Teenage Mutant Ninja Turtles* movie!

WITH HIS THUMB in action again, Beck now got together with his old keyboards chum, Tony Hymas, to work on ideas for his next album release which would feature Terry Bozzio on drums. Before it was in the can, however, Beck had an invitation to record for another movie—and this one was to include a personal appearance.

The picture was the excellent comedy *Twins*, starring Arnold Schwarzenegger and Danny DeVito. For an initial soundtrack recording of "The Train Kept A-Rollin'," he assembled Tony Hymas, (Andrew) Roachford on vocals, and Peter Richardson on drums—of whom we shall hear more later.

But this was not the group that appeared on the screen. Beck was to play the leader of a band, performing the country song "I'd Die for this Dance" (which included some outstanding soloing). With Nicolette Larson on vocals, the band was Beck's newly formed trio with Hymas and Bozzio—the movie was their first recorded outing together. They are also heard performing parts of "Green Onions" in the film, but their main contribution is as a background to the barroom brawl between the good guys and the bad guys. As Beck manfully carries on playing, moviegoers will remember that Danny DeVito snatches up his acoustic guitar from a stand—apologizing to him while doing so—and uses it to smack the gangster villain. Then he runs out, hands Beck his business card and says, "Sorry about the guitar, pal."

Since Beck had a line to speak in the movie (all of two words—"Nice hit!"), his performance earned him membership in the Screen Actors Guild. It also reminded him of the unglamorous side of moviemaking, as they sweltered for three days in a blazing hot club in Encino, California. "Don't know why we did it," says Beck, "but it was a free trip!" He would soon be seen in other cameos—this time on the small screen—when future invitations gave him the occasion to exploit that quirky sense of humor that is never far from the surface with Beck.

Buyers of the soundtrack CD were in for an additional treat that wasn't on the LP version: a glorious performance of "The Stumble" by the Beck-Bozzio-Hymas trio. Sadly, "Green Onions" never made it on any commercial release.

To round off the year, he took part in two notable jams. The first was an occasion for many old cronies to reunite, on 28 November at London's Hard Rock Cafe, when Beck teamed up with Eric Clapton, Andy Fairweather Low, Yardbird Jim McCarty, and Jimi Hendrix Experience members Mitch Mitchell and Noel Redding. This was for a special charity auction organized by Beck's former girlfriend, Celia Hammond, in aid of her Animal Trust, which was founded to run clinics for animals in distress. After a happy relationship of seventeen or eighteen years, it's good to reflect that Jeff and Celia always remained friends. Indeed, in a TV interview she attested to Beck's great patience with a constant population of rescued cats and dogs around the house, which at one time numbered over a hundred.

The second jam was just before Christmas when he guested at a benefit concert, on the stage of the Marquee, with guitarist Brian May and drummer Pete "The Spider" Richardson, backed by Richardson's band Bad News. Brian May afterwards commented, "Jeff Beck is the greatest living guitarist. I wanted to stop and watch everything he was doing. He still takes so many chances, is adventurous, and produces so much beauty. There's always greatness in what he does."

A little while later, there was a brilliant collaboration between Beck and that wonderful comedian Lenny Henry, when they got together on the stage of London's Hackney Empire to perform a sketch titled "Blues Y'All," Henry's spoof on an old blues singer à la John Lee Hooker. Producing some outrageous unaccompanied blues licks, Beck solos straight-faced throughout Henry's "Woke up one mornin'" song, until at last he cracks up when the comedian produces a blues harp and blows a strategically timed solo of his own—a single note. Beck's cream Strat on the video was his current favorite, a '59 body with a '60s rosewood neck, assembled for him some four years previously by Seymour Duncan. The show was released in LP, CD, and video formats under the title *Lenny, Live and Unleashed*. Definitely one for the collection.

BUT THESE WERE mere diversions from the ongoing preparations in hand for the new Jeff Beck album project.

The lineup was to be a trio of equals, with Tony Hymas the first to come on board, now a veteran Beck collaborator of nearly ten years standing. The new man on the scene was drummer Terry Bozzio. Distinctive in outlook and sporting an impeccable pedigree, Bozzio was the ultimate progressive who, while happy with the most minimal acoustic drum kit, was famous for experimenting with bizarre extremes of electronic rigs.

It wasn't that Beck no longer wanted to work with Simon Phillips—quite the contrary, in fact—but there never seemed to be a gap in the British drummer's heavily booked schedule. Bozzio also had commitments, but after a direct appeal from Beck he eventually agreed—with conditions. "Having heard *Flash*, which I really wasn't too pleased with, I was adamant about this being an instrumental album."

This was precisely the kind of support Beck needed, encouraging him to reassert his sense of self-direction. As a result, the album would prove to be probably his most significant piece of recorded work to date.

Bozzio's admiration for Jeff Beck was clear from the start. "Jeff's sound is what makes him special. Most guitar players follow the well-beaten path of power chords, arpeggiated chords, and blistering linear leads. Well, I say *fuck* the well-beaten path! His imagination is so staggering that it doesn't matter what equipment he uses. Technique is a good thing, but it has to be balanced with artistic concerns—Jeff is a completely balanced player."

Given the '80s obsession with solo guitar pyrotechnics, it was significant that Beck chose instead to concentrate on an integrated partnership. As Chris Gill commented in *Guitar Player*, "At the peak of shredmania, when instrumental rock guitar records ruled, Beck emphasized sparse melodies, rhythmic grooves and myriad textures, instead of wallowing in blazing displays of speed."

After the experience of *Flash*, his approach to going into the studio again was more than usually tentative. "The years were melting away. It's easy just to sit around for another year. It was like, 'Oh, well, I'll just be a has-been.' And then I'd play a guitar and think, 'Well, that didn't sound bad.' And I started becoming very uncomfortable with the fact that I hadn't really done *anything*."

It was the enthusiasm of his fans that really provided the incentive. "I went through this period of feeling, was it just time to put the guitar back in the case? Then just a few trips to America made me feel totally sick with guilt. All these kids were coming up to me saying, 'Come on, when are ya gonna do another one?' That just made me do it. So I went down to Tony's place in 15-below temperatures and sat in his little room and came up with a few things.

"I'm a little bit in awe of Tony; I find it difficult to play freely because he's so fine. I don't think he's been heard enough, he's just an incredible musician. It must be murder for him to listen to me making mistakes. But I've always thought it's better to have people miles better than you in the band: it keeps you up. I couldn't play with a guy that was so-so."

The other important thing for Beck was to have the right caliber of drummer, and this time there was no way it would be a machine! "To hear somebody play with fire is a dream. Somebody has to make your ass move. Unfortunately, grooves seem to have taken a back seat, real drummer grooves. It's just that lovely lurching thing that human beings have in anticipation. Sometimes it misses, but when it hits, it hits better than some strip of total similarity all the way through."

With no bass player in the outfit, it was Tony Hymas' job to handle the bass input. "We started writing together as a trio," he said, "and it felt right. If we had added a standard bass player, I think everything would have been done in a more traditional fashion and the music would've suffered."

Beck also found the absence of a bass was great—all he had to do was accent his rhythm parts more. "It was about a month before we noticed that we didn't have a bass player! The chemistry between the three of us was so good we decided not to rock the boat. I've noticed that, when you have four members, people tend to pair off—and that can cause trouble. We're more like triplets."

Indeed, the essential equality of the three musicians was so important on this album that the title itself was graced with all three names: *Jeff Beck's Guitar Shop with Terry Bozzio and Tony Hymas*.

THE TASK OF writing and recording was destined to span an entire year, starting in 1988 with bursts of work at Chipping Norton Studios in Oxfordshire. From the winter of 1988/89 the trio booked in at Sol in Cookham, Berkshire, as a residential studio for rehearsals and recording. Eventually they would find themselves in occupancy for eight full months. Straddling a rushing stream—it had once been a mill—the studio complex was set in delightful countryside about five miles from Windsor, and was owned by Jimmy Page. "That hurt," Beck laughed, "knowing he was getting all the bread for it!"

It took so long because the writing and rehearsing process melded inseparably with the recording. Beck: "I don't know why that happened. I think a lot of it was being too comfortable in the studio. The place was really idyllic: right by a river, a beautiful place to be. I should have been in some crappy studio that was falling to bits and have to drive there every day! When you're a resident you flop out of bed, it's all too easy, time flies by."

The three musicians shared not only the album title, but also the writing and production credits, with Leif Mases as fourth coproducer. Mases, from Sweden, was the manager of Sol and had worked with Led Zeppelin and Europe, as well as engineering for ABBA at the group's Stockholm studios; he would find himself called in by Beck on many future occasions.

Tony Hymas, Jeff Beck, Terry Bozzio: together on *Guitar Shop.*

The album opens with the title track, suffused with Beck's sharp wit: "An idea I had about the sounds that come out of a music shop on a Saturday morning, with guitars screaming and people playing in 8,000 different styles." Beck's dirty, funky riffing leads into an assault with great chunks of industrial-strength guitar, overlaid with Bozzio's deadpan sales monotone extolling the wares in our guitar mechanic's chop shop. Bozzio: "It was, like, let's have some fun! So I did that rap with my American nonregional dialect. I just flipped through a bunch of guitar magazines and thought of some terms I already knew like 'balls deluxe' and 'full shred'."

This is the only vocal input on the album apart from more spoken lines in "Day in the House," a jokey hip-hop number with a more serious undercurrent if you look for it. The House in question is of course the British Parliament's House of Lords, for which Beck mimics the plummy voices and muttered "hear-hears" of a spoof debate on the environment, punctuated by the insistent words "Nothing is being done . . ."

"Savoy" is the second track, a stylized shuffle with Buddy Rich boogie/bebop overtones, described by Beck as having a '40s-type swing, pre-rock 'n' roll. "It's got a section with a double slap bass and a Blue Caps type Gretsch guitar (I think Tony got off on being a rockabilly bass player for a few bars!). It was made with

Cliff Gallup in mind. I wanted to do something that maybe Cliff would have liked, in his sort of vein."

Then follows a Hymas composition, "Behind the Veil"—a sparse, deceptively simple song with a reggae feel in which Beck's melody weaves with constantly varying subtleties of inflection—using a guitar tone "so compressed," in the words of *Guitar Player*'s Joe Gore, "that it's about to pop."

"Big Block" (originally "Big Block Chevy") was inspired by an all-fall-down studio jam, kicked off when Bozzio delivered a press roll and Beck started steaming into it, "playing some of the best stuff I've ever done." This is a nasty blues, with a huge, wicked guitar sound which Beck describes as vintage Hendrix. "I did it, too, but he was the one who always used the wide open Marshall with a Fender Strat, and that's exactly what it is. You don't worry about the world, you just go and play."

Track five, "Where Were You," merits detailed examination and we shall return to it shortly. Meanwhile the next track, "Stand on It," is another hot rod oriented title: "Some of the hot rod slang is really tough, fun, slick, street-sounding," Beck comments. On this high-powered, stomp-along shuffle Beck produces noises reminiscent of ZZ Top, whose music he loves, especially the group's guitar slinger, Billy Gibbons. "We're sort of distant brothers—a wonderful player. He's melodic, too. 'Rough Boy' was the most beautiful solo, it could have gone on forever.

"My big love is block sounds and powerful stuff," he emphasizes. "I mean, when I heard ZZ Top do that *Eliminator* album, I realized that the simplicity is the attractive part of it." (No doubt he also thoroughly approved of the hammered '34 Ford three-window coupe pictured on the cover!)

By contrast, the moody "Two Rivers" features some incredible effects of phrasing, tone and technique, including beautiful sustained harmonics. "Two Rivers" was a prime example of the kind of off-the-cuff composing that went on. Beck had crept into a corner of the studio one morning when Tony Hymas was engrossed in rehearsing a piano solo from his classical repertoire, and had quietly picked up the guitar and headphones. Unknown to him, Hymas stopped his own playing and started to listen: "I played a short string of notes, and I heard him play a chord along with it and say, [*sternly*] 'Yes, and *then* what?' 'Well, I haven't got anything yet, Tony.' 'You better work on it: I like that.' It was just me tuning the guitar with those harmonics, and he thought it was a song! That's the way he thinks."

The last track, "Sling Shot" is an all too brief hard-driving rocker with shrieking guitar hysteria and thrash metal drum pandemonium. Joe Gore's summary is too perfect not to quote in full: "'Sling Shot,' the bad-attitude finale, combines a weird 'n' wobbly, seasick-sounding theme with long chains of crispy-crunchy pull-offs, unpredictable leaps of register, and nasty syncopations."

TO BECK'S PEERS, and to all lovers of fine musicianship, the standout track on *Guitar Shop* was "Where Were You," which we promised we would examine in more detail.

Beck was consciously trying to make the guitar a singing voice in this recording, to make it soar and tear at the heart. For this he developed an entirely new* way of producing melody: "playing" the strings with just the vibrato arm, after setting a harmonic in motion. It's an extremely difficult technique, requiring great precision in the left hand to locate and finger the harmonics, and extreme delicacy of touch in the right hand to generate all the bends and vibrato with just the whammy bar.

"The whole song is played on false [fretted string] harmonics, except for the main melody," Beck explains. "The place where I play the harmonic, where you bend the arm, you get this voice sound. I used a '59 Strat with a long repeat echo. There's no synthesized tricks on it. I wanted a dramatic, atmospheric thing, with no rumbling bass, no drums to get in the way, just this soaring singing around the auditorium. I wanted people to listen to the melody."

The sound was inspired by a recording that Hymas had introduced to him, *Le Mystère des Voix Bulgares*, a record of Bulgarian folk music sung by a female choir. "To my amazement these cascading, *brilliant* swirling voices came across, and I was very, very deeply moved. I was just completely wiped by the harmony, the colors, the voice control, the volume control."

One of the ways he emulated this singing was in lowering the whammy and hitting the note, then letting the bar rise to the desired pitch. This alone took enormous amounts of practice to get the feel and intonation right. "We sat there, the three of us in the studio, and the sweat was running down my back [*laughs*]— it was torture. We wanted a full-bodied note, as though it was coming out of heaven, from behind the mountains, you know? First of all I was playing with the volume, sneaking the note in, but Tony didn't like that at all; he said he wanted it majestic and proud."

Mo Foster (from *There and Back*) observed Beck at recordings and described what he saw with wonder: "He picks a note with his thumb, fades in the volume pot with his little finger and moves the arm into gentle vibrato. Whilst the note is still decaying, his hand seems to race all over the control area adjusting tone pots, pickup selector switch and volume pot, prior to picking the next note. And each note has a different emotional charge."

Beck: "There are parts where I'm doing four things at once—hitting harmonics, doing volume swells, manipulating the whammy bar, and muting strings! I know there are players out there thinking, 'Big deal, so you can do it in the studio. Let's hear it live, smartass!' So I'm going to play it in concert—that's where the fun will be."

Sure enough, once Beck had decided it must be done live he put untold hours into mastering it. "I didn't want to cheat. I wanted to be able to perform it

---

*Steve Vai had used a similar technique in "The Attitude Song" on his self-produced album Flex-Able, but only for a few distorted notes and not for sustained melodic lines.

live. And talk about cutting a big trench for myself. Every night I thought, 'Why did I do this damn thing?'"

His principal guitar throughout was his cream Stratocaster put together by Seymour Duncan "from the best bits he had lying about," a '59 body with a '60s neck. But there was also a new Surf Green Strat, custom built by Fender, that he later took on tour. He waited for this new guitar to finish "Where Were You," because it was equipped with a metal Wilkinson nut—the only solution to achieving the final passage, which had an open harmonic that couldn't be sustained enough with any other nut.

Other guitars on the album included Beck's '54 Tele acquired from Seymour Duncan, and an array of backup Strats including his Marriott sunburst and his trusty old white '62/'63 model. The Jackson Soloist he'd used on *Flash*, now retired, was brought out for some of the wailing guitar lines on the title track.

His amplification was mainly a Fender Twin Reverb linked to an early '80s Fender Princeton and turned up almost full. For effects he used a ProCo Rat distortion pedal, an Alesis Midiverb for reverb, and a Yamaha Rev 7 for wash behind the guitar. The occasional octaver and screamer were also on hand.

GUITAR SHOP WAS released in September 1989, and made it to number 49 in the U.S. charts. But more important was the esteem in which it was held throughout the industry. In February 1990 the album was awarded a Grammy for Best Rock Instrumental Performance of 1989.

Jeff Beck's breathtaking performance of "Where Were You" became the talk of the guitar world. Joe Gore in *Guitar Player* described every note as "a perfectly fashioned jewel. Even Beck's harmonics are soulful and vocal sounding, especially in the long chains of slurs that you would have sworn were physically impossible. This is Zen guitar playing so masterful that it seems effortless."

And of the album: *"Jeff Beck's Guitar Shop* is the work of a player who has integrated technique, emotion, spontaneity and attitude so completely that you can't begin to separate them. It's a superb rock instrumental record, one of the best ever. . . . Each note is so detailed, so imbued with personality, that he expresses more with one phrase than many players will in their entire careers. His range of tones, articulations and emotions is astonishingly broad. Each note is unmistakably Beck, but none sounds like any other Becknote."

As Gene Santoro wrote in *Pulse!*: "*Guitar Shop* doesn't avoid the problem of Beck's scattered sensibility, instead using it as a structural tool, surrounding his alternately blazing rage and heartfelt lyricism with varied styles, tempered by his inevitable wit. One of the most diverse instrumental Beck offerings ever, *Guitar Shop* ranges with gleeful, burning ease over thrash metal meltdowns, haunting balladeering, reggae riddim-riding and swaggering fusion. In some ways, it's a kind of recap of Beck's long, fruitful, erratic career."

And remembering the roots of that career, the album is noteworthy, despite its progressive and technically brilliant content, for a remarkable abundance of

Jeff Beck with surf green Signature Strat, on tour with *Guitar Shop* in 1989.

earthy blues inflections: "I tapped into some previous reserves for this album that have been there all the time; I just neglected them a bit. Now I'm going back where I belong."

Even before the release of *Guitar Shop*, the trio started tour rehearsals in a London studio where *Musician*'s Scott Isler caught up with them, commenting that the 45-year-old skinny-hipped Beck hadn't changed his shaggy hairstyle ("that bird's-nest thatch of brown hair") in twenty years, or needed to. "Beck's casual dress—jeans, work boots, open shirt over a white sleeveless undershirt—was more appropriate to the grease pit than the footlights. One could only marvel at Beck's calm grace while producing a blast furnace of sound—now leaning forward, now leaning back, only occasionally indulging in rock body language to punctuate a particularly outrageous guitar scream."

A warm-up tour of Japan started in August, where they played six joyously received concerts to 60,000 fans. Beck's immense popularity in that country remained undiminished, and the album made number one in the Japanese charts.

This was followed by an extensive 28-city tour of North America on a double bill (*The Fire Meets the Fury*) with Texas blues-rock maestro Stevie Ray Vaughan and his band Double Trouble. Neither was top of the bill, and both played full-length sets: Beck won a coin flip to take the second spot on the opening night, and afterwards they alternated. Stevie Ray Vaughan was a major Beck fan, and declared it was an honor to be on the road with his hero. For his part, Beck described Vaughan as one of the finest exponents of blues guitar. "There's no one who has that tone, and the *venom* that goes with it."

"Once onstage," Matt Resnicoff said in *Guitar Player*, "Beck is moved to the next plane. His set is a true reflection of self—kinetic, sexual, streetready. . . . But Beck is also a spectacle—with not much more than a whammy, a pick stroke, and a prayer, he knows just how to play a crowd. He zaps and stings with piercing, bent harmonics and rubbery pull-offs, all expertly punctuated with seasoned rock posturing: like his spiritual ally Nigel Tufnel of Spinal Tap, Beck knows there's far more to a show than a great solo."

Starting on 25 October in Minneapolis, the tour traveled from the Midwest to Canada, then down the Eastern seaboard to Texas and the West, ending with a 19,000-seat sellout concert at Manhattan's Madison Square Garden.

One memorable night Jeff Beck and Stevie Ray Vaughan jammed with Buddy Guy at his Chicago club, Legends. For Beck it was a tremendous thrill: "I was terrified, but in spite of that I went along, because I couldn't resist seeing [Vaughan] and Buddy playing. Seeing Buddy in his element, I didn't mind getting up there, because that is as close as you can come to the heart of the blues, as *I* know it. And the man will suddenly smile and say something so that there's no way you can *not* do it. I found my legs just carried me onstage."

The tour was a fantastic success, though Beck had been off the road so long it made him feel like an absolute beginner. "The commitment from the other two guys has been tremendous. It feels like a band. And we have a record that we're all a part of. It's been years since I went out on the road like this."

Obviously there were nights when his ingrained dislike of touring caught up with him. "Sometimes you don't really feel like playing *at all*," he confessed. "I get run down and stuff, but as soon as I hear that drum it blows it all out of my head. When your socks start going up and down, that's great—there's nothing quite like that."

Usually Stevie Ray Vaughan joined him for a brilliant encore of one of his favorite numbers, "Going Down." But it was Beck's live performance of "Where Were You" that haunted the recollections of those who witnessed these concerts—among them Eddie Van Halen, Steve Vai, Slash, Chrissie Hynde, Nils Lofgren, Albert Collins, Bonnie Raitt, Steve Lukather and David Bowie, all on one night at the L.A. Sports Arena. One guitarist was so bedazzled that he actually

The Fire Meets the Fury: Stevie Ray Vaughan joins Beck for an encore of "Going Down," 1989.

took binoculars to scrutinize Beck's technique from a seat in the fifth row, and still couldn't figure out how he was doing it. "Even Eddie Van Halen just kept shaking his head," he recalled. "And Beck was pulling it off *live*—like it was no big deal!"

From April 1990 a European tour was booked, without Vaughan and Double Trouble as they had other commitments. In fact, their final performance together the previous December was the last time Jeff Beck ever saw Stevie Ray Vaughan: on 26 August the incomparable blues master was tragically killed in a helicopter crash.

Beck's stage presentation on tour—sometimes laid-back, sometimes prancing energetically—led to an agonizing injury at his Manchester show at the Apollo Theatre in May, when pulled ligaments in his back forced him to cancel his next two sellout dates at London's Hammersmith Odeon. After several weeks flat on his back, he managed to slot them in on 28/29 July, drawing an ecstatic review from Paul Henderson:

"Jeff Beck unassumingly strolled onstage, spread his legs, and took off into what became 90 minutes of the breathtaking kind of guitar playing that the rock world has just about forgotten.

"He stalks the stage in constant search of the creative 'flash' and then, having grasped it, lets loose in a refreshingly cavalier manner with bubbling flurries, gloriously weighted chords and the most exquisite tonal colors—from his fingers rather than a rack of technology—and vibrato that stamps 'Beck' on every note he plays. Intense power blended seamlessly with spine-tingling beauty. Really, quite staggering stuff!

"Beck one minute short-circuits himself to the Bozzio/Hymas dynamo with incandescent sparks flying from his fingertips; the next minute playing with the mesmerizing delicacy of a butterfly settling on your cheek.

"There really is no one around to touch him. For those of us unlucky enough never to have seen Jimi Hendrix, Jeff Beck is arguably the next best thing. Inspirational and inspiring. Astonishing. Truly brilliant. Quite literally . . . awesome!"

15 Forward and Rewind

AS THE *GUITAR SHOP* tour got under way, Jeff Beck declared his total commitment to the trio with Terry Bozzio and Tony Hymas. "I'm truly lucky to have found them, they're such a luxury. Now I'm living and breathing music. This album will be a joke compared to where the band will be six months from now."

So what happened after 1990? Five years went by before they collaborated again. From the moment they relaxed at the end of touring, circumstances seemed to pull them apart. For a start, Hymas and his wife were just having a child; so it was important for him to spend more time with his family, which Beck could readily understand.

Then there were plans to go into the studio, "But it happened to be at the heat wave of the century. We had 103-degree weather in an unairconditioned studio. All I could think of was, 'I want to go out. I want to go driving. I'm going to go to the sea.' We were reading the great reviews that we had just got the day before, and it was all over. The party was done, at least for the time being."

The problem was that both his colleagues had careers in their own right. A year later there was one attempt to pick up the threads when Terry Bozzio flew to England. But by then Tony Hymas was already committed to other projects of his own. Beck frankly rated him the best keyboard player in the world, and a vast source of inspiration with his unique approach to writing; Hymas' parts were pivotal to the whole thing, and it was useless trying to replace him. With just a drummer, as Beck observed, "things get a little skinny there!"

So the months slipped by, and he was on his own again. Left to his own devices, his trouble had always been finding the motivation to get busy; and this was usually down to finding other musicians who would kindle the spark.

"Who are they going to be, for a start? You've got to get somebody to scratch that itch. There's no point trying to make a record without having a brotherly feeling with two or three other guys in a studio or a future band."

Back home in America, Bozzio's fellow Zappa alumnus Steve Vai had eagerly snapped him up for his awesome *Sex and Religion* album. As he said at the time: "Terry Bozzio—jeez, I've always wanted to work with him. He's been my favorite drummer forever." Interestingly, there were other signs of cross-pollination. Several Beckisms could be discerned on Vai's new album, especially in his use of whammy for the track "Rescue Me or Bury Me," on which he also explored fingerpicking to get Jeff Beck tones.

IN TERMS OF accolades, guest appearances, and invitations to perform on albums and soundtracks, Beck's personal star was in the ascendant throughout the *Guitar Shop* period and beyond.

As well as winning the Grammy, he had also won the distinction of being chosen by his peers as supreme rock lead guitarist in the Guitarists' Guitarist poll mounted by the Sunday newspaper *The Observer*. It surely must have done his heart good to be held in such esteem by his fellow musicians.

At the beginning of 1990, between *Guitar Shop* tours, he sat in with Tony Hymas on Hymas' double album *Oyaté*, which only saw release in France. Beck played on two tracks, "Tashunka Witko" and "Crazy Horse." The latter called for guitar sounds like the classic Western movies, for which he used whammy bends to get an effect reminiscent of Clint Eastwood's *The Good, the Bad and the Ugly*. Though hardly a characteristic Beck genre, strangely enough he received another request shortly afterwards to record something very similar.

It was around February/March of 1990 that he was invited to California by pop-rock icon Jon Bon Jovi, who was putting together some songs for the movie *Young Guns II*. Jon Bon Jovi had written four numbers for the film including "Blaze of Glory," and the producers wanted to release them commercially, so he augmented the collection to an album's worth of ten tracks. With the members of Bon Jovi taking a break at the time, he was free to choose a stellar lineup for the recordings. Beck was his first choice for lead guitar.

Produced by Danny Kortchmar, the result was *Blaze of Glory/Young Guns II*. Beck's guitar leads included two songs that were on the soundtrack, "Blaze of Glory" and "Billy Get Your Guns," plus five nonsoundtrack items. For one of these—"The Miracle"—there was also a video, with Beck making a brief appearance playing in a small club.

"Blaze of Glory" was very much in the vein of Bon Jovi's earlier hit, "Wanted: Dead or Alive," and showcased some much-admired down 'n' dirty Southern slide work on Beck's Strat in open D tuning. At the end of the solo it also featured one of his unique personal signatures, an item of Beckery that hadn't been much exposed lately outside of live performances (catch it in "Freeway Jam" on the *Live with Jan Hammer* album). A brief moment of farewell, echoing the shape of the song's main hook, is played high in the "Strato"-sphere above the pickups. This self-discovered technique achieves an unearthly high-pitched tone, produced by muting the strings with the left hand while tapping with the slide near the pickups, way up beyond the highest frets. The tapping position in relation to pickups and bridge has a lot to do with the quality of the effect, and of course a sensitive touch is crucial to getting the desired pitch at such altitudes.*

Acknowledgements to Dick Wyzanski for explaining this technique.

Jeff Beck in the studio with Jon Bon Jovi and producer Danny Kortchmar, March 1990.

While we're on the subject of unorthodox Beck techniques, another can be heard in a little fill on "Ice Cream Cakes" from the *Jeff Beck Group* album, where he "frets" the high E string against the neck pickup—a dry rasp kindred to the toneless effect of bowing a violin across the bridge.

Among Jon Bon Jovi's session guests was the inimitable Little Richard, and Bon Jovi couldn't help being struck by Beck's outright thrill at meeting him: "When he came in, Beck started playing 'Lucille'—and his hands were shaking." Declaring that Little Richard was the whole reason he got into the music business, Beck asked the legendary star to carve his name on the body of his guitar. The guitar in question was his favorite Surf Green Strat that first appeared on "Where Were You"—irreverently known as Small Dick from then on—which now made a non-matching pair with the pink Jackson signed by Tina Turner.

Jon Bon Jovi was just as thrilled to be working with Jeff Beck. He said he was nervous even asking him to play and, having such respect for him, felt really awkward giving him direction. But Beck appreciated it, he said: it worked. Bon Jovi could scarcely believe his control with the right hand, especially the way he used the volume and tone between chords. He was so spellbound that he actually spent some time making a videotape of Beck in action, mistakes and all.

Warren DeMartini of Ratt, who also had the chance to watch Beck in the studio, was equally amazed by his atmospherics using just volume and tone. "He would change the color in the room in a second, by switching to the bass pickup, turning the tone down, and adjusting the volume. He achieved such a radical change in sound, and it wasn't the kind where you have to mess with the tone setting on the amp. It was just so quick, and he was so at one with his guitar, which is what I've always been striving to do."

Asked how it was to work on the album, Beck said: "It was great. Jon was very nice to me. I'd go over it till I was happy while Jon was next door working his ass off singing the vocal lines. At the end of the day I'd listen to what he did and he would listen to what I did. To tell you the truth I haven't heard the album since I left the studio. We were in a cafe the other day and *Blaze of Glory* came on. It sounded pretty good."

His next film involvement, for the Tom Cruise auto racing movie *Days of Thunder*, again had him performing someone else's score: it was written by Hans Zimmer, the Oscar-winning composer of *The Lion King* soundtrack. Also recorded in 1990, it called for another of those trips abroad, this time to New River Studios in Fort Lauderdale, Florida. Four basic tracks had been laid down already, and Beck learned the melodies piecemeal, playing them as he learned them. Beck: "Hans Zimmer did the scoring for that. He must have said to the director, 'I want Beck over here.' I was flown out to Florida. Nearly got killed in a small plane crash in a thunderstorm. I thought, 'I don't like the movie business!' It was over in about four days."

Only some of this music was eventually used in the film, and Beck's instrumentals may be dimly heard at the end during the final race; unfortunately none was available on the soundtrack album.

While recounting the events of 1990, a brief mention should be made of Beck's contribution to a song recorded about the middle of the year with an outfit called Moodswings, at the invitation of Chrissie Hynde of the Pretenders. This was titled "Skinthieves," and the vocal was concerned with the plight of the endangered tiger, with Hynde—a tireless campaigner for animal rights—helping out on backup vocals. But the track never made it as intended to the album *Tame Yourself*, a release in aid of animal rights activism, and was eventually shelved for the best part of two years.

Jeff Beck's involvement was on the understanding that the song wouldn't be released as a single, but this unfortunately got overlooked when Arista later came to release an album *Moodfood by Moodswings* (in 1992), including a pared-down instrumental version of "Skinthieves"—and decided to release it as a promo single as well. Chrissie Hynde freaked when she discovered this had happened, and it had to be withdrawn in a hurry.

Later in 1990, Beck appeared in a video for his old colleague Jan Hammer, promoting Hammer's new album *Too Much to Lose*, which was released by MCA in Europe only. Also in the video were David Gilmour on bass and Ringo Starr on drums, though curiously enough none of these star guests actually played on the recording. Recalling the sessions, Gilmour said: "I'm not much of a technician and Beck is, and watching him I know I wouldn't like to play next to him. Old Clappers [Eric Clapton] is still a beautiful blues guitarist, but not in the same brilliance league as Beck."

Some more fascinating opportunities to see Beck in action presented themselves around this time, when he embarked on a number of cameo appearances in the BBC TV series *The Comic Strip Presents*, directed by his pal Peter Richardson, whose offbeat British humor appealed to Beck (you'll remember him from *Twins*, and also as Spider, the drummer with the group Bad News, actually the *Comic Strip*'s heavy metal parody band).

Beck was first seen as an airline passenger demanding *"real* food" in a two-part story titled "South Atlantic Raiders," for which he also provided some spectacular background music based on the *Guitar Shop* album. Recorded the previous year, this included an interesting early version of "Where Were You" with a bolero beat. His next appearance, in "Red Nose of Courage," featured him for a few seconds as a rowdy backbencher, wildly thrashing an inaudible acoustic guitar amidst the uproar of a House of Commons debate.

Two more episodes ensued in 1993, the first calling for Beck's guitar input to augment Bad News in the episode "Space Virgins from Planet Sex"; and the second featuring Beck in action again, in "Gregory—Diary of a Nut Case," where Beck is seen driving one of his rods (as Brad the serial killer) in a movie that Gregory is watching.

Returning to February 1991, Beck was called upon to record yet more film music—and play yet another small part—this time for a British comedy titled *The Pope Must Die*. The invitation came his way again through the multifaceted Peter Richardson, who directed, cowrote and played a part in the picture. These recordings saw Beck providing guitar and contributing original music to the score in collaboration with Anne Dudley (ex-Art of Noise). No soundtrack album was ever produced, but there was a U.K. single release of "Speedy Gonzalez," the song made famous by Pat Boone in his 1962 hit. This little gem featured some classic Beck rockin' and rollin' alongside a spirited vocal by actor Robbie Coltrane (Pope Dave). The B-side was the Dudley/Beck composition "The Pope Must Die Theme," performed by Beck with the Pro Arte Orchestra and Choir of London.

Beck's cameo in the movie has him in the part of a postman (he must have been an old hand at studio makeup by now!): look for that unmistakable profile as he appears on a bike delivering the letter that Pope Dave writes to his little friends at the orphanage. The movie was (ironically) retitled *The Pope Must Diet* for U.S. distribution, where it had a limited theater release around September 1991. Without the title change, apparently, it would never have seen U.S. release at all.

At the end of the film Jeff Beck is unspecifically credited as "featured guitar," but there's no mistaking his presence enhancing almost every musical moment. Dick Wyzanski, reporting for *The Jeff Beck Fanzine*, noted that Beck's performances ranged through no fewer than six distinct styles: classic rock, new age, rockabilly, modern classical, an instrumental soft rock ballad, and a delta blues. At one poignant moment there is also a "Sleep Walk"-ish fragment, and if that's our hero playing when the film's rock star takes the stage, you can add thrash metal to the list!

ASIDE FROM THESE dalliances, the early '90s afforded occasions to get down to some seriously satisfying music. When the first opportunity came, it gave him the chance to record with one of his lifetime heroes, Buddy Guy.

It was twelve years since his last album, and on *Damn Right I've Got the Blues* Guy had the freedom at last to do what he wanted; his past recordings somehow never did justice to his full-blooded, fire-eating originality. Guy said he felt better about this album than anything he'd done in a long time. "With the release of this new record I'm the happiest man who ever picked up a guitar. Jeff sat in. Eric [Clapton], Eric's backup singers, the Average White Band horns, and the Memphis Horns all came down. I can't even tell you . . ."

They got together in January 1991, with Beck contributing a gutsy blues performance on "Mustang Sally." He originally played on "Early in the Morning" as well, but his guitar part was not used on the release (the covers had already been printed, which accounts for his credit on that track). "Mustang Sally" also came out as a CD single and video: the video starts with Beck and Guy playing side by side in front of a casino, whereupon the girl of the title drives up in a red Mustang with license plate "Sally." A later scene in the desert finds her waited on by Beck in the guise of a gas station attendant.

Released in August, the album won Buddy Guy the richly deserved award of a Grammy for Best Contemporary Blues Album. Strangely enough, buyers in Britain would find that Beck's part was missing on the U.K. LP, although he was on the U.K. 45 single and CD single in a version different from the album recording.

Buddy Guy was full of praise for Beck's guitar work. "He did such a tremendous job on it, man, I got to go back and learn some more just to keep up with him. When *this* guy picks up a guitar, I don't care if I'm asleep or whatever, please wake me up so that I won't miss a thing." He was so turned on by working with Beck that he had the engineers keep the tape running during the rehearsals: "It was that good. In fact, it turned out to be one of the greatest sessions I was ever involved in."

With this album and his following release in 1993, *Feels like Rain* (to which Beck was unfortunately unable to contribute, due to his busy schedule), Buddy Guy suddenly found himself "rediscovered" again, with all the TV and concert tours that went with fame. "A black blues musician doesn't get on TV until he's passed away. . . . I have to pinch myself to be sure it's real!"

Both being devotees of the Stratocaster, Guy and Beck had recently been honored by the Fender company with Signature Strats to their own personal specifications. Fender had actually approached Beck with the offer as early as

Beck and Buddy Guy trading memories in 1991.

1986: that was when he placed an order for two custom Strats based on the Vintage reissue series, one of them in the same yellow as the Ford "Deuce Coupe" in a favorite film of his, *American Graffiti*. Had he accepted, the Jeff Beck model would have been the first Signature Strat they ever made. But he declined, saying he wasn't sure that he deserved it!

Nevertheless, the Fender Custom Shop made up a couple of prototypes based on his reissue specs, one of them in Beck's Graffiti Yellow (or Rebel Yella), the other with a yellow hot rod painted on the body. They presented the latter to Beck, possibly in hopes of changing his mind; when he remained unpersuaded, the model evolved into the Strat Plus.

Equipped with 22 frets, Lace Sensor pickups and Trev Wilkinson's roller nut, the Strat Plus offered features that were very much to Beck's liking. So in 1989, succumbing at last to Fender's blandishments, he based his Signature model on the Strat Plus but added a rosewood fretboard.

The process began with three prototypes: the first was a model in Midnight Purple; the second was the Surf Green model used for "Where Were You," which Little Richard autographed; and the third sported the legend *Deuce Mania* with a red roadster airbrushed against a cream background. These prototypes were equipped with three gold Lace Sensor pickups, the American Standard vibrato arm, and either Sperzel or Schaller rear-locking tuners.

When setting out his specs, Beck was insistent that he wanted a really large neck, resembling Fenders from the early '50s. "I was finding that the necks on most Strats were too thin, and because of the way my hand is, it was aching a hell of a lot. I thought, 'Why can't they make a fatter neck on a Strat?' The Fender guys offered me a guitar and I said, 'No, no, no! Just double it! Get a log, smooth it off a bit and stick it on the end there.' So they did and it was too fat [prototype number one]. Then they took it down a bit and it was okay [number two, with a neck close to one inch thick]. I think the Signature model they've got now has the fattest neck you can have without being arrested."

The prototype stage now over, the first Jeff Beck Signature models were manufactured in June 1990. A significant change here was the addition of a fourth pickup: the locations were now one in the neck position, one in the middle, and two together at the bridge, with a push-button switch to kick in the second bridge unit for a thicker sound. Jeff Beck models from 1992 incorporated the LSR nut.

"I don't know if people will enjoy playing it the way I have it set up," he says, "with the floating bridge so that I can pull the note up and down. But if people want to buy a Jeff Beck guitar, that's the way I have it. People usually pick up my guitar and say, 'Jesus! You can keep that! Take that thing outta here!'"

SIX MONTHS AFTER the Buddy Guy collaboration, Beck undertook a project that could not have been more different. In the summer of '91 he joined Roger Waters for sessions on his new album *Amused to Death*—arguably the best recording work Beck has ever done for another artist or band.

Waters had heard *Guitar Shop* and was blown away, especially by the incredible sound and atmosphere of "Where Were You." He was already working on *Amused to Death* and made up his mind that he must get Jeff Beck to put his guitar on the album.

Waters chased after Beck for several months with no response, until at last he caught him on a good day when he wasn't otherwise involved. "Look, you don't have any obligation," he said. "I'll rent a studio for you for two hours and you can go along and listen, with just an engineer to play you the tapes."

"I just work better without anybody there," Beck contends. "It leaves you free to make a judgment more accurately if the person concerned is not standing around. I don't know . . . you just hear it with *your* ears, not his." But when he heard "What God Wants" he absolutely loved it. "So I made the commitment. And I enjoyed it, I really did. It was more like a comedy half-hour every day than hard work."

Waters said that like most guitarists, Beck would continue to improvise straight through whatever he was overdubbing until asked to stop; but unlike most guitarists, Jeff Beck wanted guidance from his colleagues—and left them with performances they'd remember for the rest of their lives.

Beck's contributions were recorded in five separate trips to the studio. It was pure jamming, he said; nothing was written out. Waters wanted something akin to "Where Were You," so all Beck could do was follow producer/keyboardist Pat Leonard's chords as closely as he could, even though it meant fumbles and mistakes as they went along. The key was tapping into the emotion of the music: "That's much more important than making mistakes—so be prepared to look the chump. If you become too guarded and too processed, the music loses its spontaneity and gut feeling."

One of his most spine-tingling moments is the intro to "The Ballad of Bill Hubbard," which opens the album. Amazingly, according to Beck, this was the result of an "end-of-session messaround" which they happened to record and promptly forgot. "The story goes that Roger was driving home from the hills and he played this tape of the day's work, and at the end of it he couldn't touch the tape machine because he was driving. It ran on and suddenly this stuff came on, and he thought, '*Jesus* Christ, what's this? I want this straightaway!' Next thing, it wound up as the lead track on the album."

Though Beck's account of his work is typically prosaic, Roger Waters was positively lyrical in his praise. "A U.K. national treasure," he called him in *Goldmine* magazine, and on another occasion described him as "one of the great players of all time." Altogether Jeff Beck is credited on seven songs, of which six feature hauntingly eloquent leads. A high point is Beck's majestic, impassioned solo on "What God Wants, Part III."

Amused to Death was eventually released in September 1992, delayed by production of the accompanying animated video in which Beck can be seen briefly. A performance video in black and white is included in Waters' "What God Wants, Part I" videocassette.

The project was a characteristic Roger Waters concept album, invoking bitter images ranging from World War I to Tiananmen Square. The review in *Guitar for the Practicing Musician* was equivocal about the album, but not about Beck: "Lethargic but involving morality play saved by Beck. Jeff Beck is God, at least on this record. If you want lessons in how to steal an album, listen to the half dozen Beck leads punched into Roger Waters' latest. . . The beginning and end are saved by the appearance of Jeff Beck's gorgeously cranky guitar. Beck's warbling leads, as personal as a signature, lift this leaden album up as if weightless. His playing is like an electric shock. Borrow the CD, tape the Beck."

WE WILL INCLUDE here the third collaboration in this illustrious list, even though it means leaping forward a year or so. It was in late 1992 that Paul Rodgers (ex-Free and Bad Company) invited Jeff Beck to play on an album titled *Muddy Water Blues*, a collection of blues songs intended as a tribute to Muddy Waters. Among the galaxy of performers were guitarists David Gilmour, Buddy Guy, Brian May,

Steve Miller, Gary Moore, Trevor Rabin, Richie Sambora, Neal Schon, Brian Setzer, and Slash.

The excellent studio band boasted Jason Bonham on drums, and the outstanding fretless bass talents of Pino Palladino (later another Beck collaborator). Rodgers cited Palladino as his favorite bassist: "He's just a brilliant player. I figured that those two together would be an awesome rhythm section."

Beck had thought of working with Paul Rodgers several times before, and after Rodgers had joined the ARMS tour they even made a tentative arrangement to try getting together—sadly unfulfilled. Even now they didn't coincide in the studio, Beck's contributions being done at long distance by having the tapes flown in. He spent four days recording overdubs at The Mill Studios, with Leif Mases doing the remixes, and was the only guest guitarist used on as many as three tracks. Actually he said he was ready to do the whole album!

Beck's leads and solos bristle with excitement and intensity, the three numbers affording him the chance to home in to devastating effect with some of the wickedest blues playing he's done in many a long year. "It was real gung-ho, powerhouse blues—more English, like *Truth* or *Beck-Ola* and the old band I had with Rod Stewart." In fact, Beck probably echoed the views of many listeners when he said, "I think this has more balls than *Truth*: it's how I would have wanted the Jeff Beck Group to sound."

Rodgers: "The nicest thing Jeff said was that it took him back to the *Truth* album, which is probably my favorite Beck album of all time. Do you remember, they did 'Ain't Superstitious' and all that—whoa, great stuff!"

Keith Wyatt's review in *Guitar World* singled out the Beck songs for top billing, followed by those of Buddy Guy and David Gilmour: "Jeff Beck puts the spirit and the flesh into 'Rolling Stone,' 'I Just Wanna Make Love to You' and 'Good Morning Little Schoolgirl—Part I.' He based a career around blues with this attitude, and he lays claim to it, pushing Rodgers beyond his usual relaxed delivery right to the edge of rawness. There is the same bite as his collaborations with Rod Stewart on *Truth*, the album that made Beck's reputation as one of the few English blues players on a par with his inspirations."

Other than Beck, Guy and Gilmour, Wyatt had little praise for the work of the other guest guitarists, and gave the album only a two-star rating; in fact it deserved much better. Paul Rodgers turned in some excellent, well controlled, and in places hard-rocking blues performances, not to mention that the album offered the opportunity to compare licks from a galaxy of top-notch guitar exponents. Don't tape it—buy it.

MEANWHILE, EPIC HAD determined to put together a Jeff Beck boxed set commemorating his career in music. His fans awaited the release eagerly, but Beck dragged his heels: he was reluctant to see this kind of "tribute" produced, with all the hype that he foresaw accompanying it. "To tell you the honest truth," he says, "I wasn't into the idea of an anthology album at all.

"I got a list of the proposed tracks—some eighty tracks—and it's amazing how fast the eye can flick through a list like that and pick out the bad apples. I was amazed at the persistence of Gregg Geller, how keen he was to put this record out when I wasn't really interested. I said to Gregg, 'When I'm ready to die, put all my records out.' He said, 'No, now is the time.' He dug out all the stuff and I thought, 'Wow, I've been busy despite what people say! The amount of songs is quite impressive.' So I weeded out a few of the no-nos and let them go ahead with it."

Epic's original idea was a set of four CDs, but it was eventually pared down to three. Released in November 1991, *Beckology* was accompanied by a separate 17-track CD selection, and also a CD single. Even with only three CDs in the set, it contained a heaping helping of 55 digitally remastered tracks, spanning recording dates from 1963 to 1989. Billed as "the definitive study of the most inventive guitarist in music history," it included titles from all of Beck's groups and solo albums up to *Guitar Shop*, providing a mixture of vintage tracks, live cuts, film soundtracks, and radio recordings.

The understated design of the box was particularly impressive, being an exact copy of a Fender vintage guitar case complete with imprints of guitar strings in the lid; the photography on the cover of the booklet inside was produced to look like the guitar sitting in the case. Promotional guitar picks were also available.*

The 64-page booklet was lavishly illustrated with historic photographs, and the liner notes were excellently written by Gene Santoro with all the enthusiasm of one who obviously appreciated and understood his work, much of the material fleshed out from an interview in September 1991. Particularly refreshing was the accuracy of nearly everything in the booklet, given the clouds of obscurity that hang over so much of Beck's career.

Inevitably there were caveats about the tracks included—and omitted—from the collection. Whether they were among Beck's "no-nos," or simply dropped in the paring down process, there were several unreleased tracks that were initially considered and would have been a treat for fans. Known to be among them were additional Tridents numbers (Geller had a large selection to choose from), the "All Stars" recordings, and songs from the "Motown album."

Eventually the set had just five previously unreleased tracks: the three early Tridents numbers, and the two BBA recordings, "Blues Deluxe/BBA Boogie" live, and "Jizz Whizz" from their unfinished second studio album. But three tracks from the '60s and two from the '70s didn't constitute an over-generous offering

---

For readers interested to know the type of pick favored by Beck, on the rare occasions when he uses one, a feature in Guitar Player *in May 1985 showed an orange Ernie Ball medium bearing the name Jeff Beck, "reportedly used for one song during the tour with Stevie Ray Vaughan."*

of unreleased material in terms of what was known to be available, even ruling out bootleg recordings which would, of course, be unacceptable.

In the "CD Watchdog" column of the specialist CD magazine *ICE*, readers' recommendations mentioned rarities and deleted material such as Stanley Clarke sessions, *The Secret Policeman's Other Ball*, the ARMS tour, etc.

Gregg Geller's response in *ICE* said that all of those options were considered: "This was a project that sort of evolved over the course of eighteen years, and during that time he loosened up on using a lot of stuff that, in the beginning, he didn't want to hear about. But as with any artist, when it came down to making the final determination there were certain things that he simply didn't want on there.

"The only real way for me to make it work on three CDs was to eliminate the sessions. There was no way I could rationalize using just a few things of that nature; I would've wanted to use a lot of them. And that would have necessitated a fourth CD. Maybe there can be a *Son of Beckology* someday that would include that kind of stuff, because there certainly is an abundance of it. He did wonderful work with Stanley Clarke, Tina Turner, Donovan . . . the list is endless, going back into the '60s."

Perhaps because of the enormous variety (and disparity) of Beck's output, many reviewers climbed in with their own personal likes and dislikes. Carlo Wolff, for example, writing in *Goldmine*, was happy to see plenty of recordings with Rod Stewart, but would have preferred less BBA and *Flash*, and more of JBG2 and *Blow by Blow*. "Beck's sound, however, remains ravishing, and there's plenty of it here. You just have to slog through a lot of tired stuff to hear it clear."

On the other hand, *Musician*'s Matt Resnicoff, not a fan of the Beck-Stewart combination, would have preferred exclusion of "I've Been Drinking" and inclusion of "his vicious ARMS set, 'El Becko,' and 'Tonight I'll Be Staying Here with You.'"

With no fewer than 19 Yardbirds tracks, it seemed strange that one-third of the compilation was devoted to this period. Gregg Geller: "I'm a big Beck fan, and it's always bugged me that when people mention the Yardbirds they talk first about Eric Clapton and then about Jimmy Page, and then sometimes they mention Jeff Beck. The fact of the matter is virtually every famous Yardbirds recording—all the records that their reputation is based on—features Jeff playing guitar. I really wanted to make that clear."

Well, okay, and it did allow a selection of BBC radio recordings; but anyone who wants an entire CD's worth of Yardbirds can easily go and buy one.

It was good, on the other hand, to hear one-off soundtrack items such as "Sleep Walk" and "The Stumble." The single "Wild Thing" was a welcome inclusion, as were the less familiar—and superior—versions of "Rock My Plimsoul" (taken from the original single) and "Goodbye Pork Pie Hat" (which is different from that on the *Wired* album).

But the unaccountable choice of "Blues Deluxe/BBA Boogie" (all 16 minutes 41 seconds of it) was not only incongruous, it also denied listeners several much more desirable tracks in its stead. This writer would certainly have preferred to hear a couple more storming items from the *Blow by Blow* to *There and Back* period in addition to "Freeway Jam"—take your pick from "Thelonius," "Led Boots," "El Becko," "Star Cycle," and you still have room for something shorter from BBA.

"They weren't trying necessarily to choose the best performances," Beck defended. "I think they were categorizing them in terms of direction more than anything else. I would have loved to have put 'Star Cycle' in. I thought that was a fairly revolutionary step inasmuch as in 1978 nobody was playing digital sequence like Jan [Hammer]. And that thing gave us a lot of miles, but it never wound up on there." Nevertheless, surely the brief "Star Cycle" theme for *The Tube* could have been included, and would likely have been a revelation to listeners who were unaware of its source.

Still, in three CDs, with sessions excluded, it would obviously have been impossible to compile a truly representative selection. Perhaps this bodes well for the second retrospective that Geller hinted at, and maybe Beck will involve himself next time. Indeed, in 1994 Epic did produce an album of *Jeff Beck Session Works* with oddly assorted selections from Malcolm McLaren, Upp, Box of Frogs, Donovan, Stanley Clarke, *Twins*, and two 1993 songs with Beverley Craven—but it was only released in Japan.

As 1991 DREW to a close there appeared a resurgence of interest in the Yardbirds. A singular honor came the group's way when it was scheduled for induction into America's Rock and Roll Hall of Fame, and Sony Music Special Products released two compilation CDs which included some rare titles.

Around the same time, Warner Home Video produced an excellent 60-minute documentary videocassette which contained great vintage moments of live Yardbirds shows and TV appearances. There were interviews with their managers Giorgio Gomelsky, Mickie Most and Peter Grant, as well as contemporary footage of Eric Clapton, Jeff Beck, Jimmy Page, Chris Dreja, Jim McCarty, and Paul Samwell-Smith. Slated for release in November, it was eventually delayed until March 1992, by which time their induction had taken place in January. All the surviving members of the group were present except Clapton, who was in England recording his *Unplugged* MTV performance.

"It's peculiar," Beck reflected, "when you talk about Jimmy and Eric, we're from the same county—all within about a 12-mile distance. Maybe that part of the planet has some kind of energetic vibe about it. Or maybe it was something to do with the education system that drove us to leave school and listen to rock 'n' roll on the radio. Without that band and the exposure we all had from it, things might have been very, very different."

On the occasion of the induction there were some massive jams, though somewhat disorganized, and Beck was among the ones who didn't join in. The reason became clear when he told journalist Lisa Robinson that he was suffering from tinnitus, the terrible hearing affliction that means living with a constant, inescapable noise in the ears. Between this time and September 1992 he went to something like twenty different specialists to seek relief, but with medical knowledge at its present stage there is no known cure.

16 Frankie's Legs

As our story moves into the '90s, packaged rap and techno still dominate the charts, ever more discofied, fragmented, and infested with sampling. But style is about to take a turn to flannel shirts, knitted hats, and shapeless half-mast shorts, as advancing waves of garage bands with wildly distorting guitars emerge from damp Seattle clubs and make their move on mainstream consciousness.

The Seattle movement, spearheaded by Nirvana, acquires the appropriately anti-establishment title of grunge, soon a portmanteau term for almost any style of angry, restless, neo-punkoid grime.

That it becomes chart material is a classic oxymoron, exactly as with '70s punk. Indeed, the whole cycle has eerily repeated itself. But this time the music biz has it under control: grunge is sucked right into the commercial star-making routine of MTV and major tours. Though yesterday's punk was an anti-music music, today's grindcore shows marginally more concern for song-craft. But technique is decidedly not an issue. If shred is dead, then grunge is clearly dancing on its grave.

Whatever its validities and raw vitality, the Seattle sound of the '90s offered little that Jeff Beck had not experienced before: the pounding distortion he had himself pioneered in the '60s, the alienated primitivism he had witnessed in the '70s. If Beck had espoused any visible influences of late, they were—as we have come to expect—from the black side of the tracks. A few Prince-type grooves. A touch of hip-hop attitude. But fundamentally he was still the supreme innovator: vaunted, lauded, respected, a unique guitar voice, too often enhancing other people's creative efforts.

In 1992, however, came an invitation that gave full rein to his own creativity. It was an offer to score an entire filmed production, a fact-based Australian Broadcasting Company film made as a miniseries for television.

Frankie's House documented the edge-of-hell existence led by photo-journalists in Vietnam, a film teeming with action and violence as well as moments of aching heartbreak.

For this work Beck called in an old friend, Jed Leiber, the son of Jerry from the Leiber & Stoller songwriting/production team, whose dozens of hits included

Elvis Presley's "Hound Dog" and "Jailhouse Rock." The soundtrack was handled in its entirety by Beck and Leiber, who wrote and performed all the material. The two of them worked on it for seven weeks in virtual isolation, with Leiber providing the keyboards and synthesized bass and drums.

They had met more than ten years before, when Beck approached Jerry Leiber about the possibility of writing him some songs. "It was when Jed came to see me play on the *There and Back* tour that he woke up that I was the guy talking to his father earlier. I understood he gave up his career in astrophysics to become a keyboard player after that. He's one cat who really does believe in me, and I turn to him when I get down—I ring him. He's like a brother."

David Sinclair, interviewing Beck in *Rolling Stone*, called the album "a collection of searing and moody instrumental pieces, a soundtrack that alternates between ghostly calm and riotous frenzy, Beck's playing conjuring glorious soundscapes of pin-sharp clarity."

Working as a team was obviously the right decision, as both the medium and the music were unfamiliar territory. "It was very nerve-racking, especially as I was pinning the composing on to someone's work. It's not like you're doing a cover to order for somebody who knows what they are going to get. Nobody knew what the hell was going to happen."

Beck's first move was to saturate himself in Vietnamese tapes. The result is immediately apparent in the main theme, "The Jungle," where Beck's funky guitar is suffused with Asian overtones. "For about a month I listened to nothing else so I got those bends in my mind. They are not aesthetically correct but the feel is right. Rather than play a koto, I used the state of mind I was in from some of the Vietnamese licks. So we wrote the theme tune and we sent it over, and [director Peter Fisk] just freaked. He said, 'That's exactly what I want. The Viet feel with some modern funk groove.'"

After the initial nervousness, it was great to know they'd struck the right chord. "We got the magic phone call saying, 'Yeah, we love it,' then we were all systems go. The first episode was a breeze. We got a bit cocky with the second one. We were playing tennis, not worrying too much about the time slipping away. You can imagine the knock-on effect on the fourth episode. It was like, 'God! We haven't done 'Vihn's Funeral,' we've got to do the patrol again!'"

The plaintive "Vihn's Funeral" would prove to be one of the soundtrack's atmospheric highlights. Jeff Beck once more used his whammy/harmonics technique in this beautifully judged performance, of which *Guitar Player* published a painstaking transcription by Jesse Gress. Gress commented that, incredibly, Beck squeezed the entire piece from just ten harmonic pitches. He added that music critic Joel Selvin hit the nail on the head when he compared Beck's whammy technique to the feather-touch accelerator response on his custom hot rods. "The concepts are identical—press just a hair too hard, and you're off the road!"

Beck: "There's a purity of tone when you get a natural harmonic and a bent note and it's not interfered with by any mechanical left-hand work. It's inspiring for me to play with. You've only got to put a couple of tasty chords under there, and you're away." The real excitement of using the technique, he feels, is in being utterly original: "I mean, people use it all over the place in rock, but not with those sort of nice sweeping melodies. It's kind of my little thing I've got going, you know?"

There were nuggets of several styles to be found throughout the soundtrack. As well as featuring a short passage of delicious King Sunny Ade-type West African juju to introduce "Innocent Victim" ("I love all that"), he also quoted from his classic rocker "Rice Pudding" in the song "Cathouse." This was in response to Fisk calling for some raw, wild Beck for the barroom scenes.

In other ways he was not always happy to go with Peter Fisk's suggestions. "I know the director wanted fierce rock 'n' roll when people were getting shot, and I wouldn't do that: this obscene, *thrashing* rock when this horrible death scene was there. I wanted to underscore it, which I did—much to the director's annoyance—but I think everybody else liked it. I wanted to frame it, making the absurdity of war almost unbearable."

For almost the entire album he used a Signature Stratocaster, which, in addition to its other merits, was the perfect instrument for obtaining those harmonics. Nearly all the soundtrack was recorded direct to the console, to preserve the subtleties of the sounds. But one stand-alone track was an exception to this setup in every way: this was "Hi-Heel Sneakers," a number specifically requested by the director. "He said their researcher found that chopper pilots in Vietnam were singing it a lot. That was his nth degree of authenticity coming out."

For this joyous rock 'n' roll shakedown, Beck funked out the vocal line on guitar, using his Tele-Gib and Gretsch Duo-Jet played live through an amp. It also has a stomping Beck on bass, with Leiber boogying up a storm on keyboards ("this great stride/barrelhouse/rock 'n' roll/pub piano") in a way that even his dad, in his glory days, could scarcely have heard bettered.

As Beck takes his own solo after Leiber's workout on the ivories, you can hear another snatch of that signature high-pitched "whistling" tone he produces, to devastating effect, by tapping with the slide above the highest frets.

During April, while still working on *Frankie's House*, the duo took time out to do their own fuzz-drenched version of "Hound Dog" for the movie *Honeymoon in Vegas*, producing a one-of-a-kind instrumental just as they had with "Hi-Heel Sneakers." Again the whole thing was done by just the two of them.

Beck: "'Hound Dog' we did in our lunch hour. We needed to get away from *Frankie's House* for a while. This project came across our desk and we said, 'How the hell are we going to do that when we're doing *Frankie's House*?' I said, 'Easy,' and I rattled off the guitar part and within a flash Jed had all the drum parts."

Only the first few bars were heard in the movie's fruit machine scene; but it appeared in splendid entirety on the soundtrack album. Both "Hound Dog" and

"Hi-Heel Sneakers" were miniature classics cast from the same mold, and both received richly deserved Grammy nominations for Best Rock Instrumental of 1992.

The TV miniseries of *Frankie's House* was released in Australia in October, and in the U.S. and U.K. soon afterwards. The brilliantly evocative, sensitive soundtrack earned effusive praise from the critics, especially for the amazing range of Beck's performances. Chris Gill's review in *Guitar Player* said, "Beck soars and explores like never before. His emotional range is particularly impressive; moods shift from eerie to rowdy, from erotic to rueful. Beck pushes the guitar beyond its constraint, proving once and for all that he's not just a guitarist but a musician who happens to play guitar."

Now a third nomination came their way, this time for a prestigious British Academy (BAFTA) Award for Best Original Television Music.

Jeff Beck is known for his reluctance to attend glitzy showbiz occasions, and he'd even avoided the ceremony at which *Guitar Shop* won its Grammy. Now he intended to do the same with the BAFTA function. But Jed Leiber was determined to be there: "You don't want to go? I can't believe it! You idiot—you've got the biggest accolade that England has to offer!" And, prompted by Leiber's enthusiasm, Beck agreed that if his partner came over they would go together.

"So he made it by the skin of his teeth," Beck recalls. "Bags at the hotel, then straight down there. 'And the winner is . . .'—we couldn't believe it! Could not believe it! I went along for the ride, really, and then there's me going up there!"

AT THIS POINT in our story we come to Jeff Beck's most remarkable album project yet—the fulfillment of a dream long cherished, and in itself a triumph of one man's determination and dedication.

Beck's passion for rockabilly has recurred over and over in our narrative, and we've seen his occasional ideas for making a record in this style. At the end of *Frankie's House* he started to think about an album of classic Gene Vincent material as a tribute to Cliff Gallup, his all-time hero. And this time he had the means to make it reality.

A couple of years earlier, Beck had come across a group of musicians by the name of the Big Town Playboys who proved to be the perfect foil for his revivalist leanings. The Playboys were a six-piece authentic swing/blues/country-rock band with an established reputation and a bulging date book, founded in 1984 with the idea of playing the music of the late '40s and early '50s. They used acoustic instruments—an upright double bass, acoustic piano, and an old drum kit—and had impressed major names such as Eric Clapton and Robert Plant, who selected them as a backing band.

It was Peter Richardson who first mentioned the Playboys to Beck, and urged him to see them for himself. Mike Sanchez, the Playboys' lead vocalist and pianist, takes up the story: "Jeff came to see us on a few dates in London, and invited us to his house to jam. That early rock 'n' roll—Gene Vincent, Eddie Cochran, the Johnny Burnette Trio—was the first kind of music I really fell in love with, so it was well familiar."

Beck spent seven weeks in the studio working with Jed Leiber on *Frankie's House*, spring 1992.

The Playboys were then invited by Richardson to perform on *The Pope Must Die*, so Beck and the guys met up again. "We've played together many times at parties and rehearsals, messing around with covers and original songs," says Sanchez. "Then we came up with the idea of the Cliff Gallup/Gene Vincent tribute."

Part of the motivation for the album may have been the sad fact that Cliff Gallup had died a few years earlier, in 1988. That Gallup's death went generally unremarked was just one more proof, so far as Beck was concerned, that something needed to be done to give him the recognition he deserved.

The result was the jumpin' jivin' *Crazy Legs*, a brilliantly accurate replication of songs taken principally from *Gene Vincent and the Blue Caps*, Vincent's second (and least well known) album. A few specially chosen singles were also added, like "Race with the Devil" and "B-I-Bickey-Bi-Bo-Bo-Go"—"all the best and most adventurous tracks Cliff played on," in Jeff Beck's words.

"The songs are so strong and so radical, everything in them is a beautiful, polished and finished item. I didn't see the sense of trying to change any of the ingredients and winding up with a cake that didn't taste right. So we went for the throat and did everything the way we thought they did it originally."

This thinking reflects Beck's other loving re-creations of the past—his cars and his centuries-old English home. For those who care enough to stop and look over their shoulder, such motivation must strike a resonant chord.

That private side of Beck's existence is called vividly to mind in David

Sinclair's elegant prose, from a visit to his subject's house reported in *Rolling Stone*.

"Built in 1591 and set in eighty acres of wooded grounds, Beck's Tudor mansion is a magnificent building nestling on the border of East Sussex and Kent, the mansion of a guitar legend who has become the most reclusive of them all. Beck is currently restoring the building to its original state. The process involves stripping away various modifications and centuries-old additions to the façade to reveal the original thick wooden beams, which have supported the building since Shakespeare's time.

"Diamond-paned leaded windows stretch the entire length of the building's front, and old-fashioned red tiles make the roof look perilously uneven. Inside, the austere period feel is similarly preserved. Several dogs mill around on the stone floors, while numerous cats stir in dark corners. In a huge fireplace a great chunk of timber that Beck chopped up himself and hauled in earlier burns fitfully.

"Beck has never [re]married, but he has a young, blonde girlfriend called Sandra Jane who brings a tray of coffee and chocolate biscuits. Formerly a topless model for one of Britain's best-selling tabloid newspapers, even she seems to radiate a traditional charm—the comely wench—that chimes with the Old English surroundings."

Moving to reflections on the death of Cliff Gallup, Sinclair noted with regret that his passing went largely unreported and unlamented: "The whole guitar-playing legacy of that era has been vastly undervalued."

Beck agreed. "Scotty Moore, James Burton, and Cliff Gallup—they were all just tossed away. They were brilliant players, but no one was really aware of them. Cliff Gallup's guitar playing was absolutely phenomenal. His solos are so packed with dynamite on the wild numbers, and yet they're full of knowledge and fluidity, melodic as hell."

THIS ENDEAVOR GAVE rise to an enormous amount of fascination on the part of the music press, particularly the specialist guitar magazines. Here was the opportunity not only to interview Jeff Beck, but to delve into how the legendary sound of rockabilly was created, and how a musician of today managed to reproduce it.

Beck declared their only concession to 1990s techniques was using modern recording equipment so the sound would conform to present-day expectations. And he gave full praise to the production and engineering team led by Stuart Colman and Leif Mases.

"We could have practiced for 20 weeks, but it's still down to how the guy engineers it and records it all. All the tracks were done live, we never did a drum track or anything. We cut it with an overall feel. It didn't matter if anyone screwed up. The album existed after about four or five days."

Beck had put an enormous amount of research and experiment into his preparations, but was never able to identify exactly what Cliff Gallup's picking hardware was, or precisely what amp he used. Knowing that his guitar was a Gretsch Duo-Jet, Beck had reflected it with one that was as close as possible. But the whereabouts of Gallup's own instrument were a mystery. Beck had heard that it was stolen after one of his gigs.

It was only after the album's release that *Guitar Player*'s Chris Gill, another interviewer who visited Beck in his home surroundings, provided some of the answers. Gill had gone to the trouble of calling Cliff Gallup's widow, Doris, so he was able to confirm that Gallup's guitar was happily still safe in Doris' hands. After her husband's death she had given his amp to his best friend; the most Gill discovered was that it was a tweed Fender.

It's hard to imagine just how Beck felt as he heard these precious morsels of information. He had never in his life spoken personally to Cliff Gallup, although he would have loved to. "The *awe* I would have been in of him, and he would have been sitting there, wishing he was fishing [*laughs*]. I would have just liked to hear one syllable. His voice would have satisfied me."

As they settled in front of the fireplace, with tea, biscuits, and mushroom pies at hand—the fire crackling in the background and candles dimly illuminating the room—Gill brought out a gift from *Guitar Player*, something that Jeff Beck would treasure always: it was a set of Cliff Gallup's own guitar picks, together with a handwritten letter from Gallup himself. Beck was overwhelmed: "I'm having a religious moment. . . . Oh man, that's the best. Thank you."

Not only the guitar, but even the strings proved to be critical in reproducing the Cliff Gallup tone. In the end he turned to tape-wound strings, and suddenly the problem was solved. Another revelation was that he had to play at minimal volume levels. "For twenty-five years I'd been playing loudly," he said, "and you simply don't do that for this kind of music. As soon as I cut the volume, the whole thing started to swing."

One of the most frequent questions asked was why Beck had chosen not to include Vincent's first and greatest hit, "Be-Bop-A-Lula." The answer was simply that the album they were emulating didn't have that track on it—and if they'd included "Be-Bop-A-Lula" it would have received the most airplay. "I'm an awkward sonofabitch when it comes to doing the unexpected!"

But *Crazy Legs* wasn't entirely devoted to Cliff Gallup numbers. It also contained three tracks that paid tribute to Gallup's successor in the Blue Caps, Johnny Meeks: "Lotta Lovin'," "Say Mama," and "Baby Blue." "It shows Vincent's progression from almost traditional country rock to really *now* music. I still love the work he did. He had a killer sound." Beck brought out his white '62 Strat to recapture that sound—the sound which had turned him on to the Strat in the first place. "He was the total rock 'n' roll hooligan with the striped shirt and the quiff and the cap stuck on the back of his head.

"But so precious little was known or seen of the original Blue Caps," he lamented. "I've never seen an original film—I don't even know if any exists. This album is all for them, really. Cliff in particular. He changed my life. It's my way of saying, 'I've listened to what you did, and pretty close.'"

Released in June 1993, *Crazy Legs* took just six weeks to be recorded and mixed. During those weeks, in September/October 1992, Beck got totally saturated in the Gene Vincent period—emerging from the studio he'd be amazed to find strange looking cars in the streets!

Guitar World's Dan Forte said of the performances, "Their tone, spirit, and energy border on savant-level accuracy. Beck plays his role of latterday bop-cat to the hilt, capturing the techniques, nuances and, above all, the spirit of Gallup's snaky leads. Far from being stiff, archival fare, the music is alive."

But the critics were not unanimous in this view. Gene Santoro's review for the same publication commented: "The album feels so static. Not that it isn't fun—it is. His guitar work is beautifully pristine, exquisitely tasteful, as flawless as a carefully cut gem. It's just that there's so little of the cutter's signature style in the result. So aside from marveling once more at his versatility, even a diehard fan like me has to wonder why such a master craftsman would want to work in such anonymity."

John Millward of *Rolling Stone* took a different stance again, calling it "one of the liveliest albums of Beck's long career. Instead of dominating the music with sheer sonic muscle, Beck achieves the same end by bouncing his encyclopaedic bag of riffs off a rippling rhythm section of drums and stand-up bass. So while *Crazy Legs* is ultimately redundant, it also rocks like crazy."

Not in the mainstream of taste, naturally, and not chart material, if that is your criterion for relevancy. But ultimately redundant? In the summer of '94 the solo from "Blues Stay Away" featured in a Budweiser ad on U.S. television. And in *Musician* magazine of October that year Adrian Belew named *Crazy Legs* among the top five albums he was currently listening to.

OF COURSE, THE next question on everyone's lips was whether Jeff Beck would tour in this new incarnation of his. This depended upon a lot of factors, and one of them was the problem of his tinnitus.

"The Big T," as he called it, manifested itself as a constant hissing noise, almost like a rattlesnake. To Douglas Noble, in an interview published in *The Jeff Beck Bulletin*, he confirmed that it afflicted his left ear: "It's excruciating. It does go away, it's not true to say that it doesn't, but . . . why is it such a horrible sound? A guy scratching at a window with his nails is a horrible sound—this is worse!"

He'd heard about various drugs that might be helpful, but the problem was the possible side effects ("you get a liver that drops out and hits the floor with a thud"). For a while he got excited about the cochlear implant, only to realize it was a treatment for the profoundly deaf. Eventually the only thing that kept him going was listening to music with a Walkman—"As long as I can think of and absorb what I'm hearing in the phones, it keeps me from thinking about the tinnitus, even though I know it's there. It feels as though half my head's been shot away. It's just some stupid little hair cell in the ear that's gone. It's inner eardrum damage—the junction between the auditory nerve and your brain—

which is too damn close [*laughs*]. I can hear what you're saying as perfectly as the next guy, but if we were in a crowded room I would probably not be able to decipher it. Any more damage to my high end . . . well, it's almost unbearable now. It's so stupid not to have known about the vulnerability and how delicate the inner ear workings are."

Nevertheless he was keen to do a series of live dates with the Playboys. To take account of his fragile hearing, they would confine themselves to smaller upscale clubs. Attempts were set in motion to find suitable venues, and rehearsals were set to start in February 1993.

Their tryout date was on 23 April at the 1,400 seat La Cigale in Paris, a special live performance in a club atmosphere to herald the release of the album. It was Beck's first full-length concert since the 1990 European *Guitar Shop* tour.

The show was in roughly three parts, starting with a very tight, energetic set by the Big Town Playboys, whereupon all hell broke loose as Mike Sanchez announced, "Please welcome Jeff Beck." Beck then joined the Playboys to execute his Gallup chops with incredible precision—even more impressive when you consider that he was playing at low volume with an absolutely clean tone, using a decidedly more cumbersome guitar than his usual fast-action Fenders.

Still backed by the Playboys, Beck rounded off the set with a selection of well-loved favorites including a spellbinding performance of "The Stumble," played on his Tele-Gib, and a reinvented "Going Down" interspersed with dazzling breaks of finger-lickin' chicken-pickin'.

This performance, by the way, took place only a couple of weeks after he had sliced through the top of one of his left-hand fingers when a glass broke while he was washing it. His insurance, he revealed, ran to about a million pounds per hand.

WHILE ALL THIS planning was going on, Beck was invited to participate in a tribute to B.B. King at the hallowed Apollo Theater in New York, on the occasion of King's induction into the Apollo's Hall of Fame. Beck appeared alongside B.B. King, Albert Collins, Buddy Guy, and Eric Clapton, trading licks on "Sweet Little Angel" and "Let the Good Times Roll." Hosted by the inimitable Bill Cosby, the show took place on 15 June and was aired on NBC in August.

While in the U.S. he celebrated his 49th birthday at Jed Leiber's house in Los Angeles, assisted by such luminaries as Skunk Baxter and Jennifer Batten, who joined him for a jam on "Hi-Heel Sneakers." He also discussed with Leiber a possible new album project to include a guest track from Batten, who had visited him in England during a break in her European tour as Michael Jackson's lead guitarist. "It was a pleasant surprise when I saw Jackson, having this wild woman come out blazing away!"

Beck had seen her in action in his studio and was mightily impressed: "I thought she wouldn't know me from a bar of soap, but she knew all my licks. She's very dedicated. Embarrassing—I just see her playing away in her little house somewhere, doing nothing else. Because you can't get that good unless you do."

All this was obviously leading up to something, and it transpired that as well as touring with the Big Town Playboys, Beck also wanted to tour as "a 1993 Beck band" with Terry Bozzio and Jennifer Batten. The idea was to let the Playboys open, then Beck would join them for a *Crazy Legs* set, and after the interval he'd change persona and blaze into the Bozzio-Batten project. "So I'd be opening for myself, kind of thing!"

To protect his ears he'd have a headphone monitor system that left him free to move about while hearing a custom mix with his own guitar sound filtered in. Though there was obviously still a part of him that hankered after the bone-crunching stage assaults of the past, he'd learned a bitter lesson when last he'd been subjected to the reality. Invited to guest with Guns N' Roses at the Paris Hippodrome de Vincennes in June the previous year, he'd flown over to play on a couple of numbers with the world's most notorious heavy rock band . . . and one of the loudest.

"They said, 'Right Jeff, got your sound?' and it was a great guitar sound, one of the best I've had. Then they said, 'Okay Jeff, we'll do the drums now' and CRASSSHHH—my head nearly came off. No thanks!" The nearest anyone got to hearing that amazing lineup came in a few brief rehearsal clips on MTV, with Beck performing "Locomotive."

But a related collaboration did come about when he teamed up with Guns N' Roses bass player Duff McKagen, contributing to two songs on his solo excursion, *Believe in Me*. The first number, the picturesquely titled "(Fucked Up) Beyond Belief," was recorded right after the Paris gig.

If Guns N' Roses seemed somewhat unusual company for Jeff Beck, his next few guest sessions were a decidedly mixed bag. The first, in August 1993, was for a unique tribute album to Jimi Hendrix featuring stars from solar systems many galaxies apart. *Stone Free* featured fourteen covers of Hendrix's songs performed by artists as diverse as Belly, Buddy Guy, Pat Metheny, (Nigel) Kennedy, and rapper/rocker Ice-T of "Cop Killer" fame.

So perhaps it wasn't such an oddball idea to pair Jeff Beck on "Manic Depression" with pop-soul merchant Seal, whose record "Crazy" had recently hit number one worldwide. (Beck also contributed to later Seal recordings, including a fleeting appearance on his 1994 album, *Seal*, playing some beautifully judged background lines at the end of the first track, "Bring It On.")

The original plan was to record "The Wind Cries Mary"—perhaps a better vehicle for Seal, whose vocal strengths were not quite in the Hendrix league—but after a run-through at rehearsal Beck was keen to try something he could really sink his teeth into. The result was a raving "Manic Depression" of epic proportions.

With Jim Copley (ex-Upp) on drums and Pino Palladino holding down a mean bass, Beck's striding, snarling guitar kicks off in authentic Hendrix mold but soon surpasses the original in sheer rampant hysteria. As the song progresses, with fevered guitar and vocal exchanges, the seething brew is held back down over an insistent pedal bass while a renewed head of steam is built up . . . until the guitar's mounting frenzy clamors for a return to tempo again and a final, explosive release of tension.

Beck's interpretation lifted the performance into one of the album's high spots, and as usual came in for fulsome praise. Hendrix biographer John McDermott, reflecting on Beck's experimental Yardbirds work through to such seminal efforts as *Guitar Shop*, concluded with a thought-provoking comment: "Beck has provided Hendrix fans with a glimpse into territories Jimi might have explored had he lived."

Another two guest recordings filled the gap until something more substantial came along, and this time both were with female singers.

For the new Kate Bush album, *The Red Shoes*, he laid down several tracks, along with other guests including Prince and Eric Clapton. Only one title made it to the final release, with Beck's impassioned leads providing the climax on the torchy ballad "You're the One." The other singer was Beverley Craven, whose *Love Scenes* was produced by Paul Samwell-Smith. Of the three songs recorded, the standout track was "Love Is the Light," in which his brilliant, smoking solo assured the song of generous airplay.

The year 1993 also saw him on a video titled *The Fender Story*, which included other Fender greats such as Stevie Ray Vaughan, David Gilmour and Eric Clapton in a star-studded production. Beck's segment was filmed in London, talking about his history with Fender and performing a portion of "Where Were You."

Early the following year another guest appearance was released, this time with Roachford, with whom he had worked on *Twins*. He played on the track "Emergency" for the singer's *Permanent Shade of Blue*, a project long in the pipeline and probably recorded some two years earlier.

More sessions followed in 1994 to complete a mosaic of styles that few other rock guitarists could dream of encompassing. An afternoon was spent at Paul McCartney's, recording the Hendrix number "Driftin'" (with some great whammy bar) for the album *Oh* by bassist Will Lee, and on the same day he guested with two titles on the new Jan Hammer album *Drive*. Subsequently he turned in a ravishing performance on "Django" for John McLaughlin's *Promise*, an opportunity to work once more with Pino Palladino on bass. And at the end of the year he would guest on "No More Regrets" for the Italian powerhouse singer Zucchero.

BACK IN THE world of movies, Jeff Beck found himself in demand for three sound-tracks in a row—the first of which saw him in Los Angeles for the Nick Nolte film *Blue Chips*, once more in collaboration with his pal Jed Leiber. Unfortunately the duo didn't see eye to eye with the producer over the music, and Nile Rodgers was eventually drafted to finish the project. All that remained of Beck's work were a few incidental passages, for example in the early basketball scenes, and neither Beck nor Leiber was heard on the soundtrack CD.

A happier result came from his next soundtrack, *The Cowboy Way* with Woody Harrelson. Jeff Beck and Paul Rodgers went into the studio together in the spring of 1994 to record the Leiber/Stoller classic "On Broadway," with veteran drummer Henry Spinnetti and Big Town Playboys bassist Ian Jennings.

The third movie was *Little Big League*, on which he worked with old friend Stanley Clarke. Beck contributed additional music to Clarke's original score, as well as performing on a few well-loved classics like the Ventures' landmark instrumental "Walk Don't Run." Another surf classic, "Wild Weekend," was recorded but didn't make it to release, and Beck is mysteriously listed on "Willie and the Hand Jive" and "Wipeout" in the movie's end credits; these tracks also seem to have gone the way of "Wild Weekend." A brief moment of Beck brilliance comes at the point when mom's boyfriend Lou is benched by the film's young hero, whereupon Beck lets rip with a screaming blues break to remind us that he hasn't forgotten how to wail with the best of them.

On 24 June 1994, Jeff Beck cracked open the champagne to celebrate his fiftieth birthday with a party at home. Midsummer Day it might have been, but the weather in England takes no account of that: in the middle of everything the power was blown—and the music silenced—by a storm that produced hail the size of golf balls. But Beck has chosen to live where he does because he loves the beauty and tranquility. "I could enjoy a life of seclusion," he says." It would take a hell of a lot of hounds to get me out."

That half-century landmark was hard to believe when comparing his youthful looks with some of his famous contemporaries, though looks have never been of great concern to Beck. Nevertheless, to have emerged unscathed after a lifetime in rock is no mean achievement in itself.

AFTER TWO ALBUMS in 1992/93, he was noticeably keeping quiet about the matter of new recordings. Word came through that he was working with Tony Hymas, Paul Rodgers and drummer Stewart Copeland, on an album planned to include a first-time collaboration with Bryan Adams. By the end of '94 they had laid down nine tracks, but at that point the project seemed to stop dead while Beck headed off in a totally new direction.

Soon, in his recently completed attic studio at home, he had started working on a new concept with the aid of Sade percussionist Martin Ditcham and *Blow by Blow* drummer Richard Bailey. "Simple melody with an emphasis on quality drum sound and drum patterns," was how he described it. "It's highly rhythmic, with screaming Hendrix-type guitar. I don't want to call it jungle music—it's just really strong tribal, African sort of music."

By spring of 1995, two years after La Cigale, the Paris concert was still his one and only show. A ten-city *Crazy Legs* tour had been envisaged, starting in Cliff Gallup's home territory of Norfolk, Virginia, and ending in Los Angeles, but never came to anything. There were subsequent plans to resurrect the idea of touring with Jennifer Batten and Terry Bozzio, this time in Japan; but this didn't materialize either, perhaps owing to Bozzio's ultra-full schedule.

However, good news suddenly broke with the announcement of an invitation from Carlos Santana to join him on a major two-handed U.S. tour.

Soundcheck on 31 July 1995 at Wolftrap, Virginia, the opening night of the Santana/Beck US tour.

Beck would hit the road again in summer 1995 with old cronies Tony Hymas and Terry Bozzio, plus Pino Palladino adding magic on bass—an extensive lineup of 43 dates from 31 July to 8 October, to which *Guitar Player* devoted an entire special edition.

The sellout tour was yet another Beck triumph, and managed to convince him—somewhat to his surprise—that his fans weren't about to let him retire from view. *20th Century Guitar* reported that "Jeff Beck squeezed, tore, ripped, shredded, and played every ounce of emotion that was physically possible from his guitar . . . a clean display of virtuoso and technical prowess coupled with amazing flash and showmanship. With their long extended technical improvisations, the crowd grew more attentive with every note being played by Beck's patented killer vibrato."

One of the tour's best spin-offs for Beck was the success of his Future Sonics in-ear monitor system, protecting him from high volumes while giving perfect sound reproduction. Also high on his personal satisfaction list was getting most of the surviving Blue Caps to come and see the show in Atlanta.

The set list, however, did not include any reminiscences of Gene Vincent: it concentrated mainly on well-loved Beck material from the recent past, although it also unleashed a solitary sample—"Hurricane"—of his intriguing new African-influenced music. An album was in the works, he announced, with pieces that were "extremely complicated"; then all went silent for well over a year until he was reported recording in Los Angeles with Steve Lukather, Abe Laboreal Jr., and Lenny Castro. Tony Hymas and Pino Palladino were also slated to join the project.

In terms of recordings, Beck fans had to sit tight from then onwards and content themselves with occasional guest sessions. The first to appear, with a U.S. release in the summer of 1997, was a historic project featuring Elvis Presley's erstwhile guitarist and drummer, Scotty Moore and D.J. Fontana, under the title *All the King's Men*. Among the celebrities who adorned the recording (including Keith Richards, Steve Earle, and Lee Rocker) were Jeff Beck and Ron Wood, who guested on the track "Unsung Heroes." Moore and Fontana traveled to Ron Wood's Sandy Mount Studio in Ireland for the recording in December 1996, and Beck arrived with a Strat Plus and Playboys bassist Ian Jennings.

"Unsung Heroes" was a resoundingly funky on-the-spot composition based on a lick of Scotty Moore's, which Wood and Beck embellished with guitar fills, ad-libbing the lyrics about meeting their two heroes—and regretting the loss of that third hero who couldn't be there, Bill Black. The whole project took just a couple of nights, during which time, according to producer Dan Griffin, Beck had a big smile on his face that lasted the whole weekend.

October 1997 saw the release of Steve Vai's compilation CD *Merry Axemas—A Guitar Christmas*, which featured Jeff Beck with the London Choral Society conducted by Tony Hymas in Hymas' haunting arrangement of "Amazing Grace."

In the meantime there had been several false alarms which, though promising, failed to produce results. Among them were discussions with Terence Trent D'Arby which came to nothing, and an almost-release of a collaboration with Eric Johnson on his album *Venus Isle*. Paul Burlison was quoted as saying Beck had agreed to be on his new release *Train Kept A-Rollin'*. He was about to send the tracks he'd recorded to Beck in England when the idea was scotched by Beck's record label, Sony/Epic, which couldn't agree on the contractual details.

Licensing problems were again the obstacle when Jeff Beck's recording of "Three O'Clock Blues," duetting with B.B. King for King's album *Deuces Wild*, was pulled at the eleventh hour. The withdrawal was so last-minute, in fact, that promo copies had already been distributed containing the cut. Those who have heard it describe it as the monster track of the decade—"truly magnificent," "blistering blues," and "a barrage of raw energy and emotion."

Better news for fans came in mid-1998, with another historic compilation album which had been waiting two years for release. Producer George Martin (now age 72 and sporting a knighthood) had been putting together a farewell anthology, *In My Life*, to mark his retirement. It consisted of his favorite Beatles songs performed by his favorite artists, and Beck had been drafted in to record a version of "A Day in the Life."

Beck attended Martin's retirement party in March at AIR Studios in London, saying that he was very proud to have been chosen to play on the album: "He's such a father figure in the way his musical knowledge guides you. I'll be most upset to know that he's not continuing in music."

Also in mid-1998 came the release of a much anticipated collaboration with British guitarist Brian May, presently enjoying success as a solo recording artist after the demise of Queen. On the album *Another World*, Beck's hard rocking track, "The Guv'nor," had lyrics that were originally written by Brian May for an unrealized movie project, now adapted by him to be a tribute to the man he has always regarded as the guitar guv'nor himself—Jeff Beck.

BY LATE 1998, there were rumors of a new Beck album at last. In gestation for around three years, for much of that time its guidance had been in the hands of Steve Lukather, who worked with Beck both in Britain and at his own North Hollywood studios, The Steakhouse. "I'm there as a record producer to help him make the music the way he wants to hear it," Lukather said. "He is truly the most unique guitar player we have—so full of soul. The hum of his amp blows away most people, you know."

Subsequently, however, it appeared that production had been completely taken over by Beck in conjunction with Tony Hymas. It resulted in the March 1999 release *Who Else!* The album contained plenty to surprise us from our maverick adventurer, including a sizeable helping of ambient, electronica, and Prodigy-inspired techno. A cheeky touch of laid-back blues made an appearance in "Brush with the Blues," and two morsels of lush, lyrical balladry ended the collection, "like a cigarette after sex," as one reviewer commented.

As Beck says himself, "I'm in the fortunate position where it's become the norm for me to do something different each time; which is great because it means I'm not actually sacrificing or dumping a load of fans because I want to do this or that. I don't actually reap any *benefit* too much . . . but I'd rather take the punches."

He did, in fact, surprise us in quite another way by suddenly going on the road in the summer of 1998 for a four-week European tour of 21 dates. It started in Amsterdam on 7 July and took in Paris, Switzerland's Montreux Jazz Festival, and several venues in Italy, Austria, and Germany (in Montreux Beck was joined onstage by John McLaughlin for an encore, "Manic Depression").

His lineup comprised ex-Incognito bassist Randy Hope-Taylor and ex-Duran Duran drummer Steve Alexander, with the incredible Jennifer Batten on guitar/guitar synthesizer. Batten rendered listeners speechless as she used the synth to play what were basically all the original Tony Hymas parts, as well as ripping out "rabid, really *heavy* solos," as Beck described them, displaying the most amazing technique on straight guitar (through a rack setup one reviewer reported as one of the most elaborate he'd ever seen!). Beck's own touring hardware was his favorite Surf Green Strat played through three new Marshall DCM2000s, aided by his ProCo Rat as well as a Cry Baby Wah.

Another reviewer singled out Steve Alexander for his brilliant soloing, and said the whole band was so great he simply couldn't believe it.

The European shows were opened by the Big Town Playboys, and about half Beck's set consisted of new pieces from the long awaited album (although "Hurricane" was dropped after the first few shows). From several live recordings made on their later tour dates, two were eventually heard on the CD.

The tour was then extended to take in South America in October—Mexico, Uruguay, Brazil, Argentina, and Chile—with North American/Japanese/British dates to follow in 1999. For the Free Jazz Festival on 17 October in Brazil's Rio de Janeiro, tickets were completely sold out within six days—beating the previous record-holder, Stevie Wonder. Beck was so popular, in fact, that an extra five o'clock show was added at the last minute.

This was his first ever tour of South America, and the cheering festival audience was packed with celebrities, including Brazil's famous guitarist Victor Biglione. Wayne Shorter opened the bill, and Beck was still onstage playing encores at one a.m.

NOTHING COULD BE more fitting, to end this account of Jeff Beck's musical career, than to commemorate two distinguished accolades bestowed on him in recent years. In 1995 the respected magazine *Guitar Player* announced it had honored Beck with a Lifetime Achievement Award. And in 1996 he took his place among the all-time greats in Hollywood's Rock Walk of Fame.

Chris Gill's citation for the Lifetime Achievement Award said most of what there was to say: "Ever since he recorded the sitar-influenced lines on 'Heart Full of Soul' with the Yardbirds, Jeff Beck has continually expanded the electric guitar's horizons. He explored psychedelia with the Yardbirds, laid the foundations for heavy metal with the Jeff Beck Group, defined the jazz-rock fusion genre as a solo artist in the '70s, and remained a trend-defying iconoclast in the '80s and '90s. With an uncanny ability to coax a wide array of sounds from a simple setup, Beck plays as if his fingers were hardwired to his soul. In recent years Beck has embraced more styles than most artists span in an entire career. . . Not content to rest on his past achievements, Beck incessantly strives to create new sounds and techniques, and he consistently shatters conventional notions of guitar playing. A true musician."

Being the man he is, no doubt Beck would rather have seen the honor go first to Cliff Gallup and then follow in the great man's footsteps. (Gallup would actually receive the award in 1996.) Which is not to say his eyes are forever cast

Summer 1995, on US tour with Carlos Santana, still toting his favorite surf green Strat.

backwards; merely that, while steadfastly looking to the future, he is acutely and humbly aware of his roots.

In an earlier edition of the same magazine he said, "I never dreamt of being able to play in public when I was in my front room back home. I just thought, 'This is great. I'm enjoying myself taking what little bits I can off the records.' I never, ever thought I'd be on a platform somewhere, playing."

So where would Jeff Beck direct a young listener who wanted a broader familiarity with his past?

"That's a very tricky question," he mused, "because how can I say, 'Go down and get the '50s and work your way up'? I spent my *life* doing that, so to tell some young kid to buy Gene Vincent or Howlin' Wolf or any of the records we love might be setting them back thirty years. I would just say take what you see, and use that. Take what is going on now and use that as your platform, but always keep an ear for where we came from.

"As long as we keep a bit of the magic and the glory going in music, the job's done really . . . the guitar is sitting there—just pick it up and see what's in it for you."

Bibliography

Books and Articles

Bacon, Tony (Ed.). *Rock Hardware*, Blandford Press/Quill Publishing, 1981

Bacon, Tony and Paul Day. *The Fender Book*, Miller Freeman/Backbeat Books, 2000.

Bacon, Tony and Paul Day. *The Gibson Les Paul Book*, Miller Freeman/Backbeat Books, 1993

Clark, Dick and Richard Robinson. *Rock, Roll & Remember*, Thomas Y. Crowell, 1976

Clayson, Adam. *Beat Merchants*, Blandford Press, 1995

DesBarres, Pamela. *I'm with the Band*, Jove Books, 1983

Ewbank, Tim and Stafford Hildred. *Rod Stewart: A Biography*, Headline, 1991

Frame, Pete. *The Complete Rock Family Trees*, Omnibus Press, 1993

Frame, Pete (Ed.). *The Road to Rock*, Charisma, 1974

Gregory, Hugh. *1000 Great Guitarists*, Balafon, 1994

Hedges, Dan. *British Rock Guitar*, Guitar Player Books, 1977

Hjort, Christopher and Doug Hinman. *Jeff's Book*, Rock 'n' Roll Research Press, 2000

Hotchner, A. E. *Blown Away*, Simon & Schuster, 1990

Miller, Jim (Ed.). *The Rolling Stone Illustrated History of Rock & Roll*, Straight Arrow and Plexus, 1992

Mills, Bart. *Tina*, New English Library, 1985

Nelson, Paul and Lester Bangs. *Rod Stewart*, Sidgwick & Jackson, 1982

Norman, Philip. *The Stones*, Elm Tree Books/Hamish Hamilton, 1984

Ober, Michael and others. *Then Play On*, Michael Ober, 1992

Platt, John, Chris Dreja and Jim McCarty. *Yardbirds*, Sidgwick & Jackson, 1983

Roberty, Marc. *Clapton: The Complete Chronicle*, Pyramid/Reed Internat'l, 1991

Roberty, Marc. *Eric Clapton: The Man, The Music, The Memorabilia*, Paper Tiger/Dragon's World, 1994

Sinclair, David. *Rock on CD*, Kyle Cathie, 1992

Swenson, John. *Bill Haley*, W. H. Allen, 1982

Tobler, John and Stuart Grundy. *The Guitar Greats*, BBC Publications, 1983

Trynka, Paul (Ed.). *The Electric Guitar*, Virgin Publishing, 1993

Turner, Tina with Kurt Loder. *I, Tina*, Viking, 1986

Wood, Ron. *The Works*, Fontana/Collins, 1988

Magazines, Journals, etc

Autoweek	The Jeff Beck Fanzine
BAM Magazine	Kerrang
Beat Instrumental	Melody Maker
Blast Celebrity Magazine	Modern Drummer
Circus	Musician
Crawdaddy	Music Gig
Creem	New Musical Express
Dallas Morning News	New York Times
Disc	The Observer
DownBeat	Peavey Monitor
E C Rocker	Player Magazine
Experience Hendrix	Playboy
Faces	Pulse
Fender Frontline	Q Magazine
Goldmine	Record Mirror
Go! Pop Weekly	Record Retailer/Music Week
Guitar For The Practicing Musician	Record Review
Guitarist	Relix
The Guitar Magazine	RIP
Guitar Player	Rolling Stone
Guitar School	Sounds
Guitar World	Stereo Review
Hard Rock Video	Trouser Press
Hit Parader	USA Today
ICE	VOX
Internat'l Musician & Recording World	Yardbirds World
The Jeff Beck Bulletin	ZigZag

Photo Credits

Discography/Videography

RECORDINGS FOR AUDIO, VIDEO AND MOTION PICTURE RELEASE—
NO BOOTLEGS OR PIRATED RECORDINGS
Compilations and anthologies are not listed unless significant.

NOTES

All entries under "Released" refer to the earliest date the recording was released.
However, since this is intended as a buyer's guide, the "Reference" entries may refer to more recent releases:

1. In early LP recordings the stereo reference is preferred to mono.
2. CD releases and reissues, where available, are listed in preference to original LP catalogue numbers.
3. Only UK and US releases are listed, plus CD versions in other territories when no UK or US CD is available.

PRE YARDBIRDS

In estimated order of recording

Performer Credit	Title	Reference	Released
The Nightshift	Stormy Monday/That's My Story	Single Piccadilly UK: 7N 35264	1965
The Tridents	Keep Your Hands Off My Woman/ Trouble in Mind	Unreleased single	NA
The Tridents	That Noise/Wandering Man Blues	Unreleased single	NA
Jeff Beck	*Beckology* [Tridents 3 titles]: Trouble in Mind/Wandering Man Blues/Nursery Rhyme [live]	3-CD set Epic/Legacy UK: EPC 469262 2 US: E3K 48661	Jan 92 Nov 91
Phil Ryan & the Crescents	Mary Don't You Weep/Yes I Will	Single Columbia UK: DB 7406	Estimated 1964
Screaming Lord Sutch & the Savages	Dracula's Daughter/Come Back Baby	Single Oriole UK: CB 1962	Oct 64
	Reissued on *Screaming Lord Sutch and the Savages*	CD EMI UK: CDEMS1433	1991
Johnny Howard Band	Rinky Dink/Java	Single Decca UK: F 11925	Jun 64
Fitz & Startz	I'm Not Running Away/So Sweet	Single Parlophone UK: R 5216	Dec 64
Various artists	*Blues Anytime* [JB 2 titles]: Steelin'/ Chuckles [jam session Beck/Page] Reissued on *White Boy Blues—Classic Guitars of Clapton, Beck and Page* Reissued on *The Great / Jeff Beck and Friends*	LP Immediate UK: IMLP 019 LP Compleat/Polygram US: 672005 1 CD UK: GREAT 020	1968 1984 1994

Performer Credit	Title	Reference	Released
Chris Andrews	Yesterday Man/Too Bad You Don't Want Me [went gold in Germany]	Single Decca UK: F 12236 Atco US: 45-6385	Sep 65
	Reissued on *20 Greatest Hits*	CD Repertoire Germany: REP 4233-WG	1992
Paul Young	[You Girl]/I'm Not Running Away [JB B-side only]	Single Philips Sweden: PF 350316	1966

YARDBIRDS

In chronological order of release

Performer credit	Title	Reference	Released
The Yardbirds	Heart Full of Soul/Steeled Blues	Single Columbia UK: DB 7594 Epic US: 9823	Jun 65 Jly 65
The Yardbirds	*For Your Love* [JB 3 titles]: I'm Not Talking/I Ain't Done Wrong/My Girl Sloopy	LP Epic US: BN 26167	Jly 65
The Yardbirds	*Five Yardbirds*: My Girl Sloopy/ I'm Not Talking/I Ain't Done Wrong	EP Columbia UK: SEG 8421 CD Jimco Japan: JICK 89217	Aug 65 Mar 93
The Yardbirds	Evil Hearted You/Still I'm Sad [double A-side]	Single Columbia UK: DB 7706	Oct 65
The Yardbirds	I'm a Man/Still I'm Sad	Single Epic US: 9857	Oct 65
The Yardbirds	*Having a Rave-Up with the Yardbirds* [JB 6 titles]: You're a Better Man Than I/ Evil Hearted You/I'm a Man/Still I'm Sad/Heart Full of Soul/The Train Kept A-Rollin'	LP Epic US: BN 26177 (UK export only Columbia SCXC 28) CD Jimco Japan: JICK 89218	Nov 65 1966 Mar 93
The Yardbirds	[Questa Volta]/Pafff . . . Bum [JB B-side only]	Single Ricordi International Italy: SIR 20-010	Feb 66
The Yardbirds	Shapes of Things/You're a Better Man Than I	Single Columbia UK: DB 7848	Feb 66
The Yardbirds	Shapes of Things/I'm Not Talking	Single (withdrawn) Epic US: 9891	Feb 66
The Yardbirds	*A Yardbirds' Eye View of Beat* (unfinished studio album) Titles included: Jeff's Blues/Someone to Love/Like Jimmy/Reed Again/Chris' Number/Pounds and Stomps/What Do You Want/Here Tis/Crimson Curtain	Unreleased album	NA
The Yardbirds	Shapes of Things/New York City Blues	Single Epic US: 10006	Mar 66
The Yardbirds	Over Under Sideways Down/Jeff's Boogie	Single Columbia UK: DB 7928 Epic US: 10035	May 66 Jun 66

Performer Credit	Title	Reference	Released
The Yardbirds	*Yardbirds:* Lost Woman/Over Under Sideways Down/The Nazz Are Blue/ I Can't Make Your Way/Rack My Mind/ Farewell/Hot House of Omagarashid/ Jeff's Boogie/He's Always There/Turn into Earth/What Do YouWant/Ever Since the World Began	LP Columbia UK: SCX 6063	Jly 66
	Reissued as *Roger the Engineer* [plus Happenings Ten Years Time Ago/ Psycho Daisies on CD and mono LP]	CD Edsel UK: EDCD116 LP Epic US: FE 38455	1983 1983
The Yardbirds	*Over Under Sideways Down:* Lost Woman/Over Under Sideways Down/I Can't Make Your Way/ Farewell/Hot House of Omagarashid/ Jeff's Boogie/He's Always There/Turn into Earth/What Do You Want/Ever Since the World Began [plus Shapes of Things on Canadian version]	LP Epic US: BN 26210	Aug 66
The Yardbirds	Happenings Ten Years Time Ago/ Psycho Daisies	Single Columbia UK: DB 8024	Oct 66
The Yardbirds	Happenings Ten Years Time Ago/ The Nazz Are Blue	Single Epic US: 10094	Nov 66
The Yardbirds	*Over Under Sideways Down:* Over Under Sideways Down/I Can't Make Your Way/He's Always There/ What Do You Want	EP Columbia UK: SEG 8521	Jan 67
Various artists	*Blow-Up* [JB 1 title]: Stroll On	S'track LP MGM UK: C 8039 CD Sony US: AK52418	Apr 67 1992
	Reissued on *Rock Goes to the Movies*	CD CBS US: AK-46201	1990
Various artists	*Blow-Up* [cinema film, JB appeared performing 1 title]: Stroll On	Video: MGM/UA SO 50015	1994
The Yardbirds	*The Yardbirds' Greatest Hits* [JB 8 titles]: Shapes of Things/Still I'm Sad/New York City Blues/Over Under Sideways Down/ I'm a Man/Happenings Ten Years Time Ago/Heart Full of Soul/I'm Not Talking	LP Epic US: BN 26246 CD Germany: REP 4258-WG	Apr 67
The Yardbirds	*The Yardbirds Featuring Performances by Jeff Beck, Eric Clapton, Jimmy Page* [JB 9 titles]: Hot House of Omagarashid/ The Train Kept A-Rollin'/Jeff's Boogie/ What Do You Want/LostWoman/ Farewell/I Ain't Done Wrong/Ever Since the World Began/Turn into Earth	Double LP Epic US: EG 30135	Aug 70
The Yardbirds	*On Air* [BBC radio broadcasts, JB 21 titles]: I Ain't Got You/For Your Love/ I'm Not Talking/I Wish You Would/	CD Band of Joy Music UK: BOJ CD 200	May 91

Performer Credit	Title	Reference	Released
	Heart Full of Soul/I've Been Wrong [aka I Ain't Done Wrong]/Too Much Monkey Business/Love Me Like I Love You/I'm a Man/Evil Hearted You/Still I'm Sad/Hang on Sloopy/Smokestack Lightning/You're a Better Man Than I/ The Train Kept A-Rollin'/Shapes of Things/Dust My Blues/Scratch My Back/ Over Under Sideways Down/The Sun Is Shining/Shapes of Things [version 2]		
Various artists	*Rock 'n' Roll History—English Invasion of the '60s* [anthology, JB appeared performing 1 title]: Heart Full of Soul	Video: Good Times HomeVideo VHS 8114	1990
The Yardbirds	*The Yardbirds* [documentary, JB appeared in interviews and performed 11 titles]: I Wish You Would/For Your Love/I'm a Man/Heart Full of Soul/Still I'm Sad/My Girl Sloopy/TheTrain Kept A-Rollin'/ Shapes of Things/Over Under Sideways Down/Happenings Ten Years Time Ago/ Stroll On [footage from *Blow-Up]*	Video: A Vision Entertainment/ Warner Bros UK: 8536 50278-3 US: 50278 3	Feb 92 Apr 92
The Yardbirds	*The Yardbirds, The Train Kept A-Rollin'— The Complete Giorgio Gomelsky Productions* [JB 27 titles]: I'm Not Talking/ I Ain't Done Wrong/My Girl Sloopy/ Heart Full of Soul/Steeled Blues/Evil Hearted You/Still I'm Sad/Shapes of Things/You're a Better Man Than I/I'm a Man/New York City Blues/The Train Kept A-Rollin'/Pafff . . . Bum[version 2]/ Jeff's Blues [take 1]/Jeff's Blues[take 2]/ Someone to Love, Part Two/Like Jimmy Reed Again/Chris' Number [take 1]/ Pounds and Stomps (XYZ)/Pounds and Stomps/What Do You Want [take 1]/ What DoYou Want [take 2]/What Do You Want [take 3]/What Do You Want [take 4]/Here Tis [stereo instrumental version]/Crimson Curtain [edit of take 1 and insert]/Stroll On	4-CD set Charly UK: CD LIK Box 3	Apr 93

NB: *Roger the Engineer, On Air* plus *The Complete Giorgio Gomelsky Productions* provide the entire catalogue of official Yardbirds releases with Jeff Beck.

JEFF BECK

In chronological order of release

Performer credit	Title	Reference	Released
Jeff Beck	Hi Ho Silver Lining/Beck's Bolero	Single Columbia UK: DB 8151 Epic US: 10157	Mar 67 Apr 67
Jeff Beck	Tallyman/Rock My Plimsoul	Single Columbia UK: DB 8227 Epic US: 10218	Jly 67 Aug 67
Jeff Beck	Love Is Blue/I've Been Drinking	Single Columbia UK: DB 8359	Feb 68
Jeff Beck	*Truth*: Shapes of Things/Let Me Love You/Morning Dew/You Shook Me/ Ol' Man River/Greensleeves/Rock My Plimsoul/Beck's Bolero/Blues De Luxe/ I Ain't Superstitious Reissued with *Beck-Ola*	LP Columbia UK: SCX 6293 CD Epic US: EK 47412 Remastered: EK 66084 CD EMI UK: CDP 795469 2 CZ 374	Oct 68 Jly 68 Jly 00 Mar 91 Feb 93
Jeff Beck Group	Plynth (Water Down the Drain)/ Jailhouse Rock	Single Epic US: 5-10484	Jun 69
Jeff Beck Group	*Shapes of Things* [JBG appeared, performed]: Shapes of Things Reissued on *Hard Rock Heaven/The Best of Hard Rock*	Video: Spectrum R-2078 Video Arts Japan: VAVZ-2085	1991 1991
Jeff Beck Group	*Beck-Ola ("Cosa Nostra")*: All Shook Up/ Spanish Boots/Girl from Mill Valley/ Jailhouse Rock/Plynth (Water Down the Drain)/Hangman's Knee/Rice Pudding Reissued as *The Most of Jeff Beck* Reissued with *Truth* (q.v.)	LP Columbia UK: SCX 6351 CD Epic US: EK 47411 Remastered: EK 66085 LP MFP UK: 5219	Sep 69 Jun 69 Jly 00 Oct 71
Jeff Beck with Rod Stewart	*Best of Jeff Beck 1967-69*: Hi Ho Silver Lining/Tallyman/Love Is Blue/Beck's Bolero/Rock My Plimsoul/I've Been Drinking/Shapes of Things/Let Me Love You/Morning Dew/You Shook Me/All Shook Up/Spanish Boots/Jailhouse Rock/ Plynth (Water Down the Drain)/ Hangman's Knee/Rice Pudding/Ol' Man River/Greensleeves/I Ain't Superstitious Reissued as *Late 60s with Rod Stewart*	CD Fame UK: FA 41 3125 1 CD EMI UK: CDP 746710 2	May 85 Sep 88
Jeff Beck, Cozy Powell, James Jamerson, et al	*Unfinished studio album ("The Motown Album")* [Supposedly total of 7-8 titles]: Loving You Is Sweeter Than Ever/Reach Out, I'll Be There/(I Know) I'm Losing You/I Got to Have a Song/I Can't Give	Unreleased	NA

Performer Credit	Title	Reference	Released
	Back the Love I Feel for You/Just Like You Never Loved Me/Don't Give a Hoot		
Jeff Beck Group	*Rough and Ready*: Got the Feeling/ Situation/Short Business/Max's Tune [previous title Raynes Park Blues]/I've Been Used/New Ways Train Train/Jody	CD Epic UK: EPC 4710472 US: EK 30973	Jan 72 Oct 71
	Reissued with *Jeff Beck Group*	CD Epic UK: TFOCD19 US: PE 30973	May 89 May 89
	Reissued with *Blow by Blow*	CD Epic UK: 477252 2	1994
Jeff Beck Group	Got the Feeling/Situation	Single Epic UK: EPC 7720 US: 10814	Jan 72 Dec 71
Jeff Beck Group	*Jeff Beck Group ("The Orange Album")*: Ice Cream Cakes/Glad All Over/Tonight I'll Be Staying Here with You/ Sugar Cane/I Can't Give Back the Love I Feel for You/Going Down/I Got to Have a Song/Highways/Definitely Maybe Reissued with *Rough and Ready* (q.v.)	CD Epic UK: EPC 4710462 US: EK 31331	Jun 72 May 72
Jeff Beck	Hi Ho Silver Lining/Beck's Bolero/ Rock My Plimsoul	Maxi-single RAK UK: Replay RR3 UK: Replay RRP3	Oct 72 Sep 82
Jeff Beck	Hi Ho Silver Lining/Definitely Maybe	Single Epic US: 10938	Dec 72
Jeff Beck Group featuring Rod Stewart	I've Been Drinking/Morning Dew/ Greensleeves	Maxi-single RAK UK: RR4	Apr 73
Beck Bogert & Appice	Black Cat Moan/Livin' Alone	Single Epic UK: EPC 1251	Feb 73
Beck Bogert & Appice	*Beck, Bogert & Appice*: Black Cat Moan/ Lady/Oh, to Love You/Superstition/ Sweet Sweet Surrender/Why Should I Care about You Now/Lose Myself with You/Livin' Alone/I'm So Proud	CD Epic UK: 32491 US: EK 32140	Apr 73 Mar 73
Beck Bogert & Appice	I'm So Proud/Oh, to Love You	Single Epic US: 10998	May 73
Beck Bogert & Appice	Lady/Oh, to Love You	Single Epic US: 11027	Jly 73
Beck Bogert & Appice	*BBA Live in Japan*: Superstition/Lose Myself with You/Jeff's Boogie/Going Down/Boogie/Morning Dew/Sweet Sweet Surrender/Livin' Alone/I'm So Proud/ Lady/Black Cat Moan/Why Should I Care/Plynth (Water Down the Drain)- Shotgun [medley]	2-CD set Japan: ESCA 5067 8	Sep 73
Beck Bogert & Appice	*BBA Live in Japan*: Superstition/Going Down/I'm So Proud/Lady/Black Cat	LP Japan EPCO 58, reissued as 25.3P 57	1975 1979

Performer Credit	Title	Reference	Released
	Moan/Sweet Sweet Surrender/Plynth (Water Down the Drain)-Shotgun [medley]/Jeff's Boogie		
Beck Bogert & Appice	*Unfinished 2nd studio album* Titles included: Solid Lifter/Song for Lovely Ladies/Satisfied [aka Gonna Be Satisfied]/ Laughalong [aka Laughin' Lady or Song for Lovely Ladies]/(Get Ready) Your Lovemaker's Coming Home/All in Your Mind/Living Life Backwards/Got to Find My Woman (Time Is a Lady)/Funky Woman/Prayin' [aka Missing Word]/ The Chant Song [a version of Thelonius]/Jizz Whizz* [*released on *Beckology*]	Unreleased album	NA
Jeff Beck	*Blow by Blow*: You Know What I Mean/ She's a Woman/Constipated Duck/ AIR Blower/Scatterbrain/Cause We've Ended As Lovers/Thelonius/Freeway Jam/Diamond Dust	CD Epic UK: CDEPC 32367 US: EK 33409	Apr 75 Mar 75
	Reissued with *There and Back* and *Flash*	3-CD set Epic UK: EPC 468802 2 US: 83288	Feb 91 Mar 93
	Reissued with *Wired* and *There and Back*	3-CD set Epic US: E3K 64808	Oct 95
	Reissued with *Rough and Ready* (q.v.)		
Jeff Beck	She's a Woman/It Doesn't Really Matter [aka You Know What I Mean]	Single Epic UK: EPC 3334	May 75
Jeff Beck	You Know What I Mean/Constipated Duck	Single Epic US: 50112	Jun 75
Jeff Beck	*Wired*: Led Boots/Come Dancing/ Goodbye Pork Pie Hat/Head for Backstage Pass/Blue Wind/Sophie/Play with Me/ Love Is Green [Album nominated for Grammy 1976 Best Pop Instrumental Performance]	CD Epic UK: CDEPC 86012 US: EK 33849	Jly 76 Jun 76
	Reissued with *Flash*	2-CD set Epic UK: EPC 461009 2	
	Reissued with *Blow by Blow* and *There and Back* (q.v.)		
Jeff Beck	*Everything You Always Wanted to Hear by Jeff Beck But Were Afraid to Ask For*: Shapes of Things/Ol' Man River/Beck's Bolero/All Shook Up/Jailhouse Rock/ Plynth (Water Down the Drain)/Ice Cream Cakes/Tonight I'll Be Staying Here with You/Going Down/Black Cat Moan/ Superstition/You Know What I Mean/ She's a Woman/Thelonius/Freeway Jam	Promo LP Epic US: AS 151	Mid 76

Performer Credit	Title	Reference	Released
Jeff Beck	Come Dancing/Head for Backstage Pass	Single Epic US: 50276	Sep 76
Jeff Beck with the Jan Hammer Group	*Jeff Beck with the Jan Hammer Group—Live:* Freeway Jam/Earth (Still Our Only Home)/She's a Woman/ Full Moon Boogie/Darkness Earth in Search of a Sun/Scatterbrain/Blue Wind	LP Epic UK: EPC 86025 CD Epic US: EK 34433	Apr 77 Mar 77
Jeff Beck	*There and Back:* Star Cycle/Too Much to Lose/You Never Knew/The Pump/ El Becko/The Golden Road/Space Boogie/ The Final Peace Reissued with *Blow by Blow* and *Flash* (q.v.) Reissued with *Blow by Blow* and *Wired* (q.v.)	CD Epic UK: CDEPC 32197 US: EK 35684	Jly 80 Jly 80
Jeff Beck	The Final Peace/Space Boogie	Single Epic UK: EPC 8806	Jly 80
Jeff Beck	Too Much to Lose/The Final Peace	Single Epic US: 9 50914	Jly 80
Jeff Beck	The Final Peace/Scatterbrain/Too Much to Lose/Led Boots	EP Epic UK: EPCA 1009	Feb 81
Jeff Beck	*Flash:* Ambitious/Gets Us All in the End/ Escape/People Get Ready/Stop, Look and Listen/Get Workin'/Ecstasy/Night after Night/You Know, We Know/Nighthawks*/ Back on the Street* [*on CD, not LP] [Escape won 1985 Grammy Best Rock Instrumental Performance] Reissued with *Wired* (q.v.) Reissued with *Blow by Blow* and *There and Back* (q.v.)	CD Epic UK: 982 838 2 US: EK 39483	Jun 85 Jun 85
Jeff Beck and Rod Stewart	People Get Ready/Back on the Street/ You Know, We Know	12" single Epic UK: TA 6387 7" single US: 34 5416	Jun 85 Jun 85
Jeff Beck	Stop, Look and Listen [4'26"]/Stop, Look and Listen [3'44" UK mix]/You Know, We Know	12"/7" singles Epic UK: TX 6581	Sep 85
Jeff Beck	Ambitious/You Know, We Know	Single Epic US: 34 5595	Oct 85
Jeff Beck	Ambitious/Escape/Nighthawks	12"/7" singles Epic UK: TA 6981	Mar 86
Jeff Beck	Wild Thing/Gets Us All in the End/ Nighthawks	12"/7" singles Epic UK: TA 7271	Jly 86
Jeff Beck with Terry Bozzio and Tony Hymas	*Jeff Beck's Guitar Shop with Terry Bozzio and Tony Hymas:* Guitar Shop/Savoy/ Behind the Veil/Big Block/Where Were You/Stand on It/Day in the House/Two Rivers/Sling Shot [Album won 1989 Grammy Best Rock Instrumental Performance] [No. 1 album in Japan]	CD Epic UK: 463472 2 US: EK 44313	Nov 89 Oct 89

Performer Credit	Title	Reference	Released
Jeff Beck with Terry Bozzio and Tony Hymas	Guitar Shop [special version]/People Get Ready/Behind the Veil	7" single Epic UK: BECK 1	Oct 89
Jeff Beck with Terry Bozzio and Tony Hymas	Guitar Shop/Cause We've Ended As Lovers/Blue Wind	CD single Epic UK: CD BECK 1	Oct 89
Jeff Beck with Terry Bozzio and Tony Hymas	Day in the House/Guitar Shop [special version]/Cause We've Ended As Lovers	12" single Epic UK: BECK T1	Oct 89
Jeff Beck	*Beckology*: Trouble in Mind/Nursery Rhyme/Wandering Man Blues/Steeled Blues/Heart Full of Soul/I'm Not Talking/ I Ain't Done Wrong/The Train Kept A-Rollin'/I'm a Man/Shapes of Things [YB]/Over Under Sideways Down/ Happenings Ten Years TimeAgo/Hot House of Omagarashid/Lost Woman/ Rack My Mind/The Nazz Are Blue/ Psycho Daisies/Jeff's Boogie/Too Much Monkey Business/The Sun Is Shining/ You're a Better Man Than I/Love Me Like I Love You/Hi Ho Silver Lining/ Tallyman/Beck's Bolero/Shapes of Things [JBG]/I Ain't Superstitious/ Rock My Plimsoul [single version]/ Jailhouse Rock/Plynth (Water Down the Drain)/I've Been Drinking/Definitely Maybe/New Ways Train Train/Going Down/I Can't Give Back the Love I Feel for You/Superstition/Black Cat Moan/ Blues De Luxe-BBA Boogie/Jizz Whizz/ Cause We've Ended As Lovers/Goodbye Pork Pie Hat/Love Is Green/Diamond Dust/Freeway Jam [live]/The Pump/ People Get Ready/Escape/Gets Us All in the End/Back on the Street/Wild Thing/The Train Kept A-Rollin' [*Twins*]/ Sleep Walk/The Stumble/Big Block/ Where Were You	3-CD set Epic/Legacy UK: EPC 469262 2 US: E3K 48661, E3K 65424	Jan 92 Nov 91 Feb 98
Jeff Beck	*The Best of Beckology*: Happenings Ten Years Time Ago/Over Sideways Under Down/Shapes of Things [YB]/ Hi Ho Silver Lining/Shapes of Things [JBG]/Beck's Bolero/I Ain't Superstitious/ Rock My Plimsoul [single version]/Going Down/Superstition/Freeway Jam [live]/ Cause We've Ended As Lovers/People Get Ready/Wild Thing/The Train Kept A-Rollin' [*Twins*]/The Stumble/Big Block	CD Epic UK: 4713482 US: E3K 4275	Mar 92 Nov 91
Jeff Beck and Rod Stewart	People Get Ready/The Train Kept A-Rollin' [*Twins*] People Get Ready/New Ways Train	7" single Epic UK: 657756 7 CD single Epic	Feb 92

Performer Credit	Title	Reference	Released
	Train/The Train Kept A-Rollin' [*Twins*]	UK: 657756 5	Feb 92
	People Get Ready/Cause We've Ended	CD single Epic	
	As Lovers/Where Were You	UK: 657756 2	Feb 92
Jeff Beck and Jed Leiber	*Frankie's House* [JB played/co-wrote	S'track CD Epic	
	instrumental score for TV miniseries]:	UK: 472494 2	Feb 93
	The Jungle/Requiem for the Bao-Chi/	US: EK 53194	Jun 93
	Hi-Heel Sneakers/Thailand/Love and		
	Death/Cathouse/In the Dark/Sniper		
	Patrol/Peace Island/White Mice/Tunnel		
	Rat/Vihn's Funeral/Apocalypse/Innocent		
	Victim/Jungle Reprise [Hi-Heel Sneakers		
	nominated for Grammy Best Rock		
	Instrumental] [Album won 1993 BAFTA		
	Award for Best Original TV Music]		
Jeff Beck and the Big	*Crazy Legs*: Race with the Devil/Cruisin'/	CD Epic	
Town Playboys	Crazy Legs/Double Talkin' Baby/Woman	UK: 473597 2	Jun 93
	Love/Lotta Lovin'/Catman/Pink	US: EK 53562	Jun 93
	Thunderbird/Baby Blue/You Better		
	Believe/Who Slapped John?/Say Mama/		
	Red Blue Jeans and a Pony Tail/Five Feet		
	of Lovin'/Bi-I-Bickey-Bi-Bo-Bo-Go/Blues		
	Stay Away from Me/Pretty Pretty Baby/		
	Hold Me, Hug Me, Rock Me		
Jeff Beck	*Jeff Beck Session Works (Rock 'n' Roll Spirit*	CD Epic/Sony	
	Vol 2): Call a Wave/House of the Blue	Japan: ESCA 7550	Jly 94
	Danube/Bad Stuff/Jeff's One/I Don't Want		
	Nothing (to Change)/Back Where I		
	Started/Another Wasted Day/Barabajagal/		
	Journey to Love/Hello Jeff/Jamaican Boy/		
	Love Is the Light/Winner Takes It All/The		
	Stumble/I'd Die for this Dance/The Train		
	Kept A-Rollin' [*Twins*]		
Jeff Beck	*Best of Beck*: The Pump/People Get	CD Epic	
	Ready/Freeway Jam/Shapes of Things/	UK: 7464	1995
	Where Were You/Beck's Bolero/Going	US: EK 64689	1995
	Down/Jailhouse Rock/Goodbye Pork Pie		
	Hat/Blue Wind/Plynth (Water Down the		
	Drain)/Two Rivers/Scatterbrain/She's a		
	Woman		
Jeff Beck	*Who Else!*: What Mama Said/Psycho	CD Epic	
	Sam/Brush with the Blues/Blast	UK: 493041 2	Mar 99
	from the East/Space for the Papa/Angel	US: EK 67987	Mar 99
	(Footsteps)/THX 138/Hip-Notica/Even		
	Odds/Declan/Another Place [Album		
	nominated for 2000 Grammy Best Rock		
	Instrumental Performance]		
Jeff Beck	*You Had It Coming*: Earthquake/	CD Epic	
	Roy's Toy/Dirty Mind/Rollin' and	UK: 501018 2	Feb 01
	Tumblin'/Nadia/Loose Cannon/Rosebud/	US: EK 61625	Feb 01
	Left Hook/Blackbird/Suspension		

SESSIONS

In chronological order of release

Performer credit	Title	Reference	Released
John's Children	[Just What You Want—Just What You'll Get]/But She's Mine [JB B-sideonly]	Single Columbia UK: DB 8124	Feb 67
	Reissued on *A Midsummers Night Scene*	LP Bam Caruso UK: Kiri 095	Nov 87
	Reissued on *The Legendary Orgasm Album*	CD Cherry Red UK: CDM RED 31	1988
John Walker	[If I Promise]/I See Love in You [JB B-side only]	Single Philips UK: BF 1612	Oct 67
Paul Jones	And the Sun Will Shine/The Dog Presides	Single Columbia UK: DB 8379	Mar 68
Donovan and Jeff Beck Group	Barabajagal/Bed with Me (Trudi)	Single Pye UK: 17778 Epic US: 10510	Jun 69 Jly 69
Donovan	*Barabajagal* [JB 2 titles]: Barabajagal/ Trudi	LP Epic UK: 26481 CD US: EK 26481	Fall 69
Girls Together Outrageously (GTOs)	*Permanent Damage* [JB 3 titles]: The Eureka Springs Garbage Lady/The Captain's Fat Theresa Shoes/The Ghost Chained to the Past Present and Future (Shock Treatment)	LP Straight US: STS 1059 CD Enigma Retro US: 7 73397 2	Dec 69 1989
Screaming Lord Sutch	*Lord Sutch and Heavy Friends* [JB 2 titles]: Gutty Guitar/Brightest Light	LP Atlantic UK: 2400 008 Cotillion US: SD 9015	Feb 70
	Reissue with extra title: Would You Believe	CD Line Germany: LECD 9.00947 0	1990
	Reissued as *Smoke and Fire* [JB 3 titles]: Gutty Guitar/Would You Believe/ Brightest Light	CD Thunderbolt UK: CDTB-022	1985
Donovan	*HMS Donovan* [JB 1 title]: Homesickness	2-LP Dawn UK: DNLD 4001	1971
The Holy Smoke	If You've Got a Little Love to Give/ [It's All in the Camera] [JB A-side only]	Single Capitol UK: CL 15677	1971
Stevie Wonder	*Talking Book* [JB 1 title]: Lookin' for Another Pure Love	CD Motown UK: ZD 72011 US: MOTD 0319	Jan 73 Oct 72
Various artists	*Music from Free Creek* [JB billed as A N Other, 4 titles]: Cissy Strut/ Cherrypicker/Working in a Coalmine/ Big City Woman	2-LP Charisma UK, US: CADS 101	May 73
Eddie Harris	*E.H. in the U.K.* [JB 2 titles]: He's Island Man/I've Tried Everything	LP Atlantic UK: K 50029 CD Collectables US: COL-CD-6241	Early 74 1999

Performer Credit	Title	Reference	Released
Badger	*White Lady* [JB 1 title]: White Lady	LP Epic UK: 80009	Jun 74
		US: KE 32831	Jun 74
Michael Fennelly	*Lane Changer* [JB 1 title]: Watch Yerself	LP Epic UK: 80230	Jun 74
		US: KE 32703	Jun 74
Zzebra	*Panic* [JB 1 title]: Put a Light on Me	LP Polydor	
		UK: 2383 326	1975
		CD Disconforme	
		Spain: DISC 1955	1999
Upp	*Upp* [JB produced, played on 5 titles]: Bad Stuff/Friendly Street/Get Down in the Dirt/Give It to You/Jeff's One	LP Epic UK: 80625	Apr 75
		US: KE 33439	Apr.75
	Reissue [JB 7 titles]: Bad Stuff/Friendly Street/It's a Mystery*/Get Down in the Dirt/Give It to You/Jeff's One/Count to Ten* [*alternative versions]	CD Epic UK: 4809642	Aug 95
Stanley Clarke	*Journey to Love* [JB 2 titles]: Journey to Love/Hello Jeff	CD Epic	
		UK: EPC 468221 2	Sep 75
		US: EK 36974 2	Sep 75
Upp	*This Way* [JB 2 titles]: Dance Your Troubles Away/I Don't Want Nothing (To Change)	LP Epic UK: 81322	May 76
		US: PE 34177	May 76
	Reissue [JB 2 titles]: Dance Your Troubles Away/I Don't Want Nothing (to Change) [NOT Say Goodbye]	CD Epic/Sony Japan: ESCA 7542	Jly 94
Upp	*The Jeff Beck Band Upp, Featuring Jeff Beck* [JB 3 titles]: Jeff's One/Count to Ten/ Get to the Bottom* [*different version than *This Way*]	CD Teichiku Japan: TECX-25457	Mar 93
Upp	*The Jeff Beck Group Upp, Featuring Jeff Beck* [as Japan]	CD ISBA Canada: WISCD-104	1993
Billy Preston	*Billy Preston* [JB 1 title]: Bad Case of Ego	LP A&M	
		UK: AMLH 64587	Nov 76
		US: SP 4587	Nov 76
		CD Polydor Japan: POCM-2039	Oct 95
Stanley Clarke	Life Is Just a Game/[Hot Fun] [JB A-side only, different version than *Schooldays*]	Promo single Nemperor	
		US: NE-009	1976
Narada Michael Walden	*Garden of Love Light* [JB 1 title]: Saint and Rascal	LP Atlantic	
		UK: K 50329	1976
		US: SD 18199	1976
Dorian Passante	*Dorian Passante Zero* [JB 1 or 2 titles]: Destination Nowhere and/or Inside Looking Out	LP Amerama	
		US: A-1001	1977
Stanley Clarke	*Modern Man* [JB 1 title]: Rock 'n' Roll Jelly	CD Epic	
		UK: 468220 2	1978
		US: Tristar 80859	1978

Performer Credit	Title	Reference	Released
The Bee Gees and Peter Frampton	*Sgt Pepper's Lonely Hearts Club Band* [cinema film, JB plays 1 title on soundtrack]: You Never Give Me Money	S'track LP A&M UK: AMLZ 66600 RSO US: RS-2-4100	Aug 78 Aug 78
Stanley Clarke	*I Wanna Play for You* [JB 1 track]: Jamaican Boy	CD Epic UK: EPC 22133 LP Nemperor US: KZ 2 35680	Jly 79 Jly 79
Murray Head	*How Many Ways* [JB 3 titles]: Affairs Across a Crowded Room/Last Days of an Empire/Children Only Play Reissued as *Voices*	LP Music Lovers UK: MLP-101GB CD Get A Head Austria: GAH 102CD	Apr 81 1993
Cozy Powell	*Tilt* [JB 2 titles]: Cat Moves/Hot Rock	LP Polydor UK: POLD 2391513 US: PD 16342 CD Japan: POCP-1812	Sep 81 Sep 81 May 90
Various artists	*The Secret Policeman's Other Ball—The Music* [charity concert, JB appeared performing 4 titles]: Cause We've Ended As Lovers/Farther Up the Road/ Crossroads/I Shall Be Released	CD Castle UK: CCSCD 351 Rhino US: 71048 2	Nov 81 Apr 82
Various artists	*The Secret Policeman's Other Ball* [as above]	Video Comstock Japan: JSW 1001	Jly 88
Ph.D.	I Didn't Know/Theme For Jenny [instrumental version of I Didn't Know] [No. 1 in Italy]	Single WEA Italy: 25-9996-7	1982
Ph.D.	*Is It Safe?* [JB 1 title]: I Didn't Know	LP Warner Bros UK: WEA U0050 CD US: WEA 25-0052-1	1983 1983
Various artists	*Risky Business* [JB 1 title]: The Pump [from *There and Back*]	S'track Virgin CD UK: CDV 2302 LP US: V2302	1983 1983
Various artists	*The ARMS Concert* [charity concert, JB appeared performing 6 titles]: Star Cycle/ The Pump/Led Boots/Goodbye Pork Pie Hat/Hi Ho Silver Lining/People Get Ready *Rock Legends* [same concert, JB appeared performing 7 titles]: Star Cycle/The Pump/ Led Boots/Goodbye Pork Pie Hat/Hi Ho Silver Lining/Tulsa Time*/Goodnight Irene* [*closing ensemble]	Video Music Media M445 Rhino RNVD 1446 (2421) Video MIA V3340	1984 1991 1992
Various artists	*The ARMS Concert* [as above]	LP US: San Francisco Radio Station release	1984
Stanley Clarke	*Time Exposure* [JB 3 titles]: Are You Ready (for the Future)?/Time Exposure/I Know Just How You Feel [guitar synthesizer]	LP Epic UK: EPC 25486 US: FE 38688	Apr 84 Apr 84

Performer Credit	Title	Reference	Released
		CD Epic Japan ESCA-5236	Feb 91
Vanilla Fudge	*Mystery* [JB billed as J Toad, 2 titles]: Jealousy/My World Is Empty	LP ATCO UK: 790-149	May 84
		CD Atlantic Germany: 7567 80805 2	1998
Rod Stewart	Infatuation/[Three Time Loser] [JB A-side only]	Single Warner Bros UK: W 9256	May 84
Rod Stewart	*Camouflage* [JB 3 titles]: Infatuation/Can We Still Be Friends/Bad for You	CD Warner Bros UK: 7599 25095 2 US: 25095 2	Jun 84 Jun 84
Rod Stewart	Infatuation/[She Won't Dance with Me] [JB A-side only]	Single Warner Bros US: 29256	Jun 84
Box of Frogs	*Back Where I Started* [UK] *Box of Frogs* [US] [JB 4 titles]: Back Where I Started/ Another Wasted Day/Poor Boy/Two Steps Ahead	LP Epic UK: EPC 25996 US: BFE 39327 CD Epic Japan: ESCA 7543	Jun 84 Jun 84 Jly 94
Box of Frogs	Back Where I Started/[The Edge]/[Nine Lives] [JB 1 title]	12"/7" single Epic UK: TA 4562	Jun 84
Box of Frogs	[Into the Dark]/[Nine Lives]/Two Steps Ahead/[Just a Boy Again]/Another Wasted Day/Back Where I Started [JB 3 album extracts]	12" single Epic UK: TA 4678	Jun 84
Box of Frogs	Two Steps Ahead [long version and short version]	12" promo single Epic US	Jun 84
Tina Turner	*Private Dancer* [JB 2 titles]: Private Dancer/ Steel Claw	CD EMI UK: CDP 746041 2 Capitol US: C21Y 46041 2	Jun 84 Jun 84
Diana Ross	*Swept Away* [JB 1 title]: Forever Young	CD EMI UK: CDP 746 053 2 RCA US: 5009 2	Sep 84 Sep 84
The Honeydrippers	*The Honeydrippers Volume 1* [JB 2 titles]: I Got a Woman/Rockin' at Midnight	EP Es Paranza 7 90220-1-B Mini-CD 7567 90220 2	Sep 84 Sep 84
The Honeydrippers	[Sea of Love]/Rockin' At Midnight [JB B-side only]	Single Es Paranza US: 7-99701 (withdrawn)	Sep 84
The Honeydrippers	Rockin' at Midnight/[Young Boy Blues] [JB A-side only]	Single Es Paranza US: 7-99686	Sep 84
The Honeydrippers	[Sea of Love]/Rockin' at Midnight [JB B-side only]	Single Es Paranza UK: SAM 220, WEA YZ33	Jan 85

Performer Credit	Title	Reference	Released
Mick Jagger	*She's the Boss* [JB 6 titles]: Lonely at the Top/Running Out of Luck/Hard Woman/ Just Another Night/Lucky in Love/ She's the Boss	CD Columbia UK: 467560 2 Atlantic US: 82553 2	Feb 85 Feb 85
Mick Jagger	Just Another Night/[Turn the Girl Loose] [JB A-side only]	Single CBS UK: A 4722 Columbia US: 38-04743, 44-05181	Feb 85 Feb 85
Various artists	*Porky's Revenge* [cinema film, JB 1 title]: Sleep Walk	S'track LP Columbia UK: CBS 70265 CD Mobile Fidelity US: MFCD 797	Mar 85 Mar 85
Various artists	[High School Nights—Dave Edmunds]/ Sleep Walk—Jeff Beck/[I Don't Want to Do It—George Harrison]	12" promo single Columbia US: CDN-189	Mar 85
Mick Jagger	Lucky in Love/Running Out of Luck	Single CBS UK: A 6213, TA 6213 Columbia US: 44-05214	Apr 85 Apr 85
Various artists	*Live! For Life* [live at the Greek Theatre, L A —JB joins Sting for 1 title]: I Been Down So Long	CD IRS UK: MIRF 1013 LP US: 5731	Apr 86 Apr 86
Philip Bailey	*Inside Out* [JB 1 title]: Back It Up	CD Columbia UK: CDCBS 26903 US: CK 40209	May 86 May 86
Mick Jagger	[Ruthless People]/I'm Ringing [JB B-side only]	Single UK: 25517 5291 Epic US: 34-06211	Jly 86 Jly 86
Pete Brown	*Before Singing Lessons 1969-1977* [JB 1 title]: Spend My Nights in Armour [unreleased single originated 1973]	2-LP Decal UK: LIKD7	1987
Mick Jagger	*Primitive Cool* [JB probably on all titles]: Throwaway/Let's Work/Radio Control/ Say You Will/Primitive Cool/Kow Tow/ Shoot Off Your Mouth/Peace for the Wicked/Party Doll/War Baby	CD Columbia UK: 460123 2 Atlantic US: 82554 2	Sep 87 Sep 87
Mick Jagger	Let's Work/Catch As Catch Can	Single CBS UK: 651028 Columbia US: 38-07306, 44-06926	Sep 87 Sep 87
Mick Jagger	Throwaway/Peace for the Wicked	7"/12"/CD single CBS UK: THROW 1, T1, C1 Columbia US: 38-07653, 44-07492	Nov 87 Nov 87

Performer Credit	Title	Reference	Released
Mick Jagger	Say You Will/Shoot Off Your Mouth	7"/12" single Columbia US: 38-07703, 44-07570	Jan 88
Various artists	*Twins* [JB 3 titles on CD]: The Train Kept A-Rollin'/I'd Die for this Dance/The Stumble [LP version does not include The Stumble; neither CD nor LP includes Green Onions]	S'track CD WTG US: SP 45036	Dec 88
Various artists	[No Way of Knowing—Henry Lee Summer]/The Train Kept A-Rollin'/ The Stumble [from *Twins*—JB latter two only]	Promo CD single WTG US: PSK 1391	1988
Various artists	*Twins* [cinema film, JB appeared and played 4 titles]: The Train Kept A-Rollin'/ I'd Die for this Dance*/The Stumble/ Green Onions [*performed in vision]	Video MCA 80873	1989
Lenny Henry	*Lenny, Live and Unleashed* [JB 1 title]: The Blues Y'All	CD Island UK: CID 9937	1989
Lenny Henry	*Lenny, Live and Unleashed* [JB 1 title]: The Blues Y'All	Video Palace UK: PVC 4031A	1989
Malcolm McLaren & the Bootzilla Orchestra	*Waltz Darling* [JB 2 titles]: House of the Blue Danube [instrumental]/Call a Wave	CD Epic UK: EPC 460736 2 LP US: OE 45247	Jly 89 Jly 89
Malcolm McLaren & the Bootzilla Orchestra	House of the Blue Danube [dub mix]/ House of the Blue Danube [shorthouse mix]/House of the Blue Danube [album mix]	7"/12"/CD single Epic UK: Waltz C4 / 4 US: 49-73146	Nov 89 Nov 89
Tony Hymas	*Oyaté* [JB 2 titles]: Crazy Horse/Tashunka Witko Tashunka Witko reissued on *A Sense of Journey*	2-CD set NATO France: 53010 2 CD: 112 010	1990 May 95
Jon Bon Jovi	*Blaze of Glory/Young Guns II* [album/ soundtrack from cinema film *Young Guns II*, JB 7 titles]: Miracle/Justice in the Barrel/Never Say Die/Bang a Drum/ Dyin' Ain't Much of a Livin'/Billy Get Your Guns*/ Blaze of Glory* [*from soundtrack]	CD Vertigo UK: 846473 2 Mercury US: 846473	Aug 90 Aug 90
Bon Jovi	*Cross Road* [JB appeared performing 1 title]: Miracle	Video Polygram Japan PHVS-5007	1994
Jon Bon Jovi	Blaze of Glory/[You Really Got Me Now] [JB A-side only]	CD single Vertigo UK: JBJ 1 Polygram US: 875896	Aug 90 Aug 90
Jon Bon Jovi	Miracle/[Blood Money] [JB A-side only]	Single Mercury US: 878 392	Oct 90

Performer Credit	Title	Reference	Released
Jon Bon Jovi	Miracle/[Going Back (Live)] [JB A-side only]	12" picture disc Vertigo UK: JBVJ 2	Nov 90
Various artists	*Young Guns II* [cinema film, JB 2 titles]: Billy Get Your Guns/Blaze of Glory	Video CBX Fox 1902	1991
Various artists	*Days of Thunder* [JB played/wrote part instrumental score for cinema film, no audio release; 1 track in movie]	Video Paramount/ PolyGram 631 690 3	Feb/Jly 91
Robbie Coltrane	Speedy Gonzalez/The Pope Must Die Theme	7"/12"/CD singles PMD Records UK: POPE2001-3	Jly 91
Buddy Guy	*Damn Right I've Got the Blues* [JB 1 title]: Mustang Sally	CD Silvertone UK: ORECD 516 Jive US: 1462 2	Aug 91 Aug 91
Buddy Guy	Mustang Sally/[Trouble Don't Last] [JB A-side only]	Single Silvertone UK: ORE 30	Sep 91
Buddy Guy	Mustang Sally [single version]/[Trouble Don't Last]/Mustang Sally [album version]	CD single Silvertone UK: ORE CD 30	Sep 91
Rod Stewart	*Rod Stewart—The Videos 1984-1991* [JB appeared performing 2 titles]: Infatuation/People Get Ready	Video Warner Reprise 7599 38283 3	Dec 91
Various artists	*The Pope Must Die(t)* [cinema film, JB played 2 titles and other soundtrack music, appeared in cameo role]: Speedy Gonzalez/The Pope Must Die(t) Theme	Video UK: Columbia Tristar CVR 23220 US: Fox Video M012881	Feb 92 Feb 92 Feb 92
Spinal Tap	*Break Like the Wind* [JB 1 title]: Break Like the Wind	CD MCA UK: MCAD 10514 US: MCAD 10514	Mar 92 Mar 92
Moodswings	*Moodfood by Moodswings* [JB 1 title]: Skinthieves	CD Arista UK: 74321 111702 US: 18619 2	Aug 92 Aug 92
Various artists	*Honeymoon in Vegas* [cinema film, JB 1 title]: Hound Dog [Hound Dog nominated for Grammy Best Rock Instrumental]	S'track CD Epic UK: 471925 2 US: EK 52845	Aug 92 Aug 92
Roger Waters	*Amused to Death* [JB 7 titles]: The Ballad of Bill Hubbard/What God Wants, God Gets Part I/What God Wants, God Gets Part III/Watching TV/Three Wishes/It's a Miracle/Amused to Death	CD Columbia UK: COL 468761 2 US: CK 47127	Sep 92 Sep 92
Roger Waters	*What God Wants, God Gets Part I*	Video Sony SMV 9V 49148	Aug 92
Roger Waters	What God Wants, God Gets Part I/What God Wants, God Gets Part I [5'50" version]	Single Columbia UK: 65813902 US: 38K 74363	Aug 92
Paul Rodgers	*Muddy Water Blues* [JB 3 titles]: Rollin' Stone/Good Morning Little Schoolgirl— Part One/I Just Want to Make Love to You	CD Victory UK: 828414 2 US: 383 480 013 2	Apr 93 Apr 93

Performer Credit	Title	Reference	Released
Duff McKagen	*Believe in Me* [JB 2 titles]: Swamp Song/ (Fucked Up) Beyond Belief	CD Geffen UK: GED 24605 US: GEFD 24605	Sep 93 Sep 93
Kate Bush	*The Red Shoes* [JB 1 title]: You're the One	CD EMI UK: CDEMD 1047 Columbia US: CK 53737	Nov 93 Nov 93
Beverley Craven	*Love Scenes* [JB 3 titles]: Hope/Love Is the Light/TheWinner Takes It All	CD Epic UK: 474517 2 US: 57745	Oct 93 Oct 93
Various artists	*Stone Free* [JB 1 title]: Manic Depression	CD Reprise UK: WBCD 1779 US: 9 45438 2	Fall 93
Various artists	*Guitar Legends* [JB appeared, performed]: Definitely Maybe	Video: Rhino US: R3 2070	1993
Various artists	*The Fender Story* [JB appeared performing 1 title]: Where Were You	Fender promotional video	1993
Various artists	*Blue Chips* [JB occasional soundtrack input]	Video CIC Victor PHF 0575	1995
Roachford	*Permanent Shade of Blue* [JB 1 title]: Emergency	CD Columbia UK: 475842 2 US: CK 475842 2	Apr 94
Seal	*Seal* [JB 1 title]: Bring It On	CD Warner Bros UK: 4509 96256 2 SIRE/WB US: 9 45415 2	Jun 94 Jun 94
Various artists	*The Cowboy Way* [JB 1 title]: On Broadway	S'track CD Epic Soundtrax UK: 476822 2 US: BK 64379	May 94 May 94
Various artists	*Little Big League* [JB 3 titles]: Lou Benched/ Walk Don't Run/Comiskey Park	S'track CD RCA US: 07863 66460 2	Jly 94
Various artists	*Little Big League* [JB credited with 3 titles plus additional soundtrack music]: Lou Benched/Walk Don't Run/Comiskey Park	Video Castle Rock Entertainment 9510	1994
Will Lee	*Oh* [JB 1 title]: Driftin'	CD Polystar Japan: Go Jazz PSCS 5015	Nov 94
Jan Hammer	*Drive* [JB 2 titles]: Drive/Underground	CD Miramar US: 2501	1994
Vanilla Fudge	*Coca-Cola Commercials* [JB 2 versions]: Things Go Better with Coke	CD Coca-Cola US: CC1	1995
Zucchero	*SpiritoDiVino* [JB 1 title]: No More Regrets	CD London UK: 527 785 2 Polydor US: 314 529 271 2	Oct 95 Jan 96

Performer Credit	Title	Reference	Released
Various artists	*Fender's 50th Anniversary Guitar Legends* [JB 1 title]: Where Were You	CD Virgin US: 72438 42088 2	1996
John McLaughlin	*The Promise* [JB 1 title]: Django	CD Polydor US: 529828 2	Feb 96
Scotty Moore & D J Fontana	*All The King's Men* [JB 1 title]: Unsung Heroes	CD Polydor UK: 539066 2 Sweetfish US: SWET 0002 2	Dec 97 Aug 97
Various artists	*Merry Axemas* [JB 1 title]: Amazing Grace	CD Epic UK: 4891692 US: EK 67775	Oct 97 Oct 97
George Martin	*In My Life* [JB 1 title]: A Day in the Life	CD Echo UK: ECHCD20 Echo/MCA US: 11841	May 98 Jly 98
Brian May	*Another World* [JB 1 title]: The Guv'nor	CD Parlophone UK: 494973 2 Hollywood US: HR 62103 2	Jun 98 Jun 98
The Pretenders	*Viva El Amor!* [JB 1 title]: Legalise Me	CD WEA UK: 3984 27152 2	May 99
ZZ Top	*XXX* [JB 1 title]: Hey Mr Millionaire	CD RCA UK: 74321 69372 2 US: 07863 67850 2	1999 1999
Sharon Sheeley	*Songwriter* [JB 4 titles, recorded 1960s]: Mrs Mac/Something Different/Baby Went Wrong/Cheers Love	CD RPM UK: RPM 206	Aug 00
Stevie Ray Vaughan	*Stevie Ray Vaughan & Double Trouble* [JB 1 title]: Going Down [live at Tingley Coliseum, Albuquerque, New Mexico, during *Fire Meets Fury* tour 1989]	3-CD set Epic/Legacy UK: EPC 5009302 US: E4K 65714	Dec 00 Dec 00

Index